Dedicated to:

Pauline, Holly and Sophie (A. P.)

and

Ann, Sarah and Ruth (T. C.)

The authors and publishers would like to thank
British Birds and *Birding World* for their generous
assistance with the production of this book.

BIRDS NEW TO BRITAIN
1980–2004

ADRIAN PITCHES

AND

TIM CLEEVES

T & A D POYSER
London

Published 2005 by T & A D Poyser, an imprint of A&C Black Publishers Ltd.,
38 Soho Square, London W1D 3HB

David Bakewell (82); **Andy Birch** (119, 172); **Nik Borrow** (56); **Brian Brown** (61); **Hilary Burn** (178); **Trevor Charlton** (40); **Mike Frost** (75); **John Gale** (202); **Alan Harris** (37, 94, 158, 160, 183, 188, 237, 259, 306); **Ren Hathway** (46, 125, 170); **John Holloway** (29); **Richard Johnson** (32, 64, 70, 73, 155, 167, 220, 222, 224, 226, 228, 254, 257, 265, 268, 270, 279, 282, 285, 287, 303, 316, 318, 320, 323, 325); **Alan Kitson** (21); **Ian Lewington** (1, 168, 245); **Jeff Lunn** (57); **Richard Millington** (33); **Killian Mullarney** (100, 127); **Dave Nurney** (47, 65, 97, 102, 121, 123, 136, 141, 149, 151, 211); **Mike Parker** (35); **Bruce Pearson** (134, 139); **David Quinn** (73, 240); **Brian Small** (299); **Gordon Trunkfield** (93); **Erik van Ommen** (111); **D.I.M. Wallace** (42, 301).

ISBN-10: 0-7136-7022-3
ISBN-13: 978-0-7136-7022-6

A CIP catalogue record for this book is available from the British Library.

A&C Black uses paper produced with elemental chlorine-free pulp, harvested from managed sustainable forests.

www.acblack.com

Typeset and designed by RefineCatch Limited, Bungay, Suffolk

Printed in Great Britain by The Cromwell Press Ltd, Trowbridge, Wiltshire

10 9 8 7 6 5 4 3 2

CONTENTS

PREFACE

Black Lark on Anglesey. It was 6 pm on Sunday 1st June 2003 and those four words caused pandemonium across Britain. The pager message had alerted birders to arguably the Mega of all Megas. A male Black Lark on a clifftop on Anglesey – at the beginning of the working week…

This iconic First for Britain generously stayed for a week and thousands of birders (or twitchers or listers, call us what you will) made the pilgrimage to North Wales to see it.

Seeing a First for Britain is a very special experience for the keen birder. *Finding* a First for Britain is a quantum leap beyond. This book is a compilation of the finders' accounts for 76 birds new to Britain that were first published in *British Birds* or *Birding World*. It's the successor to *Birds New to Britain and Ireland* by Tim Sharrock and the late, great Peter Grant, which was published in 1982. That book spanned the 35 years between 1946 and 1980 and detailed 83 Firsts. This book picks up where that one left off (March 1980) and covers the 25-year period 1980–2004.

It's remarkable that this compilation, covering a period ten years shorter than that of the previous book, nevertheless comprises the finders' accounts for almost as many species. And this book covers only Britain – we have not included Firsts for the British Isles that arrived in Ireland, following the decision to separate the British and Irish Lists in 1999. Although we have restricted our remit to England, Scotland and Wales (and also excluded the Isle of Man), we have listed the Irish and Manx Firsts that have yet to occur in Britain in Appendix 1.

As our period is the years 1980–2004, we have placed all Firsts within this timeframe, using either the finding date of the widely accepted First or the date of its elevation to the British List to place it. Hence the account for Yellow-browed Bunting appears in 1980, although the 1975 Norfolk record was subsequently accepted as the First (and this account appears too). Likewise, Black Lark appears in 2003, although an earlier record from East Yorkshire in 1984 has subsequently been elevated to the First. Southern ('Steppe') Grey Shrike appears in 1996 – the year it was admitted to the British List following its split from Great Grey Shrike – but we reproduce the account of the original sighting on Fair Isle in 1956: yet another entry in the annals of Firsts for the late Kenneth Williamson.

This device may appear artificial but we wanted to focus on the period 1980–2004 and the dramatic developments in birding that have taken place during this time. In 1980 there was an informal telephone 'Grapevine' amongst a few hundred birders, and a couple of useful field guides. Since then, world travel, improved field guides and access to the internet have all vastly improved our knowledge of birds. And with Birdline, pagers, mobile phones and digiscoping, the broadcast of rare bird news now takes minutes rather than days.

The pace of change has been just as rapid in taxonomy, with the advent of mito-chondrial-DNA analysis – the most widely accepted upgrades to species status are reflected in these pages. However, if the First record is 19th century or before (e.g. Green-winged Teal, Pacific and American Golden Plovers), then it is not included here. And there are many more 'splits' in the pipeline with gulls, wildfowl and wagtails prime candidates for promotion.

Finding a First for Britain is a great achievement for the finder; if it stays beyond that first sighting, it can provide great pleasure for the many people who come to see the bird. And occasionally it can be very important in conservation terms.

The Black Lark is a mythical bird of the Central Asian steppes. It could be the forerunner of further records – like the recent upsurge in Pallid Harriers from the same area – that may show something is amiss in the grasslands of the former Soviet Union following the demise of collective farming. Another First of even greater significance was the first-summer Slender-billed Curlew in Northumberland in May 1998. This record proved that, somewhere in Siberia, this Critically Endangered species bred in 1997, holding out the slim hope that the species may still survive.

There are as many lists as there are listers in modern birding. In an attempt to establish some consistency, we have followed the official British List maintained by the British Ornithologists' Union Records Committee (BOURC), although we *have* stuck our necks out with the most recent Firsts that have yet to be officially rubber-stamped. For an insider's view of the whole record assessment process, see the Foreword by Eric Meek, Chairman of the BOURC.

The casual observer could be forgiven for assuming that the number of new birds to arrive in Britain from all points of the compass would plateau; that there are only so many migrant species that could potentially arrive on our shores. It would seem that this is not so! New species for Britain keep on appearing but when or where the next one will turn up is anyone's guess, and that is what makes seeking out one's own birds so exciting. However, there are familiar islands and headlands which will always be the first landfall for windblown vagrants. Shetland and Scilly, at opposite ends of the country, accounted for the lion's share of Firsts for Britain in 1946–80 and they continued to do so in 1980–2004.

After a relatively quiet period since the late 1970s/early 1980s, Fair Isle returned to form in spectacular style in October 2004 with two Firsts within a week. Lundy – and Cliff Waller – managed two Firsts within three days in June 1966 (Spanish Sparrow and Eastern Towhee), but it was the Isles of Scilly that delivered three Firsts within four days in October 1987. For any birder seeking the immortality – and eternal gratitude of their peers – that comes with a First for Britain, then Scilly, Shetland or Lundy would be a good bet. And if you choose 7th October, your chances might improve further: Ovenbird, Wood Thrush, Blackburnian Warbler, Short-toed Eagle and 'Brown Skua' all appeared on this date!

We hope that the excitement of finding a First is communicated within these pages. But we wanted to provide more than a compilation of the finders' accounts. The two features that differentiate this book from its predecessor are an account of each birding year in the quarter century 1980–2004, and a series of birders' years commissioned from friends and colleagues in British birding. Among the writers of these 25 accounts are hardened listers, dedicated patchwatchers and professional conservationists, all of whom share the highs and lows of 'their' year. We thank them all for these highly read-able insights into their birding lives.

And we express particular gratitude to Roger Riddington and the directors of *British Birds* – and to Steve Gantlett & Richard Millington at *Birding World*. The opportuni-ty to reproduce the finders' accounts of all those Firsts for Britain for a wider audience is much appreciated.

Likewise, we are also indebted to the artists and photographers whose work is repro-duced within these pages. Special thanks to Richard Johnson & Alan Harris for their artwork – and to John Belsey, Dave Cottridge, Jon Green, Iain Leach, Tim Loseby, Phil Palmer, Martin Scott & Steve Young for their help in finding photos.

Tim Melling & Jimmy Steele provided useful guidance as the book took shape and Eric Meek kindly wrote the Foreword.

We must also thank Nigel Redman for commissioning this book, Marianne Taylor for initiating the editing task – and Jim Martin for completing it. Caroline Dudley did an excellent job as copy-editor; any errors are those of the authors.

Finally, we must express our gratitude to the birders who have found Firsts for Britain. Whether on Fair Isle, on Scilly or on a housing estate in Kent, these people had the alertness, the identification skills and often the sheer dogged persistence to clinch a sighting that would subsequently enrich the lives of their fellow birders.

Adrian Pitches and Tim Cleeves
Tynemouth, June 2005

FOREWORD
By Eric Meek

This is a book about dreams – indeed it is more than that, it is a book about dreams come true! For it surely must be every birder's dream to add a new species to the much-revered 'British List', a dream that comes second only to the nigh-impossible aspiration of finding a species new to science. Within these covers are the accounts of those whose dreams did come true, they did attain their nirvana and the sheer excitement of the experience jumps out of every page of these essays.

It nearly happened to me! Many years ago, on a dark November afternoon in 1970, two friends and I drove the Heligoland trap tucked away behind a small wood on the Northumberland coast. It was to be the last drive of the day and as we approached the trap's catching end, I could see a small *Phylloscopus* warbler fluttering against the netting. My immediate reaction was that it was a Yellow-browed Warbler but, even in the increasing gloom, I could see that it was too dull in colour, only had a single wing-bar and very little in the way of tertial edgings. The legs were dark and, fleetingly, I wondered about some form of Greenish Warbler. But no, it had to be a 'Yellow-browed' of some sort. Duly boxed then bagged, the bird was taken to the ringing hut for examination. In those 'pre-Svensson' days, the ringer's and migrant-hunter's bible was Ken Williamson's *Identification for Ringers: The Genus* Phylloscopus. It told us what we really already knew from hours of browsing its contents on long dark nights or birdless days of westerly weather – our bird in the bag fitted perfectly the description of *Phylloscopus inornatus humei*, a race of Yellow-browed Warbler found in what Williamson described as the 'higher wooded parts of the NW Himalayas at 8,000 to 10,000 feet'.

But surely it couldn't be – there was no precedent for a bird from that mysterious corner of Asia making it to British shores. Description and measurements taken, the bird was released before it got any darker, and it wasn't seen again.

The memory of it, however, remained with me and was brought back into sharp focus almost eight years later when, in February 1978, I paid my first visit to India. There, foraging in the woodlands and gardens of Rajasthan, was the very bird I had seen in November 1970 – our Northumberland bird had to be *P. i. humei*.

On my return, a quickly penned note to *British Birds* was to begin a saga that would last for almost another 20 years and will be familiar to many birding addicts. The initial write-up drew other records out of the woodwork, increasing foreign travel allowed the field characters to be more clearly defined, and BBRC eventually acknowledged that the taxon was identifiable in the field and gave consideration to a batch of claims. The BOURC, ever-careful, noted the occurrence of Yellow-browed Warblers of unusual appearance in late autumn but initially felt that overlapping characters precluded accurate field identification. Eventually, however, even they had to admit that increasing knowledge did now allow us to be certain and, moreover, their Taxonomic Sub-committee recommended that Hume's Yellow-browed Warbler, Hume's Leaf Warbler or, simply,

Hume's Warbler, as it had come to be known, was worthy not just of being admitted to the British List, but also worthy of elevation from subspecies to species status. At last it was there and the saga was at an end after almost 30 years but, in that time, unfortunately (for me!), our Northumberland record was no longer a 'first' but a 'third' – a bronze medal rather than a gold. Others from East Sussex (1966) and Norfolk (1967/68) had overtaken it in the race but the race had been both fun and instructive.

The whole saga of this 'first' Hume's Warbler perhaps encapsulates the attitudes and feelings that birders have towards the British ornithological establishment. Once the identity of our Northumberland bird was quite certain in our own minds, we then had to convince the British Birds Rarities Committee (BBRC) – the 'ten rare men', or the 'House of Commons'. This, to our minds, took a frustratingly long time. To be fair, we didn't have a brilliant description – a few hastily scribbled notes and measurements taken in the failing light before having to release the bird before it got too dark – and no photographs. Worse still, our bird was never heard to call, although at that time the significance of transcribing a slightly different call-note might well have been lost on us. The East Sussex bird that eventually became the real 'first', however, was a classic example of incredibly detailed observation in the field (it was never trapped), together with a spot-on description of the different call. Nonetheless, it was to be almost 20 years after details of this record first appeared (and 31 years after it had been seen!) before its official acceptance by BBRC in 1997. By that time, there had been no fewer than 27 records with a couple of others pending and a couple more considered unproven. On reflection, of course, this apparently inordinate delay allowed a very necessary process to take place. Although to modern birders the identification of a Hume's Warbler is a fairly straightforward business (though not without its pitfalls!), very little was known about its field characters in the '60s and '70s. However, by that time, a growing number of birders were travelling to more and more remote corners of the globe and the necessary knowledge of a whole host of species was growing apace and, just as importantly, beginning to be published in a vast array of notes and papers that left many struggling to keep up with the detail of it all.

If the role of BBRC in the saga was to carefully gather enough information to ensure that the identification of the now-burgeoning number of records was sound, what of the role of the British Ornithologists' Union Records Committee (BOURC), the 'House of Lords'?

Tasked with being the 'keepers' of the official British List, the BOURC frequently incurs even more wrath than BBRC over the slowness of its deliberations and the conservativeness of its decisions. The story of Hume's Warbler and how it clawed its way onto Category A of the British List is a classic of its kind. The 10th Report of the BOURC, published in *Ibis* in October 1980, noted three claimed records of *P. i. humei* but spoke of a cline between *inornatus* and *humei* and a broad zone of intergradation, concluding that, 'at best, it can be said that some vagrants to Britain, of unknown provenance, appear to approach *humei* in plumage tones; the late arrival of such birds (with Pallas's Warblers *Phylloscopus proregulus*) is noted'.

And there things remained, or appeared to do so to frustrated observers such as myself who felt that there had to be more to it than that! What is not always obvious to the outsider looking in, of course, is the tremendous amount of work going on in the background unseen by the great majority. Studies of *Phylloscopus* taxonomy were proceeding apace, with Scandinavian workers to the fore, and a milestone was the appearance of the fourth edition of Lars Svensson's *Identification Guide to European Passerines* in 1992, with its detailed guide to the in-hand identification of *humei* and its conclusion that the taxon warranted recognition as a full species.

This, taken together with a wealth of other material by then appearing in various journals, especially the key paper by Hadoram Shirihai & Steve Madge in the November 1993 edition of *Birding World*, allowed the BOURC to conclude in their 23rd Report (*Ibis*, January 1997) that elevation of *humei* to specific status was, indeed, the correct step. By the following year, BBRC had completed its review of claimed records and BOURC, in its 24th Report (*Ibis*, January 1998), admitted the species onto Category A of the British List with the East Sussex bird acknowledged as the first record.

The Hume's Warbler story had been a memorable journey through the dark realms of ornithological officialdom and one on which I reflected as I attended my first meeting of the BOURC at Swanwick in December 1999, having been elected onto the Committee a few months earlier. The feeling of 'poacher turned gamekeeper' was strong in me but, as I looked round the table at the faces of the other members, I realised that they, to a man, had all been poachers too. But here they were, armed with their knowledge and experience (and, in my case, age), prepared to give up enormous amounts of their spare time to ensure that the 'British List' remains the most accurate possible account of the British avifauna – the last word in birding.

There have been monumental changes in the birding scene since the late '60s and early '70s. Apart from the vast increase in knowledge in the form of the ever-increasing number of guides and journals, we have seen the advent of digital photography, and especially digiscoping, which has allowed for careful study of minute details of individual birds after the event, and sound-recording that allows the analysis of sonograms of individual calls. But the basics don't change – it is still hard to beat a good field description, as the final acceptance of the East Sussex *humei* showed.

And what of the British List itself? What is its relevance? It has a legal relevance, of course, especially in relation to conservation legislation, the official BOU List being the one that is used for this purpose. However, to most birders, it is the marker by which they gauge the results of their passion, and for this reason, as much as any other, it is essential for the list to be as refined and immaculate as it is possible for it to be – and if it sometimes takes a long time for a decision to be reached, so be it. Actually, in recent times, the vast majority of decisions are reached within a year, only the more problematic files taking longer to circulate. Taxonomic questions, of necessity, often take longer to answer and BOURC is acutely aware of birders' frustrations over, for example, the 'large white-headed gull' complex. Be patient – we're nearly there! Only now, as the insider looking out, rather than the outsider looking in, can I see just how much is being done to resolve such issues and my admiration for the skills and expertise of those involved in such resolutions increases daily.

Eric Meek is Chairman of the British Ornithologists' Union Records Committee.

BIRDERS' MAP OF BRITAIN

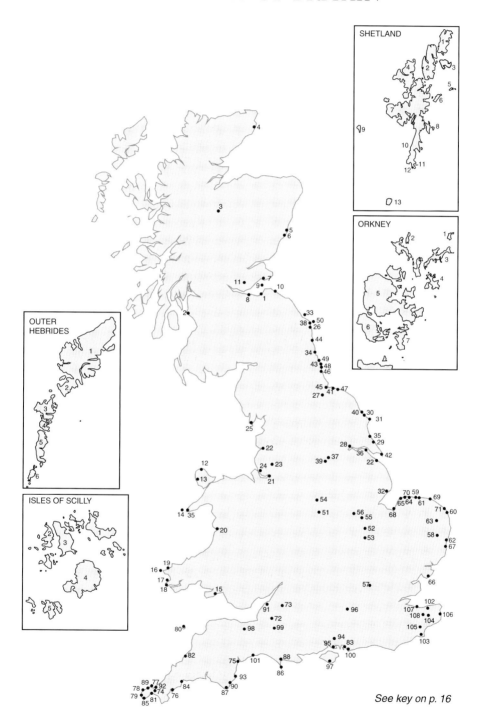

SHETLAND

OUTER
HEBRIDES

ORKNEY

ISLES OF SCILLY

See key on p. 16

KEY

1. Aberlady
2. Irvine
3. Aviemore
4. Wick
5. Aberdeen
6. Cove
7. Kilrenny
8. Musselburgh
9. Isle of May
10. St Abb's Head
11. Loch Leven
12. Cemlyn Bay
13. South Stack
14. Bardsey
15. Kenfig
16. Ramsey
17. Skomer
18. Skokholm
19. Dinas Head
20. Ynys-hir
21. Frodsham
22. Martin Mere
23. Pennington Flash
24. Seaforth
25. South Walney
26. Bamburgh
27. Billingham
28. Blacktoft
29. Easington
30. Filey
31. Flamborough Head
32. Gibraltar Point
33. Holy Island/Lindisfarne
34. Holywell
35. Hornsea
36. Humber Estuary
37. Langsett
38. Newbiggin
39. Potteric Carr
40. Scarborough
41. South Gare
42. Spurn
43. Tynemouth
44. Druridge Bay
45. Hartlepool
46. Sunderland
47. Teesmouth
48. Whitburn
49. Whitley Bay
50. Farne Islands
51. Chasewater
52. Ditchford
53. Earl's Barton
54. Nottingham

55. Rutland Water
56. Eyebrook Res.
57. Rye Meads
58. Beccles
59. Blakeney Point
60. Breydon Water
61. Cley
62. Dunwich
63. Gimingham
64. Holkham
65. Holme
66. Landguard
67. Minsmere
68. Snettisham
69. Sheringham
70. Titchwell
71. Waxham
72. Cheddar Gorge
73. Chew Valley Lake
74. Drift Res.
75. Exe Estuary
76. Falmouth
77. Hayle Estuary
78. Kenidjack
79. Land's End
80. Lundy
81. Marazion
82. Nanquidno
83. Pagham Harbour
84. Plymouth
85. Porthgwarra
86. Portland
87. Prawle Point
88. Radipole
89. St Ives
90. Slapton
91. Slimbridge
92. Stithians Res.
93. Studland
94. Dummer
95. Farlington Marshes
96. Staines Res.
97. St Catherine's Point
98. Stanpit
99. Swindon
100. Beachy Head
101. Winspit
102. Cliffe
103. Dungeness
104. Grove Ferry
105. Rye
106. Sandwich Bay
107. Sheppey
108. Stodmarsh

Shetland
1 Unst
2. Yell
3. Fetlar
4. North Mainland
5. Out Skerries
6. Whalsay
7. West Mainland
8. Noss
9. Foula
10. South Mainland
11. Pool of Virkie
12. Sumburgh Head
13. Fair Isle

Orkney
1. North Ronaldsay
2. Papa Westray
3. Sanday
4. Stronsay
5. Mainland
6. Hoy
7. South Ronaldsay

Outer Hebrides
1. Lewis
2. Harris
3. North Uist
4. Benbecula
5. South Uist
6. Barra

Isles of Scilly
1. St Martin's
2. Bryher
3. Tresco
4. St Mary's
5. St Agnes

THE BIRDER'S YEAR

Adrian Pitches

Birders embarking on their year list in 1980 were spoilt for choice. **Belted Kingfisher** in Cornwall? Or a drake **Steller's Eider** in the Outer Hebrides? A quarter of a century later, birders were still awaiting the next British Belted Kingfisher … until 12 noon on 1st April 2005 (but that Staffordshire bird was not an April Fool). Incredibly, the Cornish bird, a first-winter male, was found in October 1979 at the same location as the first British record in 1908. It remained until late August 1980. The late 1970s were also notable for a yet-to-be-repeated long-stayer: **Wallcreeper**. An obliging bird overwintered in Cheddar Gorge, Somerset, in 1976/77 and again in 1977/78.

With these memories fresh in their minds, birders looked forward to new rewards in 1980. The first was a **Pied-billed Grebe** in Dorset in late January, only the seventh for Britain, which stayed until April. It coincided with a first-winter **Ivory Gull** on Portland. Also in late January, back in Cornwall, Brian Cave saw a tern far out in the bay off Falmouth. He had a further inconclusive sighting in February but finally had good views of the bird on March 9th. It was Britain's first **Forster's Tern**, a first-winter bird that probably crossed the Atlantic the previous autumn. It remained a further nine days and was responsible for the first mass twitch of the 1980s.

Wintering wildfowl included: two adult **Lesser White-fronted Geese** at Slimbridge, Gloucestershire; male **Black Duck** in Gwynedd (and the resident female on Scilly); three Scottish drake **King Eiders**; ten **Ring-necked Ducks** (a further 29 arrived in the autumn/winter prompting the comment in *BB* that 'Colonisation is hopefully imminent'); and a male **Bufflehead** on South Uist, Outer Hebrides, for four days in March.

In Kent, the two long-staying **Glossy Ibises** continued their sojourn at Stodmarsh. Britain's third **Greater Sand Plover** overwintered at Chew Valley Lake – the First was only a year before (Dec 1978/Jan 1979) in West Sussex, followed by the second in Orkney in June 1979. A male **Two-barred Crossbill** in Staffordshire was a big draw until March – but one that got away in March was an unreported **Evening Grosbeak** in Highland.

Spring brought a sparse scattering of southern herons: five **Night Herons** (including two immatures together in Merseyside), one **Little Bittern** and one **Great White Egret** (the 21st record for Britain and Ireland, 11 of which had occurred since 1974). A total of five **Little Egrets** was recorded throughout 1980: the *BB* summary was that Little Egret 'has sadly declined here since the mid 1970s …'. From the vantage point of 2005, we can appreciate the irony. Little Egret colonised Britain in the 1990s and there were almost 200 breeding pairs in 2004. Likewise, the ultra-rare Great White Egret of 1980 has also become commonplace.

Late spring in 1980 produced two wonderful birds. First there was an inland **Sooty Tern** at a Northamptonshire gravel pit which was taken into care on its second day. How many ticked it in its cardboard box?! The second bird was a lot more difficult: a male **Scops Owl** holding territory in a Hampshire village for two months. Locals initially reported the persistent bleeps to the telephone company, but there were no wires running to that particular tree. When 'resident Scops' was diagnosed, the locals then experienced late-night pilgrimages by birders, who trained their car headlights on the tree in question.

Attention switched back to Cornwall in July, as an unprecedented passage of **Cory's Shearwaters** got underway. There were 2,735 past Porthgwarra on the 19th, the vanguard of a movement that lasted for a month. The final tally was 17,230 birds – ten times the combined total for the entire period 1958–80! Also in July, Britain's sixth **Franklin's Gull** was found on the Scottish west coast, in North Ayrshire. On the Scottish east coast, a **Black Stork** appeared in Perth & Kinross in August. And then there was the **Rufous Bush Robin** at Prawle Point, Devon on 9th August.

The autumn wader season saw the lion's share go to Cornwall, where there were **Semipalmated** and **Solitary Sandpipers**, all three of the year's **Baird's Sandpipers**, all three '**Lesser Golden Plovers**' (all Americans), three **Lesser Yellowlegs**, two **Wilson's Phalaropes**, a flock of four **Buff-breasted Sandpipers** and the best wader of the year: a **Cream-coloured Courser** seen only by its three finders on 8th October. The courser was the first since 1969, but a twitchable one was only four years away … In September, Britain's fifth **Black-and-white Warbler** was a one-day bird on Skomer, Dyfed. More accessible was an **Isabelline Wheatear** in Northumberland, only the fourth for Britain (the second had been in 1977–90 years after the first – and the third had been in 1979).

The Scilly season produced a **Yellow-billed Cuckoo, Red-eyed Vireo** and **Sardinian Warbler** and two of the year's four **Olive-backed Pipits**, taking the British total to 18. But attention was about to shift dramatically to Shetland. The discovery of a male **Yellow-browed Bunting** on Fair Isle prompted the first-ever twitch from Scilly to Shetland. Those brave pioneers, travelling the length of Britain by car and ferry, were also greeted with a **Pine Bunting** and a live **Brünnich's Guillemot**. At the end of the Yellow-browed Bunting's 12-day stay, 20 observers had seen the bird. A long-staying First for Britain with just 20 admirers: there's no better illustration of birding in a different era.

For British listers, the Fair Isle hat-trick marked the end of an era and the beginning of a scarcely credible new one. When Ron Johns saw the Fair Isle buntings, his British List soared to an unprecedented 400 species, the four-minute mile of British birding.

A quarter of a century later, several birders have broken through the 500-species barrier, the equivalent of a three-minute mile when seen from the perspective of 1980. Although overshadowed by events on Shetland, Orkney also had a remarkable October, with not one but two **Tengmalm's Owls** – the first in Britain for more than 20 years.

The year ended with a two-day **Ross's Gull** in North Yorkshire and an overwintering **Spotted Sandpiper** in Gwent. A **Black Brant** which settled in Essex at the year's end was only the fourth ever. (This bird was first seen in Suffolk in 1977.)

A TWITCHER'S DIARY
Richard Millington

1980 saw the dawning of a new decade in ornithological history and, for one birder at least, the year heralded a brand new era of birding in Britain. Sure, I had been birdwatching all my life, and twitching on and off since 1969, but by the late seventies I had caught myself backsliding into the dark abyss of normality. It was no good being a dude; this phase had to stop, so towards the end of 1979 the equivalent of a 'life laundry' brought Hazel and me to Norfolk in search of a new start. 1980 was then to be my first whole year as a Norfolk resident, although ensuing events ensured that it actually turned out to be a year seemingly spent everywhere else but!

Being a struggling bird artist meant that I was working night shifts in a factory at that time and driving a condemned car (an ancient Hillman Minx with only one working door), so it was fortunate that Steve Gantlett lived just 15 miles away from my New Buckenham home. Happily for me, he had decided that 1980 was just the year to target the year list record and was looking to at least break the then near-mythical '300 birds in a year' barrier. Okay, the record now stands closer to 400 than 300, but a quarter of a century ago things were rather different. There was no Birdline back then, and the 'Grapevine' consisted of only a small number of hard-won contacts, plus Ethel up at Nancy's Cafe in Cley. Organised mass twitching was still a thing of the future and most life lists were comparatively feeble, but the upside was that new birds came along relatively frequently!

As well as second helpings of the wintering Belted Kingfisher in Cornwall, January 1980 was notable for a beautiful male Two-barred Crossbill at Cannock Chase in Staffordshire and a 'two-tick day' in Dorset: a juvenile Ivory Gull on Portland and an elusive Pied-billed Grebe at Radipole Lake. A wintering Greater Sand Plover at Chew Valley Lake was February's star bird, but March was a far more exciting month as it produced the ultimate prize: a First for Britain!

Today, now that the species is an annual visitor here, it is difficult to imagine the excitement engendered by that first-ever Forster's Tern at Falmouth, but it really was a newsworthy twitch and a photograph of a modest crowd perched on a Cornish clifftop even appeared in a national newspaper!

Most of the spring was spent in Norfolk, but a summer-plumaged Red-throated Pipit in Gloucestershire, the still-resident Glossy Ibises in Kent, a Great Reed Warbler in Hampshire and a Red-rumped Swallow in Essex were amongst the out-of-county temptations. A Broad-billed Sandpiper at Breydon Water on May 28th was notable for being a 'birthday lifer', but late May also produced two of the year's most memorable highlights: a Sooty Tern in Northamptonshire (at Ditchford gravel pits) and a singing Scops Owl in Hampshire (at Dummer).

Travelling further afield during the summer of 1980, Laughing and Franklin's Gulls (in Cornwall and Ayrshire respectively) were added to the list, and so too were the long-staying drake Steller's Eider on the Outer Hebrides and a Black Stork in Perthshire. Norfolk did, however, produce two new birds: a Gull-billed Tern at Titchwell and a Sabine's Gull at Sheringham.

The pace of year listing hotted up during the autumn, with a Solitary Sandpiper and Lesser Yellowlegs at Drift Reservoir, Cornwall, on August 31st kicking off a good wader spell which included Wilson's Phalarope in Essex, Buff-breasted and Spotted Sandpipers in the Midlands and, back in Cornwall, Semipalmated and Baird's Sandpipers.

Passerines were not to be ignored though, and the second half of September produced an Aquatic Warbler (in Cornwall), a Sardinian Warbler (in Norfolk) and a rollicking roadside Roller (at Redisham, Suffolk). The obligatory Scilly season added a host of goodies to the year list, the best of which included Red-eyed Vireo (then only the eighth British sighting), Booted Warbler (only the fourth away from Shetland), Yellow-billed Cuckoo, Isabelline Shrike and Olive-backed Pipit. In retrospect, it was not a classic Scilly October by any means, but was still exciting enough at the time ... Norfolk's first Citrine Wagtail (formally accepted 17 years later), a Pallas's Warbler and a Ring-billed Gull (both still official rarities in 1980) were the final big birds as the year's total struggled towards the magic 300.

There were plenty of birds I didn't see in 1980 of course, including the summering Black-browed Albatross and Snowy Owls in Shetland (I didn't need them as lifers), Pine Bunting and Yellow-browed Bunting together on Fair Isle, and the Bufflehead on South Uist (I've seen them all since). There are two that still irk though: Tengmalm's Owl in Orkney and Evening Grosbeak at Nethybridge ... maybe the next decade or two will see them fall?

But no time to stop and reflect, as it was time to crack on with the next project: *Twitcher's Diary*. Famously censored by the RSPB (who blacked-out the title of the book when it appeared in a book-club advert on the back cover of *Birds* magazine), *A Twitcher's Diary – the Birdwatching Year of Richard Millington* was another personal milestone. Although challenging to the then vehemently anti-twitching hierarchy of the RSPB, it did seem to strike a chord amongst some keen birders of the day. Not great literature, not the most lifelike of illustrations, but that glorified version of my 1980 notebook is why I can still remember the year so well (even if it is an unshakeable ghost that has shadowed me ever since ...). I found a copy in a second-hand bookshop the other day, but I'm still some way from tracking them all down and finally retiring them.

Richard Millington lives in Cley, Norfolk. One of Britain's top listers, he runs Birdline *and is assistant editor of* Birding World. *Together with Steve Gantlett, he found Britain's first Rock Sparrow in 1981.*

OCTOBER 1980

YELLOW-BROWED BUNTING ON FAIR ISLE

Alan Kitson and Iain Robertson

For the small band of observers remaining on Fair Isle, Shetland – the observatory warden, two assistants and two visitors – 12th October 1980 was already a hectic day, fresh arrivals including a Short-toed Lark *Calandrella brachydactyla*, three eastern Stonechats *Saxicola torquata maura/stejnegeri*, two Red-breasted Flycatchers *Ficedula parva*, a Rustic Bunting *Emberiza rustica* and a suspected Little Bunting *E. pusilla*. It was, however, to become a sensational day, dare we say a 'red Setter day'.

Discovery and identification

At about 15.30 GMT, ARK was walking along the edge of the turnip crop at Setter, vaguely in search of a Little Bunting which had been reported heading in that direction some two hours earlier. A small bird hopping around under the turnip leaves caught his eye. Fragmentary views suggested a bunting *Emberiza* and he suspected that it might be a Little, but when its head came into full view he was startled to see a blaze of yellow over and in front of its eye and a white central crown-stripe between black lateral crown-stripes. As he gently walked the bird along the rows of turnips, three possible identities presented themselves: Yellow-browed Bunting *E. chrysophrys*, Little Bunting and White-throated Sparrow *Zonotrichia albicollis*. The last was quickly eliminated, for, although this bird had a yellow head mark, it clearly could not be an adult White-throated Sparrow, since its underparts were streaked, and immatures lack the yellow; besides, it 'felt' like a bunting. From research prior to his Mongolian trips, ARK knew that Yellow-browed Bunting has a pale crown-stripe and a yellow supercilium, which fitted this bird very well; but could it not perhaps be an unusually well-marked Little Bunting? In spring, at least, Little can show quite vivid orange on the fore-supercilium, have blackish lateral crown-stripes and be flecked underneath similar to this bird. During the advance, it was briefly flushed and heard to call: a high metallic 'tic' just like Little. Of course, most features were at variance with normal Little: no eye-ring, brown ear-coverts heavily bordered black, white crown-stripe, and most of all the yellow fore-supercilium; also, the bill: surely it was too large and was pink at the base?

ARK watched it for about 15 minutes, then ran to the phone in the Setter cottage, only to find no answer from the observatory. He watched the bird for some further minutes, leaning more and more towards Yellow-browed, then took leave for a few minutes to look up a probable Citrine Wagtail *Motacilla citreola* which had flown over as he was watching the bunting. It was now that he met P. J. Ewins and K. M. Morton, both elated over the putative Citrine, but due to become even more so over the bunting.

It was easily found again in the turnips. The possibility of an aberrant Little Bunting was not upheld by PJE, and the probability was that this bunting with black-and-white crown and dash of lemon on the face was a Yellow-browed, a first for Britain and Ireland. PJE went to the phone to try to reach ISR at the observatory, only to learn that he was out. The message which did eventually reach him referred to a 'Yellow-browed WARBLER' *Phylloscopus inornatus*, so that he was still to remain blissfully unaware of the excitement at Setter. Since the light was beginning to fade and the bird was approachable, PJE decided that they (now joined by A. del-Nevo) should catch the bird, which they did easily in a 20-foot single-shelf net. Back at the observatory, it was examined in the hand by ISR, and the measurements and plumage were found to be in good agreement with those for Yellow-browed Bunting in Dementiev & Gladkov. We thus became certain of its identity. It was dark by the time the examination was over, so the bird was roosted overnight and released back at Setter the next morning, where it was to remain throughout most of its stay, moving to a similar crop at Field for the last few days, when disturbed by crop-lifting at Setter. It was last seen on 23rd October, by which time it had been seen by about 20 observers.

Field description

The Yellow-browed Bunting was quite confiding, allowing approach as close as 2m at times. On 12th and 13th October, it was seen in good light and (remarkably for the Northern Isles) gentle breeze, through 9x and 10x binoculars, when the following description was taken:

> *Size and Shape* Small- to medium-sized bunting, nearer in size to Rustic than Little. No crest. Bill rather large, accentuated by pale pink base.
>
> *Plumage* Head pattern most striking: crown black, with narrow white crown-stripe widening on hind crown; supercilium broad, bright lemon yellow in front of and over eye, becoming whiter farther back; ear-coverts brown (quite warm in bright light, but not chestnut or rufous as on Little Bunting), with broad blackish outline extending backwards from eye, around rear edge and

forward along lower edge in point towards gape without quite reaching it, considerably more extensive than border of ear-coverts on Little Bunting; whitish spot in upper rear corner of ear-coverts, more conspicuous than on any other west Palearctic bunting; lore pale brownish, partly invaded by yellow of supercilium; no eye-ring; submoustachial stripe off-white, diffusing around ear-coverts patch; malar stripe fine and inconspicuous, of blackish flecks. Underparts sullied white with brownish invasion across sides of breast and flanks, overlaid with fine blackish flecks from chin to belly, smallest on chin and throat, boldest on flanks. Upperparts rich brown, having chestnut tinge in centre of mantle, with black streaks probably extending onto rump, and a pair of inconspicuous buff 'braces'. Wings: lesser coverts brown; median and greater coverts with dark centres, buff edges and whitish tips, latter forming two narrow wing-bars; tertials edged buff; primaries and secondaries edged brown. Tail with white on outer feathers.

Bare Parts Bill with flesh-pink base and grey tip. Legs flesh-pink.

Call 'Tic' or 'tic tic', probably indistinguishable from Little, Rustic and Yellow-breasted *E. aureola* Buntings. Three observers (KMM, Ad-N, ISR) thought a 'tink' note was given at times, possibly different from the 'tic'.

Kitson, A. R. & Robertson, I. S. 1983. Yellow-browed Bunting: new to Britain and Ireland. *British Birds* 76, 217–225.

An earlier record of Yellow-browed Bunting, in Norfolk in 1975, was subsequently accepted as the First for Britain and a short note appeared in BB *in October 1990:*

OCTOBER 1975
YELLOW-BROWED BUNTING IN NORFOLK
David Holman

On the late afternoon of 19th October 1975, Mike Parker (MP) met John Kemp (JBK) and myself (DJH) in the Dell at Wells Woods (Holkham Meals), Norfolk, and excitedly informed us that he had located what he considered to be a Rustic Bunting *Emberiza rustica* around the edge of the nearby caravan site. We quickly returned to the spot, seeing nobody else along the way.

We soon arrived at the area of scrubby bushes and tall fruiting weeds and split up to try to locate the bird quickly, since the sun was already low in the sky. Almost instantly, a bunting appeared before me and gave the distinctive rare bunting 'tic tic' call note. As it sat in view in tall weeds only about 6 m from me, I hailed JBK and MP and started viewing.

My initial impression was indeed of Rustic Bunting, but by the time the others had joined me I had realised that it was something far more interesting, so I advised the others to make careful notes, which JBK duly did; MP, however, hung back as he had made his notes earlier.

With evening drawing on, we concentrated on the bird; fortunately it obligingly sat up in weeds and bushes when gently pushed from cover, but would drop back down into ground cover if left, or fly a short way to a small group of low bushes if pushed too hard. It allowed views down to about 3 m over a period of about half an hour up to dusk. Although extensively looked for the next day, it was most unfortunately never seen again.

The relative brevity of views and excitement of the moment meant that certain contentious features in our three descriptions could never be rechecked against the bird. It was these discrepancies that caused the very delayed acceptance of this record. I believe that if it were not for the extremely well documented and very similar-plumaged Fair Isle bird of 1980, this record would have been lost.

After the sighting, we could initially find only a brief description of Yellow-browed Bunting *E. chrysophrys* in Peterson, Mountfort & Hollom (*A Field Guide to the Birds of Britain and Europe*) but this fitted our bird perfectly.

The British Museum (Nat. Hist.) kindly sent some skin specimens of various Palearctic buntings and all three observers independently selected a Yellow-browed Bunting, although MP selected a different individual from the one picked by JBK and me.

The weather at the time of our sighting was perfect for eastern vagrancy, as a look at the 1975 rarities report will more than testify.

Holman, D. 1990. Britain's first Yellow-browed Bunting.
British Birds 83, 430–432.

Yellow-browed Bunting is a scarce breeder in eastern Siberia and winters in eastern China.

There have been three subsequent records:

Orkney North Ronaldsay, 22nd–23rd September 1992
Scilly St Agnes, 19th–22nd October 1994
Orkney Hoy, 4th–5th May 1998

1981

THE BIRDER'S YEAR

Adrian Pitches

An influx of **Cattle Egrets** was the first headline of 1981. Four had arrived in mid-December 1980 (two in Cornwall, one in Dyfed and one in Hereford & Worcester). A further two were discovered in Gwynedd in January and three more were found in Gwent, Dyfed and North Yorkshire in March/April. The predominantly western distribution of the records suggested that they were American birds displaced by severe weather on the east coast of the USA in late 1980.

Also in January, a leg with a ring on it was found under wires in Fishburn, County Durham. It was the leg of a **Tengmalm's Owl** ringed as a nestling in Norway in June of the previous year. The bird probably arrived in autumn 1980 in the same influx that brought those two other Tengmalm's Owls to Orkney.

February 1981 served up a Valentine's Day present in Cleveland: an adult **White-billed Diver** in Hartlepool docks. An English mainland 'banana bill' was a gift and this confiding bird stayed for a week, feeding on fish scraps discarded by the local fishing fleet.

There was a flurry of Firsts for Britain in 1981, with no fewer than nine by the year's end – the highest number ever found in one year. But before all that excitement there was a distinctly unexciting **American Coot** in Ireland which tempted many British birders across the Irish Sea.

Back in Britain, it was Fair Isle which picked up where it had left off – following the previous October's Yellow-browed Bunting, the first First of 1981 was a **Sandhill Crane** which spent two days on the island in late April. The only previous record of this stately American species in Britain & Ireland was a bird shot in Co. Cork in September 1905. A decade after the First record, Britain's – and Shetland's – second Sandhill Crane turned up in September 1991.

Coinciding with the crane's arrival, there were fierce northeasterly gales which wrecked seabirds from the North Sea across central England. There were 57 displaced **Gannets**, including one in Buckinghamshire, 110 km from the nearest coastline. One that crash-landed on a motorway was 'coned off' by traffic police as a hazard to motorists!

25

Two **Squacco Herons** in April – in Devon and Cornwall – were exceptionally early birds, whereas a **Killdeer** in Nottinghamshire in late April was one of the latest ever.

May and June 1981 were full of eastern promise. Britain's First **Little Swift** appeared in Cornwall on 16th May and the second was on Skokholm off the Dyfed coast a fortnight later (some compensation for the Welsh record in November 1973 now judged *not* to be the definitive First for Britain).

Late May saw the appearance of two **River Warblers** – one on Fair Isle and the second in Norfolk; a third bird, in East Yorkshire in August, took the British tally to double the previous total. The Norfolk River Warbler has a famous, if not infamous, place in British birding history. It was found at Roydon Common in a hedgerow bordering a field of rye and the finders attempted to suppress the news. But the news spread, the hordes descended and the cereal crop was flattened. The twitch was a media event that gave twitchers a bad name but, like the River Warbler, it was an extreme rarity. Virtually all big twitches from that day to this have been well managed and today 'twitcher' is a word of mild amusement to non-birders and the media – not a term of abuse.

Britain's third **Trumpeter Finch**, a male, was on Sanday in Orkney in late May, a decade after the first two in May/June 1971 in Suffolk and Highland. On 14th June, a Sunday morning walk along the beach at Cley, Norfolk, paid dividends for Steve Gantlett and Richard Millington. Their **Rock Sparrow** has yet to be repeated and the bird's speech bubble on Richard's sketch in the log at The George in Cley said it all: the bird's call was "grip, grip…"

Following Norfolk's star bird, Suffolk achieved the extraordinary feat of three Firsts for Britain (well, two plus an honorary third) within a month. On June 19th, an exhausted swift with a white rump landed on a gas-platform 45 km (28 miles) off the Norfolk coast. It was flown to the Beccles heliport in Suffolk where birder Mike Parker worked. He alerted Cliff Waller but the two were mystified and, as the bird had revived and it was getting dark, they released it. That night they consulted books and independently realised that the fork-tailed swift had been a **Pacific Swift**! Cliff briefly saw it again nearby the following day. Although its progress to the mainland was human-assisted, this First for the Western Palearctic had naturally occurred within the 200-mile limit of the British coastline.

Three days after the swift crash-landed onto the British List, David Burns found a pratincole at Dunwich which seemed to be a Collared. But it lacked a white trailing edge to the secondaries … A fortnight later it was re-identified as an **Oriental Pratincole** and it lingered in East Anglia until October, when it was last seen in Essex.

On the last day of June, another First was found in Suffolk. The **Lark Sparrow** at Landguard Point seemed to have hopped off a ship from North America at nearby Felixstowe docks – or had it been a captive bird? Ten years later, another east-coast Lark Sparrow – in Norfolk in May 1991 – strengthened its credentials.

Spring/summer 1981 had been pretty eventful – what would the autumn hold? On August 5th, an adult **Sora** trapped itself in the observatory Heligoland trap on Bardsey – only the second modern British record after one on Scilly in 1973.

If the spring had been dominated by birds from the Near and Far East, the autumn was dominated by birds from the West. The first North American gem was a two-day

Magnolia Warbler on Scilly in late September, another First. Meanwhile, a problematic godwit with a dark underwing had been troubling the warden of Blacktoft Sands RSPB Reserve in East Yorkshire for nearly three weeks. Andrew Grieve finally confirmed it as Britain's First **Hudsonian Godwit** on 27th September, but it disappeared a few days later. Remarkably, it was refound by Exeter University student Gary Wright on the Exe estuary in Devon seven weeks later and stayed until January 1982.

Another shorebird on another RSPB reserve completed the tally of Firsts for Britain in 1981 – but this one was not available to the masses as the RSPB imposed a news blackout. The **Grey-tailed Tattler** on the Ynys-hir RSPB reserve in North Wales stayed for a month from mid-October. There's more in Chris Harbard's *The tattler's tale.* (Britain's second tattler finally appeared in Moray in November 1994.)

The 1981 Scilly season yielded **Yellow-billed Cuckoo, Common Nighthawk** and an **Orphean Warbler**, the fourth for Britain. In Cornwall there was an immature male **Scarlet Tanager** – the third after birds on Scilly in 1970 and 1975. Fair Isle responded with a first-winter **Pallas's Reed Bunting** (the second for Britain – and Fair Isle – after a similar-aged bird in 1976) and a **Red-flanked Bluetail**, the first for a decade.

Meanwhile, in Norfolk, a **White-winged Lark** spent three days near King's Lynn in late October – the fifth for Britain and the first since 1955. Another influx of rare herons rounded off the autumn – not Cattle Egrets this time but **American Bitterns**! A long-staying bird at Magor in Gwent, from the end of October into January 1982, was very popular. Another was in Strathclyde for a similar period.

In late December, at the end of an extraordinary year, there was just one more surprise: a flock of three **Great Bustards** (plus a singleton) in Kent. 1981 had been phenomenal. It seemed impossible that any subsequent year could equal it. But there wasn't long to wait…

THE TATTLER'S TALE
Chris Harbard

Looking back to 1981 brings many memories. My diary for that year bears witness to the old 'Grapevine' … chock-full of phone numbers from institutions like Nancy's café to a long list of Christian names – many of them belonging to birders I have totally lost contact with or now speak to only occasionally: Clive, Dave, Edwin, Gerry, Graham, Phil, Steve…

I worked for the RSPB at The Lodge back then, which meant that word of a rarity always reached me quickly, and there was often a ready-made carful. However, most of the keenest staff had sizeable lists and if I was the only one who needed the bird, it could also mean a lonely, expensive drive … or no trip at all!

I have never been a year lister and so lack the compulsion to mop up all of the previous year's leftovers; however, there was one which attracted me, and so it was that 1981 started badly. Yes, it was yet another trip to Slimbridge to look for a Lesser White-fronted Goose. I seemed to do it every winter and this time it was the usual story ... "It was just in the left-hand bunch of White-fronts and has gone into a dip ... It'll be out again soon ..." Some dip. It wasn't. Some dip it was.

So it was a quiet January, and February would have been the same if not for the arrival of a White-billed Diver at Hartlepool. A good old 'banana bill' – a fantastic bird, and extremely obliging – no need for a scope! Thank you Tom Francis and Co.! At the same time, news broke of an American Coot in Ireland – too far for me, but perhaps not the most inspiring bird! March passed uneventfully as far as I was concerned but with April came my first Nearctic bird, in the shape of a Bonaparte's Gull in Dorset.

May and June brought me Great Reed and River Warblers – great birds to hear in song! Then in mid-June word reached RSPB of an odd warbler singing in Priory Park, St Neots, only a stone's throw from my house. An RSPB staff member had heard it and thought it might be a Marsh Warbler; along with colleague Tim Stowe, I went to investigate. We soon located the bird, which was merrily warbling away in a patch of trees at the top of the park and it was, without doubt – an Icterine Warbler! What a little cracker!

Midsummer was livened up with the appearance of a Lark Sparrow in Suffolk – only a short twitch away and a nice-looking bird, even though it was to be categorised then as ship-assisted ... and its status is still being debated!

Black-winged Pratincole was a nice birthday present in August – found by Mike Everett, who saw it fly-over his car on his route between Hemingford Grey and Sandy. As a result, a long line of RSPB staff was standing by the road after work, when who should drive by but a bemused Ian Prestt, RSPB Director, who must have imagined it was some strange kind of RSPB social activity!

In September, an Arctic Warbler was found at Spurn, which gave me the ideal excuse to go back to my old stamping ground where my birding had really started. The Arctic performed well in the churchyard and as a bonus I jammed in on a Booted Warbler along the peninsula. Magic!

Quandary is one of those rather nice words ... but not a nice state to be in. It started with an innocent-enough phone call to the RSPB library, which was where I worked at the time. Reg Thorpe, an RSPB warden, telephoned with an urgent request.

"I need some information ... about tattlers," he said. A copy of the appropriate North American bird book was found.

"How do you distinguish between Grey-tailed and Wandering?" he asked. There was a disturbing lack of calmness to his voice...

The salient points were gone through and then, when asked why he wanted to know, he said: "Because I've got one at Ynys-hir!"

It was Britain's first Grey-tailed Tattler and what subsequently happened is well documented. The warden in charge of the reserve was away at the time, and with limited parking facilities and sensitive landowners, the news was kept quiet for a few days.

Then a decision was made to release the news on the Saturday night, which would mean a busy Sunday and then quieter subsequent days. Perfect, I thought, I'll go on the Saturday before any crowds. On the Friday, the senior warden returned and vetoed the release of news because of local sensitivities. What should I do? Go and be one of the select group of RSPB people to see it (which would risk censure from many of my non-RSPB birding mates)? Or do the decent thing and respect the suppression by not going? I was in a quandary! I chose not to go … and as I never made it up to see the subsequent Scottish individual, I still think wistfully of that day back in 1981! (Nice word, wistful.)

As the year quietly edged towards its end, a surprise arrival in the form of an American Bittern resulted in the first major (or is it Magor?) twitch to Wales for this magnificent and obliging bird. This was followed rapidly by the last twitch of the year, this time to the Southwest, for a second Nearctic mega, the Hudsonian Godwit, whose appearance cheered the many who missed the bird at Blacktoft.

And what else did I miss in 1981? Well it's a long list of goodies which includes Sandhill Crane, Rock Sparrow, Orphean Warbler, Magnolia Warbler, Pallas's Reed Bunting … Many of them weren't twitchable, some were … but I still need them all!

Chris Harbard lives in Cambridgeshire. A voice of the RSPB for many years, and the author of the 'Coot and Corncrake' quiz books, he is now mainly writing and travelling.

APRIL 1981

SANDHILL CRANE ON FAIR ISLE

Nick Riddiford

There was little sign of any migrant activity on Fair Isle, Shetland, early on the morning of 26th April 1981. The light northwest wind had brought nothing but a series of snow flurries, falling from a leaden sky.

But, at 10.00 GMT, D. G. Borton reported seeing a crane flying over Ward Hill, though in poor weather conditions he had been unable to ascertain which species.

An hour later, the bird appeared over the Observatory building. At this stage, we assumed that it would be a common Crane *Grus grus*. Even when directly under it, however, we strained unsuccessfully, in driving snow and poor visibility, to see the expected striped neck pattern. Indeed, the initial impressions of I. S. Robertson and C. D. Rowley were that the entire plumage, including neck and face, was uniform grey with red on the forepart of the head, apparently reaching the base of the bill. Having gathered this puzzling information, we were left to ponder, for the bird disappeared northwards.

At lunchtime, ISR, familiar with the species in Texas, suggested the possibility of Sandhill Crane *Grus canadensis*, but no-one was prepared to consider this seriously until better views of the bird had been obtained. As if on cue, the clouds rolled back, the sun came out, and shortly afterwards the crane reappeared, soaring against a blue sky over Landberg. Lunch ended suddenly.

During the next four hours, the bird circled continuously over the island. For long periods, it spiralled over Field and Busta. This allowed us to position ourselves to best advantage and we were at last able to obtain accurate details of its plumage. We soon realised that we were indeed looking at a Sandhill Crane: a pale sandy and grey crane with uniform sandy neck apart from a red patch running from the forepart of the crown to the base of the bill and a narrow whitish fan over the ear-coverts. It was a large, rakish-looking bird, how large we came to appreciate when it was joined in its spiral by a Grey Heron *Ardea cinerea*: the crane was considerably bigger.

It was not until 19.00 hours that we saw the bird on the ground. It was extremely wary, but nevertheless everyone at the Observatory had good views from 150 m as it stood in Homisdale. It roosted at Easter Lother Water and was still present the following morning, until the 09.30 plane arrived and put it up. Competition from this larger aerial beast apparently proved too much, as the crane flapped and sailed steadily northeastwards until lost from view.

During the day, we noted the following details:

General appearance Clearly a crane, but with very thin neck and thin legs momentarily suggesting flamingo *Phoenicopterus* in outline, though wings broad and fingered. Generally held wings straight when circling and gliding, and, with well-demarcated and equal fingers, wings seemed rectangular as in Griffon Vulture *Gyps fulvus*. Neck jutted out in front, and legs extended as far behind. Head not very much thicker than neck, and this, with dagger-shaped bill, emphasised thinness of the protruding parts.

Head Forehead, surrounds of eye, and upper half of lores red. In some lights, shade of red over eye appeared darker and deeper than on forehead, and at times 'eye patch' appeared virtually black, presumably effect of shadow. 'Face' (*i.e.* lower part of lores, ear-coverts and up towards nape) very pale off-white, this area being fan-shaped, and broadest at upper and hind margins of ear-coverts. Off-white face contrasted markedly with rest of head and neck.

Neck Long, thin neck held outstretched at all times in flight. On the ground, it was held upright and straight, and was kept straight even when preening. Uniform beige-buff, apart from entire hindneck, which was mid-grey.

Upperparts Appeared beige to sandy buff throughout, but in good light it became evident that the 'saddle' (mantle, back and scapulars) was mottled grey. In flight, saddle contrasted as darker than wing-coverts and appeared to have longways mottling or diffuse streaking. On the ground, saddle appeared mottled grey on beige background, with grey predominant (a pale to mid grey, similar in tone and coloration to the hindneck). Grey did not appear to extend to rump/uppertail-coverts. Short, fanned tail appeared in flight to be sandy buff above with indistinct dark terminal border. On the ground, tail hidden by long tertial and tertial-covert plumes.

Upperwing Secondaries and primaries, including 'fingers', dark, dull grey-black, forming relatively narrow borders to trailing edge and tip of wing. Rest of upperwing, comprising all the wing-coverts, appeared uniform sandy buff. On the ground, primaries and secondaries completely covered by tuft of downcurving feathers (plumes): elongated tertial-coverts and perhaps tertials. Thus, on the ground, visible part of wing was sandy buff, contrasting with grey of saddle.

Underparts Whole underparts from chin to undertail-coverts appeared sandy buff, with suggestion of cinnamon wash to breast and belly. Tail from below (seen when bird in flight) pale, with more marked dark terminal border than from above.

Underwing Secondaries and primaries, including 'fingers', dark but not as intense as on upperwing, and border to trailing edge becoming far less distinct on inner wing. Five or six 'fingers' (tricky to count). Underwing-coverts sandy buff, but dark tips to one set of coverts, probably median underwing-coverts, produced indistinct diagonal line from near wing tip towards axillaries. No contrast apparent between sandy buff of underwing-coverts and underparts.

Bare Parts Bill dagger-shaped, looking pale yellow-brown in some lights, particularly distal two-thirds, but in fact dull grey (trick of the light). Similarly, legs appeared in some lights, particularly when bird airborne, as dull orangey-brown, but on ground were dull grey-green. In flight, feet visible as 'clenched fists' or 'bunch of grapes' attached to thin, straight legs.

Call Heard on a number of occasions: honking, rolling 'carr-rooo', reminiscent in tone of Canada Goose *Branta canadensis*.

Riddiford, N. 1983. Sandhill Crane: new to Britain. *British Birds* 76, 105–109.

Sandhill Crane is a widespread breeder in North America and also breeds in northeast Siberia. Migratory populations winter in the southern USA.

There has been one subsequent record:

Shetland Mainland, first-summer/second-winter bird, 17th–26th September 1991

MAY 1981

LITTLE SWIFT IN CORNWALL

Harry Kay-Robinson

On arriving at Skewjack, Cornwall, on 16th May 1981, I started to check through the mixed flock of hirundines and swifts that was circling over the pools. This flock comprised some 75 Swifts *Apus apus*, 40 Swallows *Hirundo rustica*, 25 House Martins *Delichon urbicum* and ten Sand Martins *Riparia riparia*. The birds were flying down to the pools from the north over fields and a sallow carr. After a few minutes, I noticed one bird which was different from the others, the main features being: pale crown and throat; dark upper body; pale brown upperwings; prominent white rump; and dark, square-cut tail, looking very short. Its wings were like Swift's but shorter. By jizz, it was a species of swift and I believed it to be a Little Swift *Apus affinis*.

After watching the bird for some time, I left and moved on to Porthgwarra to find other local birders. W. R. Hirst, J. H. Johns, L. P. Williams and others were looking at a Woodchat Shrike *Lanius senator*; this they promptly left and came back with me to Skewjack. The bird was quickly relocated and was seen for most of the day hawking insects in the area. It was photographed by W. R. Hirst and J. H. Johns. The following detailed description was obtained:

Size Much smaller than Swift, perhaps slightly larger than Swallow.

Shape Very different from a Swift, with body heavier, but not tapered at rear. Tail seemed an appendage, rather than a continuation of the body lines as on Swift. Wings seemed proportionately shorter than Swift's.

Flight Unlike any other birds in view, glided endlessly into, across and down wind, with exceptionally a series of very shallow, rapid wing-beats. For much of the time, wings held bowed down and back. Whilst it patrolled the pools, it seemed to follow a particular route for 2–3 minutes and would then change to a completely different pattern. Flight was often level, about 1 m above the water, although at times it would lift up quite high only to drop back again. Never seen to dip to the surface.

Plumage Forehead and crown pale brown; throat also pale, but tinged grey. Mantle, scapulars and back appeared black, with marked sheen. In contrast, upperwings pale brown. Whole of rump white, the white extending down to sides of the rear flanks. Tail dark grey, but outer tail feathers slightly paler (these could have been slightly shorter, thus rounding the edges of the squared tail). Breast grey. Belly and flanks appeared black. Undertail-coverts and underwing a paler grey. Eye dark.

Examination of the photographs indicated a number of features not noted in the field. The bird had a marked, but thin, pale supercilium; the uppertail-coverts were black; the black on the belly extended to the vent, only the undertail-coverts being a paler grey. The bird's plumage was in poor condition, with worn primaries and no visible secondaries, the latter presumably lost through moult.

No trace of this bird was found after 16th, despite checking of a number of other sites in western Cornwall; a Little Swift located two weeks later, on Skokholm, Dyfed, could, however, have been the same bird.

Robinson, H. P. K. 1984. Little Swift in Cornwall. *British Birds* 77, 261–262.

Little Swift is an abundant bird across Asia and Africa. The nearest breeding birds are in southern Spain, northwest Africa and Turkey.

There have been 18 subsequent records up to the end of 2003, including a bird that stayed for four days in Nottinghamshire in May 2001.

JUNE 1981

ROCK SPARROW IN NORFOLK

Steve Gantlett and Richard Millington

At 08.00 GMT on 14th June 1981, we were walking from the 'North Hide' at Cley, Norfolk, towards the Coastguard's carpark. RGM idly lifted his binoculars to look at a couple of small birds feeding on the ground under the Eye Field fence. Without speaking, he intimated that it might be worthwhile for SJMG also to raise his binoculars.

One of the birds was a male Linnet *Carduelis cannabina*, but the other was a sparrow-like bird with a boldly striped head. The initial thoughts that it might be a Lapland Bunting *Calcarius lapponicus* were quickly superseded by thoughts of Nearctic sparrows and various rare buntings. RGM then suggested that it might be a Rock Sparrow *Petronia petronia*. At this point, the bird flitted up onto the fence, exhibiting a shortish dark tail tipped with prominent white spots, which confirmed the identification for SJMG, who was familiar with Rock Sparrow in Europe.

For the next ten minutes, we watched the bird, at ranges of about 50–100 m, as it fed along the ruts in the turfed gravel strip between the beach and the field. It flitted up onto the fence a few times and we both compiled detailed descriptions. SJMG then left to alert other observers: J. McLoughlin, M. Eldridge and C. Jones were fortunate to arrive in time and joined RGM still watching the bird. At 08.30 it flew up, for no apparent reason, and headed strongly westward across the Eye Field. It was never seen again, in spite of much searching.

It was a sandy-brown sparrow similar in size to House Sparrow *Passer domesticus*, but plumper in proportions, with the strikingly striped head the most obvious feature. The following detailed description is compiled from notes made at the time and immediately afterwards:

Head Broad crown-stripe creamy/off-white. Dark brown lateral crown-stripes of even width, meeting just above bill. Supercilium long, extending from before eye, flaring out broader behind eye and curving down onto sides of nape, clear buffy-white with distinct yellowish-peach wash towards rear. Dark brown eye-stripe extending back from eye, broadest immediately behind eye and at rear (where forming large dark area on upper rear ear-coverts). Narrow, but distinct, pale creamy eye-ring. Ear-coverts and lores warm buffish-grey, bordered below by slightly darker smudgy grey moustachial stripe. Submoustachial stripe and chin off-white, with pale grey-brown smudgy malar stripes.

Upperparts Mantle and scapulars buffish-grey strongly streaked with blackish-brown and with yellowish feather edgings. Strong pale cream-coloured 'braces' down either side of mantle. Rump and longish uppertail-coverts buffish-grey streaked lightly with dull brown. Median and greater coverts dark-centred, edged sandy-brown and with whitish tips forming double, narrow but distinct, wing-bars. Upper wing-bar stronger and paler, lower narrower with yellowish-peach wash (as supercilium). Primaries and secondaries dark brown, edged paler. Large tertials blackish, edged broadly with pale warm sandy-brown and with distinct white spots on tips. Tail shortish and notched, blackish-brown with prominent creamy-white spot showing on tip at rest. White spot at tip of each tail feather, showing in flight as broken white bar at end of tail.

Underparts Off-white with subdued pale greyish-brown wash and with a distinctly darker brown smudge on sides of upper breast. Dull buff mark across throat. Flanks strongly streaked with dark brown. Small, oblong, pale clear yellow patch visible on centre of upper breast only when bird looked up when face-on, otherwise apparently obscured by throat feathers.

Bare Parts Fairly large, conical, sparrow-like bill flesh-pink, darker grey-brown on upper mandible and tip. Eye dark. Legs and feet flesh-yellow and strikingly thick and sturdy.

An active and nervous bird, it fed on the ground in a horizontal, hunched posture, when it was stouter-looking than House Sparrow, but of a similar size. Though having a rather shuffling gait on the ground, it was bold and alert-looking when perched on the fence.

In Norfolk, 14th June 1981 was clear and sunny with a very warm southwesterly wind of about force 5. The whole of Continental Europe was bathed in a high-pressure system and, in particular, Iberia (a possible area of the bird's origin) was experiencing an exceptional heatwave at this time: Lisbon's temperature of 102°F was the highest for 13 years and in Seville it reached 111°F.

There was much visible migration in progress at Cley during the morning. Starlings *Sturnus vulgaris* were passing west at the rate of about 2,000 per hour; Lapwings *Vanellus vanellus* and Turtle Doves *Streptopelia turtur* were also passing west. The Rock Sparrow, too, was probably on passage: it was not seen at 07.30 when we walked past the same spot, and it clearly left at 08.30.

Gantlett, S. J. M. & Millington, R. G. 1983. Rock Sparrow: new to Britain and Ireland. *British Birds* 76, 245–247.

Rock Sparrow is found across southern Europe, eastwards through Turkey and Iran to the Himalayas, and also in northernmost Africa. It is a resident and partial migrant.

There have been no subsequent records.

JUNE 1981

PACIFIC SWIFT IN THE NORTH SEA

Mike Parker

On 19th June 1981, R. Walden was on the deck of the Shell BT gas-platform on the Leman Bank at 53°06'N 02°12'E, about 45 km off Happisburgh, Norfolk, when a bird attempted to land on his shoulder. It then flew past him and clung to a wall on the rig. He caught the exhausted migrant at about 13.30 GMT, and sent it ashore on the next helicopter flight for release, as caring rig-workers often do. At 19.30 GMT, the helicopter arrived at Beccles Heliport in Suffolk, where I work. Mrs S. Irons rang me from the passenger terminal to say she had just been handed a swift which seemed unable to fly; knowing I was a birdwatcher, she asked if I could help. To my astonishment, the bird lying on her cardigan was indeed a swift, but with a startling white rump and all the upper body feathers pale-tipped, giving a very scaly appearance. My colleagues were somewhat startled when I reacted by running around closing all the windows.

MIKE PARKER

At first, I assumed that it was one of the two European white-rumped species – Little Swift *Apus affinis* or White-rumped Swift *A. caffer*. This bird, however, had an obvious forked tail, so I discounted Little Swift. I phoned C. S. Waller, who promptly arrived, measured, photographed and took a description of the swift. At this point, identification as White-rumped Swift was also discounted because of the dimensions, but CSW had information only on European birds with him, so the bird's identification remained a mystery.

While we were measuring and examining the swift, it revived a little. Since dusk was approaching, we decided to release the bird, to give it time to feed before nightfall. At about 21.00 hours, CSW threw it into the air, and to our relief it flew off and immediately started to catch insects. It continued feeding low over the grass and along the hawthorn hedge surrounding the heliport. As the light faded, all we could see of the bird was its white rump, until finally it was lost to view in the dark.

That night, from our reference books, we both independently came to the same conclusion, that the swift was *A. pacificus*, known then, very confusingly (since *A. caffer* was also sometimes called 'Fork-tailed Swift'), as Fork-tailed Swift, but now known as Pacific Swift. CSW saw the bird briefly again the next day, at Shadingfield, about 4½ km southwest of Beccles Heliport.

Field description

In dull light and without binoculars, the size and shape were very similar to those of the common Swift *A. apus*. The flight and behaviour were also similar, but perhaps a little more sluggish; CSW noted the flight as 'more lazy and jerky'. The only obvious difference in the field was the patch of white on the rump, which also wrapped around towards the undertail-coverts, so that it was clearly visible when the bird was viewed side on. CSW considered that the size seemed the same as Common Swift, but that the plumage looked 'a little darker', in direct comparisons at a range of about 400 m on 20th.

Detailed description

Examination in the hand was brief, to expedite the bird's release before darkness fell; the following details were noted by CSW:

Upperparts Head brownish with pale edges to feathers on forehead. Mantle blackish-brown with buffer edges to feathers. Rump white, with brown shafts to feathers, reached right around and under to legs. Width of rump band was 15 mm in centre and 12 mm on edges. Tail comprised of ten feathers, brown with pale outer edges to outer feathers.

Wings Primaries brownish-black, with buffer inner edge; secondaries similar, with narrower pale edge. Primary and secondary coverts similar, with buffish tips, inner feathers being darker than outer. Median coverts blackish; lesser coverts blackish brown, showing paler than blacker bastard wing. Tertials similar to secondary coverts, and the tiny feathers along the leading edge of the wing were scalloped grey and brownish-black.

Underparts Throat white. Belly and breast brownish, with broadish white tips, some showing rufous tint. Undertail-coverts paler and buffer. Flanks also scalloped, and underwing-coverts grayish-brown, edged with white.

Bare Parts: *Bill* dark blackish-horn; *Tarsus* blackish; *Claws* dark horn; *Soles of feet* purplish-flesh, much paler than legs; *Eye* brownish-black; *Gape* flesh-coloured.

Parker, M. 1990. Pacific Swift: new to the Western Palearctic. *British Birds* 83, 43–46.

Pacific Swift breeds in east Asia and winters in southeast Asia and Australasia.
There have been two subsequent records:
Norfolk Cley, 30th May 1993
Northamptonshire Daventry Reservoir, 16th July 1995

JUNE 1981
ORIENTAL PRATINCOLE IN SUFFOLK
David Burns

On Monday 22nd June 1981, while on a week's holiday, I was taking a walk along the coastal marshes from Dunwich to Walberswick, in Suffolk. I had gone only a few hundred metres when I stopped to scan the marshes behind me. In the far distance I picked up what appeared to be a brown tern *Sterna/Chlidonias* flying directly towards me, and I kept my binoculars on it as it flew right past me, passing very close; I had excellent views of a chestnut underwing and a creamy-white rump. Collared Pratincole *Glareola pratincola* immediately sprang to mind. When it was some distance away, I lowered my binoculars to get a better idea of where it was going to land; it appeared to drop down deep in the marshes (which were out of bounds to birders). I continued my walk, keeping an eye on where the bird had landed. I noted the time as 10.05 GMT. The bird was relocated at 10.25, standing on the ground in an open area of the marsh just off the path. I watched it for 45 minutes, taking down a description and making a few sketches; it was quite approachable. I decided to return to my car to fetch my camera.

When I returned 30 minutes later, the bird was in the same place. It appeared quite nervous this time, and I could not get very close before it flew off, landing in the far distance; I continued on towards Walberswick. On my return, I was amazed to find the bird in exactly the same spot: I stalked it and got to within about 15 m, from where I took a few photographs of it perched and then waited for it to take flight; as it lifted off, I managed to get one more photograph (when developed, this showed an upstretched wing revealing all the underwing). The bird made several short flights, but always returned to the same spot. I crept away quietly, leaving it standing on its favoured piece of ground.

As I had not seen any other birders all day, I decided to go to Minsmere to break the news. Nobody there, however, showed much interest, so I left. In the evening, I was in the public hides at Minsmere when the assistant warden, Zul Bhatia, came in, together with John Grant and Jenny Berry. I told them of my find, and we arranged to meet at the carpark at Dunwich. I found the pratincole at 19.45 hours, in the same location as before. It spent most of the time just standing hunched up, very like a miniature skua *Stercorarius*, occasionally moving its head from side to side and bobbing it up and down. Suddenly it took wing, flew towards the sea, caught a large moth, and returned to its favourite spot to eat this. It would also snap at insects that flew past.

Description

The following description is taken from my own notes made during several periods of observation, with additional material from other observers (D. J. Britton and J. Miller) who saw the bird and sent in their notes to the British Birds Rarities Committee.

Shape In flight resembled a tern. When perched, could be likened to a miniature skua.

Head At distance, appeared to have dark eye-stripe, but closer observation showed this to be a shadow formed by the fold of its feathers. Dark line from gape continued under and past eye, then dropped down to form complete necklace around creamy-white throat patch; close views again showed necklace to be broken (almost formed by small spots).

Upperparts Olive-brown (pale sandy-grey or pale greyish-fawn: DJB). Rump, uppertail-coverts and tail base creamy-white. Primaries (long) and leading edge of folded wing very dark, almost black. In flight, upperwing-coverts and mantle appeared very dark sand; contrast between coverts and outer wing not very strong (JM); dark brownish-black primary colour extended along tips of secondaries (JM). Dark outer wing, less dark inner wing, but contrast not always evident (DJB). No hint of white trailing edge to secondaries.

Underparts Creamy buff-brown, obviously lighter than upperparts; belly and undertail-coverts creamy-white. Undertail white with black terminal band.

Underwing Coverts and axillaries chestnut-red. Leading edge of wing to first primary black; primaries and secondaries mousey-brown, secondaries slightly darker.

Uppertail At rest, shorter than primaries (about 1–1.5 cm short of wingtips: JM). Generally fanned in flight, showing little fork, but on landing briefly showed fork of about Black Tern *Chlidonias niger* proportions (DJB).

Bare Parts Bill short, slightly curved, with hooked tip; large gape. Very dark, almost black, with deep-red base. Legs dark brown. Eye dark brown.

On returning to my cottage in the evening, I looked up Collared Pratincole in the only book I had available at the time, *The Hamlyn Guide to Birds of Britain and Europe* (Bruun & Singer 1970). Certain identification points did not fit the bird I had just been watching; most obviously, the latter lacked a white trailing edge to the second-aries, and its tail was shorter than the folded primaries. Nevertheless, I telephoned home to put the news out. From the following day, 23rd June, a steady stream of bird-watchers came to see the pratincole, and I observed it daily thereafter in the same loca-tion. On Thursday 25th, I noticed when it took flight that one of its secondaries was missing from its right wing; from this I assumed that the bird was in moult, and that this accounted for the lack of a white trailing edge (worn off by abrasion) and the short tail-streamers. I could not locate the pratincole the following day, probably because of the heavy rain, and I left for home on Saturday 27th June.

On 5th July, some friends and I were at Landguard Point, Suffolk, from where we made our way to Dunwich via Minsmere. On arrival at Minsmere I met ZB, who informed us that the pratincole was now considered by some to be an Oriental Pratincole *G. maldivarum*. We were not familiar with this species, nor were other birders who were at the site.

Burns, D. W. 1993. Oriental Pratincole: new to the Western Palearctic.
British Birds 86, 115–120.

Oriental Pratincole breeds from India across Asia to northeast China; eastern populations winter in Indonesia and Australia.

There have been two, or possibly four, subsequent records:

Kent Harty, 21st or 22nd June to 3rd September then Elmley to 3rd October1988

Norfolk Gimingham, 14th May to 3rd June then other sites to 17th August 1993

East Sussex Pevensey Levels, 29th–30th August 1993

Suffolk Havergate Island, 4th and 19th September 1993

JUNE 1981

LARK SPARROW IN SUFFOLK

Trevor Charlton

Landguard Point in coastal Suffolk has, over recent decades, proved to be the county's most important migratory watchpoint. Indeed, so much so that in 1984 an unofficial bird observatory developed, steered by a strong force of local ornithologists. Fortunately, this commitment still continues to this day.

Through its flourishing popularity and intensive coverage since the early 1980s, Landguard has played host to an impressive variety of rare birds from both the East and the West. Perhaps the most memorable of these was the Lark Sparrow *Chondestes grammacus*: an individual whose arrival was to provoke much controversy, and which was set to embark upon a prolonged passage before entering Category A of the British List.

The following account highlights the occurrence of this Lark Sparrow, which turned out to be Landguard's first major crowd-pulling bird.

On the warm and sunny afternoon of 30th June 1981, my wife Lesley (LHC) and I decided to visit Landguard Point with the intention of an afternoon's casual birding. Not surprisingly, as it was late June, there were few birds to see, so we switched our attention to the reserve's flora. This was, however, short-lived as, whilst walking the open short grassy sward near the Coastguard's Cottage at 14.45 BST, we flushed a flock of about 20 House Sparrows *Passer domesticus*, a Sky Lark *Alauda arvensis* and an intriguing, slightly smaller and darker bird. The tantalisingly brief flight view of the smaller bird suggested a bunting *Emberiza*, with a relatively long tail which, when fanned, showed an extraordinary amount of white on its edges and corners. The bird landed about 100 m away in a cluster of Yellow Horned-poppies *Glaucium flavum* on a raised shingle bank, where it remained completely concealed for a few tantalising minutes. As we approached to within 30 m of the poppies, the bird momentarily peeped out through the foliage, revealing a rather complex face-and-head pattern, recalling Rustic Bunting *E. rustica*, only to retreat again into obscurity. Being conscious of recent predominantly westerly weather, time of year and unusual tail pattern, I considered that Rustic Bunting was unlikely. So what could it be? Moments later, the bird showed again, this time out in the open, revealing all, including a startling dark breast-spot.

Having seen many of the American sparrows in the USA some years earlier, I realised that we were watching a British 'first', one of North America's few sparrows to sport such a breast marking; but which one?

Following rapid sketching and note-taking, I telephoned Derek Moore, then Suffolk's County Bird Recorder, from the Coastguard's Cottage. News of an unidentified Nearctic sparrow was quickly passed to local birders, and shortly afterwards the late Messrs Arthur Westcott and Harry Lee arrived, armed with a field guide. From the book, I was able positively to identify the bird as Europe's first Lark Sparrow.

Over the following eight days, the bird was well watched by many hundreds of observers. The bird allowed prolonged and sometimes close views which provided ideal opportunities for note-taking and photography (*Brit. Birds* 74: plate 236; 86: plate 201; 88: plates 112–114). The following description is based on field notes taken by TDC and LHC over several days.

Size and Shape Similar in size to a House Sparrow, though notably slimmer, longer-legged and longer-tailed. Head shape recalled typical bunting, often showing peaked rear crown.

Head Pattern Very striking indeed. Crown-stripe creamy on forehead, merging with creamy-buff on crown and becoming greyer towards nape. Lateral crown-stripe appeared black forward of eye, becoming dark chestnut towards rear. Supercilium creamy, slightly buffier along upper edge. Eye-stripe black and thin, extending from bill through eye to rear edge of ear-coverts. Ear-coverts dark chestnut, beginning at base of bill, grading to paler chestnut towards rear, where prominent white spot present. Malar stripe black, starting very thin at bill base and thickening towards end. Submoustachial stripe white. Eye-ring white and broken, with most prominent area below eye, formed by white crescent. Nape greyish-brown, blending to warm buff breast sides.

Upperparts Mantle, scapulars, back and rump grey-brown, perhaps a shade darker than those of female House Sparrow, with irregular blackish streaking extending to rump. Lesser and median coverts darker brown than mantle, grading darker towards tips of median coverts, forming line of about five blackish spots with cream tips, resulting in thin but distinctive wing-bar. Outer greater coverts black-centred, grading paler brown towards innermost coverts.

All greater coverts edged pale brown, including tips, which formed indistinct wing-bar. Alula appeared completely dark brown. Greater primary coverts dark brown, edged pale brown. Primaries, secondaries and tertials dark brown, all edged pale brown, with secondaries and tertials darker than primaries. Short off-white notch recalling that of Wood Lark *Lullula arborea* present directly below closed greater primary coverts.

Underparts Chin and throat white. Upper breast white with conspicuous central black spot. Breast spot had white cleft on top side, forming horseshoe shape. Breast sides warm buff, with lower breast and belly greyish-white, shading to buff on flanks and vent. Vent bounded by dark brown chevron on each side of body, though not meeting on the underside, a feature not illustrated in field guides. Undertail-coverts creamy.

Tail Blackish-centred, with most visible rectrices showing brown fringe, except outermost, which was white on outer web and broadly tipped white. White tips to each rectrix reduced in size towards centre of tail. Undertail appeared white.

Bare Parts Eye appeared black. Bill pale lead-grey with slightly paler lower mandible. Legs flesh-coloured with bluish-grey feet.

Voice On the few occasions that we heard the bird call, it gave a quiet, disyllabic, nasal or coarse 'tsssi-tsssi', 'tssit-tssit' or 'prrrip-prrrip', repeated two to four times in succession.

Behaviour

The Lark Sparrow was fairly approachable and occasionally offered views down to about 4 m. It fed mainly on its own, out in the open, either on a short-grass sward interspersed with Common Restharrow *Ononis repens* and Lady's Bedstraw *Galium verum* or on sandy-shingle ground, paths and road. It occasionally fed alongside House Sparrows and Linnets *Carduelis cannabina* in a rather typical bunting-like fashion, being crouched and showing very little, if any, leg. The bird most often hopped but on occasions ran, stopping sharply to peck at the ground in a rather plover-like manner. It sometimes scurried short distances across open ground in pursuit of low-flying insects, flicking its wings and tail in the process. When alarmed, it stood erect, stretching its head upwards.

Charlton, T. D. 1995. Lark Sparrow in Suffolk: new to the Western Palearctic.
British Birds 88, 395–400.

Lark Sparrow breeds in western North America; it winters south to Central America. There has been one subsequent record:
Norfolk Waxham, 15th–17th May 1991

SEPTEMBER 1981

HUDSONIAN GODWIT IN EAST YORKSHIRE

Andrew Grieve

On 10th September 1981, I entered the Xerox hide at the RSPB Blacktoft Sands Nature Reserve, Humberside, at about 07.00 GMT, to check the

waders present on the lagoons. A group of six godwits *Limosa* was quickly picked out sleeping in a shallow part of the lagoon and appeared to be five Black-tailed *L. limosa* and a single Bar-tailed *L. lapponica*. The latter was smaller, with a large patch of very dark red plumage on the underparts, covering the belly and extending beyond the legs towards the vent as on summer-plumaged Bar-tailed Godwit. Since the birds were sleeping, few other details could be ascertained, though this smaller godwit was much greyer on the back.

Whilst checking the other waders present, I noticed the six godwits flying off towards the River Humber about half an hour later and was surprised to note that the small godwit showed a similar wing and tail pattern to Black-tailed Godwits, so my initial identification was presumed wrong, the bird on this second sighting appearing to be a small Black-tailed Godwit.

I was puzzled by this bird and checked a few reference books later in the day, but the only American field guide in my possession (Robbins *et al.*, 1966, *Birds of North America*) was not particularly helpful with its illustrations of American godwits, as they were either in full summer or winter plumage, and the bird at Blacktoft was obviously losing its summer plumage, having red underparts restricted to the belly area in the main. The *Guide to the Identification and Ageing of Holarctic Waders* (Prater *et al.*, 1977) indicated, however, that only one other species of godwit was that similar to Black-tailed Godwit, the Hudsonian Godwit *L. haemastica*, but only a few brief identification notes were given. Robbins *et al.* showed that Hudsonian Godwit had a whiter face than Black-tailed Godwit in both summer and winter plumage, which was not the case with the small Blacktoft godwit, and it also showed that Hudsonian Godwit had the summer plumage extending to the undertail-coverts, whereas the Blacktoft bird had whitish undertail-coverts, though it may have lost the red plumage from this area. Prater *et al.* gave measurements of the various races of Black-tailed Godwit, and one of these *L. l. melanuroides*, was smaller than either the nominate race or the Icelandic race, and also had more extensive red underparts and was greyer on the back: thus, it could not be ruled out on the details seen on the small godwit at Blacktoft.

Over the next few days, this small godwit was observed with up to five Black-tails on the lagoons for up to four hours a day, usually sleeping, but occasionally feeding, staying on the lagoons over the high-tide period, but absent when the tide was low, presumably feeding out on the Humber estuary at that time. The few times that it was seen flying were usually when it left the lagoons, and the underwing pattern was not seen because of the angle of flight. Prater *et al.* noted that Hudsonian Godwit has 'axillaries and most of underwing black', but also stated that 'chestnut-red in summer plumage extends to belly and under tail coverts', whereas the Blacktoft bird had mainly white undertail-coverts, and this, taken with the lack of white in the face of the Blacktoft bird, caused me to doubt that it was a Hudsonian Godwit. Many other observers saw this bird during its stay, but, although the possibility of its being Hudsonian Godwit was often discussed, lack of information together with the fact that I was not claiming it as Hudsonian perhaps put others off from claiming it. Many were unhappy about the bird, as I was, but up to this time, the underwing pattern had not been seen, and the eastern race of Black-tailed was still a possibility.

The bird was absent from the lagoons during 21st–23rd September, but returned with higher tides from 24th September. At this time, I paid little attention to it, but the nagging doubts returned, and on 27th September I determined to see the underwing pattern. Again for an hour or so it slept when I watched it from the Xerox hide, but, when it departed, I paid particular attention to the underwing pattern and was able to observe the dark under forewing and black axillaries. At this stage, I discussed this bird with Steve Madge, as I had done earlier, and he was able to confirm, on information just received, that the eastern race of Black-tailed Godwit, which is smaller than the European races, had the same pale underwing pattern of the Icelandic and European races. This removed one of the main problems, and I was now in a position to claim that this bird was Hudsonian Godwit.

On 1st and 2nd October, I spent several hours observing the bird and obtained a more detailed field description, Keith Atkin being present with me on 2nd October.

Size Intermediate between Bar-tailed and Black-tailed Godwit. When standing next to Black-tailed Godwit, noticeably smaller, and on one occasion that Bar-tailed Godwit also present (though not alongside) it was slightly bigger than that species, so perhaps nearer to Bar-tailed Godwit in size.

Shape Similar in shape to Bar-tailed Godwit, with same shorter leg length, body size, and length of bill, though slimmer-looking than that species (perhaps due to the wings projecting beyond tail).

Shape in Flight Intermediate between Black- and Bar-tailed Godwit, though more similar to Black-tail, with blunter wing tip, but legs projecting beyond tail as on Black-tail, though not so pronounced.

Upperparts Mostly dark grey, darker than on adult Black-tailed Godwit in summer plumage. Some traces of summer plumage on sides of back, feathers with black centres.

Underparts Throat buffish, giving way to pale off-white upper breast. Lower breast and belly deep chestnut-red, very dark. This extended between legs to vent, but gave way to off-white undertail-coverts, with a few faint dark cross bars on undertail-coverts. Sides of flanks off-white, with dark barring running down to be exposed below folded wing.

Head Generally grey-buffish, darker on crown, but similar to Black-tailed Godwit, with pale supercilium, more prominent just in front of eye and fading out behind eye. Throat buffish, only slightly paler than rest of head.

Bill Thinner than Black-tailed Godwit and not quite so long, slightly uptilted from base and coming to finer point than Black-tail. Also thinner than Bar-tailed Godwit, but similar uptilting to that species. Dark along most of length, but pale orangey colour near base.

Legs Black, not so long as Black-tailed Godwit's, similar in length to Bar-tail's, perhaps slightly longer.

Upper Flight Pattern Very similar to Black-tailed Godwit, with pale wing-bar, black primaries, black-and-white tail pattern. Wing-bar thinner and less marked than on Black-tail. Tail pattern not quite so striking as on Black-tail, with less white on upper tail. Legs projected beyond tail, more so than on Bar-tail, but did not project as much as on Black-tail.

Underwing Pattern Probably most important distinction between Hudsonian and Black-tailed Godwit, with much darker underwing pattern than Black-tail. Central pale wing-bar noticeable, but rest of underwing sooty-grey, darker on under forewing than hindwing, with sooty black axillaries merging into under forewing.

Voice Largely silent, but on one occasion uttered a soft 'chow chow' in flight, similar to Bar-tail's call, but less strident, and much softer, with no similarities to various calls of Black-tailed Godwit.

The general impression was of a much darker bird than Black-tailed Godwit, accentuated by the dark underwing pattern and the less striking wing-bar and tail patterns. Obviously, however, this species could be overlooked at a distance, as it was to start off with at Blacktoft Sands. In retrospect, I should have been sharper with it, but at least it was sorted out carefully before being claimed.

On 3rd October, hordes of birdwatchers descended upon Blacktoft, and consequently some disturbance was caused when the bird again flew in at high tide, which caused all the birds to fly up from the lagoons. After alighting briefly, the Hudsonian Godwit took off, flew back out towards the Humber and was not seen again.

The bird was considered to be an adult male (or perhaps a first-summer male) on plumage and size: the tone of the summer plumage on the underparts was a very dark chestnut-red, whereas the female lacks this richness of colour on the underparts (Bent 1927, *Life Histories of North American Birds*, page 297; and Williamson & Smith, 1964, 'The Distribution and Breeding Status of the Hudsonian Godwit in Alaska', in *Condor* 66: 48). Size is very variable in all species of godwit, but the small size of the bird at Blacktoft compared with Black-tailed Godwit was also indicative of its being a male.

Grieve, A. 1987. Hudsonian Godwit: new to the Western Palearctic.
British Birds 80, 466–473.

Hudsonian Godwit breeds in northern North America and winters in southern South America. The Blacktoft bird was relocated at Countess Wear, Devon on 22nd November 1981 and remained until 14th January 1982.

There have been two subsequent records:

East Yorkshire Blacktoft Sands, 26th April-6th May 1983; presumed same as 1981

Aberdeenshire Slains Pools, Collieston, 26th September 1988

MAGNOLIA WARBLER ON SCILLY

Shane Enright

I was walking along Barnaby Lane, St Agnes, on 27th September 1981, with Alaric Sumner, after an uneventful morning's birdwatching, when we spotted a small bird perched close to the top of a *Pittosporum* bush. My first impression was of a Warbler with bright yellow underparts, grey-green upperparts and a broad double white wing-bar. Before I could get a better look, the bird 'flipped' over the hedge, and I was left puzzling. Clearly it was not a species I had seen before, but I was inclined to think that it was a New World Warbler, probably a Northern Parula *Parula americana*, or one of the closely related *Dendroica* warblers.

In general appearance, the bird had very bright plumage with contrast between the upperparts and underparts. The rump was not, however, very obvious in the field, as it was generally hidden by the wings, and was well seen only in flight. Nor was the tail pattern particularly evident on the feeding bird, probably owing to the fact that the outer tail feathers forming the white patches were folded under the all-dark central tail feathers at rest. As a result, these patches were clearly visible only when the bird fanned its tail when landing. In addition, the streaking on the flanks, which appeared brownish at very close quarters, seemed, to my eyes at least, to look black at moderate range.

The following description is based on my observations on 27th and the following day:

The bird was longer than a Chiffchaff *Phylloscopus collybita*, about the size of a Wood Warbler *P. sibilatrix*. The breast was, however, slightly deeper and the tail proportionately longer, about a third as long again as that of a Wood Warbler.

The crown, ear-coverts and nape were a smooth blue-grey colour, unmarked save for a distinct, though not particularly broad, complete, white eye-ring around the dark eye. The blue-grey of the head merged into an olive-grey on the mantle and lower back. The uppertail-coverts were a bright yellow colour forming a distinct square yellow rump, which contrasted strongly with the lower back and tail. The tail was black with the exception of two square white patches halfway down its length. These patches are easiest described as being formed by a broad white band, running across the tail and taking up about one-third of its length, the band being divided in two by the black central tail feathers. The undertail pattern seemed to be quite different, though, being whitish with a broad dark band close to the tip, and a narrow whitish terminal band. The wings were a dark olive or slate colour with two broad white wingbars formed by pale edgings to the coverts, the lower bar being longer than the upper.

The chin and throat were a very bright yellow colour which contrasted strongly with both the blue-grey of the upper head and the olive-grey of the upperparts. This yellow continued down the breast, flanks and belly to a little beyond the legs, and was free of any markings except on the flanks, which were moderately streaked brown. The undertail-coverts were an off-white colour.

The bill was dark, fairly short and fine. The legs were dark.

The bird was very active; it was almost continuously in motion close to the top of the hedgerows in which it fed. It rarely flew for long distances, preferring to flit and hop through the bushes. Whilst feeding, it occasionally flicked its wings. Often, it perched with its tail seemingly raised above the horizontal, giving it a posture sometimes reminiscent of that of a Red-breasted Flycatcher *Ficedula parva* or some *Sylvia* warblers. Because of its feeding technique, it often disappeared out of sight along the hedgerows.

Enright, S. D. 1995. Magnolia Warbler in Scilly: new to Britain and Ireland. *British Birds* 88, 107–108.

Magnolia Warbler breeds in North America and winters in Central America and the Caribbean.

There have been no subsequent records.

OCTOBER 1981

GREY-TAILED TATTLER IN WALES

Reg Thorpe

A Grey-tailed Tattler *Heteroscelus brevipes* frequented the Dyfi Estuary, Gwynedd/ Dyfed (Ceredigion/Meirionnydd), from 13th October to 17th November 1981. It was seen by 35–40 people, of whom P. E. Davis, A. D. Fox and M. Stott submitted notes. The record was accepted as the first for Britain and Ireland, in Category A.

Circumstances

On 13th October 1981, I was walking away from the Saltings Hide at the Ynys-hir RSPB Nature Reserve on the Dyfi Estuary with two voluntary wardens when I noticed two Common Redshanks *Tringa totanus* and a smaller, greyer wader flying north along the River Dyfi. I watched the three birds until they went out of sight, my attention attracted by the unusual appearance of the grey individual. On this brief view, its uniform grey upperparts and white underparts did not suggest any species with which I was familiar. Thankfully, after a short period of time, I noticed the bird in question flying back towards us and landing in view some 250 m away. On the ground, the initial impression was of a bird showing the structural characters of a Redshank, but with plumage more reminiscent of a Red Knot *Calidris canutus*. After a few minutes, it flew again and this time landed on a small raised bank, bobbing in typical *Tringa* fashion. With mounting excitement, I attempted to obtain details through a telescope, but again the bird flew, landing this time some 200 m in front of the Saltings Hide. We returned to the hide and obtained further views. It did not come any closer, but a call note was heard. After some discussion with a visitor in the hide, I was still unsure of its identity, but the possibility of its being a tattler was discussed, although that suggestion seemed too far-fetched. As the views had not been ideal, there was still a lingering doubt that it might be an aberrant individual of a common species, but I returned home and consulted Don Roberson's *Rare Birds of the West Coast* (1980) and, on turning to the tattler photographs on page 148, I was shocked to realise that the bird that I had just seen on the reserve was almost certainly a Grey-tailed Tattler.

As the tide had now dropped, there was no way to observe the bird until the following day, so I set about obtaining more information on the separation of the two tattler species, discussing the bird with other birders and informing several local people whom I thought might be interested in seeing it.

The following day, the bird was seen again at high tide by R. Q. Skeen and me. Much better views were obtained, and by now I was reasonably certain that it was a Grey-tailed and not a Wandering Tattler *H. incana*.

As soon as I was happy that the identification was beyond doubt and the bird appeared settled, I began to make plans to cope with the expected large influx of birders. Local birdwatchers, who had seen the bird, were requested to keep the information to themselves until additional help was organised to supervise what was expected to be a major 'twitch'. Unfortunately, the planning came to nothing when the reserve warden made the decision that under no circumstances could the news be released. This decision was based on several factors, including severe access problems with very limited car-parking space and potential risk of disturbance to the wintering wildfowl on the estuary in the vicinity of the tattler's favoured feeding area. It was also considered that a large influx of people and vehicles to the reserve would be detrimental to the already delicate relationship between the reserve and its tenant farmer. As one who has travelled to see many rarities found by others, I personally found it very difficult to be involved in this restriction of information, but, as a RSPB employee, I had to respect the decision of the warden.

The bird remained in the area during the next week, but was visible only at high tide. On 23rd October, it was disturbed by a Peregrine Falcon *Falco peregrinus* and flew off towards the mouth of the Dyfi. It was then recorded on the reserve only on the highest tides, being seen for the last time on 17th November. A full description follows, based on my own notes and those submitted to the British Birds Rarities Committee by P. E. Davis, A. D. Fox and M. Stott.

Size About two-thirds that of Common Redshank. Similar in shape, but slimmer. (Neck often stretched, even raised in flight, giving a curious shape on the wing; at rest, primary tips reached only to tip of tail, although it looked long-winged in flight, ADF.)

Head Pattern Head-on, a white area above the bill where distinct, but thin, supercilia met. Rest of forehead grey, with white feather tips visible at close range. Grey of crown slightly darker than grey nape (slate blue-grey, ADF), setting off the supercilium well. (Supercilium very obvious, narrow and fading behind eye, with no sharp termination, ADF; drawn as strong and well marked to above ear-coverts by MS.) Sides of face grey, except for an off-white area extending from below the bill across to the eye. Thin black line through the lore extending to just behind the eye, creating a well-marked striped pattern of dark crown, pale supercilium and dark eye-stripe.

Upperparts Mantle grey, feathers tipped white, giving a scaly pattern at close range and in good light, but appearing uniform at a distance. On closed wing/ scapular region, a pale area contrasted with surrounding grey, a useful pointer when locating the bird at long range. Primaries tipped black. Rump pale grey and uniform, with no indication of barring. Tail uniform grey.

Underparts Throat and chin white, fading into grey suffusion on the breast, which ended in a distinct pectoral band, but with a slight extension of grey beneath the closed wing. Belly and undertail pure white.

Wings Upperwing pattern difficult to determine, varying according to light and hard to see because of the bird's wing action. Appeared uniform grey, with darker primary tips, and an indication of a very slight pale 'flash' at the base of the primaries and a thin, pale bar along the edge of the secondary coverts (coverts darkening to primary coverts, contrasting slightly with paler secondaries and primaries, ADF).

Underwing striking, with thin black line on axillaries and very dark grey (often appearing black) underwing-coverts contrasting with whitish or very pale grey flight feathers (with faint brownish wash, ADF). Primaries darker towards tip.

Bare Parts Bill about $1\frac{1}{4}$ to $1\frac{1}{3}$ times the length of the head and dark, except for $\frac{1}{3}$ to $\frac{1}{2}$ the length of the lower mandible, which was yellow. The nasal groove was seen well from 15 m away using a telescope in excellent light and was a distinct, but shallow oval, extending from the nostril for, at most, half the length of the yellow on the lower mandible (*i.e.* less than one-quarter the length of the bill). Legs long (but shorter visible tibia than on Common Redshank), yellow or greenish-yellow in some lights.

Call The call was heard on several occasions: a note written as 'chew-ee', like a cross between calls of European Golden Plover *Pluvialis apricaria* and Grey Plover *P. squatarola* (*i.e.* with the quality of European Golden, but with the intonation of Grey) (not unlike Grey, but more plaintive like European Golden, MS; 'too-ee', very like European Golden, PED). On one occasion, this was repeated quickly, with three or four notes run together. (Series of notes led to two-note whistle, something like 'dwer-di, dwer-di, der-di dloo-weet'; 'wi-wee-wee' given on the ground and remarkably piercing 'dweeeeeee' with rising inflection, ADF.)

Behaviour On the ground, the tattler fed by picking food from the surface of mud or grass and spent most of its time dashing about at great speed. On its favourite feeding area, it would chase away any Redshanks that came too close, lowering its head and rushing at the intruder with its bill held horizontally. On landing, or when nervous, it would bob its tail once or twice and on one occasion, when perched on a floating branch, it bobbed for several seconds.

In flight, its wing action was distinctive, with very deep, flicked beats of long wings (flick of Common Sandpiper *Actitis hypoleucos*, but more reminiscent of Ruff *Philomachus pugnax*, MS; downflick with slow upstroke reminiscent of Black Tern *Chlidonias niger*, frequent glides on arched wings, ADF).

Identification of the bird on the Dyfi as either a Grey-tailed or a Wandering Tattler was relatively straightforward, once the initial shock of finding such an exceptional bird had worn off. The separation of these two species was slightly more problematical as, at the time, the literature was confusing and access to many references difficult. Mainly on the basis of its call note and head pattern, I was, however, able to conclude that it was a Grey-tailed.

Thorpe, R. I. 1995. Grey-tailed Tattler in Wales: new to Britain and Ireland. *British Birds* 88, 255–262.

Grey-tailed Tattler breeds in northeast Siberia and winters in southeast Asia and Australia.

There has been one subsequent record:

Moray Burghead Bay, juvenile, 27th November–27th December 1994

1982

THE BIRDER'S YEAR

Adrian Pitches

Both **American Bitterns** that arrived in October 1981 obliged year listers until early January, when severe cold weather moved them on. And the **Hudsonian Godwit** kept company with the wintering Black-tailed Godwit flock on the Exe estuary, Devon, until mid-month. Back at Blacktoft Sands, East Yorkshire, where the godwit first appeared, the pair of **Penduline Tits** that arrived in November 1981 survived the freezing conditions until at least 4th January. They were the fifth and sixth for Britain (the First was at nearby Spurn in October 1966). The long-staying **Glossy Ibises** at Stodmarsh, Kent (one first recorded in 1975 and joined by the second in 1979), continued to oblige and at Slimbridge, Gloucestershire, there was a pair of **Lesser White-fronted Geese** plus another immature bird. In the Outer Hebrides, the male **Steller's Eider** off North Uist (first seen in 1972) lingered, while the drake on Papa Westray, Orkney (first recorded in 1974), called it a day this year and was not seen again after July.

The undoubted highlight of January was a **White-tailed Eagle** in Suffolk, the first British record for almost a decade. It ranged between Minsmere and Sizewell nuclear power station and the *BB* Rarities Report notes: 'The Suffolk bird generated a great deal of excitement and the scene at Sizewell resembled an anti-nuclear demonstration …' Remember those? Another White-tailed Eagle was in Yorkshire at the end of February.

Serin made its last appearance in the Rarities Report for 1982 because it was occurring too frequently to be considered a rarity. A pair in Kent at the end of February was the forerunner of 44 birds recorded during the year, including the returning breeding pair in south Devon which reared seven young from two broods. Breeding Serin is a distant memory now and the bird is once again a rare migrant in Britain.

In March there was a **Killdeer** on Bardsey, Gwynedd, and the Welsh island scored a notable success in early June with Britain's first **Crested Lark** since 1975. After the outstanding haul of nine Firsts for Britain in 1981, it seemed wildly optimistic to think that 1982 would yield similar bounty. But as spring migration got underway,

51

Portland Bill in Dorset once again proved its magnetism to rare birds. Steve Broyd encountered a streaky bunting on the clifftops on 11th April which he quickly identified as a **Savannah Sparrow** from North America and the First for the Western Palearctic. A confiding bird, it was trapped and measured and assigned to the race *princeps,* known as 'Ipswich Sparrow'.

A moor in the south Pennines would not be a good bet for a First for Britain, particularly if that bird undertook relatively short migrations around the Mediterranean. But Midhope Moor, South Yorkshire, is where Gary Lee found a singing male **Marmora's Warbler** on 15th May and it stayed for two months, holding territory in heathland vegetation not unlike the Mediterranean maquis.

The supporting cast for this overshooting southern species were **Subalpine Warbler, Sardinian Warbler**, no fewer than four **Lesser Grey Shrikes** … and a **White-crowned Black Wheatear** in Suffolk! On the evening of 4th June, Mr and Mrs Tarry attended the monthly meeting of the Lowestoft RSPB members group and described a black wheatear they'd seen at Kessingland that afternoon which sounded like a Black Wheatear. A trio of birders decided to miss the meeting after all! They relocated the bird that evening but its tail pattern was wrong for Black Wheatear and a single white feather on the bird's forehead pointed to its true identity. It stayed one more day.

Three Firsts for Britain in the first six months of 1982 – and a fourth came in July. On 13th, a tern-ringing session on Anglesey was enlivened by a **Lesser Crested Tern** among the Arctic Terns. It showed only to its two finders but was followed by another bird in Norfolk in 1983.

Autumn is usually well underway by August on the birding calendar, so anyone who headed off to the Med on the Bank Holiday weekend in August 1982 missed a pair of wonderful waders from eastern Siberia. On 28th August, Teesmouth stalwarts Tom Francis and John Dunnett found an intriguing small shorebird on Saltholme Pool. It failed to reappear the following day, but did return on the Bank Holiday Monday, and was confirmed as a juvenile **Long-toed Stint**. The 'Grapevine' was alerted and birders converged on northeast England.

Also on Bank Holiday Monday, in South Wales, Steve Moon and David Dicks discovered a small curlew at Sker Point, Kenfig, which had crown-stripes but lacked a white rump. The following day they identified it as Britain's First **Little Whimbrel** (or Little Curlew). This was impressive enough – but they had to eliminate the possibility that it was the mythical Eskimo Curlew first! It was a long round-trip for twitchers intent on seeing both the stint and the whimbrel.

In amongst all the excitement, another First for Britain also landed on the List that memorable Bank Holiday weekend. But this was a single-observer record – and the sighting was very brief. Ted Griffiths found a **Northern Mockingbird** in Saltash, Cornwall, on 30th August that was blown away by the northwesterly gale on which it had arrived within five minutes of his initial sighting. Earlier records in Norfolk in 1971 and West Glamorgan in 1978 – both also seen in August – were not considered valid wild birds. Perhaps the most bizarre record of 1982 was Britain's third **Blue-cheeked Bee-eater**, which appeared out of the fog to one lucky observer in a lorry park in Peterborough, Cambridgeshire, on 17th September.

The American influence on the autumn persisted with a run of superb rarities that petered out only in December. Shorebirds included: eight 'Lesser Golden Plovers'; two **Semipalmated Sandpipers**; two **Upland Sandpipers**; at least 23 **Buff-breasted Sandpipers**; and another Killdeer, while Scilly had a one-day **Sora** in September. Another one-day Sora was on Foula, Shetland, on 30th October.

Scotland also secured an excellent passerine record: an **Orphean Warbler** trapped in Aberdeen on 10th October. But the autumn of 1982 will be best remembered for Nearctic passerines and near-passerines. Scilly produced two **Black-billed Cuckoos** (and there were two more, in Devon and Merseyside), and a **Common Nighthawk** for the second year running, which drew an appreciative crowd to St Agnes. The October haul of songbirds on the islands included **Red-eyed Vireo, Blackpoll Warbler, Northern Waterthrush** and **Scarlet Tanager**. But mainland Cornwall was not to be outdone: **Citrine Wagtail**, another Red-eyed Vireo, a **Black-and-white Warbler, Bridled Tern** and Britain's second **Forster's Tern** were the forerunners – with the best yet to come.

Away from the Southwest, Britain's third **Tennessee Warbler** was trapped on Orkney by Eric Meek – and Roy Dennis had a **Yellow-rumped Warbler** on North Uist, the seventh for Britain. A **Northern Parula** found moribund at Wigan Infirmary, Greater Manchester, was rushed to A&E but ended up in Liverpool Museum. It was the first inland record.

Back in Cornwall in late October, there was another First: **Chimney Swift**, with one, then two birds fluttering over Porthgwarra – the finders had also seen Britain's First Little Swift the previous year. Three weeks later, a white-and-grey *Zoothera* thrush discovered at Nanquidno proved very puzzling. But lateral thinking by Steve Madge, who substituted orange and black for white and grey, resulted in the identification of Britain's First **Varied Thrush**, all the way from the West coast of America. This aberrantly plumaged bird stayed a further ten days.

And November still had two Nearctic treats in store – but both were on the East coast. An **American Redstart** at Gibraltar Point, Lincolnshire, stayed a month (another, a one-day bird, was on Islay) and then a **Green Heron** turned up just to the north, at Stone Creek, East Yorkshire. This bird shared a drainage ditch with a **Great White Egret**!

Shetland was distinctly overshadowed in the autumn of 1982 but did manage three special thrushes: **Grey-cheeked Thrush, Black-throated Thrush** and **American Robin**. There was another American Robin on Lundy, Devon – the island's third, which included Britain's First in October 1952.

The late autumn of 1982 was also notable for three major invasions – more than 200 **Common Cranes** crossed the North Sea (including a flock of 40 over Dungeness, Kent), there was an influx of **Parrot Crossbills** to northeast Britain and a coincidental arrival of approximately 130 **Pallas's Warblers**. These eastern sprites were formerly a great rarity and the 1982 influx was understandably described as 'absolutely staggering' in *BB*.

In the wider world, 1982 was the year Britain sent a task force to the South Atlantic to reclaim the Falkland Islands from their Argentinean invaders. The returning fleet brought a delightful avian reminder of the sub-Antarctic to Plymouth docks: a **Snowy Sheathbill**. The late Laurel Tucker lamented the bird's ineligibility for inclusion on the British List. Her lovely sketch evokes the bird she described as a cross between a Cattle Egret, an Ivory Gull – and a Dodo.

At the end of 1982 there had been another nine Firsts for Britain, equalling the record set in the previous year. If that sheathbill had been admitted, it would have been the perfect ten. However, one species that could have been admitted to the List – and seems to have been overlooked – is referred to in the 1982 Rarities Report. A '**Blue-winged Teal**' trapped and ringed at Abbotsbury, Dorset, in October 1979, identified as an immature female, was subsequently shot in northern France in February 1981. The now-adult bird, complete with British ring, was identified as a male **Cinnamon Teal**! So maybe 1982 should have seen a tenth First added to the British List. The record certainly adds spice to the male Cinnamon Teal found on Lewis in the Outer Hebrides in May 2004.

HITCHING AND TWITCHING
John McLoughlin

Mid Wales to deepest Lincolnshire wasn't the most enjoyable cross-country drive, but by dawn we had arrived. We were in luck as the boy, or should I say the baby, was still there! After a 20-minute wait, the American Redstart appeared at close range, flashing and shining its sulphur tail-flashes in the gloom of that November morning. American Redstart, what a bird, what a twitch, does it get any better than this?

Six months earlier, 17th May to be exact, we were northward-bound heading for the Pennine peaks of South Yorkshire. After a three-mile scramble, we found our quarry: Britain's first Marmora's Warbler. Next morning, cracking views of a first-summer male Red-footed Falcon at Potteric Carr were in order. That afternoon, I hitched down to Cley and my final lift was pillion on the back of a Triumph Bonneville, another tick of a kind. Being dropped off in Salthouse was perfect for an evening walk along the coast to Cley. Perfect because feeding on the pools adjacent to the Iron Road was a spanking Terek Sandpiper.

After celebrating in the White Horse in Blakeney, I was up at 5 am the next day. Following my good fortune of the previous evening, I proceeded to dip on Spoonbill, Buff-breasted and Pectoral Sandpipers, Temminck's Stint and a Red-throated Pipit which were all seen at Cley that day. But in my notebook one species still stands out, Turtle Dove: I counted no less than 700 flying west.

Back in Wales, the team were well and truly gripped but the fun didn't stop there as the year evolved into one of the classic years of British twitching. Boy, did we get our share of it, despite our rather backwater location. In the early hours of 26th June, we were woken by Cardiff birder Mike Powell. An Elegant Tern had been discovered in Ireland and we were watching it at Greencastle Pier, Co. Down that evening.

July was the post-field work Shetland Trip. I had spent the spring and summer surveying birds along Welsh rivers. Up at four each morning, and now it was time for a rest. But no, we had big birds to see and two were especially in our sights. En route to Aberdeen for the Lerwick ferry, I made a quick detour in a taxi to see a Roller at Kington near Galashiels.

The afternoon of 6th July was spent dodging Bonxies at Hermaness, and from an elevated perch we looked down at Albert the famous Black-browed Albatross. Later, on Fetlar, we grilled a summer-plumaged Bonaparte's Gull after savouring one of the resident female Snowy Owls.

I was back at Cley for the August Bank Holiday. The highlights were cracking views of Baird's Sandpiper and the breeding Cranes at Horsey. However, the buzz of the weekend was an unidentified wader on Teesside. Initially reported as a White-rumped Sandpiper, Britain's first-ever Long-toed Stint was identified on Bank Holiday Sunday. That night, we kipped out in Seaton Carew bus station following three nights sleeping rough in the beach shelter at Cley; I was used to this by now.

Following a frantic wait, I settled down to watch this beauty for five hours at very close range. At midday, news broke of another mega, a Little Whimbrel in Wales. However, the Grapevine was still scratchy and Nancy's news was that it was just a Hudsonian Whimbrel, so panic over. Or so I thought until I got back to mid Wales that evening. My housemate John Martin had been down to Cardiff for the weekend and had been involved in the identification of what was indeed a Little Whimbrel, so panic on!

The next morning, 1st September, the Little Whimbrel flew in at 07.15 and I watched it in the rain and drizzle for nearly two hours. Relief! I could rest at last after three days of non-stop twitching from Wales to Norfolk to Teesside and back to Wales. Two of the best birds I have seen in Britain, and the Long-toed Stint has yet to fall 23 years later.

September was non-stop: a Paddyfield Warbler at Walney on the 12th followed by a Sharp-tailed Sandpiper on the Humber on the 19th. A detour on the return to Wales took in the Falklands Snowy Sheathbill at Plymouth Docks on the 21st.

Then came Scilly. I had made my first trip to the magic isles in 1978 and I had seen some good birds, most notably the St Agnes Semipalmated Plover and most memorably the Nighthawk in 1981.

My first trip was for a Red-eyed Vireo on the 25th, which I dipped initially but caught up with two days later. I paid a heavy price for refinding the vireo as I missed the Sora Rail only yards away at Porth Hellick. The Sora brought many of the generation's young twitchers to Scilly and we spent the next two days staking out Porth Hellick, but to no avail. However, fortune dealt a kinder hand as Britain's third-ever Northern Waterthrush was found on Bryher.

It was time to return to work, so I reluctantly left the Isles but managed to see both Forster's Tern – Britain's second – near Plymouth and a Semipalmated Sandpiper in Somerset on the way!

Ten days later I was back in the heliport in Penzance and, despite the force nine winds, eventually made the crossing to St Mary's. At Holy Vale that evening the rain had stopped and the wind had calmed and, luckily for me, the Scarlet Tanager (more of a mucky green tanager) appeared on cue. There was a good disco at the Porthcressa that night and my luck was still in the following day as a Blackpoll Warbler was found on Peninnis as I walked past.

My final trip to Scilly that month produced Black-billed Cuckoo, Upland Sandpiper (to make up for the one I dipped on the Lizard), Killdeer, another Nighthawk and a probable Marsh Hawk. What a haul! And to cap it all, not one but two Chimney Swifts at Porthgwarra when I came off.

Things went quiet until the Yankee Redstart that was followed by the Green Heron near Hull. I was straight on the scene for an odd thrush at Nanquidno, Cornwall, on 20th November. It took a six-hour search to relocate Britain's first Varied Thrush; it can't get any better than that!

'Johnny Mac' lives in West Yorkshire where he works for the optics company In Focus. A member of the BB Rarities Committee, he is the voice of Birdline Northeast.

APRIL 1982

SAVANNAH SPARROW IN DORSET

Steve Broyd

At 06.08 GMT on 11th April 1982, at Portland Bill, Dorset, Gary Edwards saw a small bird land about 15 m away. Although he and three other observers watched it for about one minute down to 2½ m or so before it disappeared beneath a rock, none was able to identify the species. About 12 minutes later, a group of observers which included Keith L. Fox and Ron King noticed a small, streaky passerine on some nearby rocks. Their views were brief, as the bird quickly disappeared. Some suggested that it was a Little Bunting *Emberiza pusilla*, and others that it was a strange-looking

Meadow Pipit *Anthus pratensis*, but the presence of yellow about the supercilium prevented specific identification. A search of the immediate area revealed only a female Yellowhammer *E. citrinella*, and the mystery bird was soon forgotten.

Later that afternoon, I was searching for migrants along the East cliffs of the Portland Bird Observatory recording area when I noticed a small, streaky bird feeding in short grass at the cliff-edge. It was half obscured, so I approached closer; as I did, it turned towards me, revealing its small triangular bill and very noticeable yellow supercilium. Its boldly streaked underparts and pink legs helped me to identify it as a Savannah Sparrow *Passerculus sandwichensis*, a species I had seen commonly in North America. I quickly attracted the attention of my wife and J. Tilbrook, who were close by. As soon as it was clear that the sparrow was settled in the one area, I hurriedly returned to the observatory to alert others. A small crowd quickly gathered, including RK, who felt fairly sure that the sparrow was the bird he had seen earlier that morning at the Bill.

During the course of the afternoon, I took the following field notes:

Size and Structure Smaller than accompanying Rock Pipits *Anthus petrosus*, seeming closer to Little Bunting in size. The notched tail looked shorter than that of Little Bunting, and the legs slightly longer. The tail was shorter than the total wing length. Five primary tips were visible on the closed wing, the tip of the longest extending only just beyond the tip of the longest tertial. The head and its triangular bill were small.

Plumage: Head Supercilium yellow, extending from base of bill to well beyond the eye, narrowing and suffusing to creamy-white towards the nape. Lateral crown-stripes brown with finer dark brown streaks, contrasting with a fine pale straw-coloured median crown-stripe, which also showed a few fine darker fleckings. Median crown-stripe most noticeable when viewed head-on. Nape greyish-straw with very fine greyish-brown flecking. Lores and ear-coverts greyish-straw, bordered by thin dark brown lines above and below, which did not meet at rear edge. The upper border formed an eye-stripe, which became more prominent behind the eye, and the lower formed a moustachial stripe beginning at the base of the bill and ending at the nape. Submoustachial stripe white, contrasting with a dark brown malar stripe, which was thin at the base of the bill but widened to form a triangular area at side of throat. Throat and chin white. *Underparts* White, with bold brownish-black streaking radiating out from malar stripes to form distinct gorget across breast. Two broad streaks stretched the length of the flanks and were noticeably more brown. Belly, vent and undertail-coverts unmarked. *Wings* Median coverts brown with buffy fringes and off-white tips. Greater coverts similar. Both sets of tips formed pencil-thin wingbars, detectable only at close range. Primaries and secondaries brownish. Tertials dark brown with pale buff fringes. *Upperparts* Mantle and scapulars brownish-grey, with two very noticeable off-white 'braces' running parallel towards the rump. Both braces edged brown, adding to their prominence. Rump greyish-brown with darker brown streaks. Tail brown, light at base, darker towards tip.

Bare Parts Eye dark and beady, with thin yellow eye-ring. Bill dark horn on upper mandible with pink lower edge; entirely pink on lower mandible. Legs pink, but looked orange in some lights.

The sparrow remained in the area until 16th April, during which time it was watched by several hundred observers. On 12th April, it was trapped and ringed by M. Rogers.

Throughout its stay, the sparrow remained very confiding, which enabled close study. It ran about actively in search of food, in a similar manner to that of the resident Rock Pipits, and even established a small territory, which it defended with short bursts of song delivered from the top of large limestone blocks, under which it roosted at night. P. J. Grant noted this song as a two-second, buzzy 'tit-tit-titti seee seee', with the penultimate syllable up-slurred and the final one down-slurred.

Broyd, S. J. 1985. Savannah Sparrow: new to the Western Palearctic. *British Birds* 78, 647–656.

Savannah Sparrow is a widespread bird in North America; northern populations winter in the southern USA.

There have been two subsequent records:

Shetland Fair Isle, first-winter *P. s. sandwichensis*, 30th September–1st October 1987

Shetland Fair Isle, first-winter, race undetermined, 14th–19th October 2003

MAY 1982
MARMORA'S WARBLER IN SOUTH YORKSHIRE
Jeff Lunn

In the late evening of 15th May 1982, G. Lee telephoned me to say that, during that day, at Mickleden Clough, Langsett, South Yorkshire, he had watched a small Warbler which he could identify only as a Marmora's Warbler *Sylvia sarda*. At 07.00 GMT on the following morning, I located the bird and watched it for about 35 minutes before losing sight of it; shortly afterwards, it was found about 400 m down the valley by other observers, including J. E. Dale. Its identity was confirmed as Marmora's Warbler. Throughout the next few months, until 22nd July, the Warbler was watched by many hundreds of observers. It was photographed by A. V. Moon (*Brit. Birds* 75: plates 145 & 146), John T. Belsey, S. G. D. Cook and John Hewitt.

Description

First impressions were of a small Warbler, strikingly blue-grey in colour, closely resembling a Dartford Warbler *S. undata* in shape, and with a noticeably long tail.

> *Plumage* Striking: at a distance appeared uniform blue-grey, recalling adult Cuckoo *Cuculus canorus*, this emphasised by dark vegetation background. At closer range, head appeared darker, especially around lores, and at close quarters various grey-blue hues of varying quality and intensity visible on head and neck. Underparts slightly paler, especially towards belly. Wings grey; remiges often appeared paler, especially in bright light (this effect perhaps caused by outer webs or feather shafts being paler, or reflecting light). Tail variously described as brown-washed grey or buffy-grey; feather tips appeared abraded.
>
> *Bare Parts* Legs originally described as straw-yellow, later as yellow-orange (difference perhaps due to lighting effects?). Bill appeared sharply defined pale at distance, accentuated by dark background and grey plumage; at closer range, upper mandible pale horn, base and lower mandible pale yellow. Eye blood-red, surrounded by blood-red orbital ring, conspicuous at close quarters. Mouth pale straw-yellow, striking when bird singing.

Habitat

Mickleden Clough is a steep-sided gritstone valley situated at 1,400 feet (426 m) in the southern Pennines. A small, fast-flowing stream meanders northwards through the valley bottom, where the vegetation is dominated by grasses (*Nardus, Agrostis* and *Molinia*) and wet flushes of moss *Sphagnum*, rushes *Juncus* and cottongrass *Eriophorum*. The valley sides are dominated by Heather *Calluna vulgaris*, Bilberry *Vaccinium myrtillus*, Cowberry *V. vitis-idaea* and Bracken *Pteridium aquilinum*. Small rocky outcrops and quarries are also a feature of the habitat, as too is an almost complete lack of tree cover apart from isolated Rowans *Sorbus aucuparia* and Hawthorns *Crataegus monogyna* on the slopes and a line of mature mixed deciduous trees for about 400 m in the valley bottom.

General habits and behaviour

Throughout its stay, the warbler frequented the steep eastern side of the valley, and was only occasionally recorded in the valley bottom. It occupied almost exclusively an area of about 400 m × 50 m (its apparent territory) comprised mainly of Heather about 0.5 m tall and Bilberry interspersed with grass patches and Bracken. It was generally very active within this whole area, continuously moving short distances through the vegetation and then flying 30–40 m. The warbler frequently perched and sang, usually on top of some Heather, but was out of sight to the stationary observer for considerable periods of time. When perched it occasionally cocked its tail to about 45° in Dartford Warbler manner.

The Marmora's Warbler frequently gave display. This was very much like that of a Common Whitethroat *S. communis*: a steady fluttering ascent to 4–7 m above the Heather at an angle of 60–70° to the horizontal, with legs trailing, singing continuously, followed by a very steep undulating dive to alight usually farther down the slope. Display was noted over the whole length of the warbler's territory, and no particular song perches were used exclusively. Collection and carrying of nest material (dry grasses and cobwebs) was seen on a number of occasions, especially during the early part of the bird's stay.

The warbler attempted to catch flying insects just above the vegetation, and also moved through the vegetation as if foliage-gleaning. On one occasion, I observed it moving over bare ground under the Heather in the manner of a Dunnock *Prunella modularis*, apparently foraging.

No agonistic interactions were reported with any of the breeding Meadow Pipits *Anthus pratensis*, Skylarks *Alauda arvensis* and Whinchats *Saxicola rubetra*. Only one other *Sylvia* Warbler was noted in the vicinity: a Garden Warbler *S. borin* on 16th May; again, no encounter was observed.

Voice

The Marmora's Warbler frequently sang throughout the day, at times almost continuously, and often this was the only indication of its presence. The individual song seemed to comprise a two-to-three-second phrase of a weak warbling quality, lacking both strong notes and rich tone; a diagnostic trill, recalling a weak or distant snatch of Wood Warbler *Phylloscopus sibilatrix* or Tree Pipit *Anthus trivialis* song, often punctuated and invariably terminated the song. The tonal range was narrow, and the total impression was of a weak quality, recalling Dunnock.

A call note was heard infrequently. I described it as a sharp 'twik', typical of *Sylvia*, but having a more chat-like quality.

Origin

The occurrence of a Marmora's Warbler some 2,100 km north of its previously known range immediately raises questions concerning its origin. The most likely solution seems to be a spring overshoot of the nominate race, which would correspond closely to records on the French and Italian Mediterranean coasts in mid or late April. Climatic conditions prevailing at and just before the time of the Yorkshire bird's arrival, with high pressure building on the Continent and a warm southerly airstream originating well to the south, also support this view.

Lunn, J. 1985. Marmora's Warbler: new to Britain and Ireland. *British Birds* 78, 475–481.

Marmora's Warbler breeds in Corsica and Sardinia and winters in North Africa; it is also present in Spain on the Mediterranean coast. The sedentary form found on the Balearic Islands has been split as a separate species, Balearic Warbler Sylvia balearica.

There have been four subsequent records:

East Yorkshire Spurn, 8th–9th June 1992

Borders St Abb's Head, 23rd–27th May 1993

Norfolk Scolt Head, 12th & 18th May 2001

Suffolk Sizewell, 29th May 2001

JUNE 1982

WHITE-CROWNED BLACK WHEATEAR IN SUFFOLK

Brian Brown

At about 18.15 GMT on 4th June 1982, A. C. Easton and R. Conner were told by Mr and Mrs R. Tarry of Kessingland, Suffolk, that they had seen what they thought was possibly a Black Wheatear *Oenanthe leucura* to the north of the pumping station at Kessingland. Their description was good, so ACE telephoned me and we went to investigate.

The bird was easily found, in the exact spot that Mr Tarry had described. It was quite approachable, and we instantly identified it (at that time) as a Black Wheatear. Since it was all-black, with a white rump, uppertail- and undertail-coverts, and a white tail except for black central feathers, we did not consider the possibility that any other species could be involved or needed to be eliminated. We had, however, noted a single white feather on the forehead; and that the white on the outer tail feathers extended to the tip with, apart from one or two small marks, no terminal black band.

The wheatear was frequenting a small pit which was being used to dump farm rubbish and pieces of disused machinery, and a flat grassy area around this. While we were watching it, a gentleman on holiday at Kessingland came along and told us that he had observed the bird for the past two days; he had no idea what it was, believing it to be a freak Northern Wheatear *O. oenanthe*. The supervisor of the nearby pumping station confirmed that it had been there for a few days before it was reported.

After we had watched the wheatear for about an hour, we went off to spread the news. When we arrived at my home, we checked our notes against various books. It was then that we realised that our initial identification was wrong. Looking at the illustration in Heinzel *et al.* (1972, *The Birds of Britain and Europe with North Africa and the Middle East*), we concluded that our bird must be a White-crowned Black Wheatear *O. leucopyga*. This is the only species which has a combination of all-black body (in non white-crowned specimens) and all-white sides to the tail. The single white feather on the forehead of our bird then became much more significant.

The wheatear was watched by a large number of people on 5th, but as many more missed out on 6th, by which time it had disappeared. This was the first record of White-crowned Black Wheatear in Britain and Ireland, and the species' most northerly occurrence by around 1,700 km.

DESCRIPTION

Head Black, more or less tinged brownish, except for one white feather just right of centre on forehead.

Body Rump, lower back, uppertail- and undertail-coverts, vent and rear flank white, this extending well up back and much farther than I have seen in photographs of Black Wheatear; at times, the white showed in rough T shape between tertials when wings folded. Rest of body black, more or less tinged brownish, with no noticeable bluish gloss; black appeared to extend back to just between legs.

Tail White, except for central feathers which were black. All outer feathers unmarked, apart from one on right-hand side which had small black mark at tip. Underside of each feather appeared to have small dark marks at tip, but only fleeting glimpses obtained, so accurate description cannot be given.

Wings Blackish-brown and paler than rest of body, looking reminiscent of Ring Ouzel *Turdus torquatus* at a distance. Coverts sooty-brown, edged slightly paler brown, but this noticeable only at close range; primaries sooty-brown, perhaps slightly paler than coverts; secondaries appeared to be a bit darker than primaries, but this difficult to confirm.

Bare Parts Eye black. Bill and legs black, but appearing quite grey in some lights.

Size and Shape No direct comparison with any other species, but appeared to be slightly larger than Northern Wheatear. Shape and stance as in typical Northern Wheatear, but appeared quite pot-bellied at times.

Behaviour Similar to Northern Wheatear. When we watched at close range during first evening, flicked wings quite often and 'waved' tail up and down slowly. This behaviour not seen on following day (perhaps anxiety reaction to my close approach on previous evening).

Age and Sex Probably first-summer.

Peter Clement has commented (*in litt.*) that 'the bird was most likely to have been of the nominate race *O. l. leucopyga*, from North Africa, on tail pattern. The state of plumage does not help subspecific identification and only measurements in the hand would have confirmed. Many birds from Egypt and Sinai are intermediate between the two races.'

The wheatear stayed in the vicinity of the small pit and the surrounding area of flat stony ground, which was covered to a varying extent with short grass and dune-type flora. The pit was being gradually infilled with farm rubbish, including pieces of concrete, metal, wood, tyres, bricks, a trailer, and soil which was being dumped on the afternoon of 5th and which may have been the cause of the bird's departure. The vegetation in the pit was much lusher than in the surrounding area and the bird obtained much of its food there. It was seen to feed mainly on brownish and greenish caterpillars, which it persistently bashed and squeezed before swallowing. Other observers reported seeing it eating earthworms.

Weather, and occurrence of associated species

The weather during May and June 1982 was abnormally dry and sunny. Only small amounts of rain fell between 7th and 27th May, and in a warm southwesterly airflow temperatures soared to 75°F (24°C) on 16th. The temperatures in the first week of June were the hottest for 35 years, and a very warm air-stream originating from North Africa and the Mediterranean raised temperatures to over 80°F (27°C) in Suffolk.

There seems little doubt that this weather pattern was the cause of the vagrancy of the White-crowned Black Wheatear. A number of other southern species occurred in Britain at the time, but the Marmora's Warbler *Sylvia sarda* at Langsett, South Yorkshire, from 15th May (Lunn 1985) is most significant: it could have come from the same area, on the same air-stream. It is quite possible that our bird had been at Kessingland for up to a couple of weeks, as the spot is virtually unwatched, particularly in summer; most birders visiting Benacre, to the south, stop short of the pumping station. It may seem amazing that two unexpected 'firsts' should have arrived in Britain at the same time, but the possibility was foreseen (Sharrock & Grant 1982, Editor's summary, *Birds New to Britain and Ireland*): 'One year, perhaps, we shall get whatever weather pattern is needed to bring rarities such as Hoopoe Lark *Alaemon alaudipes* pouring northwards to us from the deserts of North Africa.'

Brown, B. J. 1986. White-crowned Black Wheatear: new to Britain and Ireland.
British Birds 79, 221–227.

White-crowned Black Wheatear breeds across the Sahara from Morocco east into Arabia. It is mainly resident.

There have been no subsequent records.

JULY 1982

LESSER CRESTED TERN ON ANGLESEY

Clive Hurford

On the morning of 13th July 1982, John Chester and I were awaiting the arrival of ringers on the beach of Cymyran Bay, Anglesey, Gwynedd, using the time to count recently fledged Arctic Terns *Sterna paradisaea* that were gathered along the shoreline, when my attention was caught by the presence of a large, yellow-billed tern amongst them. I called John over and, after watching the bird for a short while, he suggested, to his eternal credit, that we had better take some field notes, at which point the following details were noted:

> *Size and Shape* Considerably longer than Arctic Tern, though slightly smaller than Sandwich Tern *S. sandvicensis*, both of which were available for direct comparison. Upright stance recalled that of Sandwich Tern, and, at rest, wingtips extended beyond shallowly forked tail.
>
> *Upperparts* Head heavy and Sandwich Tern-like, with dense black cap running from base of bill, through eye, and ending at rear of crown in short ragged crest, giving head square-ended appearance. Shoulders, mantle, rump and tail uniform medium grey, noticeably darker than that of Sandwich Tern. Upperwing in flight appeared pale whitish-grey, with three or four dark shafts showing in outer primaries, recalling upperwing pattern of Roseate Tern *S. dougallii*. Underwing appeared generally pale, with only trace of darker shading near wingtips.
>
> *Underparts* Chin, 'cheeks', throat, breast, belly, flanks and undertail-coverts all white.
>
> *Tail* In flight, appeared very short and barely forked. On one occasion, as bird was alighting on beach, tail was fanned and looked almost rounded, losing all semblance of a fork.
>
> *Bare Parts* Bill orange-yellow, length approximately that of Sandwich Tern's bill, but heavier and slightly downcurved. Legs and feet black.
>
> *Behaviour* Flight heavy and ponderous (in comparison with Arctic Tern's). No call heard.

For the greater part of the time that the bird was present (probably no longer than ten minutes in total), it stood with the Arctic Terns on the shoreline, preening occasionally. It undertook two short flights, each of approximately 50 m along the beach, and, on alighting from the second of these, it stood directly alongside a Sandwich Tern, making direct comparison possible. One or two minutes later, it flew off southwest towards Rhosneigr and was not seen again.

Initial thoughts on the identification of the bird turned to Elegant Tern *S. elegans*, purely on the strength of the knowledge that a tern of that species had been present in Ireland during the period immediately prior to the sighting. Later, on referring to the literature, Elegant Tern was ruled out by the medium grey uniformity of the mantle, rump and tail on the bird that we had observed (Elegant Tern showing a white rump and tail, and also a deeply forked tail and a proportionately longer, more slender bill). Both Caspian Tern *S. caspia* and Royal Tern *S. maxima* were discounted on size and never seriously considered. Cayenne Tern *S. s. eurygnatha* was ruled out on the strength of bill shape and coloration and the uniform medium grey upperparts. This left only Crested Tern *S. bergii* and Lesser Crested Tern *S. bengalensis*, and Crested Tern was ruled out on size and bill colour.

The field notes taken indicated that the bird was in fact an adult Lesser Crested Tern in summer plumage, the combination of size, bill shape and coloration, and the uniform medium grey of mantle, rump and tail eliminating all other species.

Hurford, C. 1989. Lesser Crested Tern: new to Britain and Ireland.
British Birds 82, 396–398.

The nominate race of Lesser Crested Tern breeds from the Red Sea and East Africa east to Sri Lanka; the race to which the Anglesey bird is assigned, S. b. torresii, breeds in Australia and southern New Guinea, Pakistan and, the Persian Gulf – and in the Mediterranean, with large numbers in the Gulf of Sirte, Libya, and a few pairs in France, Spain and Italy.

There have been at least 15 subsequent records, including a female which summered on the Farne Islands, Northumberland from 1984–97.

AUGUST 1982

LONG-TOED STINT IN CLEVELAND

John Dunnett

At about noon on Saturday 28th August 1982, at Saltholme Pool, Cleveland, Tom Francis and I discovered independently a lone wader with structure and feeding behaviour typical of a Wood Sandpiper *Tringa glareola*.

Other similarities with that species included a small, squarish head, ample neck and longish pale-coloured legs. On the other hand, a bright chestnut crown and upperparts, clear supercilia and an indistinct pectoral band, together with prominent white mantle and scapular lines ('V's), were plumage features one would associate with either juvenile Pectoral Sandpiper *Calidris melanotos* or Sharp-tailed Sandpiper *C. acuminata*. The combination was puzzling.

Having to contend with both an exceptional heat haze (inhibiting full use of a telescope) and shortage of time, we risked a closer approach, whereupon the bird flew to the opposite end of the pool. TF and I both believed that we had seen a white rump, a feature which was seemingly substantiated when the bird (now at long range) started preening, revealing prominent white lateral tail-coverts. Hastily accepting this as a juvenile White-rumped Sandpiper *C. fuscicollis*, albeit a strange one, we departed, although not until numerous observers had witnessed and agreed with our presumption.

Later, in the evening, I returned to the pool. Viewed for a second time and at much closer range, I was amazed – indeed shocked – at the bird's stint-like size and proportions. Initially, from farther afield, it had appeared larger, a curious phenomenon which was later experienced by numerous observers. Now accompanying Dunlins *C. alpina*, the strange bird was bodily only three-quarters of their size, but, owing to its more upright posture and significantly longer legs, was of equal height. I also discovered the absence of a white rump.

Despite extensive searching on the following day, the bird was not relocated. After perusal of the limited literature that I had available, however, and following several telephone conversations, I expressed my views on the probability of Long-toed Stint *C. subminuta* to C. Sharp, who subsequently related this to a colleague, and that evening I received a telephone call from R. T. McAndrew offering a supporting description.

Fortunately, the next morning (Bank Holiday Monday), the stint was relocated and, following a brief period of observation with Ian Mills, we agreed that 'the Grapevine' should be notified. This was carried out shortly before noon. The bird was last seen on 1st September.

During its five-day stay, the bird was observed only on Saltholme Pool, despite, in its absence, being sought elsewhere. It showed great site-fidelity, almost always feeding on the same edge of the pool, affording excellent opportunities for viewing and photography.

DESCRIPTION

Size and Shape Marginally larger than Little Stint *C. minuta* (though direct comparison not obtained), more upright stance with longer neck, especially so when extended (cf. *Brit. Birds* 75: plates 215–217), more attenuated towards the tail, and longer-legged, creating problems when attempting accurate size comparison. When viewed from farther afield, seemingly grew in stature and, combined with small, squarish head (owing to steep forehead), flattish back, ample belly and attenuated rear, bore uncanny resemblance to Pectoral Sandpiper, an impression iterated by most observers.

Head Central forehead and crown black, with bright chestnut lateral fringes extending from base of upper mandible, creating striped effect (three on either side). Supercilium white, starting short of forehead and extending onto sides of upper hindneck, with increasing amounts of brownish streaking; distinctly rounded or bulbous in front of eye, almost bisecting lower grey-brown loral line, the latter being a continuation of the black/brown forehead extending backwards and widening (crescent-shaped) in front of and slightly below eye before expanding onto ear-coverts, forming distinctive oval brown patch with lower buffish fringes. In bright sunlight, 'split supercilium' effect formed owing to the fusion of fore part with lower chestnut fringes of crown.

Upperparts Chestnut tones of crown terminated on nape in downward point. Hindneck and sides of neck grey, with delicate grey-brown flecking. Mantle black with chestnut-buff streaking, neatly framed either side with broad white/cream fringes, forming prominent lines or V (as on juvenile Little Stint), apparent at long range and further accentuated by alignment of black-centred outer mantle feathers and neat top row of black scapulars, forming two solid black parallel lines. Lower back, rump and central tail feathers black, with contrasting white lateral tail-coverts and greyish outers. Scapulars black/brown-centred with downwardly increasing amounts of chestnut fringes, the lower two rows having broad orange-chestnut fringes with white leading edges and tips, forming two broken yet prominent white scapular lines.

Wings Tertials black with chestnut fringes, long and at all times cloaking primaries, almost reaching, apart from a couple of millimetres, tip of tail, which was black where visible. Lesser and median coverts with black/brown centres, whitish-buff edges and dark tips. Greater coverts similar to tertials, having black centres, but marginally paler fringes more orange in tone with whitish tips. Whilst observing the bird preening at close range on 1st September, I was able to detect a white shaft to the longest primary, a feature specifically looked for, having previously read of this in the literature (Wallace 1974). The primary feathers were blackish, and the remainder of the shafts were either brown or grey. When viewed in bright sunlight, chestnut tones of crown and fringes of tertials were radiant; the supercilium and mantle lines appeared whiter than the underparts.

Underparts Chin and throat white, narrow collar of fine greyish-brown streaks encircling lower throat and breast, forming gorget which ended in downward point. Streaking heavier, more pronounced and of browner tone towards sides, and extended onto upper flanks. Sides of breast and upper flanks, however, partially separated by inverted V of white underparts; streaking on upper flanks more sporadic and of warmer brown tone, and suffused with general buffish-orange wash. Remainder of underparts, lower flanks, belly and undertail-coverts white.

Bare Parts At exceptionally close range and in bright sunlight, yellowish suffusion on basal area of lower mandible (apparent in some photographs). On all other occasions, bill appeared black, slightly downcurved towards tip, appearing approximately three-quarters length of head. Iris dark brown or black. Arguably, most significant feature was leg length, owing largely to the amount of tibia visible: yellow legs and toes, even hind toes, seemed conspicuously long.

Behaviour Feeding technique akin to Wood Sandpiper, appearing sedate and erect, frequently extending its longish neck, picking rather than probing and generally lacking the rapidity of a feeding Little Stint. During one period of observation when on dry terrain, with neck extended parallel to the ground and attenuated rear pointing skywards, was most reminiscent of a feeding Wilson's Phalarope *Phalaropus tricolor*. Whenever wading (occasionally up to underparts) or feeding in soft mud, appeared to show some difficulty in extracting its feet, a characteristic which was seemingly substantiated by its eagerness to perch on any convenient stone. Indeed, when initially sighted it was resourcefully using a discarded wooden plank as a platform from which to feed.

Flight When flying with Dunlins, smaller size and quicker flight apparent, the prominence of the white lateral tail-coverts, emphasised by the dark upper-parts, being the most striking feature; whitish tips of greater coverts formed indistinct wing-bar. Rump and central tail feathers black with greyish-white outer tail feathers.

Call Similar to that of Curlew Sandpiper *C. ferruginea*, but lower in pitch: rolled 'terrup, terrup'.

Dunnett, J. B. 1992. Long-toed Stint: new to Britain and Ireland.
British Birds 85, 431–436.

Long-toed Stint breeds in northeast Siberia and winters in southeast Asia and Australia. There have been no subsequent records but there was one previous record (in Cornwall in June 1970), previously identified as Least Sandpiper, that was re-identified and accepted as the First for Britain:

JUNE 1970
LONG-TOED STINT IN CORNWALL
Philip Round

The weekend of 5th–7th June 1970 was extraordinary by the standards of the time, and especially exciting for me. I was still at school and in the midst of sitting my GCE A-level examinations. On the evening of Friday 5th June, I thought that, by way of a break from my studies, I would have a look at my 'home patch', Marazion Marsh, Cornwall. I expected it to be fairly quiet as the weather was clear and settled, and, moreover, the marsh was, at that time, fairly dry with exposed wet mud and surface water restricted to little more than a small puddle at the eastern end. To my great surprise, however, I found a Temminck's Stint *Calidris temminckii*, only the fourth twentieth-century record for the county. Furthermore, other observers (while looking for the Temminck's) found a Little Stint *C. minuta* at Marazion on the following day, and two more on the Hayle estuary that same weekend. There were only four previous spring records of Little Stint for the Cornish mainland.

When I revisited Marazion Marsh on the late afternoon of Sunday 7th June, the original Temminck's Stint had gone, but another small, yellow-legged stint was present together with a Yellow Wagtail *Motacilla flava* showing the characteristics of the ashy-headed race *cinereocapilla*. J. H. Johns arrived at the site shortly after, and both he and I spent about two hours watching the new stint that evening. It was much brighter and more strongly scaled on the upperparts than the Temminck's, lacked the clear white outer tail feathers of that species, and differed in shape, proportions and call.

On the following day, we both spent several more hours observing the stint, which was tame and could be approached down to about 6 m. During this period, JHJ obtained an excellent series of photographs, both monochrome and colour. The bird was last observed on the evening of 8th June. During its stay, it was seen by at least seven other observers, including the late J. E. Beckerlegge, E. Griffiths, the late R. G. Hadden, P. R. G. Marriott, the late A. G. Parsons, B. Pattenden and L. P. Williams.

JHJ and I both reached the conclusion that the bird was a Least Sandpiper *C. minutilla*, although at that time neither of us had any experience of any of the rarer stints. Details of the sighting were sent to the British Birds Rarities Committee by JEB, JHJ, PRGM and PDR, and the record was subsequently accepted as the first spring record of Least Sandpiper for Britain *(Brit. Birds 64: 351)*.

The possibility that the bird might have been the similar Palearctic species, Long-toed Stint *C. subminuta*, was not then considered. At that time I was unaware of the existence of Long-toed Stint, and none of the three other observers' submissions to BBRC made any mention of that species. Ironically, though, JHJ's and my descriptions both drew attention to the unusually long toes shown by the bird. Further, within only a week or two of the sighting, I met D. J. Britton at Marazion Marsh and he asked me whether I or any other observer had satisfactorily excluded the possibility of Long-toed Stint. My doubts did not really begin to accumulate, however, until 1974, when I read D. I. M. Wallace's ground-breaking paper on stint identification *(Brit. Birds 67: 1–16)*.

In autumn 1975, I discussed my misgivings with JEB and JHJ, and JHJ made his transparencies, monochrome negatives and prints available for renewed scrutiny. Comparison of these photographs with skins in the British Museum, consultation with other ornithologists and, finally, experience of Long-toed Stints wintering in Thailand in January 1979 led me to believe that the Marazion bird had indeed been a Long-toed Stint in breeding plumage. I summarised my views *(in litt.* to BBRC, 27th March 1979): 'Of all the features examined here, there is none which unequivocally points to the original identification of Least Sandpiper as being correct. The size, length of legs and toes, and call all strongly indicate that the bird was probably a Long-toed Stint C. *subminuta*, while many of the plumage characters lend some support to this hypothesis. A re-examination of the record by the Rarities Committee would seem appropriate.'

Round, P. D. 1996. Long-toed Stint in Cornwall: the first record for the Western Palearctic. *British Birds* 89, 12–24.

AUGUST 1982

LITTLE WHIMBREL IN MID GLAMORGAN

Steve Moon

Sker Farm, near Sker Point, Mid Glamorgan, lies on the southern edge of extensive sandhills and slacks comprising Kenfig Pool and Dunes Local Nature Reserve. David E. J. Dicks and I were walking along a track adjacent to Sker Farm at about 15.45 GMT on 30th August 1982, when we disturbed two birds from nearby dunes. DEJD said 'Whimbrel' and both of us glanced at them through binoculars. One was indeed a Whimbrel *Numenius phaeopus*, showing extensive white on its lower back and rump, but, to my surprise, I could see that the accompanying bird had completely brown upperparts. The Whimbrel flew away, but the second bird settled nervously about a hundred metres from us and, after a while, began feeding: a delicate picking of items, including small worms, from the dune-turf. My impressions through binoculars at this range were of a long-legged, elongated, small-headed, brown wader reminiscent of an Upland Sandpiper *Bartramia longicauda*.

Excited, I set up my telescope and was amazed to see that the bird resembled a Whimbrel: it had a down-curve to its bill and possessed a crown-stripe and a super-cilium. We were able to approach to within 50 m, but, since the bird was now on its own, it was difficult to make an accurate assessment of size, although I had previously thought that it was distinctly smaller than the accompanying Whimbrel. DEJD carefully stalked the bird and took several photographs, while I made the following brief field-description:

Very like Whimbrel without white rump, but with striking pale crown-stripe and pale supercilium over large, dark eye. Bill much shorter than Whimbrel's, straighter, and with down-curve near tip; flesh-pink on basal half of lower mandible. Distinctly long-winged look; closed wings extending just beyond tail. Very pale-faced; trace of dark brown mark between bill and eye, and thin pale eye-ring, most marked behind eye, where it contrasted with dark brown patch across ear-coverts. Finely streaked neck and breast, strongest on breast-sides. Barring on flanks, strongest towards rear. Mantle, scapulars, rump, wing-coverts and tail the same dark brown, mottled, spotted and barred with pale buff-brown and white. Underparts pale sandy-brown. Legs long and greyish. In flight, resembling Ruff *Philomachus pugnax*. Long, pointed wings, with (except for suggestion of paler trailing edge) uniformly dark upper surface. Outermost long primary apparently white. Underwings pale greyish, somewhat darker than pale belly. Call a shank-like 'quip-quip-quip', much less rapid than Whimbrel's trill.

Initially, I considered that the bird could be the American race of the Whimbrel, *N. p. hudsonicus*, which lacks the white rump of the European race, but the size-discrepancy and the short bill forced us to consider Eskimo Curlew *N. borealis*. This seemed fanciful! That same evening, the bird was seen again by A. E. Hopkins, H. Nicholls, D. C. Palmer and N. M. Powell, but in fading light the views obtained were inconclusive. On the morning of 31st August, J. P. Martin, DCP, M. C. Powell and NMP relocated the bird and, after reference to accessible literature, identified it as a Little Whimbrel *N. minutus*. The bird remained in the area until mid-morning of Monday 6th September and was seen by well over a thousand observers from many parts of Britain. A comprehensive series of notes, sketches and photographs (*Brit. Birds* 75: plate 237; 76: plates 183–186) was soon obtained, and the description below is compiled from notes taken by DEJD, P. G. Lansdown, JPM, SJM and W. N. A. Nelson.

Size Resembled small, short-billed Whimbrel; slightly smaller than Lapwing *Vanellus vanellus*, and only half height of and quarter bulk of Curlew *N. arquata*.

Head Crown-stripe off-white and clean-cut, widening from just behind bill-base and extending over crown onto rear crown, bordered by dark brown lateral crown-stripes above clean-cut off-white supercilium; thin dark brown line between bill and eye, and thin off-white eye-ring, most prominent immediately behind eye where it contrasted with small dark brown triangle across ear-coverts; rest of head off-white, making eyes appear large and 'face' very pale.

Upperparts Neck buff-grey, densely flecked with brown; mantle, rump and tail dark brown, mottled with pale buff, brown and white.

Wings Upperwing-coverts generally grey-brown, with pale buff-white edgings, though some towards bend of wing more blackish-brown with thinner white edgings; scapulars dark brown with off-white spots around edges, a few of these feathers showing traces of chestnut-brown between dark and light areas; tertials pale brown, strongly barred dark brown; secondaries and inner primaries chequered brown and pale brown; outer primaries and lower edge of closed wing uniform dark brown. In flight, entire upperparts dark brown with darker leading edge; underwing dull grey, slightly darker than grey-brown underwing-coverts.

Underparts Neck and breast pale grey-brown finely streaked and mottled dark brown, strongest on breast-sides, where a few dark chevrons, the pattern much like pectoral band peaking downwards onto belly; undertail-coverts grey-brown with sparse, indistinct spotting; rest of underparts pale sandy-brown with several long, thin, vertical, well-spaced dark brown bars along flanks, strongest towards rear.

Bare Parts Bill blackish-brown with flesh-pink basal half of lower mandible; bill also comparatively much shorter than bill of Whimbrel as well as thinner and straighter: gentle down-curve to distal quarter only. Legs pale grey, tinged blue.

The bird frequented an area of dune-turf as well as nearby pasture fields and golf-course fairways. On a few occasions, it was located on Sker Rocks, a nearby rocky promontory on the coast. At other times, it rested and fed in a stubble field which appeared to become more attractive the more it was ploughed, rolled and seeded by the farmer. There, it sometimes associated with Lapwings, Golden Plovers *Pluvialis apricaria* and Starlings *Sturnus vulgaris*.

Moon, S. J. 1983. Little Whimbrel: new to Britain and Ireland.
British Birds 76, 438–445.

Little Whimbrel is a rare breeder in eastern Siberia. It winters in eastern Indonesia and Australia.

There has been one subsequent record:

Norfolk Blakeney, Cley and Salthouse area, adult, 24th August–3rd September 1985

AUGUST 1982

NORTHERN MOCKINGBIRD IN CORNWALL

Ted Griffiths

First seen at 07.30 GMT on 30th August 1982, flying down from a tall conifer from which it had been disturbed by a couple of Carrion Crows *Corvus corone*. It was about the size of a Blackbird *Turdus merula*, but with a slimmer body and a long

tail, generally grey in colour, with whitish underparts and white wing patches. It called 'chack' a couple of times as it dropped into some small trees. In flight, it had broad rounded wings with large white wing flashes, white underparts, and a long narrow tail which from above was dark grey with white on the outer feathers, the white getting wider towards the distal third of the tail; below, the tail showed a lot more white than it did from above. The flight seemed slow. The bird settled in the lower part of an apple tree, about 1 m above the ground. I went on hands and knees to a small hedge and looked through, from which position I watched the bird at a range of about 4 m for four or five minutes.

When the bird was perched in the open on the lowest branch, I noted the following details:

Head, back and wings grey, with two white wing-bars and a white patch below the longest wing-bar near the edge of the wing; primaries blackish-brown. Underparts a dirty-white with a bit of a greyish wash across the breast and on the flanks. Undertail-coverts white. Legs dark grey to blackish; eye dull yellow with dark iris. Bill black. The bird was slim and did not seem to be particularly long.

When the bird flew off, being chased by Magpies, the wing pattern was very striking, with a large white wing patch and white wing-bars; the amount of white in the tail suggested that it was on at least two and perhaps three of the outer feathers. Finally, it called two or three times, a harsh 'chack' as it was blown away over Saltash town by the force 7–8 northwesterly gale, and was not seen again.

Cobb, P. R., Rawnsley, P., Grenfell, H. E., Griffiths, E. & Cox, S. 1996. Northern Mockingbirds in Britain. *British Birds* 89, 347–356.

Northern Mockingbird is a common bird in southern North America and Central America.

There has been one subsequent record:

Essex Horsey Island, 17th–23rd May 1988

OCTOBER 1982

CHIMNEY SWIFT IN CORNWALL

Laurie Williams

At about 14.30 GMT on 21st October 1982, G. C. Hearl and I arrived at Porthgwarra in west Cornwall. As I stepped from his car, I glanced towards the house at the top of the valley and saw something flitting about over its roof. I managed to focus my binoculars on the movement and was astonished to see what appeared to be a large bat. Unfortunately, it was immediately lost to view. After some 20 minutes, however, GCH saw what he quickly recognised as a very small swift flying towards him. His first thoughts were that it was a Little Swift *Apus affinis*, but he then saw that it had a dark (not white) rump and what appeared to be small spines projecting from the end of its tail. He also noticed that its mode of flight was very different from that of the Little Swift which we had both seen in west Cornwall in spring 1981. He quickly called me over and we then watched the bird for the next two hours. For the most part, the bird fed around the area of the houses, but eventually it moved to the nearby clifftop, where it continued to feed before suddenly going to roost, apparently on the cliff face. It was observed at ranges down to 10 m, flying overhead near the houses, and below us when feeding along the edge of the cliff. For the first few minutes, we were joined by another birdwatcher and his wife; he told us that he thought the bird might be a Little Swift, but GCH pointed out the dark rump and, after a few minutes, the other observer left the area. After watching the swift for some minutes, we discussed its identity. We ruled out Little Swift, Needle-tailed Swift *Hirundapus caudacutus* and runt Swift *Apus apus*, and quickly came to the conclusion that it was probably a Chimney Swift *Chaetura pelagica*, an identification which we independently confirmed on returning home and consulting our literature. Over the following days it was seen by hundreds of observers, who all agreed with this identification. Amazingly, it was joined by a second Chimney Swift from 23rd to 25th. It was last seen early on the morning of 27th October. The following description is a combination of the field notes of the two original observers.

Size Very small swift, about size of Little Swift, but with much plumper body.

General Coloration Difficult to specify exactly: at distance looked black, but at closer range and in good light looked sooty-brown. Slightly darker plumage around eye, giving slight masked effect.

Body All-dark, sooty-brown, with just faint lightening of colour on chin and throat, difficult to see except in good light and at favourable angle. Shape likened to short fat cigar or torpedo.

Wings Long for length of body, well swept back, slightly lighter than rest of body.

Tail Very small, so difficult to determine exact shape, but looked slightly rounded. When bird close overhead, GCH pointed out what appeared to be three or four spines projecting from tail (although most authors state that these cannot be seen in the field, they are well shown in the excellent photographs taken by S. C. Hutchings).

Bare Parts Eye dark. Bill small, dark.

Call None heard.

Flight Bird's most striking character. At times, when swooping after prey, amazingly fast and agile and very bat-like. When not hunting, however, held wings bowed down, in manner of Common Sandpiper *Actitis hypoleucos*. On a few occasions, hovered after prey, with tail fanned.

Confusion species

The three *Chaetura* swifts (Chimney *C. pelagica*, Vaux's *C. vauxi* and Chapman's *C. chapmani*) are closely related. Vaux's Swift, however, is smaller and is more extensively and obviously pale on the throat and upper breast. Chapman's Swift has a paler back and rump. The only other North American swift likely to be confused with Chimney Swift is the Black Swift *Cypseloides niger*, which is larger and has a slightly forked tail. Given a good view, Chimney Swift should be easily identifiable.

Williams, L. P. 1986. Chimney Swift: new to the Western Palearctic.
British Birds 79, 423–426.

Chimney Swift is a widespread breeding bird in North America east of the Great Plains; it winters in Central America and northeastern South America.

There have been ten subsequent records: eight in England and two in Scotland.

NOVEMBER 1982

VARIED THRUSH IN CORNWALL

Steve Madge, Graham Hearl, Stuart Hutchings
and Laurie Williams

On 14th November 1982, E. Grace was leading an RSPB field meeting at Nanquidno, near St Just-in-Penwith, Cornwall. At about 14.00 GMT, one of the ladies in the group drew his attention to an unusual thrush, which was dark grey with a white throat and supercilium, greyish breast-band and white wingbars. Consultation of field guides did not help; the nearest thrush to it seemed to be Dusky Thrush *Turdus naumanni*, but several features did not fit. Despite further searches by local birdwatchers, it was not seen again until the morning of 17th, when it was relocated by the late Bernard King, and later, independently, by GCH, SCH (who obtained a series of photographs, *Brit. Birds* 76: plates 37–39; 83: 109–111) and LPW. The possibilities of Siberian Thrush *Zoothera sibirica* or an escaped Aztec Thrush *Z. pinicola* (a Mexican species) were then considered, but the white throat, upper breast and prominent wingbars were inexplicable.

On the evening of 18th, SCH telephoned SCM and described the bird. It sounded as if it was some weird escape, possibly a peculiar plumage stage of Pied Ground

Thrush *Z. wardii* (an Indian species). The following morning saw a handful of us gathered at the spot; when the bird appeared, its banded underwing certainly suggested a species of *Zoothera*, but it was clearly none of the above possibilities, and we were all totally perplexed.

Returning home and looking at the literature, it suddenly dawned on SCM that the markings fitted Varied Thrush *Z. naevia* perfectly, and that, if the latter's orange areas were whitish, then that was the Nanquidno bird. Luckily, the markings were distinctive enough to show that no other thrush could possibly fit: it was indeed an aberrantly coloured Varied Thrush. The thrush regularly visited Nanquidno Farm to feed on berries of a cotoneaster *Cotoneaster* in the garden. It had first been noticed by Miss Phillips of Nanquidno Farm, on 9th November, almost a week before being spotted by birdwatchers, and was last seen on 24th. During its stay, it was watched by a large number of people but many others were reluctant to travel to see what seemed to be an unlikely vagrant in an aberrant plumage.

DESCRIPTION

Size and Shape A large, plump thrush, appearing a little smaller and slightly shorter-tailed than Blackbird *T. merula*.

Head Pattern Forehead, crown and nape dark grey; lores, ear-coverts and sides of crown a darker slate-grey. Broad white supercilium from just above eye running back and curving down rear of ear-coverts, broadening above rear ear-coverts and ending abruptly.

Underparts Throat and upper breast clean white and unmarked. Relatively wide, dark grey breast-band below white of upper breast. Underparts below breast-band creamy-white; extensive grey overlapping scaling along flanks, widening towards rear to extend to tibia feathering and vent, merging with grey upper-tail-coverts; central undertail-coverts unmarked white.

Upperparts Mantle and back dark grey, with slight brownish cast. Rump, uppertail-coverts and tail dark grey, latter with small white tips to outermost feathers.

Wings Upperwing dark grey, with two prominent white bars formed by tips of median and greater coverts; white patch at base of outer primaries, surrounded by a blackish shade; folded primaries and secondaries showed extensive brownish-grey-white panel along central portion of feathers, becoming darker grey towards tips and bases. Underwing whitish, with dark grey band along lesser coverts, greyish flight feathers, and grey band along centre of wing (precise pattern difficult to describe, as only glimpsed in flight).

Bare Parts Bill blackish-brown, with paler yellowish base to lower mandible; legs fleshy-yellowish; iris dark.

It was a shy bird, spending most of its time feeding not far from cover, but it could often be seen in the open, feeding on fallen apples in a small orchard or devouring the berries of a cotoneaster in the garden of the farm. On one occasion it perched for some 30 seconds on the tip of a 14-m-high tree. When it flew, it kept low, skimming walls and flying between trees. It called rarely, but SCH twice heard a call, which he described as a low 'chuur, chuur'.

Age and sex

Ageing and sexing the bird was difficult. Male Varied Thrushes have a broader and blacker breast-band than females; the Nanquidno bird had a broad, but grey, breast-band, hardly darker than the upperparts. A comparison of the photographs with skins at the British Museum (Natural History), Tring, indicated that the bird was a first-year, and probably a male: the greater-covert bar is stepped, with smaller white tips to newer, innermost, feathers compared with larger white tips to older, outermost, feathers (adults would have greater-covert tip markings of equal size); the width of the breast-band, which appears slightly darker than the mantle in some of the photographs, suggests that the bird was a male.

Plumage aberrations and escape potential

Clearly, the Nanquidno individual was abnormal in plumage coloration: it completely lacked the stunning orange pigmentation so characteristic of Varied Thrush. Suggestions that its abnormal plumage was due to diet or captivity, although highly unlikely, cannot be totally discarded. It was a first-winter bird, and so must have been some five or six months old: perhaps too young for a captive diet to have had such a total effect on its coloration? At this age, if captive feeding were responsible, it seems likely that some orange would have been present somewhere, as only during moult would colourless feathers replace the normal orange ones. More plausible is the theory that the bird was a genuinely aberrant individual.

Madge, S. C., Hearl, G. C., Hutchings, S. C. & Williams, L. P. 1990. Varied Thrush: new to the Western Palearctic. *British Birds* 83, 187–195.

Varied Thrush breeds in western North America from Alaska south to northwestern California; birds winter chiefly from southern British Columbia to California.

There have been no subsequent records.

The second for the Western Palearctic, a male in normal plumage, was in Iceland in May 2004.

THE BIRDER'S YEAR

Adrian Pitches

The previous two years had each seen nine new species added to the British List, but the hat-trick was not completed in 1983. However, there was a First for Britain in the autumn and arguably one of the most controversial episodes in recent birding history. Rather than wildfowl, it was the dainty **Ross's Gull** that attracted attention in early 1983: there were four across northern England and northern Scotland. Meanwhile, **Ring-billed Gull**, first recorded in 1973, had reached 'plague' proportions by 1983 with 84 records.

Two striking passerines distracted birders from gulls at the beginning of the year. A male **Two-barred Crossbill** on the Derbyshire/South Yorkshire border stayed from early January until late February. The earliest-ever **Rock Thrush**, a male in Kent on 5th February, was more problematic, particularly as it lingered for two months. (Another male occurred in Hertfordshire in May.)

But real controversy came in March. A **Tengmalm's Owl** at Spurn stayed for the entire month, indeed it may have been present since late January, but the Yorkshire Wildlife Trust suppressed the news. Following storm erosion of the peninsula in February, the shingle spit was in a parlous state. Emergency repair work by bulldozers was underway to keep the point connected to the mainland. Understandably, the Trust did not want hundreds of birders swarming over their reserve during this period – there's a letter of explanation in September 1983's *BB*. More than 20 years later, Tengmalm's Owl remains near the top of most birders' 'Most Wanted' lists.

The traditional spring influx of overshooting long-legged birds from southern Europe included a record 17 **Night Herons**, single **Squacco Heron** and **Cattle Egret**, three **Black Storks**, a pair of **Black-winged Stilts** in Cheshire – and three together in Cornwall. A fondly remembered friend reappeared at Blacktoft Sands, East Yorkshire, on 26th April, after more than a year's absence: the **Hudsonian Godwit** that was first recorded there in September 1981 and then wintered on the Exe estuary, Devon. It stayed ten days but never put in another appearance.

Britain's second **Pallid Swift** was over Farlington Marshes, Hampshire, on 20th May. And in late May there was a remarkable influx of **Dark-eyed Juncos** to southern England – three were found in gardens in Cornwall, Dorset and Somerset. Earlier in the month a **White-throated Sparrow** was trapped at Spurn.

But the star bird of the spring was a **Needle-tailed Swift** (White-throated Needletail) that zoomed over Orkney on 11th June – it was the first British record for more than a century. Six **Collared Pratincoles** in late spring equalled the previous peak in 1973 and eight **Black Kites** in spring/summer 1983 was a good showing.

The autumn kicked off with a **Sharp-tailed Sandpiper** at Frodsham, Cheshire, in late August that was skilfully re-identified after most had dismissed it as a Pectoral Sandpiper. And a **Least Sandpiper** in landlocked Cambridgeshire was a great find by RSPB staffers Ian Dawson and Richard Porter.

As if the English mainland Tengmalm's Owl that got away was not bad enough, the Shetland **Hawk Owl**, belatedly identified in September after a lady complained that something was killing her local Kestrels (!), rubbed salt in the wound.

Attention then inevitably switched to southwest England. On 3rd September, after a howling westerly gale, seawatchers at St Ives in Cornwall picked out a **Wilson's Petrel** among an estimated 10,000 Storm Petrels wrecked in the bay. On 27th September, a **Pechora Pipit** on Portland, Dorset, was the first south-coast record.

In September/October on Scilly there was a juvenile **Solitary Sandpiper**, long-staying **Thrush Nightingale, Swainson's** and **Grey-cheeked Thrushes, Arctic Warbler**, not one but two **Parula Warblers, Blackpoll Warbler, Rose-breasted Grosbeak, Bobolink** and **Northern Oriole**. And a **Cliff Swallow** – the First for Britain. It arrived on St Mary's via St Agnes on 10th October and fed along the Garrison wall. A garbled message on the birders' CB radio network was initially dismissed as 'Cliff Waller on the Garrison'! The bird stayed until 27th October. And then there was the ludicrously tame **Upland Sandpiper** that took earthworms from birders' hands – and one from a brave soul's mouth! And there was a First of a distinctive form of Greenish Warbler – a '**Green Warbler**' – which stayed a week in October. Mainland Cornwall had some quality birds too: **Black-and-white Warbler** on the Lizard and **American Redstart** at St Just, the third in two years! Real quality came with a one-day **Dusky Thrush** near Bude in November.

There was a **Penduline Tit** in Northamptonshire, and Dorset had a real purple patch with a **Common Nighthawk** at Studland on 25th October followed by a **Little Swift** in the same place on 26th November – the third for Britain. A male **Little Crake** which resided in Nottinghamshire for two weeks was another November highlight.

Autumn on the East coast produced a **Pied Wheatear** in Norfolk, and **Black-eared Wheatear** and **Pallas's Grasshopper Warbler** were goodies for Bill Oddie in the first week of October on Out Skerries, Shetland.

The east coast also produced two out of the three **Red-breasted Geese** which arrived in November and December. Besides birds in Norfolk and Suffolk, there was also an adult in Hampshire. All three stayed into 1984.

FOUR LIFERS IN ONE DAY

Richard Thomas

1983 was a big year – I turned 21, survived my finals, found two BBRC rarities and somehow squeezed in 26 lifers. January, and the day after my 21st birthday I was nursing a hangover and watching a drake American Wigeon in Northants. The first weekend of February saw me freezing at Caesar's Camp, Bucks. A local birder arrived: 'No use getting here before 10.45,' he said. Sure enough, at 10.50, four Parrot Crossbills flew in. A fortnight later came a weekend I'll never forget. An icy northern blast had resulted in a Little Auk wreck … accompanying them was the ultimate Arctic waif … After an hour's nerve-wracking wait on Filey Brigg, the Ross's Gull loomed out of the mist and circled in front of its admirers. It was a magical moment. Next, the Wirral, where a Little Bunting would have been bird of the day if it hadn't been earlier outclassed.

In early March it was off to Sheppey, Kent, for a Rock Thrush (that was missing a toe). Nearby Cliffe held a Kentish Plover which, along with a Baird's Sandpiper at Staines, and a Temminck's Stint at Rutland Water, completed a trio of unusual waders I saw that winter. The end of March saw me heading for the Outer Hebrides, crammed into a Nissan Estate with four Notts birders on what became affectionately known as the 'Insane Trip'. We lived mainly off cold rice pudding, and camped or slept aboard inter-island ferries. The first night I awoke to snow *inside* the tent, and I didn't warm up for a fortnight. But the birding was brilliant. First, a 'blue' Snow and a small Canada Goose. Then, after three days searching, I don't know whether it was the cold or the elation that had me quivering when the male Steller's Eider landed close inshore. Three days later we were at Valtos on Harris. But our first fry-up for days (the sausages by now were turning green) was interrupted. A flash of orange, black and white off-shore. 'I've got a male King Eider' – what an excellent way to open my *BB* rarity account. One afternoon in Stornoway produced 25 Iceland and six Glaucous Gulls, whilst the journey south took in Surf Scoter, Ring-necked Duck at Loch Insh (help-fully flushed out by a Peregrine), and – surprisingly – a Med Gull at Musselburgh.

April produced little save my second Kentish of '83, at Portland, and a Great Grey Shrike in the New Forest. In May, I was obliged to visit Wraysbury, Berks, twice in a week – for Night Heron and Alpine Swift. Towards the end of the month, a Collared Pratincole put on a fine display near Blunham in Beds.

There are few more exciting birding moments than finding a *BB* rarity on your local patch. On 12th June, at Port Meadow, Oxon, a male Red-footed Falcon flew low over-head. It was a thrill I shall never forget. Later in June, a day's birding produced Purple Heron and Collared Pratincole (the Beds bird?) at the Ouse Washes, a female Wilson's Phalarope at Titchwell and a male Red-backed Shrike in the Brecks.

A late July 'on spec' trip to Teesmouth, and I dipped into White-rumped and Pec Sands. Then off for a three-week trip to southern Ireland. I saw my second Night Heron, Pec Sand and Wilson's Phalaropes of the year, three Spotted Crakes, a Dotterel, nine Melodious and one Icterine Warbler, Scarlet Rosefinch, a couple of Ortolans and a Short-toed Lark. Out to sea were scores of Storm Petrels, Great and Cory's Shearwaters, plus, most frustratingly, a distant small, dark petrel…

Late September, and birds were building up on the Scillies. The 1st of October saw me intending to day-twitch the islands … As I watched a Solitary Sandpiper, someone arrived, breathless. 'Parula, Tresco' … I decided to mop up on Mary's first – a bad decision. Bobolink (and two Buff-breasts) on the Golf Course, (Western) Bonelli's at Longstones, and, in the nick of time, the Sprosser at Rocky Hills. Four lifers in an afternoon! As I rushed quaywards, I met Andy from Notts. 'Can I crash in your tent? I can't leave – too many birds.'

Dawn saw me, but alas no Parula, on Tresco. But things soon looked up – Green Warbler relocated on the Garrison, but I decided on Aggie first. The Subalp appeared shortly before the Baltimore Oriole. Then it was back to Mary's for the Green, a couple of Tawny Pipits and a Woodchat for good measure, then return to the mainland and a fortunate lift home.

The pace continued: a Roller in Lincs, a Red-necked Phalarope at Cley. But pressure was mounting on Scilly … October 16th and another four-lifer day: Britain's first Cliff Swallow on Mary's, a flighty Upland Sandpiper, which eventually settled down (so much so that it fed from the hand), a Richard's Pipit (my bogey bird!) and a Grey-cheeked Thrush in Lower Moors.

Next day, on Aggie, a first-winter Rose-breasted Grosbeak, then back to Mary's for a run … 'What are we running for?' 'Swainson's.' It was the thrush, not the hawk. Two days later we were running again. 'Sora, Tresco.' To save time, the boatman grounded the boat, put a plank over the side and we leapt overboard into the surf. Soon, more than 500 of us were gawping at the UK's first twitchable Sora.

Off Scilly and a cold night at Drift was followed by a Spotted Sand, then on to St Just where the immature male American Redstart put on a stunning display in the early morning sunlight. 'Just like the '82 bird,' we all agreed. Stithians was next. Twenty Golden Plovers flew close by. 'Let's hope the next group has the Lesser in it,' said someone. And so it did!

Following a Red-breasted Goose in Norfolk in mid November, there was one final twist to '83. A mass trip to Studland for a Little Swift dip. Two Dartford Warblers scolded us in nearby scrub – my last year-tick of 1983.

But my account wouldn't be complete without mention of Bob Burgess, who drove on many trips, Pete Allen, Robin Brace, Dave Chalmers, Andy Collins, Pete Kaspar, Chris Park, and the 'Durham Lads'. Thanks. You all helped make my 1983.

Richard Thomas lives in Cambridgeshire. He is a keen world birder and has his dream job: Communications Manager for BirdLife International.

OCTOBER 1983

CLIFF SWALLOW ON SCILLY

Michael Crosby

During the early afternoon of 10th October 1983, several people had brief views of an unusual hirundine on the islands of St Agnes and Gugh in the Isles of Scilly. Only Paul Vautrinot saw the bird well enough to make a detailed description, but it was of an unfamiliar species which he was unable to identify. Later in the afternoon, P. Morrison, M. Opie and D. N. Smith noticed a small flock of Swallows *Hirundo rustica* flying in off the sea on the eastern side of the Garrison, St Mary's. PM noticed that one bird in the

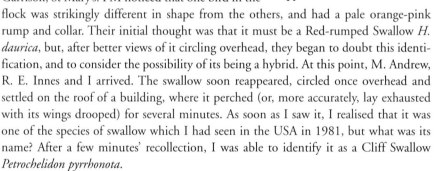

flock was strikingly different in shape from the others, and had a pale orange-pink rump and collar. Their initial thought was that it must be a Red-rumped Swallow *H. daurica*, but, after better views of it circling overhead, they began to doubt this identification, and to consider the possibility of its being a hybrid. At this point, M. Andrew, R. E. Innes and I arrived. The swallow soon reappeared, circled once overhead and settled on the roof of a building, where it perched (or, more accurately, lay exhausted with its wings drooped) for several minutes. As soon as I saw it, I realised that it was one of the species of swallow which I had seen in the USA in 1981, but what was its name? After a few minutes' recollection, I was able to identify it as a Cliff Swallow *Petrochelidon pyrrhonota*.

The news spread quickly (and caused some confusion because many of the birders on the islands had never heard of this species), and by late afternoon a crowd of several hundred was enjoying excellent views of the swallow feeding low over the Garrison Wall. The following day, it moved to Lower Moors, and, during its stay, visited several parts of St Mary's, particularly favouring the Higher Moors and Longstones area. It was present until at least 27th October, and was closely observed and photographed (*Brit. Birds* 77: plates 14 & 15; 81: plate 216).

> *Size and Structure* Similar in length to Swallow, but much more stockily built, with broader wings, particularly at base. Tail short and square-ended, with shallow notch, which was difficult to see in flight. When perched, wings projected almost 1 inch (2.5 cm) beyond tip of tail.
>
> *Head Pattern* Crown, forehead and 'face' sooty blackish, apart from small, oval, buff-brown patch just above bill. In some lights, area around eye, and the ear-coverts, looked darker than rest of 'face', forming masked effect. Nape and

sides of neck an even, pale grey-brown, forming pale collar. Chin black. Throat deep orange-buff, with few small, scattered white spots.

Upperparts Mantle and upperwing sooty black, without sheen of accompanying Swallows. Narrow white edges to scapulars formed faint, pale lines on back, and two similar lines ran up centre of mantle. Narrow pale edges to greater and median coverts. Tertials edged pale brown, and tipped white. Large orange-pink rump patch. Tail sooty black.

Underparts Underwing dusky, greyish-brown. Breast, upper flanks and undertail-coverts orange-buff. Rest of underparts white.

Bare Parts Legs, bill and eye black.

The flight action was typically a series of rapid, deep wingbeats interspersed with long glides. Its structure and flight were reminiscent of a Crag Martin *Ptyonoprogne rupestris*.

The head pattern, lack of blue sheen on the upperparts and pale edges to the coverts and tertials indicated that it was a juvenile. Both Cliff Swallows and Cave Swallows *Petrochelidon fulva* migrate south in the autumn in juvenile plumage, not moulting until they reach the wintering grounds.

Crosby, M. J. 1988. Cliff Swallow: new to Britain and Ireland.
British Birds 81, 449–452.

Cliff Swallow is a widespread breeding bird in North America; it winters mainly in South America.

There have been eight subsequent records:

Cleveland South Gare, juvenile, 23rd October 1988

East Yorkshire Spurn, juvenile, 22nd–23rd and 28th October 1995

Scilly Tresco, juvenile, 4th–5th December 1995

West Sussex Church Norton, juvenile, 1st October 1996

Scilly St Mary's, 28th–30th September 2000

Dorset Portland, 29th–30th September 2000

Hampshire Titchfield Haven, 1st October 2000, possibly same as Dorset bird

Scilly St Agnes, St Martin's and St Mary's, juvenile, 26th–30th October 2001

The First for Ireland was at Dunmore Head, Co. Kerry on 16th November 1995.

1984

THE BIRDER'S YEAR

Adrian Pitches

There was no First for Britain in 1984 – the first blank year in the decade so far. Nevertheless, there were some fabulous birds, including **Cream-coloured Courser, Needle-tailed Swift**, an inland **Bridled Tern** and two **Common Yellowthroats** – the second and third for Britain, 30 years after the First. But perhaps the bird of the year was a single-observer historic sighting on Portland Bill…

A **White's Thrush** in south Devon was a very special garden tick for one lucky couple on 12th January. On 27th February, 'Albert' the lonesome **Black-browed Albatross** returned for his annual solitary sojourn in the Hermaness gannetry on Unst, Shetland. First seen in 1972, this was his 13th season sitting on his mud-bowl nest awaiting the female albatross that had yet to cross the Equator from the southern hemisphere to join him.

That other dependable long-stayer, the Hebridean **Steller's Eider**, also first seen in 1972, decided to call it a day in 1984 and was never seen again after 12th August. Amazingly, he *had* attracted female attention – there were *two* female Steller's Eiders accompanying him in April 1974! Another fail-safe had been a Slimbridge **Lesser White-front**, but none appeared in Gloucestershire for only the fifth time since 1958, although an adult bird was in Kent in March.

One bird that did put in an appearance was a **White-tailed Eagle** in the Home Counties. The Brill eagle (location *and* description) flapped around the Bucks/Oxon border from late November 1983 until mid-February. Another bird, first seen in Suffolk on 14th April, was shot in north Norfolk in May and died in care. It had been ringed as a nestling in Germany. A **Stilt Sandpiper** at Frodsham on 16th April was greatly appreciated. The first since 1976, it lingered in Cheshire until 3rd October.

May and June always produce quality birds and 1984 was no exception. The Spurn ringers trapped a male **Rock Thrush** and Britain's first spring **Blyth's Reed Warbler**. A **Trumpeter Finch** at Church Norton, West Sussex, had stayed six days in May when it was taken by a Sparrowhawk, a common fate for vagrant birds. In the third week of

May, Britain's third and fourth **White-tailed Plovers** (White-tailed Lapwings) graced Cleadon, Tyne & Wear, and a withheld Shropshire location.

Another late-May arrival was that **Needle-tailed Swift**: it spent nearly a fortnight at Quendale, Mainland Shetland – ample compensation for the one-day bird on Orkney in 1983. The day after it disappeared, a male **Common Yellowthroat** arrived on nearby Fetlar, the second for Britain following another male on Lundy, Devon, in November 1954.

There were two male **Collared Flycatchers** in late May – in Kent and Scilly – and a male **Lesser Grey Shrike** was on Fair Isle, Shetland, in early June. Amazingly, the two other records of this shrike in 1984 were both on urban Tyneside – in July and November. In landlocked Rutland, there was a **Bridled Tern** at Rutland Water on 8th–9th June and on 9th July there was a **Sooty Tern** on the Kent/East Sussex border.

Arguably THE bird of the year was flushed by Grahame Walbridge on Portland, Dorset, on 10th June. It was an **Egyptian Nightjar**, only the second ever and 101 years since that first sighting in Nottinghamshire in June 1883.

Another southern species which provided a special record in 1984 was **Little Bittern**. A pair took up residence at Potteric Carr, South Yorkshire, in June and bred! They produced three young. The male returned in 1985 but the female did not.

After the invasion in 1982/83, **Parrot Crossbills** stayed to breed in 1984. Pairs with juveniles were seen in Norfolk and Suffolk. Nine adult **Rose-coloured Starlings** in England, Wales and Scotland brought a splash of colour to the summer birding scene from June through to August but intriguingly there were no juveniles recorded in 1984.

The summer was further enlivened by a wandering **Lesser Crested Tern** in northeast England which took up residency on the Farne Islands in Northumberland. 'Elsie' (*LC* Tern) paired with a Sandwich Tern in subsequent summers.

Hadleigh Marsh in Essex was the venue for the most appreciated bird of 1984: a first-winter **Cream-coloured Courser** that arrived on 29th September and stayed four days. Apart from the one-day bird in 1980, this was the first courser since the long-staying bird in 1969: a 15-year gap. But it was to be another 20 years, almost to the day, before another one arrived: on Scilly in September 2004.

Also in September, Fair Isle proved its worth yet again with its second record of **Red-flanked Bluetail**, this time a female, the first for the island having been in September 1981. And another island, that underwatched hotspot Lundy, turned up the first **Bobolink** for Devon towards the end of the month. The island also produced a **Blackpoll Warbler** in October which, together with two on Scilly, briefly became the most frequently recorded Nearctic passerine in Britain. It took the crown from **Red-eyed Vireo**, one of which was at Dungeness, Kent, in early October: the first east-coast record. The second **Common Yellowthroat** of the year, another male, was on Bryher, Scilly, for a fortnight in October. Scilly also recorded seven **Little Buntings**, part of a record haul of 38 in Britain in 1984. The lion's share (17) was on Shetland, including 11 on Fair Isle. And Fair Isle also had an invasion of **Arctic Redpolls**: 25 arrived in October.

Scilly had a colourful **Rock Thrush** in October and a very drab – but very exciting – **Eastern Olivaceous Warbler**, found by Chris Heard. A one-day **Hermit Thrush** on St Mary's on 28th October was a great find: the second for Britain, the First having been on Fair Isle in June 1975. Scilly also recorded two other *Catharus* thrushes: single **Swainson's** and **Grey-cheeked Thrushes**. And St Mary's logged a male **Eyebrowed Thrush**; another was on Orkney.

One Scilly speciality that turned up in Greater London was a **Common Nighthawk**! A moribund adult male was picked up on Barnes Common. Another Nearctic find in the stockbroker belt was an **American Robin** in Haslemere, Surrey, on 12th October.

Back on Portland, on 10th November, Martin Cade found two **Pallid Swifts** travelling together – the third and fourth for Britain and reminiscent of 1982's pair of Chimney Swifts. A further two were logged in Dyfed and Kent that same week, taking the British total to six. But perhaps THE bird that all birders dream of finding was on South Ronaldsay, Orkney, on 13th November: a male **Siberian Thrush**. On the same day, a **Lanceolated Warbler** was trapped in Prior's Park, Tynemouth, Tyne & Wear: only the third English record.

In December, a rave from the grave: a tideline corpse of a juvenile female **Capped Petrel** was picked up at Barmston, East Yorkshire. Also known by the fabulous name of *Diablotin* on its native Hispaniola in the Caribbean, this enigmatic *Pterodroma* was already on the British List following a bird allegedly caught on a heath near Swaffham, Norfolk, in March or April 1850 (a previous claim of Capped Petrel in the Atlantic 50 nautical miles southwest of Rockall on 26th February 1980 is still under consideration). As it is assumed from the condition of the corpse that the Capped Petrel died in British waters, the mysterious stranger on the beach has become the first reliable record of the species in Britain.

So the year ended with no *new* Firsts. But with the Capped Petrel and the ghostly Egyptian Nightjar that drifted up from the Sahara to Portland in June, providing the only modern-day record of that species, 1984 could perhaps be credited with two *honorary* Firsts for Britain.

THE DESSERT COURSER
Dominic Mitchell

As one of the more active years in my then relatively youthful birding 'career', 1984 was certainly among the most memorable. Not that it seems significant for entirely birding reasons – immortalised as the title of George Orwell's vision of the future, 1984 also brings to mind such defining images of the decade as the miners' strike, Band Aid and the famine in Ethiopia. On a personal level, it was also a landmark in that, after a rather itinerant period ('the wilderness years' to my birding friends), I finally put down roots with the purchase of my first flat, pursued a steady job in office administration and returned full-time to the birding fold.

Not that I'd ever really left, of course, though in those pre-technology days if you didn't actively make the effort, you were soon out of the loop. With no internet, birdlines, pagers or even birding magazines to buy in the shops, it was a case of who you knew to find out what was being seen where. Fortunately, I had a connection to the Grapevine through Roy Beddard, who as leader of the North London RSPB Members' Group in the late 1970s had done much to start broadening my birding horizons.

I don't recall the details now, but it was very probably Roy who tipped me off about my first big bird – in every sense – of 1984. An overwintering White-tailed Eagle at Brill, Buckinghamshire, was a great opportunity to get the year off to a flying start. I set off clutching my first telescope, a Bushnell Spacemaster bought with money generously loaned by my brother Laurence, for an outing up the M40 from London. It wasn't my first twitch, but watching that impressive raptor as snow flurries descended on the slopes of the Chilterns was certainly one of the best.

February's highlight was no less impressive. Having yet to visit Scilly, Shetland or Asia, I could not have anticipated that my first Olive-backed Pipit would appear in a garden on a housing estate in Berkshire in winter. But like many others, I made the pilgrimage to Dave Parker's living room in Bracknell to witness what was then an unprecedented occurrence.

Next month saw two forays to the Peak District, where Black Grouse was the much-wanted quarry. At the second attempt I finally saw three birds at Swallow Moss, but sadly the dwindling population there was consigned to history within a few years. However, spring also brought a more upbeat experience – the Mediterranean. I had birded in The Netherlands twice before and casually mopped up a few goodies when working elsewhere in Europe, but two weeks in Mallorca in April was a definite step upwards. Black Vulture, Eleonora's Falcon, Thekla Lark, Spectacled and Marmora's (now Balearic) Warblers, Rock Sparrow – my eyes were opened to a whole new world of birds, from which there would be no going back.

The Continental feeling continued back home in May, a highlight being Red-breasted Flycatcher – my first – at Holkham, Norfolk. A nice double in the offing was the smart male Collared Flycatcher found in Margate, Kent, on 24th, but a first attempt at twitching Thanet brought only the very decent consolation prize of a Broad-billed Sandpiper at Pegwell Bay. The following weekend I made a second attempt, this time by train (I was 'between cars' at the time), and remarkably jammed in on the elusive flycatcher almost immediately at Northdown Park. Assuming I'd seen its best showing of the day, I headed back to the station – too quickly, as it turned out, because I later heard that Marsh Warbler and Red Kite were both noted by the masses in Margate.

After a memorable spring for birding, summer was somewhat anti-climactic and dominated by preparations for moving home, a process finally completed in July. Come early September, however, the pace picked up, and on 2nd a memorable moment in a hide at Minsmere, Suffolk, gave me two lifers out of different windows – a Pectoral Sandpiper from one, and a Great White Egret (then a real rarity) from the other. Visits to Norfolk on the next two weekends brought the likes of Sabine's Gull and Red-backed Shrike, while a morning excursion on the last day of September to London's Staines Reservoirs produced two more 'Pecs'.

Satisfied with the month's haul, at lunchtime that same day I caught a bus to my mother's house for a family gathering. I can still remember her words now, mentioned in passing some time after I arrived. "Oh, Roy called … something about a bird." Why had he tried to track me down here, I wondered – what bird? "I can't really remember – maybe a cream-coloured something?" Oh no … please. I called Roy and he confirmed the worst: it was indeed a Cream-coloured Courser, near Southend, and he was on his way out the door. I couldn't rush straight out, but my downcast expression at lunch must have said it all. My mother quietly leaned over, handed me her car keys and said: "Bring it back by six, and don't drive too fast." Thanks a million – within an hour I was watching the bird of my dreams as it fed incongruously in a ploughed field in Essex.

It wasn't until Scilly 20 years later that the next one, the islands' first, finally appeared. In 1984, Scilly had another first: me. Regaled by friends' stories of former glories such as Cliff Swallow, Orphean Warbler and Scarlet Tanager, I finally succumbed to the temptation of the Fortunate Isles and spent a week based on St Mary's. At the time I remember feeling it hadn't quite lived up to expectations, but looking back at the tally that seems harsh. It was the heyday of two much-missed luminaries, Peter Grant and David Hunt, and though not a vintage year there was plenty to look at. On the second day a Blackpoll Warbler on St Agnes became my first-ever Nearctic landbird, while Solitary and Semipalmated Sandpipers were scarcely less impressive. Bird of the trip was unquestionably Britain's third Common Yellowthroat, made all the more satisfying because after a day of dipping out on acceptable views with hundreds of others, it showed very well to a much smaller crowd – me included – the following morning. My personal haul on Scilly that October also included Dotterel, Pectoral Sandpiper, Grey Phalarope, Melodious, Barred and Yellow-browed Warblers, Red-breasted Flycatcher, Common Rosefinch and Lapland Bunting, and with American Golden Plover and another Yellow-browed Warbler in Cornwall on the way home, I had seen enough to convince me to return the following year (and what a year *that* was).

The tail-end of autumn and early winter was inevitably quiet by comparison, but two Little Auks at Snettisham, Norfolk, on 11th November were a welcome final life-list addition for 1984. With a Black Redstart at Staines Reservoir seeing the old year out on 30 December, it was all set to be 'in with the new' once more in 1985…

Dominic Mitchell is publisher and editor of Birdwatch *magazine and author of* Where to Watch Birds in the London Area.

1985

THE BIRDER'S YEAR

Adrian Pitches

Scilly was destined to have a memorable autumn in 1985 and the islands laid down a marker from the outset with, on New Year's Day, the first-ever January record of an **American Golden Plover** – this one had lingered on St Mary's since November 1984. It would be another 20 years before another January American Goldie: at Slimbridge in January 2005. On 2nd January, St Agnes recorded an immature **Gyr Falcon** which toured the islands until April. In Devon, Robin Khan found a Gyr in February, exactly ten years after the previous one he found in the county.

In early March, Cuckmere Haven in East Sussex attracted a female **Little Crake**, a very confiding bird that stayed for ten days. And in Kent a **Sociable Plover** was another early spring migrant/vagrant. In the Isles of Scilly, a male **Pine Bunting** on St Mary's in April was followed within days by Britain's third **Calandra Lark** (the other two were also April birds: on Portland in 1961 and on Fair Isle in 1978).

A **Stilt Sandpiper** at Minsmere, Suffolk, in early May stayed a week (another was in Kent in late August). Meanwhile, a bird few had heard of – apart from Paul Harvey – landed on Fair Isle on 7th May. The **Daurian Starling** (Purple-backed Starling) also landed on the British List as a First for Britain but was subsequently demoted as a captive origin for this Siberian starling could not be discounted. Mid-May 1985 will best be remembered for an east-coast bonanza of **Bluethroats**, accompanied by two male **Collared Flycatchers** (in Suffolk and North Yorkshire), five **Thrush Nightingales** in northeast England and Scotland – and half a dozen **Rustic Buntings**. But the best of the bunch was a male **Wallcreeper** at St Catherine's Point, Isle of Wight, on 16th May. It didn't stay. On the same day, the female **Lesser Crested Tern** returned to the Farne Islands, Northumberland. Another bird, at Dawlish Warren in Devon in July, while 'Elsie' was still up north, took the number of British records to four.

A **Needle-tailed Swift** over Fairburn Ings, West Yorkshire, on 27th May made it three years in a row for this Eastern Palearctic vagrant. A **Little Swift** was in Fife two days later. Another **Little Swift** was at Slapton, Devon, in mid-August.

June produced two Firsts for Britain on Scottish isles, but news emerged later: see the accounts for **Blue Rock Thrush** and **Cedar Waxwing** below. Meanwhile, Britain's third **Eleonora's Falcon**, a male, was seen on South Uist, Outer Hebrides, on 14th June by Corncrake census workers.

There were two **Greater Yellowlegs** in spring/summer 1985: a one-day bird on Skye, Highland, in May and a bird that appeared discontinuously at Minsmere for six weeks from early July. A third bird was on Islay, Inner Hebrides, in late October.

The east coast had an excellent autumn wader passage. There were three **Sharp-tailed Sandpipers**: at Elmley, Kent, in late July, and in Lothian and Lincolnshire in August. A **Greater Sand Plover** in the Cley/Blakeney area of Norfolk was the seventh for Britain. It was first seen on 30th July; birders seeking to relocate it on 24th August stumbled across Britain's second **Little Whimbrel** instead! Like the 1982 bird, this one turned up on an August Bank Holiday weekend – but stayed for a fortnight.

On 21st September, Essex man Gary Wright found a **Trumpeter Finch** at Foulness – the first autumn record. But the previous day, Michael and Val Peacock found an even better bird: their **Chestnut-sided Warbler** on Fetlar, Shetland, was the First for Britain and the first Nearctic passerine to make landfall in autumn 1985. And attention stayed focused on Shetland with another First for Britain. On 30th September, Mark Chapman found a **Brown Shrike** at Sumburgh which stayed a further two days. This was a stunning achievement as he had also found what was probably another Brown Shrike on Shetland in 1981, but that record had been rejected. The same day as the eastern shrike was found, the flood of birds from the West resumed with a **Blackpoll Warbler** on Shetland and a **Northern Parula** in Dorset.

October then turned out to be the best-ever month for rare birds in Britain and Ireland. Scilly's transatlantic haul included two **Yellow-rumped Warblers**, another Northern Parula, **Bobolink, Rose-breasted Grosbeak**, four of a record nine **Red-eyed Vireos** recorded in Britain this autumn, three **Yellow-billed Cuckoos** and a single **Black-billed Cuckoo**. It was only the second time that both cuckoo species had coincided – 1965 was the other occasion. Two other Yellow-billed Cuckoos were found dead: in Cornwall and Hampshire.

The Cornwall/Devon border was scoring highly too: Britain's First **Wilson's Warbler** was a one-day bird at Rame on 13th October and it was followed by another Northern Parula at Cawsand four days later. And the one that got away was a freshly dead **Ovenbird** found just across the Tamar at Wembury, near Plymouth, on 22nd October. Elsewhere in Cornwall there were three Red-eyed Vireos and a **Grey-cheeked Thrush**. In Devon, Lundy had another Grey-cheeked Thrush and a Rose- breasted Grosbeak. An **American Redstart** at Winchester College water meadows, Hampshire, in early October continued the recent run of this Nearctic wood-warbler. A **Common Nighthawk** found exhausted in Cheshire on 11th October managed a reverse migration across the Atlantic care of the RAF. It was released a fortnight later on its wintering grounds in Belize. And a **Forster's Tern** at Musselburgh, East Lothian, in October/November was the first for Scotland.

Birds from points east did arrive too: Scilly had an **Eastern Olivaceous Warbler** for the second year running, Shetland had a **White's Thrush** and Northumberland had a **Pallas's Grasshopper Warbler** on the Farne Islands on 26th October – the latest ever.

On the same day, a **Sora** was found at Pagham, West Sussex, which stayed until Christmas – the second small crake to delight the crowds in 1985. On 27th October, an immature **White-tailed Eagle** was tracked down the East coast from Cleveland to Lincolnshire via North Yorkshire and East Yorkshire. The late-autumn highlight was an influx of **Nutcrackers**; there were birds in Cambridgeshire, Kent and a long-staying individual at Westleton, Suffolk, which was very partial to apples.

In late November, a first-winter male **Pied Wheatear** repeated the appearance of the 1983 bird on the same stretch of Norfolk coast at Sheringham. And Norfolk was THE destination in December when an 'animated humbug' appeared at How Hill, Ludham. That **Black-and-white Warbler** in a most unlikely location put the seal on a landmark year for Nearctic landbirds.

FANFARE FOR THE COMMON BIRD
Mark Cocker

1985 was memorable partly because, after two lengthy trips to India and Nepal in consecutive years, I finally got my first proper job. It was the beginning of a short-lived career in conservation – a development I owed directly to a striking bull-necked finch at Holkham, Norfolk. No, not the fabulous frosted *exilipes* Arctic Redpoll, which stayed several weeks among a large mixed redpoll flock and whose feathered tarsi made it seem like a diminutive Ptarmigan; it was the year's other celebrity bull-necked finch at Holkham, the pair of Parrot Crossbills.

By the time the Arctic Redpoll had appeared in late February, the crossbills had shown every sign of wishing to nest again in the pines by Wells carpark. They'd enjoyed a double success the previous year, generously assisted by the hanks of beard donated as nest-lining by Norfolk birder, Bryan Bland. The RSPB had further boosted their chances by finding a temporary warden to live in a minuscule caravan adjacent to the nest tree. In 1985, for about £13 a day, I shared guard duties with Reg Land. We maintained a daily log on the birds' progress and acted as information service to the steady stream of visitors. I also found a loophole in the contract to abscond for a Sociable Plover that appeared on the outskirts of London, near Dartford, in late March.

But the most memorable part of the wardening stint happened each night. We'd rigged up a cot listening device beneath the tree in order to help foil any nocturnal assault on the eggs. The speaker end of the contraption sat next to my bed and while it never revealed any nefarious activities, it kept me in night-long touch with the northerlies soughing through the pines and the odd hysterical Oystercatcher, which came through the speaker with the volume of a low-flying B52 … at least my charges slept soundly.

After the Parrot Crossbill work it seemed a natural development to take the seasonal wardening job at Holkham with the Nature Conservancy Council. My main task was to look after 200 pairs of Little Terns, over 10 per cent of the national total, spread along the shoreline. I quickly discovered that Little Terns were vulnerable to a completely unreasonable number of nest predators including squirrels (one found on the beach a mile from the nearest tree), hedgehogs, foxes, gulls, Oystercatchers, Carrion Crows (I saw one spot some eggs with supernatural precision while flying c. 30 metres above), not to mention high tides and spring showers.

There seemed more grounds for hope in searching for migrants in any off-duty moments and the effort produced a handsome return in a trio of spring rarities. One of these was a Great Reed Warbler in mid June. The bird marked my debut as a suppressor because I found it while censusing *Acrocephalus* in a patch of wetland (known as Decoy Carr) entirely surrounded by cattle pasture and completely off limits. Several local regulars were given permission but I was told to repel all other comers. Unfortunately the bird took to advertising its presence with that wonderful stentorian song. You couldn't miss it even a mile away. I sometimes wonder how many people heard it unconsciously but, in a moment of lapsed concentration, dreamed they were in Majorca.

The least expected of my three came on 23rd May, when I heard a harsh tacking call, then a strange song, from a bird in the upper canopy of some birches. I was thinking of nothing more exceptional (if unseasonal) than a Red-breasted Flycatcher but it proved to be a *Phylloscopus* warbler. Having delivered a few phrases of a cheerful ditty it then reverted to its default personality and skulked for the next 90 minutes. I pieced together an identikit image. It was a Dusky Warbler singing in May – still only the third spring record ever.

Yet I suppose the nominal headline bird of my 1985, only the twelfth for Britain at that time, was the third of my Holkham rarities. To call it 'mine', however, is wildly overstating my part. I was certainly the first to nail it as an 'interesting passerine'; it was Richard Grimmett who merely added as a qualifier – 'Collared Flycatcher'. Sadly this stunning little gem showed one too many greyish tips to its nape feathers and since the collar was marginally incomplete it languished for 20 years in the rare-bird debating chambers (for long periods as a hybrid Collared × Pied) and was only rehabilitated as the genuine article in 2003. Was it tenacity or faith that let me cling to its identity all these years?

More likely it was laziness, or perhaps indifference. Because running through my identity as a seeker of rarities, like a fault line through a seam of rock, was a realisation in the same year that rare birds can sometimes excite you far less than ordinary everyday birds. True to that insight, I can barely remember now the Little Whimbrel or the Greater Sand Plover or the Wilson's Phalarope all scooped later in the autumn at Cley. However, I can clearly recall the Holkham Barn Owls floating over fields of barley, whose ripe, late-summer colours they closely echoed. I also remember House Martins tottering around the Holkham puddles like weird pied mice as they came down for a thousandth pellet of mud.

Perhaps, most of all, I remember a Song Thrush that performed outside our Holkham cottage. Can I possibly nominate it as the outstanding bird of 1985?

I'll explain. I've just completed *Birds Britannica* and in its quarter of a million words that Song Thrush is the only bird of 1985 which I felt warranted inclusion. The thrush was memorable then – it's unforgettable still – because it used to produce a strange captivating sequence of notes that were remarkably similar to the loud asthmatic call of an Indian bird, Grey Francolin *Francolinus pondicerianus*. And I could never hear them without being transported momentarily to those wonderful, bird-filled, mist-shrouded winter dawns of Rajasthan. For me it exemplified the powerful emotional impact of that simple song.

Mark Cocker lives in Norfolk. A founder member of the Oriental and African Bird Clubs, he is the author of the classic Birders – Tales of a Tribe *and the monumental* Birds Britannica.

JUNE 1985

BLUE ROCK THRUSH IN STRATHCLYDE

Rob Hume

On 14th June 1985, Mrs Elizabeth McConnell wrote to the British Trust for Ornithology from Girvan, Ayrshire. The first lines of her letter caused immediate excitement: 'Enclosed please find "bird": we think it is a Blue Rock Thrush.'

The letter gave brief details, and John Marchant responded with considerable interest: it was, indeed, a Blue Rock Thrush *Monticola solitarius* and, as such, potentially the first record for Britain. The specimen had arrived safely, but had begun to decay.

Initial details given were that it had arrived at Skerryvore Lighthouse, Strathclyde, on 4th June and had been found dead by A. McConnell on 8th, after which it had been kept in a deep-freeze. The weather was fine, occasionally sunny, during the bird's stay, and it hopped about on the rocks of the small island. Mr McConnell suggested that dehydration might have been the cause of death, as there is no fresh water available on the island.

Further correspondence revealed that Skerryvore is a pillar lighthouse on a rocky base with space for a helicopter pad and some small rocky areas, which are all completely awash in rough weather. There is no terrestrial vegetation at all. There were five or six birds present at the time the Blue Rock Thrush appeared, but it remained separate from them; it was not heard to call. A dish of fresh water was ignored by all the birds, and the rock thrush spent its time picking insects from the rocks. It was nervous when approached, always flying off out of sight behind the rocks when it realised it was being watched. It appeared to seek a crack in the rocks at night.

Other birds on the rock usually include a few wagtails *Motacilla*, although they seem not to survive: the McConnells had previously found dead Common Snipes *Gallinago gallinago* and Oystercatchers *Haematopus ostralegus* after at least 60 waders had flown around the light at night, and noted a small variety of passerine migrants, too, on occasion, often attracted to the light and not infrequently being killed by collisions with it.

John Marchant examined the bird and considered that the amount of wear and the lack of damage to feathers around the bill or to the bill, claws and toes gave no cause to suspect captive origin. The specimen was transferred to a deep-freeze at the British Museum, Tring, but was too decayed to allow the preparation of a skin.

Hume, R. A. 1995. Blue Rock Thrush in Strathclyde: new to Britain and Ireland. *British Birds* 88, 130–132.

Blue Rock Thrush is found from southern Europe to Japan. Birds winter in north Africa, Arabia, south and southeast Asia.

There have been four subsequent records:

Gwynedd Moel-y-gest, male, 4th June 1987

Scilly St Mary's, male, 14th–15th October 1999

Cornwall Cot Valley, St Just, male, 25th October 1999 (Possibly the Scilly bird)

Cornwall Pendeen, first-summer female, 14th–18th May 2000

JUNE 1985

CEDAR WAXWING ON SHETLAND

Clive McKay

In the summer of 1985, I was employed as the Nature Conservancy Council's Warden on Noss National Nature Reserve, an island east of Bressay, Shetland, Scotland. On the afternoon of June 25th, two visitors, Mr and Mrs P. Leward, returned to the

Visitor Centre after walking around the island, and informed me that they had seen a waxwing *Bombycilla*. They had obtained good views of the bird, and it was obvious from their verbal description that it was indeed a waxwing: they described the bird's general brown coloration, prominent crest, yellow tip to the tail, and even the red tips to some of the wing feathers. The date indicated that there was little likelihood of its being a wild Bohemian Waxwing *B. garrulus*, and I suggested that it might be an escaped cagebird.

I immediately searched the north coast of the island, and found the bird feeding amongst Thrift *Armeria maritima* on the top of a sheltered rocky headland. It was obviously not a Bohemian Waxwing, having no white on the primaries, and possessing pale sulphur-yellow underparts. Dredging up my scant knowledge of American birds, I suspected that it was a Cedar Waxwing *B. cedrorum*, and I proceeded to take a field description. After watching it during 16.30–17.30 GMT, I hurriedly left the island to telephone local birders. Unfortunately, none was at home, but I was not too worried by this, since I assumed then that the bird was an escape from captivity.

I also, however, telephoned a friend in Sheffield, Keith Clarkson, who had spent some time on a small island off Newfoundland in the summer of 1982, studying Brünnich's Guillemots *Uria lomvia*. He told me that the Cedar Waxwing is migratory, and that he had seen small flocks on the island in June, well away from their normal habitat. At home, I flicked through *The Shell Guide to the Birds of Britain and Ireland* and was surprised to find that, at that time, several species of Nearctic passerine vagrant had occurred in Britain either occasionally or exclusively in June (e.g. Hermit Thrush *Catharus guttatus*, Cape May Warbler *Dendroica tigrina*, Eastern Towhee *Pipilo erythrophthalmus*, Fox Sparrow *Passerella iliaca*, White-crowned Sparrow *Zonotrichia leucophrys* and White-throated Sparrow *Z. albicollis*). I began to consider the possibility that this Cedar Waxwing might be a genuine vagrant. Fortunately, it was still present on 26th, and, together with Susan Crosthwaite, I watched it during 08.30–10.30. I paid particular attention to the condition of the bird's plumage and to its feeding behaviour. It bore no colour rings or marks of any kind, nor did it show any obvious plumage aberrations that might have suggested a captive origin. I was able to obtain some photographs of it. We made no attempt to catch the bird, as I had been able to make satisfactory observations of it in the field. It could not be found on 27th.

Description
The following details were supplied to the British Birds Rarities Committee.

> *Structure and Behaviour* Wary when approached, but afforded good views when stalked carefully. Size similar to Common Starling *Sturnus vulgaris*, but smaller. Flight also similar to starling. General structure like that of a short-legged Redwing *Turdus iliacus*. When relaxed, short-necked and hunched, with wings held stiffly along sides and the wing-tips drooping below level of tail, exposing the rump. When active, posture sleek and elegant, with wings

held close to the rump/tail. Hopped around boldly on ground, with little elegance, and generally preferred to remain stationary between fly-catching sallies or lunges. Fed actively, taking food (thought to be mostly flies) either from the ground, from plant stalks and flower-heads (picked off delicately), or in flight. Fly-catching sallies from ground only, not from wall or other perches. Regularly sat on top of a broken-down dry-stone dyke when preening or after being flushed. Often mobbed by the local resident Rock Pipits *Anthus petrosus*, and attracted attention of Twites *Carduelis flavirostris*, but not mobbed by them. Ignored by Common Starlings, and never seen to associate with any other species.

Plumage In very good condition, truly immaculate, typical waxwing 'feather-perfect' appearance. The black mask and bib gave the bird a very bold appearance, whilst the rest of the plumage was characterised by the very subtle way that one colour merged into another, enhancing the bird's beauty.

Head Typical waxwing head pattern, with a distinctive crest, usually held drooped and closed over the back of the head, but raised slightly from time to time. Facial pattern particularly beautiful when seen head-on. Black mask from lores extending through eye and upwards behind eye towards back of head. Anterior two-thirds of mask bordered above and below by a thin cream-coloured line, this line a little thicker where it formed a short creamy moustachial stripe. Short black bib merging imperceptibly into pale bronze of breast (a female characteristic?). Rest of head a rich metallic bronze.

Upperparts Nape and mantle dull bronze, merging imperceptibly into lead-grey rump and uppertail-coverts. Lesser and median coverts dull bronze. Greater coverts and primary coverts brown-grey, six or seven of the former with red waxy tips. Tertials grey-brown, fringed with creamy-white on their inner margins. Primaries dark brown-black with blue-grey leading edges to basal half of feathers, forming a narrow panel on leading edge of wing. Basal half of tail lead-grey, distal third-quarter black, distal quarter yellow.

Underparts Black bib merging imperceptibly into pale bronze breast and chest. This in turn merging imperceptibly with pale sulphur-yellow on belly. Vent and undertail-coverts creamy-white. Tibial feathering white.

Bare Parts Bill clean and gun-metal blue-black. Legs short (much shorter than those of Common Starling or Song Thrush *Turdus philomelos*, for example), clean and black. Eye appeared to be all black, and difficult to see against the black facial mask.

Call A thin, feeble 'Schreet', heard twice immediately after the bird took flight.

Comments

The wind had been east or southeast at Noss since 20th June, swinging around to SSW on the afternoon of 25th, clearing away the fog that had persisted for several days. The wind backed to southeasterly again on 26th, when clear weather provided excellent conditions for observations.

The bird showed no obvious behavioural traits or plumage characteristics to suggest that it was of captive origin. On the day on which it arrived, there was also a small influx of three or four Common Crossbills *Loxia curvirostra* to Noss.

McKay, C. R. 2000. Cedar Waxwing in Shetland: new to the Western Palearctic. *British Birds* 93, 580–587.

Cedar Waxwing is a widespread bird in North America.

There has been one subsequent record:

Nottinghamshire Nottingham, first-winter, 20th February–18th March 1996

SEPTEMBER 1985

CHESTNUT-SIDED WARBLER ON SHETLAND

Michael Peacock

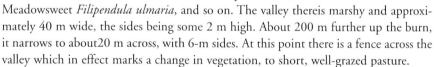

At about 13.30 GMT on 20th September 1985, having seen a Pied Flycatcher *Ficedula hypoleuca* at the end of the Burn of Feal on Fetlar, Shetland, I decided to walk up the burn, a walk I often did to look for migrants. The burn runs at the bottom of a valley which is distinctly steep-sided, giving a lot of shelter from the wind and, at the Wick of Houbie end, a fair amount of cover: docks *Rumex*, thistles *Cirsium*, Yellow Iris *Iris pseudacorus*, Meadowsweet *Filipendula ulmaria*, and so on. The valley thereis marshy and approximately 40 m wide, the sides being some 2 m high. About 200 m further up the burn, it narrows to about20 m across, with 6-m sides. At this point there is a fence across the valley which in effect marks a change in vegetation, to short, well-grazed pasture.

I found the Pied Flycatcher again at the end of the burn and then walked into a patch of irises and flushed a Garden Warbler *Sylvia borin*, which flew farther up the burn to a large patch of thistles. As I approached the point where I had last seen the Garden Warbler, I saw another warbler moving through the thistles. It then flew from the thistles to the fence. It was unlike any warbler I had ever seen, having double yellow-white wing-bars, a bright green-yellow head, back and rump, and white-grey underparts. It perched on the fence with its tail erect and wings slightly drooped.

When the bird had worked its way to the end of the thistles where the fence crosses the burn, it flew back to the iris patch some 200 m away. Throughout the period of watching, the warbler would work its way up the burn to the point where the vegetation changed and then fly back to the Houbie end, sometimes in one continuous flight, or in stages. When the bird flew the longer distances, it had a slightly undulating flight, the wing-bars were very distinct and some white was visible on the outer tail feathers.

The warbler seemed to prefer to perch on vantage points, such as the fence, tops of docks, and thistles. It would then fly down into the vegetation to find insects before returning to a vantage point. When on the fence, the warbler would hop short distances with its tail erect and wings drooping slightly, flicking its wings intermittently. When its tail was held in this position, white on the undertail-coverts was very distinct. The warbler would also fly up into the air, flycatching, and then return to near the original take-off point, very like a flycatcher.

After viewing the bird for about 30 minutes, I returned to the house a few hundred metres away to get my telescope, with which I was able to observe a lot more detail, including a very distinct white eye-ring and the fact that the grey-white of the 'cheek' extended slightly above the eye.

After further observations, I returned again to the house, at about 15.00 hours, to ask my wife, Val, to come and look at the bird, as she was the only other birdwatcher on the island at the time. We both got excellent views of the bird in good sunlight.

At 16.30 hours, we returned to the house and I telephoned, among others, Mike Walker, the RSPB warden for Fetlar, who was on holiday – on Fair Isle! He managed to get off and return to Fetlar that evening, but arrived after dark. We went out at first light (05.30 hours) on 21st, to be joined later by other birders from the Shetland Mainland, but, despite thorough searching, the bird was not seen again. My last sighting had been at about 17.30 hours the previous evening.

Although I was reasonably certain that the bird was an American Warbler of some kind, I lacked a North American field guide, and it was not until my telephone conversation with Fair Isle that the species, Chestnut-sided Warbler *Dendroica pensylvanica*, was determined, the first to be recorded in Britain and the Western Palearctic.

Description
The following description is based on my field notes taken at the time, supplemented by my wife's notes.

Size Slightly smaller than Pied Flycatcher that it perched next to.
Head and Neck Forehead, crown and upper part of nape bright green-yellow (moss-green). Ear-coverts and 'cheek' grey-white, extending to just above eye and also to side of neck and onto lower nape. Fairly distinct white eye-ring, no eye-stripe.
Upperparts Mantle, back and rump all bright green/yellow, slightly duller than head and nape, and unstreaked.
Wings Primaries and primary coverts dark grey with possible greenish tinge. Secondaries grey-green, edged dull yellow. Tertials greener than secondaries

and with more yellow edging. Lesser coverts green, greater and median coverts green with two yellow-white wing-bars, the lower bar being slightly larger than the upper (both very distinct on open and closed wing).

Tail Dark grey, possibly with some green. Some white on outer tail feathers, thought at the time to be probably on outer webs, but actually occurs only on inner webs (Dr A. G. Knox *in litt.*).

Underparts Chin white, throat and upper breast grey/white, becoming white on lower breast and belly, but greyer towards flanks. Undertail-coverts white and very conspicuous when tail held erect.

Bare Parts Legs grey. Bill brown and typical warbler shape, upper mandible appeared lighter than lower, but this probably effect of light. Eye large-looking and dark.

Behaviour Perched frequently on fence or other vantage point, flying down into surrounding vegetation to catch insects, also up in air like flycatcher. Often hopped short distances with tail erect and wings drooped, sometimes flicking wings. Appearance recalling Wren *Troglodytes troglodytes* when tail held erect.

The plumage was very fresh-looking, with little wear. After consulting North American bird guides, the age was confirmed as first-year. Apart from the conspicuous chestnut flanks which give the bird its name, both adult male and female also have a boldly streaked mantle.

Peacock, M. 1993. Chestnut-sided Warbler: new to the Western Palearctic.
British Birds 86, 57–61.

Chestnut-sided Warbler is a summer visitor to North America east of the Rockies; it winters in Central America.

There has been one subsequent record:

Devon Prawle Point, 18th October 1995

SEPTEMBER 1985

BROWN SHRIKE ON SHETLAND

Rob Hume

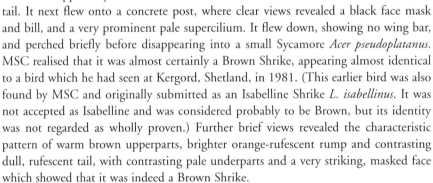

A Brown Shrike *Lanius cristatus* was present at Grutness, Sumburgh, Shetland, from 30th September to 2nd October 1985. It was discovered and identified by M. S. Chapman. This short paper is based upon his original account, submitted to the British Birds Rarities Committee.

During fine, calm weather (except for occasional light showers) on 30th September 1985, MSC was checking the garden at Grutness, Sumburgh. As he walked towards a small patch bordered by roses, a shrike *Lanius* flew away around a corner. Brief views showed an apparently adult shrike with a dull rufescent tail. It next flew onto a concrete post, where clear views revealed a black face mask and bill, and a very prominent pale supercilium. It flew down, showing no wing bar, and perched briefly before disappearing into a small Sycamore *Acer pseudoplatanus*. MSC realised that it was almost certainly a Brown Shrike, appearing almost identical to a bird which he had seen at Kergord, Shetland, in 1981. (This earlier bird was also found by MSC and originally submitted as an Isabelline Shrike *L. isabellinus*. It was not accepted as Isabelline and was considered probably to be Brown, but its identity was not regarded as wholly proven.) Further brief views revealed the characteristic pattern of warm brown upperparts, brighter orange-rufescent rump and contrasting dull, rufescent tail, with contrasting pale underparts and a very striking, masked face which showed that it was indeed a Brown Shrike.

MSC telephoned several people, including Fair Isle Bird Observatory, and went in search of A. F. T. Fitchett and G. J. Fitchett, whom he had met earlier ['to his eternal credit, he hired a taxi to come to look for us': GJF]. By dusk, excellent views had been obtained by about 12 observers, including J. D. Okill, P. Ellis, J. Eames and R. J. Johns (although GJF mentions an agonising hour-long search with the weather deteriorating to driving rain, followed by good views later). By 2nd October, the shrike had been seen by about 80 observers, photographed by Dennis Coutts and drawn by GJF.

Description

Very smart adult shrike, about size of Red-backed *L. collurio*. Upperparts rich, warm brown. Crown warmer, reddish-brown, merging evenly into mantle, fading towards nape (mantle medium brown: GJF). Rump bright orange-rufescent, contrasting markedly with mantle and tail (formed clear oblong between mantle and tail: GJF). Lower rump merged into uppertail-coverts, duller rufescent-brown, similar to tail, which was dull but distinctly rufous-brown, brightest at base and slightly darker at tip (extreme tip buff: GJF).

Wings rich, dark brown, edged conspicuously pale on tertials, with broad, pale edges washed pale rufous-buff at base, creamy-white at tips. Rest of wing, including coverts, uniform, with no pale edges. Wings as a whole contrastingly darker and colder brown than rest of upperparts, though contrast not marked (primaries/secondaries forming dark panel: GJF). No trace of any pale patch on the primaries.

Striking facial pattern. Black mask (lores and ear-coverts), white forehead (very narrow: GJF) and broad pale supercilium, broadening and flaring slightly behind eye (white, washed grey along upper border). Dark bill reinforced contrasted effect.

Throat white; rest of underparts sandy-buff with faint buff speckling on upper flanks.

Bill black except for small, greyer area at base, visible only at close range. Legs blackish.

The bird looked distinctively large-headed and heavy-billed, the bill heavier than on Isabelline, with a longer, more prominent hook and a longer, more bulging lower mandible.

The tail appeared long and slim, almost disproportionately narrow from the side. In a rear view, the individual feathers looked narrow; tip rounded. On 1st October, MSC paid special attention to the tail and noted the outer two pairs of tail feathers as distinctly shorter than the rest (by an estimated 25 mm) and paler, sandier brown.

Identification
Distinguished from Isabelline Shrike by:
(1) Combination of solid black face mask and complete lack of white wing bar
(2) Basically warm mantle colour
(3) Strong contrast between bright orange-rufescent rump and duller (but still rufous) tail
(4) White forehead (black on male Isabelline)
(5) Underparts washed sandy-buff, not pinkish-buff
(6) Very bold, distinctly large-headed structure
(7) Large bill with prominent hook (overlaps on skins, but on this bird particularly striking)
(8) Long, slim, rounded tail

Weather and associated birds
The weather maps for the few days prior to 30th show a large high-pressure system over the Baltic, with a smaller one approaching from the north on 27th September, giving easterly winds on that date.

There was an arrival of birds in Shetland on 27th/28th September, with small numbers of Continental migrants and several Yellow-browed Warblers *Phylloscopus inornatus*, Common Stonechats *Saxicola torquata* of one of the eastern races and, on

Fair Isle, three Pechora Pipits *Anthus gustavi* and a Lanceolated Warbler *Locustella lanceolata* prior to 28th. On 30th, birds were seen arriving at Grutness, with Common Redstart *Phoenicurus phoenicurus*, Yellow-browed Warbler, Chiffchaffs *Phylloscopus collybita*, Blackcaps *Sylvia atricapilla* and a Barred Warbler *S. nisoria* around the small garden.

Hume, R. A. 1993. Brown Shrike in Shetland: new to Britain and Ireland.
British Birds 86, 600–604.

Brown Shrikes of the nominate race breed in Siberia and Mongolia; they winter in southeast China, southeast Asia, Borneo, the Philippines and India.

There have been three subsequent records:

Shetland Fair Isle, first-winter female, 21st October 2000

Scilly Bryher, first-winter, 24th–28th September 2001

Shetland Whalsay, 19th–24th September 2004 (BBRC decision awaited)

The First for Ireland was an adult female at Ballyferriter, Co. Kerry, from 22nd November–10th December 1999.

OCTOBER 1985

WILSON'S WARBLER IN CORNWALL

Roger Smaldon

On 13th October 1985, after a good morning's birding at Rame Head, Cornwall, I left V. R. Tucker and R. Burridge and headed homeward at about 10.00 GMT. On the way, I stopped to check the hedge and trees around Rame church, which regularly hold migrants. In the cover of the roadside hedge, I found nothing but a small flock of Blue *Parus caeruleus* and Great Tits *P. major* with one or two Goldcrests *Regulus regulus*. I was about to leave when a small bird on the far side of a Hawthorn *Crataegus monogyna* hedge caught my attention. It was facing away from me and partially hidden by foliage, but I was intrigued by what I could see of the upperparts, which showed a bright olive-green on the mantle and coverts and a darker shade on the flight feathers; no wingbar was visible.

Within a second or two, the bird changed position in the Hawthorn to reveal its head and underparts. The effect was completely stunning. The underparts were a bright yellow, and the head, which was also basically yellow, had a neat black cap and a prominent black eye. It was, I was sure, an American wood-warbler (Parulidae), but, thinking rather frantically of all the American warblers on the British and Irish List, I realised that I could not put a name to it. The bird dropped quickly into cover, and when, after a few minutes, it did not reappear I dashed back to Rame Head to tell VRT and RB.

We all returned quite quickly to the church and spent nearly two hours searching the small area where the bird had been seen. These were, without doubt, ornithologically the longest and most excruciating two hours I have ever experienced. As the total cover in the area amounted to only about 50 m of hedge and a few adjacent trees, we reluctantly came to the conclusion that the bird had probably departed.

When giving details of the brief views that I had obtained, RB had at once suggested Wilson's Warbler *Wilsonia pusilla*, and so it was with great relief that I heard him shout the name when a small yellow-and-green warbler eventually appeared in the topmost branches of a small Ash tree *Fraxinus excelsior*, not 20 m from the original location. We had very good views for a few minutes before it again disappeared into cover; it was seen to drop into an area of hedge covered in ivy *Hedera helix*, and this was where it stayed for most of the day. Although the bird was watched by ten local people during the course of the day, and indeed was seen to go to roost in the ivy, unfortunately it could not be relocated by the much larger number of birders present from before dawn the next day.

As well as being seen by RB, who had experience of the species in the United States, the bird was also watched and photographed on 13th by K. Pellow (see *Brit. Birds* 81: 576, plate 301), who had seen Wilson's Warblers in Bermuda and who confirmed the identification.

Description

The following description is based on field notes taken by RS, VRT, S. C. Madge, M. Rayment and A. H. J. Harrop.

Size and Shape Although never seen directly beside any other species, considered to be about size of Chiffchaff *Phylloscopus collybita*. Shape altered perceptibly depending on bird's actions: it could, while in the higher foliage, look a slim warbler, but when it fed low in the ivy, flitting about with drooping wings and flicking tail, it looked markedly rounded and plump. The tail, which had rounded corners and was slightly notched, was perhaps proportionately a little longer than Chiffchaff's.

Head and Neck Head, which had a gently rounded appearance, basically bright yellow with small, clearly defined, glossy black 'skull-cap' type cap on crown; tips of rear feathers in cap fringed brownish. Lores and ear-coverts a subtle olive-green, shading into the surrounding yellow. Wide yellow supercilium extending whole length of cap. Nape and hindneck an olive greenish-yellow, merging into olive of mantle. Under optimal conditions, VRT noted a very narrow, bright yellow eye-ring.

Upperparts Mantle and upperwing-coverts bright olive-green; tertials and secondaries olive-brown, primaries a darker olive-brown. Tertials and greater coverts indistinctly and narrowly tipped paler, as were outer webs of secondaries. No wingbars present.

Underparts Throat to undertail-coverts bright rich yellow. In some lights and at certain angles flanks could appear less yellow, but sustained watching proved this to be illusory.

Tail Colour somewhat difficult to assess. Uppertail contrasted greatly with bright olive-green of upperparts: AHJH thought uppertail blackish; RS also did at first, but later considered it more a dark olive-brown. Undertail paler, probably a paler shade of olive-brown, but looking greyish or even whitish at times.

Bare Parts: Legs Long and substantial; looked orange/flesh in most lights, but exceptionally good views (by VRT) revealed front of leg to be a dark horn, with rear paler, and feet pinkish; *Eye* Black, beady and large; *Bill* Not noticeably fine or long, but broad-based, sharp-tipped and quite substantial; upper mandible dark horn, lower fleshy pink with darker tip.

Voice Two types of call were heard. (i) A loud, rather liquid 'twick', uttered singly: this reminded VRT of the alarm of Cetti's Warbler *Cettia cetti*, and he noted that it was given from cover; to SCM this note recalled a cross between the single note of Goldfinch *Carduelis carduelis* and Grey Wagtail *Motacilla cinerea*, or even Ortolan Bunting *Emberiza hortulana*. (ii) In the open, the bird would utter a short series of 'kick-kick-kick' calls resembling those of Red-breasted Flycatcher *Ficedula parva*.

Behaviour Always very active, moving at great speed through cover. Regularly performed flycatching, when snapping of bill easily heard. Also seen to pick insects from branches, and at least once foraged on ground. Drooped wings as it moved around branches, and flicked tail regularly. After appearing in the Ash tree, it kept in low cover for most of rest of day, giving good, if at times tantalisingly brief, views down to ranges of 5 m.

Discussion

From its well-defined glossy black cap, the Cornish Wilson's Warbler was obviously a male. It should, however, be noted that females can have black on the crown and this can be quite extensive, but generally it is admixed with olive (particularly at rear of crown) and so forms a diffuse, non-glossy cap (Pyle *et al.* 1987, *Identification Guide to North American Passerines*). Two points were raised by this individual's plumage. First, the illustrations of Wilson's Warbler in National Geographic Society (1983) show male and female with blackish tails, and the text points out that one of the better characters distinguishing females from those of Hooded Warbler *W. citrina* is the lack of white in the tail. As the Rame Wilson's showed a paler undertail, looking whitish at times, this statement is perhaps a little confusing, at least with certain individuals; more correctly stated, Hooded Warbler (of both sexes) shows not only a white undertail, but also, more importantly, white upper surfaces to the outer rectrices.

Secondly, an interesting question was first raised by AHJH: although the bird was clearly a male in adult-type plumage, why, if it had gone through a breeding season, a transatlantic crossing, and perhaps a migration across the North American continent, was it in such bright, immaculate plumage? If the bird was adult, one would have expected a worn, faded plumage, not the vivid crisp colours of the Rame individual. Yet neither could it have been an immature if all the statements in the literature are correct. The answer is probably to be found in Pyle *et al.* (1987), who show that many adult North American passerines, including Wilson's Warbler, have a complete 'prebasic' (post-breeding) moult prior to migration; with Wilson's Warbler, this takes place in June-August and could thus explain the fresh plumage of a bird in Britain in mid October.

Smaldon, R. 1990. Wilson's Warbler: new to the Western Palearctic.
Birding World 83, 404–408.

Wilson's Warbler is a widespread summer visitor in North America; it winters in the southern USA and Central America.

There have been no subsequent records.

1986

THE BIRDER'S YEAR

Adrian Pitches

An overwintering **Sociable Plover** that arrived on Hallowe'en in 1985 saw in the New Year in West Sussex. In Cornwall, a female **King Eider** in January was the first for the county and only the sixth in England since 1915. Eight 'new' King Eiders in 1986 was the best total since 1977. And the six **Bonaparte's Gulls** in 1986 – starting with the first-winter in Cornwall in January – was the best total ever for this dainty North American gull. But for gull aficionados, the Northeast was the place to be. A bitterly cold Arctic blast brought an immature **Ivory Gull** to Saltburn in Cleveland on 31st January and the next day a **Ross's Gull** was found at Hornsea, East Yorkshire.

On 22nd February, an **Upland Sandpiper** at Topsham, Devon, was the first-ever late-winter record of this American wader. And the first-ever overwintering **Least Sandpiper** was an instructive bird. It lingered at Portscatho, Cornwall, from early February until late April, moulting from first-winter to first-summer plumage during that time. And the Southwest had an even greater treat in store: the **Gyrfalcon** which stayed for ten days at Berry Head in south Devon from 31st March.

There were a record 13 **Black Kites** in Britain in 1986, and 21 **Woodchat Shrikes**, the majority of both species being seen in the spring. Another southern species making landfall was a **Great Spotted Cuckoo** on the Isle of Wight at the end of May. Meanwhile, from the north, yet another **Tengmalm's Owl** arrived in Orkney on 31st May. It was found dead a month later.

There were four **Terek Sandpipers** in 1986 – a pair in June and another pair in September. A long-staying male **Sardinian Warbler** at Gibraltar Point in Lincolnshire from early July until the end of August was a repeat of the bird which also skulked in the Sea Buckthorn at Gib Point from June to September 1979.

Late July saw the year's only First for Britain. Scrupulous work by Brett Richards delivered a **Red-necked Stint** at Blacktoft Sands, East Yorkshire, which others had lacked the tenacity to identify. For joyful listers there was an added bonus: nearby at Tetney, Lincolnshire, was Britain's first **Pacific Golden Plover** since the 'Lesser Golden Plovers' had been split. And it was alongside an **American Golden Plover!**

In late September, Fair Isle recorded its first **Bobolink**, which was almost overlooked amongst a flurry of six female/immature **Yellow-breasted Buntings**. The other east-coast American passerine was a **Red-eyed Vireo** at Dungeness, Kent – the second east-coast record following the first, also at Dungeness, in 1984. The only other Red-eyed Vireo of the autumn was on Scilly.

After the amazing autumn of 1985, Scilly had a relatively quiet 1986. The highlights were two juvenile **Semipalmated Sandpipers**, an **Upland Sandpiper** and a **Rose-breasted Grosbeak**. And then there were the **Grey-cheeked Thrushes**. At least eight arrived on Scilly in late October, together with three in Cornwall and one on Lundy, Devon. Few other American landbirds were involved in this influx, which exceeded the previous record for any one species of American landbird in Britain: ten Blackpoll Warblers in 1976. The flock which scattered over Scilly suffered calamity after calamity: one was taken by a cat, while another was washed off a rock and drowned as it finally made landfall after its transatlantic crossing.

There were other influxes in October 1986: 18 **Glossy Ibises**, including a family party of two adults and three juveniles on the Hayle estuary in Cornwall – and 12 **Cattle Egrets** arrived too. A group of three first-winter **Lesser White-fronted Geese** arrived in Essex in October, while down the coast in Kent there was a male **Pied Wheatear**. In November, a **Desert Wheatear** on South Walney in Cumbria was the first record for northwest England. Also in November, a **Black-winged Pratincole** at Eyebrook Reservoir, Leicestershire, was the latest record ever; a **Collared Pratincole** in mid-October on the Camel estuary in Cornwall was the second-latest record of that species.

A **'Steppe' Grey Shrike** at Landguard, Suffolk on 6th December was the third record for Britain of this race following birds on Fair Isle in 1956 and 1964. Ten years later the shrike would be upgraded to species status (see 1996) making the Landguard bird a satisfying 'armchair tick' for Suffolk birders.

On the last day of the year, a First for Britain reappeared in Hampshire, after its first appearance in Somerset at the beginning of the year. It was a **'Whistling Swan'**, the nominate North American race of Bewick's Swan. This adult bird, first seen on Curry Moor on the Somerset Levels on 5th January 1986, spent January 1987 at Ibsley, Hants, before presumably heading off to Siberia; it returned to Somerset in December 1987.

BIRDING WITH SANTA

Tim Melling

Throughout 1986 I was based at Newcastle University and was in the thick of the Tyneside birding scene. For me, the most sought-after birds were not always the rarest. They were often birds that your birding friends had seen but you hadn't, but they were especially desirable if they helped complete a 'gettable' set. Ivory Gull was one such bird that fitted all these criteria, so when news came through of one at Saltburn in Cleveland I was sent into a blind panic. It was mid-afternoon on 31st January when the call came through. The bird was a good hour away, the days were short, and I didn't have my car handy. Fortunately, my friend the late Paul Greenwood (who had the hide on Lindisfarne named in his memory) was visiting and was just about to drive back to Durham. He didn't take much persuading and we hurtled down to Saltburn as the light was fading. It was after 4 pm when we arrived but to our relief the bird was still there, shining like a beacon, and feeding down to 10 metres on a dead Guillemot. A fantastic black-spotted first-winter bird, and no other birders there to share it. Fortunately the bird hung around until 8th February.

On 11th February, I was travelling back down to Cleveland, this time to see an Arctic Redpoll. It seems funny looking back that Arctic Redpolls were once considered such a rare bird, but their separation from 'Mealies' was still considered problematical. In fact, sight-only records were near impossible to get through the Rarities Committee. Fortunately, this individual had been trapped and was seen to have the requisite 10 mm of unstreaked white rump as described in the then current edition of Svensson's Ringers' Guide. We saw the bird no problem, but it was a bit of a disappointment. I left with the awful feeling that I had previously thrown one or two away as Mealies because they didn't appear frosty enough.

Next day I was watching the long-staying Laughing Gull at Newcastle General Hospital. It had been present since 1984 and the staff had now become accustomed to people staring up at the buildings with binoculars. A young bird-watcher approached me to tell me that he had just found a Ring-billed Gull just a few yards down the road. Now what are the chances of two American gulls arriving at the same urban site more than ten miles from the sea? That's what I thought too, and raised an incredulous eyebrow, but went along expecting to put him straight. Instead I ate a large slice of humble pie as he had indeed found a Ring-billed Gull.

The 22nd of February saw my first long-distance twitch of the year, down to Penzance for a Bonaparte's Gull. It seems ridiculous now, but Bonaparte's was then a very rare bird, and I was keen to 'do' all the gulls. We drove down through the night and called in at dawn at Portscatho for a long-staying Least Sandpiper. We also picked up a female King Eider nearby before continuing down to spend a cold, fruitless day at Drift Reservoir. I was cold, wet and miserable having not slept and hardly eaten for more than 24 hours. Then word came through that the bird was showing at Newlyn Harbour. We raced down there in fading light just in time to see the bird. My big mistake then was going to celebrate in a local hostelry on an empty stomach with two big drinkers. I don't remember much after that, apart from having difficulty sleeping, despite my total lack of sleep the previous night. This was largely due to sharing a small B&B room with Dave Beaumont and Mike Wilson, who snored like a chainsaw with a broken silencer all night long. I vaguely remember seeing the Bonaparte's Gull again the following morning with a punishing hangover. I had no difficulty sleeping all the way back to Tyneside.

March 31st brought the arrival of the ultimate prize: a twitchable Gyrfalcon. There had been many records of Gyrfalcons in Britain but they were nearly always seen only by the lucky finders. This bird spent ten days roosting in a quarry at Berry Head in Devon. I remember it turned up on a Monday and I had to wait an agonising five days until we could get down to see it. This bird was so popular that we teamed up with birders from Teesside and ended up hiring a minibus. We sped down through the night and joined a crowd of hundreds in pitch darkness lined up along the ancient battlements of Berry Head. It was a clear night and I remember scanning the cliff face opposite in the half-light and finding a white blob that gradually materialised into the most charismatic bird I had ever seen. It sat in full view for the best part of an hour before taking flight right over our heads. It followed its usual pattern of disappearing for the rest of the day before returning to roost late in the evening. Nearly 18 years on, I can still remember Richard Millington's description of 'The ermine-clad executioner from the high Arctic wastes' from his *Birdwatching* column.

Spring migration was quite good in the Northeast that year. I remember birding with Ken Shaw on Lindisfarne and finding our own Rough-legged Buzzard, and dashing back up there to see three White Storks that my friend Maurice Hepple had watched flying in off the sea. Hoopoe, Temminck's Stint, Great Grey Shrike and a full summer-plumaged male Lapland Bunting was a good back-up cast in the Northeast that spring. It seems odd now, but a Black-winged Stilt on Teesside really set the pulses racing. This was before the breeding birds at Holme, and long before one took up permanent residence at Titchwell.

A female Subalpine Warbler at Spurn, quickly followed by a Broad-billed Sandpiper at Fleetwood in Lancashire were important enough to lure me out of Northumberland. But these were completely eclipsed by a Terek Sandpiper that spent three days at Hauxley in Northumberland from 29th June.

An unexpected find came on 11th July while I was photographing orchids on Lindisfarne. It was a hot, calm day so I wasn't expecting birds when I came across an adult Long-tailed Skua. It wasn't on the sea, but hunting over the fields. I remember it hovering like a Kestrel, with its long tail whipping to and fro. I imagined that this was how they hunted for lemmings on the tundra.

The only British First of the year arrived at Blacktoft Sands on 22nd July in the form of a Red-necked Stint. Unfortunately, it wasn't conclusively clinched as such until five days later. A couple of birds had previously been misidentified as Red-necked Stints, most notably a bird on Fair Isle that proved to be a Sanderling. This left observers feeling rather cautious and hesitant over what, with the benefit of hindsight, was a screamingly obvious summer-plumaged Red-necked Stint. Everyone had been aware of the bird's presence, but it was almost a standing joke that there was a dodgy Red-necked Stint at Blacktoft. Then at lunchtime on Sunday 27th July, the jokes ceased abruptly and the whole world raced across to Blacktoft to see it before the weekend ended. It remained just two more days following its correct identification. My abiding memory is of a long queue outside the hide with wardens allowing just five minutes' viewing before the next shift was allowed in.

Late August saw the tail end of an early Caribbean hurricane buffeting Britain's shores. Most sensible people stayed indoors but I remember venturing out and seeing three Red-necked Phalaropes together on a coastal pool, alongside hundreds of Little Gulls, with a single Wryneck nearby. I then dashed up to Lindisfarne where I found no less than five more Wrynecks among numerous Pied Flycatchers and Garden Warblers.

The early hurricane seemed to deposit several American waders in Britain, and I remember seeing Baird's, Pectoral and Buff-breasted Sandpipers along the Northeast coast that autumn.

Then came the Scilly season. 1986 was a relatively quiet year when compared with the previous four years, which still stand out as being exceptionally good. There were a couple of Western Bonelli's Warblers, Rose-coloured Starling, Richard's Pipit and a Little Bunting. From America there were Semipalmated and Upland Sandpipers, Rose-breasted Grosbeak and a Red-eyed Vireo, but the star of the season was surely Grey-cheeked Thrush.

At least eight were on the Scilly Isles, with another three on mainland Cornwall. I arrived with a boatload of birders from St Agnes on 21st October eager to see the first of these rare thrushes, only to be greeted on the quay by news that a cat had just eaten it. The air turned blue, but we didn't need to wait too long before other Grey-cheeked Thrushes started appearing.

I also remember returning from Tresco with Paul Dukes having seen the Rose-breasted Grosbeak. Paul had found the very first British record on St Agnes 20 years previously and clearly held this species in great reverence. So when a breathless birder ran up and asked 'Is the Grozzer showing?' Paul's face was a picture. We jokingly discussed that anyone demeaning such a wonderful bird with the name 'Grozzer' should have his tongue removed. A Chimney Swift appeared in early November after most birders had left, and stayed long enough to tempt a good few back.

My birding year finished with a surreal experience early on Christmas morning. Late Christmas Eve I was called by my friend Tom Brereton, who told me of a Cattle Egret near New Mills in Derbyshire. I was at my parents' in Bolton for Christmas so decided I would slip across for the bird early on Christmas morning. I reached the spot well before first light as I didn't want to miss it leaving its roost. After a few minutes, another car arrived. I was just about to get out to check that I had found the right spot, when a man in full Santa Claus outfit got out of the car, slung a sack across his shoulder and went to call at a nearby house. It was just getting light and as I looked back towards the fields I saw the Cattle Egret fly from its roost and land by some nearby cattle. What a great way to start Christmas Day.

Tim Melling lives in West Yorkshire. A conservation officer for the RSPB, he is Secretary to the BOU Records Committee.

JULY 1986

RED-NECKED STINT IN EAST YORKSHIRE

Brett Richards

O n leaving my home on the outskirts of Hull, Humberside, on 23rd July 1986, the weather was fairly nasty: cool, overcast and raining, sometimes heavily. The choice for me lay between seawatching at Hornsea or visiting Blacktoft Sands RSPB Reserve; only at the last moment did I decide on the latter.

On arriving at Blacktoft, I learned that the 'Little Stint *Calidris minuta*' reported the previous day was still present in front of Xerox hide, but I was in no hurry to see it, and did not enter that hide until 10.30 GMT. On seeing the stint, I immediately suspected that it might be a summer-plumaged Red-necked Stint *C. ruficollis*. The uniform chestnut-red colour of the chin, throat and upper breast, completely unmarked by any dark streaking or spotting, and the border of dark speckles below this on the white background of the lower breast, seemed quite wrong for Little Stint; the legs also appeared rather short for that species, and I therefore took a careful description of the bird.

Description

Size and Shape Noticeably smaller than Dunlin *C. alpina*, but direct size comparisons with Little Stint not obtained. More attenuated rear-end than on Little Stint, owing to longer wings and tail. Longer tertials, and shorter primary projection beyond them, than on Little, but this difficult to see. Head longer than that of Little Stint, with flatter and more sloping forehead and slight bulge over front of eye. Head held below line of back, giving more hunched appearance than Little, which carried its head more or less level with mantle. Red-necked deeper-bodied at lower belly, with 'step' between vent and undertail-coverts, unlike more smoothly curved appearance of Little.

Head and Neck Chin (to bill base), throat, foreneck, upper breast and sides of 'face' unmarked chestnut-red (paler at sides of bill base, under eye and on ear-coverts), this colour extending onto side of neck as broad wedge; dark brown loral line and eye-stripe, latter ending in diffuse blob at top rear corner of ear-coverts. Supercilia whitish-buff, with very faint orangey wash, continuous across forehead, widening towards eye, and broader behind eye owing to eye-stripe being at lower level than loral line. Viewed from side, supercilia seemed to fade out at rear, at same time looking fairly square-ended, but actually continuing onto nape, where just about meeting immediately below rear of crown, although very thin there and perhaps a shade more orangey. Crown finely streaked dark brown and white, with dark streaks being very slightly the wider. Hindneck streaked dark brown and white, as crown, but both dark and pale streaks slightly broader, almost continuous from crown, and separated only by supercilia. At sides of hindneck, these streaks met by spotting of lower-breast border.

Upperparts Mantle dark brown, very sparsely and thinly streaked whitish in centre, almost uniform dark brown towards sides, and showing thin, but distinct creamy-white line down each side. Centre of back to rear mantle lines often showed strongly rufous. Tail and rump dark-centred, with white sides to rump, pale grey sides to tail, perhaps paler than on Little Stint. Upper visible row of scapulars brownish-black with conspicuous rufous inner edges, pale buff tips and pale outer edges. Middle row of fore scapulars velvety-black, with whitish-buff edges and tips, rest of scapulars centred dark brown, with more pronounced and wider whitish-buff edges and tips towards rear scapulars, giving more scaly effect.

Wings Tertials darkish grey-brown with buff-white outer edges and tips. Primary projection blackish. Greater coverts blackish-brown, a shade darker than tertials, with buff-white edges and tips, slightly wider than those of tertials. Median and lesser coverts grey-brown with broad whitish edges and tips; appearing generally rather greyish from a distance. Alula dark brown. Distinct wing-bar, as extensive and prominent as Little Stint's.

Underparts Dark spotting of lower-breast border extending into angle formed by chestnut-red of upper breast and bend of wing; this border consisting of broad band of fine dark brown (greyish from a distance) speckles immediately below chestnut-red of upper breast. Very thin white area, curved towards right side of bird, separated two halves of border in centre of lower breast. Spots on ends of border at sides of lower breast sparser, larger, blacker, at times aligning to form broken 'V's pointing towards head. Spotting here continued down sides of lower breast, almost forming streaks at times, depending on lie of plumage. All this spotting on white background; rest of underparts also white.

Bare Parts Bill length approximately 1.75 times loral distance, with almost straight culmen, curved just perceptibly at the tip. Lower mandible very slightly decurved along lower edge, with very slight gonys bulge just discernible at close range. No lateral expansion at tip when viewed from front; not particularly deep-based, but fairly blunt-tipped; appeared generally short and stubby compared with that of Little Stint, especially at close range. Iris black or dark. Shorter-legged than Little Stint. Legs and feet grey-black, marginally paler than black bill.

Behaviour Shorter legs than Little Stint resulted in different feeding action, holding its body horizontal and moving only its head up and down in rapid pecking motions; Little had more pronounced pecking action, pivoting its body slightly each time, describing larger arc of movement with its head.

That evening, I called on Steve James and checked my description against Cramp & Simmons (*BWP* Vol 3, 1982) and Hayman *et al.* (1986). This left me in little doubt that the bird was, in fact, a Red-necked Stint, my only reservations being caused by the contrary opinions of more experienced birdwatchers, who considered it to be a Little Stint.

The lack of dark streaking or spotting on the chestnut-red colour, and the fact that all the dark speckling was on a white background and not 'overlain on orangey wash at sides of breast' (Hayman *et al.* 1986, describing Little Stint), apparently eliminated Little Stint. The lack of a white throat was also diagnostic, Little Stint 'always' having a white chin and throat, whereas Red-necked usually has chestnut-red throat; also the 'chin ... sometimes, also mainly rufous' (Cramp & Simmons 1982). The short legs also suggested Red-necked Stint.

I returned to Blacktoft the next day (24th) to make a more detailed description, but, unfortunately, I could not discuss it with the warden, Andrew Grieve, as he was away for a few days. During the course of my study of the bird on this day, I became convinced beyond any doubt that we were watching Britain's first, long-awaited Red-necked Stint, and, after much discussion, some of the other birders in the hide seemed favourable to this identification.

I again returned to Blacktoft the following day (25th), and, on this occasion, Bryan Dodsworth, who had been impressed with the wader on the previous day, announced that he also was sure that it was a Red-necked Stint, having studied Jonsson & Grant (1984). He had brought this paper along with him, and we were able to use it to confirm our identification. A Little Stint had also arrived at Blacktoft, accentuating the differences in shape of the Red-necked, and enabling us to detect a difference in feeding action.

General recognition of this bird as a Red-necked Stint came on 27th July, and, thanks to Andrew Grieve's expert management of the resulting twitch, at least 1,872 people were able to see it, raising £573 for the RSPB in the process. The stint departed on the evening of 29th July, when a low-flying light aircraft disturbed all the birds on the scrape, and it was not seen subsequently.

Richards, B. 1989. Red-necked Stint: new to Britain and Ireland.
British Birds 82, 391–395.

Red-necked Stint breeds in the Siberian Arctic; it winters in southeast Asia and Australasia.

There have been five subsequent records:

Norfolk Cley, adult, 29th July–3rd August 1992

Shetland Fair Isle, juvenile, recently dead, 31st August 1994

Northumberland Wansbeck estuary, adult, 12th–13th August 1995

Shetland Pool of Virkie, Mainland, adult, 18th–21st July 2000

Cambridgeshire Somersham, adult, 21st–22nd September 2001

The First for Ireland was at Ballycotton, Co. Cork, on 2nd–5th July 1998.

1987

THE BIRDER'S YEAR

Adrian Pitches

The year 1987 will long be remembered – by those who were there – for an unprecedented three Firsts in four days on Scilly in October (although the second, Eastern Bonelli's Warbler, was a slow burner). But there was much more to 1987, with superb rarities in almost every month of the year.

It 'bustard' into life in spectacular style on 16th January when the first of up to nine male **Great Bustards** were sighted in Suffolk. The flock led birders a merry dance across the county, finally settling near Minsmere, only to be flushed by birders on 21st February. The final sighting, of an immature male, was at Sudbourne on 7th March.

Meanwhile, Norfolk equalised with two immature male Great Bustards at New Buckenham from 7th–10th February. Very convenient for Norfolk residents Richard Millington and Steve Gantlett, who had just launched a service that would transform birding in Britain. Two decades later, Birdline (launched as Bird Alert) is an institution.

From the outset the rarity hotline was red hot: on 16th January, as that squadron of bustards touched down, a first-winter male **Harlequin Duck** in Sullom Voe, Shetland, had set birders' pulses racing. It was the first since a pair on Fair Isle in 1965. This bird stayed until late February; a second – a female – arrived on Islay in late October.

Shetland kept up the pace in February when eagle-eyed Chris Heard spotted a **Brünnich's Guillemot** off Hamnavoe, Burra. And it was alive! It stayed four days; another, dead, Brünnich's was also found nearby. On 13th February there was a **Nutcracker** in a Cambridge garden.

It was a landlocked Midlands county which yielded the first First of 1987, a tricky immature *Aythya* on Chasewater, Staffordshire, on 8th March which was resolved as a male **Lesser Scaup**. It stayed until 26th April, just overlapping with the next First of the year, this time on Lundy off the north Devon coast. Another puzzling American, this was an **Eastern Phoebe** that did its Orphean-Warbler-cum-flycatcher act from 24th–25th April. Incredibly, it – or another – had been sighted at Slapton Ley on the south Devon coast two days previously by Welsh wizards Ken Croft and Alan Davies … but this record was not accepted.

Influxes were a theme of 1987. After the bustards came **Red-rumped Swallows**, in two waves. The spring influx was led by a bird that arrived in Cley, Norfolk, on 8th April. The autumn influx in October/November was more spectacular with a flock of seven on Scilly in late October. Birds straggled as far north as Shetland, with two in Lerwick until 8th November. In total, 60 or more Red-rumped Swallows arrived in Britain this year. There was another mini-influx in late April: two male **Little Crakes**, both in Wales, one in Clwyd and one in Dyfed. Following the hirundines and the crakes was a spring influx of **Gull-billed Terns**, with nine arrivals from Cornwall to South Uist in the Western Isles.

But it was gulls rather than terns that stole the headlines in May 1987: a pair of **Slender-billed Gulls** took up residence at Cley for four days in mid-May. They departed late on the Friday, disturbed by a skua, disappointing many Saturday twitchers. There was some compensation the following day when a pair of **Black-winged Stilts** arrived along the Norfolk coast at Holme. The pair stayed to breed and fledged two young.

Attention switched back to Shetland in May and June, where there were two **White-throated Sparrows**. And a cracking male **Lesser Kestrel** on Fair Isle on 23rd June was a fortunate find for this author on his first visit to the magic isle. On Holy Island, Northumberland, another lucky observer found a male **Trumpeter Finch** on 1st August. While the stilts were rearing young (the two juveniles were subsequently seen in Staffordshire in early September), a **Stilt Sandpiper** appeared at Cliffe, Kent, on 18th August and stayed a week. Kent scored again with another ultra-rare wader in early September: a **Sharp-tailed Sandpiper** at Sandwich Bay. Meanwhile, late August saw a twitchable **Great Snipe** on Blakeney Point, Norfolk, and the first of four on Fair Isle in autumn 1987.

Fair Isle would be eclipsed by events in southwest England this autumn, but nevertheless served up five **Yellow-breasted Buntings**, two **Pine Buntings** and Britain's second **Savannah Sparrow**. A further two Pine Buntings were on Orkney.

The Scilly season started with a male **Black-headed Bunting** on Tresco in September. In October, Tresco had a **Blackpoll Warbler** – and Britain's First **Philadelphia Vireo**. Three days before, on 7th October, a select band of birders saw Britain's First **Wood Thrush** on St Agnes before gales swept in and prevented boats reaching the island from St Mary's. It wasn't seen again. From the East, a 'Bonelli's Warbler' with an unfamiliar call was on St Mary's, probably from 30th September; in time it was recognised as Britain's First **Eastern Bonelli's Warbler**. St Agnes scored again the following week with Britain's third **Hermit Thrush**, which *did* stay, from 15th–16th October. With a **Swainson's Thrush** on St Mary's, there was a chance that the full set of North American *Catharus* thrushes would give themselves up in October 1987.

Indeed, Britain's second **Veery** appeared on Lundy (the First was in Cornwall in October 1970), along with another Swainson's Thrush. The Veery stayed for a month. And Lundy had a **Yellow-billed Cuckoo** for the second year running. Another Swainson's Thrush was in the Cot Valley, Cornwall, but Grey-cheeked Thrush failed to appear in 1987 after the record influx of 12 in 1986.

Also on the mainland, a **Black-and-white Warbler** spent a week at East Prawle, Devon, and there was a **Northern Parula** at Nanquidno, Cornwall, for ten days, while Britain's fourth **Chimney Swift** was seen near Truro, Cornwall, on 18th October.

The third record of **Green Heron** was a freshly dead bird at Tyninghame, Lothian, on 25th October.

Back on the Isles of Scilly, there were two **Eyebrowed Thrushes** and a male **Black-throated Thrush** (another male was on Shetland). The final flourish on Scilly was Britain's First **'Two-barred' Greenish Warbler** on Gugh at the end of October (although a bird at Holme, Norfolk, in October 1976 was probably of this race). In fact, 1987 was the best year to date for nominate **Greenish Warbler**, with one on Fair Isle in late June the first of 19, most of which arrived in August.

In autumn 1987, Fair Isle's warbler haul included both **Blyth's Reed Warbler** and **Paddyfield Warbler**. Another Blyth's Reed was trapped in Prior's Park, Tynemouth, on 20th October. Another late-autumn influx, which coincided with the Red-rumped Swallows, was one of **Olive-backed Pipits**. There were 20 birds from Scilly to Shetland, almost treble the total (seven) in the previous best year, 1984. More than half were on Fair Isle alone, where there were up to 11 'OBPs'. Later still came another **Pallas's Warbler** influx – 40 birds was the best annual total since the 1982 invasion. The autumn wheatear roster was one **Pied Wheatear** in Kent on 7th November and two **Desert Wheatears** – a female in Essex on 12th October and a male trapped and ringed at Landguard, Suffolk, on 23rd October which was relocated at East Prawle, Devon, three days later.

After an excellent autumn that lasted well into November, some special birds arrived in December. There was a **Dusky Thrush** on Skomer early in the month – and then the year had one final surprise. On 20th December, three **Little Bustards** were sighted at Sudbourne, Suffolk – the same place where the last Great Bustard was seen in March. Another Little Bustard was in Dorset from 30th December into 1988, enhancing the New Year celebrations for the lucky few who saw it.

THE BIRTH OF BIRDLINE

Steve Gantlett

January 1987 saw the combined launch of Birdline and *Twitching* magazine – the latter to be renamed *Birding World* in just a year's time. In partnership, Richard Millington was to be the mainstay of Birdline and I was to be the editor of the magazine. I had a long-booked foreign trip to undertake first, however: 1st January 1987 found me in Cape Town, halfway through a month-long birding tour of the whole of South Africa and Namibia. It was one of the most intensive birding trips I have ever been on – but also one of the most rewarding. With a group of friends, it was birding all day, every day, from dawn till dusk, with often quite long drives at night. I finally arrived back in England on 25th January: exhausted, but with a far greater knowledge of the birds of southern Africa than I had had before.

My British birding year began in earnest from that Heathrow 'What's the news?' call. The answer was Britain's first-ever twitchable Harlequin Duck at Sullom Voe, Shetland. Unable to go immediately because I had to do some work for the partnership, I sweated it out for a few days until the weekend, and then headed north.

Three days on Shetland produced good views of the Harlequin, plus a King Eider and Harp Seal as a bonus. I was back in Norfolk for just three days and then back up to Shetland again on 6th February after news broke of a Brünnich's Guillemot at Hamna Voe. This was another successful twitch, with this weekend visit also producing White-billed Diver, Surf Scoter and repeat views of the Harlequin Duck. After several failed visits on other occasions, I also saw the famous long-staying adult Laughing Gull at Newcastle General Hospital on the way home.

But it was a delightfully hectic winter: just a day later I was grateful to be back in Norfolk and not still on Shetland. News broke on two Great Bustards in the sugar beet fields at New Buckenham. After some searching, I finally caught up with these magnificent beasts. After a mid-February visit to Pitsford Reservoir, Northamptonshire, for a drake Falcated Duck found with a flock of about 100 Wigeon (surely a wild bird!), the 21st of the month found me enjoying three more East Anglian Great Bustards in a roadside rape field at Theberton, near Minsmere.

Next up, in mid March, was Britain's first-ever Lesser Scaup, at Chasewater in Staffordshire. This bird proved to be an obliging long-stayer and, although both its identification and its origin were initially subject to considerable debate, there were no real doubters in the end. So far so good: there were more than enough top-class birds to keep Birdline essential listening and *Twitching* essential reading! In between twitches, there was work on the magazine to be done, as well as local Norfolk birding. And local Norfolk at last came good on 8th April, when Eddie Myers found an early Red-rumped Swallow hawking over Pat's Pool at Cley in the early morning. It was to prove to be a popular long-stayer, and famous for lingering over the village green, in front of The Swallows pub, and for being photographed roosting in the porch of Cley church.

Over Easter, I took a quick trip to Belgium, hoping for Tengmalm's Owl. The trip was a dip for this main target, but good views of Black Woodpecker provided fine compensation. Upon arriving back in England, Cornwall immediately beckoned: the lure of a summer-plumaged adult Bonaparte's Gull at Marazion and a Gull-billed Tern on the Hayle estuary was too much to resist. Both performed beautifully, which cannot be said of the next bird: on 24th April the male Little Crake at Shotton Marsh, Clwyd, had already gone...

May 1987 proved not to be the greatest May ever, but it still had its moments. The 3rd produced a drake Ring-necked Duck at Hardley Flood, Norfolk, and an Ortolan Bunting skulking in a bean field at Lowestoft, Suffolk. A week later, Suffolk was well worth visiting again for a Caspian Tern on Minsmere scrape, while Cley again struck gold with an adult female Wilson's Phalarope on Pat's Pool from 9th until 11th. In contrast, 12th May seemed quiet at Cley, so Richard Millington and I were tempted over to west Norfolk to see a Hoopoe at Snettisham Country Park. Very nice it was too, but the drive back to Cley was somewhat less than gentle when Robert Aberdein phoned with the news of a pair of Slender-billed Gulls there!

Five days later, when a Savi's Warbler was singing beside Cley East Bank, a pair of Black-winged Stilts arrived at Holme Hun Pool. These were the icing on the cake of an excellent Norfolk May, which, for me, also produced three red-spotted Bluethroats, a male Kentish Plover on Arnold's Marsh, Cley, and the first of a series of Caspian Terns at Hickling.

On 8th June, I found a delightful female Red-necked Phalarope on the North Scrape at Cley, in the middle of the day dipped on a Subalpine Warbler at Landguard, Suffolk, and then enjoyed a female Woodchat Shrike at Holme Dunes in the evening.

Four days later, I saw the famous breeding pair of Red-backed Shrikes in their usual bushes at Santon Downham carpark. Another visit to Holme was in order on 16th June, however: the pair of stilts was on display with their three chicks newly hatched that day – bumble bees on stilts! The month closed with two more surprises at Cley: a drake American Wigeon with six Wigeon on Pat's Pool on 22nd and a Tawny Pipit inside the beach just west of the end of East Bank on 24th.

For the first three weeks of July, I took some Americans on a round Britain birding tour (though I scarcely had time; this had been booked before the launch of *Twitching*). We saw a fine selection of Britain's birds, but didn't bump into any rarities. It did almost cost me Blue-cheeked Bee-eater, however (one was suppressed in Devon at the beginning of the month), so my enthusiasm for further commitments was dampened. On 20th July, a further visit to Holme produced further views of the Black-winged Stilts, plus their now recently fledged three young. Surely one of these was the bird now known as Sammy and resident at nearby Titchwell? Two days later, an adult Marsh Sandpiper arrived on Pat's Pool at Cley and stayed until the month's end.

Early August was quiet (or was I busy doing some work?), but mid month found me in the Western Approaches, as usual. This year's annual three-day pelagic trip on the MV *Chalice* with Peter Harrison produced seven Wilson's Petrels, numerous Great Shearwaters, two Sabine's Gulls and 54 Grey Phalaropes on a truly glass-calm sea, the like of which I have never seen before or since! On 19th August, an evening visit to Cliffe Pools, Kent, produced good views of the target bird: a fine summer-plumaged Stilt Sandpiper. The following week, north Norfolk was back in vogue, with a confiding Great Snipe, Wryneck, Icterine and Greenish Warbler all on Blakeney Point. On 11th September, I found a Pectoral Sandpiper on Pat's Pool, Cley, but the second half of the month was time for my then annual trip to Fair Isle. This year, the trip produced a good haul, headed by Blyth's Reed, Paddyfield and three Lanceolated Warblers, Great Snipe and three Yellow-breasted Buntings.

October 1987 proved to be an absolute classic. As usual, most of the action was on the Isles of Scilly, but first, a brief visit to Norfolk en route from Fair Isle to the extreme southwest produced good but brief views of a Radde's Warbler twitched at Wells Woods at midday on 2nd, and then, due to the moderate easterly wind, I spent the rest of the afternoon on Blakeney Point, where I found both a Richard's Pipit and an Olive-backed Pipit. Two days later I saw a Dusky Warbler in the hand on Blakeney Point. I spent the middle of the month on Scilly, however, and what a classic year it was! Wood Thrush and Philadelphia Vireo topped the bill, but on this visit I also saw Eyebrowed, Hermit and Swainson's Thrushes, Blackpoll Warbler and Red-eyed Vireo plus American

Golden Plover, three Red-rumped Swallows and Booted, Subalpine and Radde's Warblers. I was home in Norfolk only for a day, though, when it was necessary to go back again! On the morning of 25th October, I was on Gugh watching Britain's first 'Two-barred' Greenish Warbler but, on the following day, it was over to Lundy for the Veery (and another Swainson's Thrush and a Short-toed Lark). Back at Cley on 29th October, there was a superbly confiding Pallas's Warbler on the fence by the Eye Pool.

November was much quieter, of course, but it began with an Isabelline Shrike just west of Wells town and then there was another Pallas's Warbler at Waxham on 7th and a Dusky Warbler at nearby Happisburgh the next day. December was also quiet, though an adult Red-breasted Goose at Cley, which arrived with the Dark-bellied Brent Geese and was joined by a Black Brant, enlivened the proceedings, while a two-week trip to Morocco, which began at the turn of the year, produced a fine selection of birds, but dips on Slender-billed Curlew (this trip) and Arabian Bustard (which, sadly, was never realistically looked for ever again).

Steve Gantlett lives in Cley, Norfolk. One of Britain's top listers, he is editor of Birding World. *Together with Richard Millington, he found Britain's first Rock Sparrow in 1981.*

MARCH 1987
LESSER SCAUP IN STAFFORDSHIRE
John Holian and John Fortey

At about 09.45 GMT on 8th March 1987, JJH stopped at Jefferys Swag, Chasewater, West Midlands, to look for a long-staying male Scaup *Aythya marila*. He found, instead, a small, immature Scaup-type duck asleep amongst the wintering flock of Tufted Ducks *A. fuligula*. As there was obviously something 'different' about this bird, he brought it to the attention of A. D. Barter and J. J. Oliver, who were also present. Together they set about examining it in greater detail. After half an hour or so, they were still uncertain about the identity of this duck and so decided to obtain a comparison with the drake Scaup which had, by then, been located on the main pool. After studying the Scaup for a while, they returned for another look at the small bird on the Swag and spent an hour observing it and taking field notes. Unfortunately, the bird was asleep most of the time, but the following points were noted:

Small Scaup-type duck, similar in size to Tufted Duck. Vermiculated back, 'broken' brown breast markings and brownish primaries, indicative of immature drake. Head not so noticeably rounded as that of Scaup, having pronounced 'bump' at rear, and looking uniformly dark in colour without any sheen (maybe owing to dull conditions). Habitually held tail erect, showing ragged tail feathers. Undertail buffish or off-white, with hint of darker brown on feather tips. Bill Scaup-like, blue/grey in colour, with small black nail. Eyes yellow, but somewhat duller than those of adjacent Tufted Ducks.

After some discussion, they agreed that the bird was probably a Scaup × Tufted Duck hybrid. Later in the day, the bird was independently observed by another regular Chasewater birdwatcher, G. Evans, who subsequently came to the same conclusion.

Over the next week, the bird received scant attention until, on the evening of 15th March, JEF, T. E. Giles, A. Keatley and A. I. Whatley, unaware of the bird's presence, paid a brief visit to the Swag to have a quick look at the ducks before moving on to view the gull roost on the main pool. They soon saw the adult drake Scaup and then noticed a second *Aythya* some distance away, under overhanging willows. At first they thought that it resembled Pochard *A. ferina* × Tufted Duck hybrids with which they were all familiar, but, although the crown shape was similar, the bird's head looked blacker and lacked any red coloration, and the mantle was paler. A Scaup × Tufted Duck hybrid was suggested, although this combination was not known to any of them. Lesser Scaup *A. affinis* was jokingly mused, but, as more and more identification features were seen that they could remember as characteristics of that species, that possibility seemed increasingly likely. The bird was distant and offered tantalising views as it swam in and out of the cover of the overhanging willows. The low sun gave the bird's head a greenish gloss, which seemed a slightly worrying feature, but Tufted Ducks' heads looked similar in this light. Its bill was all blue, with a narrow black nail, making a hybrid origin unlikely. AK and JEF had brief views of strong black vermiculations on the scapulars, and noted that the bird's size was slightly less than that of drake Tufted Ducks. When the bird flew a short distance, TEG and AIW saw the upperwing wingbar, which looked white on the secondaries and grey on the primaries.

That evening, JEF and TEG examined a slide taken at Slimbridge and consulted the available literature, and became fairly certain that the bird was a Lesser Scaup. The following evening, JEF and GE – who had considered the bird to be a hybrid – discussed the identification and came to the conclusion that it was a Lesser Scaup.

News of this brought people to Chasewater from places as far apart as Scotland and the Continent, but no-one seemed to have any literature relating to the immature plumage of the species. Many hours spent observing the bird seemed to raise more unanswered questions about various aspects of the plumage. Available reference books suggested that the Lesser Scaup should have a dark purple gloss to the head, something that the Chasewater bird showed in good light. There was, however, also a noticeable green sheen around the cheek area that seemed to extend down onto the sides of the neck.

On 22nd March, the bird was quite active, giving comparatively good views of its head, including a new feature: a small, pale blue margin, much paler than the rest of the bill, situated immediately behind the black nail. This feature had also been noted by E. G. Phillips, but we had no idea whether this 'fitted' Lesser Scaup; we were also concerned about the colour of the undertail. The only way to resolve the various problems was to compare the bird at Chasewater with other specimens of Lesser Scaup, so on 29th March JJH visited Slimbridge to examine those in the collection. Unfortunately, there were no immatures present, but it was a bright day and the glossy purple sheen on the drakes' heads was obvious; all of the drakes observed also had the green sheen on the cheeks, and it did indeed extend down onto the sides of the neck in the same manner as on the bird at Chasewater. All of the drakes also showed the pale area on the bill, behind the nail, although this did vary in extent from one individual to another. By 11th April, two small, dark spots were noticeable on the undertail; as the days passed, this flecking increased, until, by 25th April, it had become very prominent. The bird was last seen at Chasewater on 26th April, and was photographed (*Brit. Birds* 80: plate 175; 85: plates 146–149).

Holian, J. J. & Fortey, J. E. 1992. Lesser Scaup: new to Britain and Ireland.
British Birds 85, 370–376.

Lesser Scaup is a widespread breeding bird in North America; it winters on both coasts and south to Central America and the West Indies.

Clearly overlooked in the past, there have been more than 70 subsequent records to the end of 2004.

APRIL 1987
EASTERN PHOEBE ON LUNDY
Colin McShane

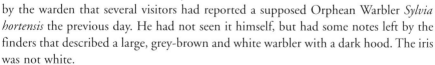

On 25th April 1987, K. J. Mitchell & A. J. Wood and I arrived on Lundy and were told by the warden that several visitors had reported a supposed Orphean Warbler *Sylvia hortensis* the previous day. He had not seen it himself, but had some notes left by the finders that described a large, grey-brown and white warbler with a dark hood. The iris was not white.

A preliminary search of St John's Valley revealed nothing, so we proceeded to set up mist-nets in the area and in the neighbouring Millcombe valley. At 14.00 GMT the nets were furled, and most of the group retired to rest after a tiring all-night journey. At 16.00, I entered St John's Valley and immediately saw a bird fitting the warden's description, but, even after just a few seconds, it was obviously not an Orphean Warbler; indeed, it was not a warbler at all.

I watched it for 15–20 minutes in superb light, with 7 × 50 binoculars, as close as 5 m. It behaved in typical 'flycatcher' fashion, with an upright stance, 'sitting on its feet', and making fluttering sallies to catch insects on the wing and on the ground, each followed by a short flight to another exposed perch. There was an audible 'snap' of its bill each time that it caught a fly. It used rabbit-proof cages around several saplings as perches. It had a slow, deliberate tail-wagging, rather than tail-flicking. I made a description and then went back to find more people.

KJM and AJW came with telescopes and we watched the bird on and off for an hour in superb light, making notes and drawings. After we had reset the mist-nets, the bird perched on the poles, on the guys and even, once, on the top shelf string, but refused to get caught and, at 18.00, flew into the next valley; it was never seen again.

It was certainly larger than any typical warbler, estimated at 6–7 inches (15–17.5 cm). The wingtips reached about one-quarter of the way down the tail, which was neither especially long nor short; in fact, the shape and proportions were reminiscent of a large Spotted Flycatcher *Muscicapa striata*. The tail had a slight indentation at the tip. The bird was essentially grey-brown above and white below. The head was dark chocolate-brown, creating a hooded effect, with a clear-cut lower edge from the base of the bill under the eye to the side of the neck, leaving a white 'diamond' shape on the chin and throat as seen from in front. The hooded effect became more or less obvious according to the angle of light, sometimes merging into the mantle and sometimes looking quite clear-cut. The back was plain grey-brown. The angle of light also affected the contrast between the depth of colour of tail and wings compared with that of the back and rump: at most there was only a faint darkening of the wings and tail. The edges of the tertials, greater coverts and secondaries were faintly lighter brown. The outer tail feathers also seemed a little lighter than the rest, especially at the base. There was no wing bar at rest or in flight. The underparts were white, but the sides of the breast showed a greeny-grey suffusion, almost meeting in the middle; with the 'scope, this was seen to be composed of very faint blotchy streaks.

The eyes were large and very dark, tinged red/brown at close range; there was no eye-ring. The black bill looked well proportioned for the size of the head, not over-large, and with no hook at the tip. The black legs were relatively short.

This description fitted none of the British and European flycatchers, and we had to wait until we had left Lundy to check field guides to other parts of the world. Various North American guides illustrated the Eastern Phoebe *Sayornis phoebe* with the characters that we had noted. One reference also quoted a behavioural trait that we had noticed: it plunged into a small stream on a couple of occasions.

The notes made the previous day, 24th April, by J. Crook and another (unnamed) observer were detailed and included several sketches: they are exactly comparable with those that I made, even to the paler outer tail feathers ('fawn') and the changing appearance in the contrast between the hood and the mantle. Obviously, it was the Eastern Phoebe, understandably not properly identified at the time. The observers noted that the size and general pattern looked like those of Orphean Warbler (the dark eye suggesting a first-year individual), but the absence of white outer tail feathers and the persistent flycatching behaviour could not be reconciled with such an identification. JC said to his companion: 'Hey! This bird does not exist.' At first it was skulking and often lost to sight in the upper branches of trees, but then the size and behaviour – pouncing onto an insect on the ground – recalled a shrike *Lanius*. They noted 'flicking' of the tail rather than the slower 'wag' that I described. It was first seen at 06.30 GMT, found again at 09.00, and once more at 12.00, always in St John's Valley.

McShane, C. 1996. Eastern Phoebe in Devon: new to the Western Palearctic. *British Birds* 89, 103–107.

Eastern Phoebe breeds in eastern North America and winters south to Mexico. There have been no subsequent records.

OCTOBER 1987
WOOD THRUSH ON SCILLY
Paul Dukes

On 7th October 1987, a morning of rain and strong winds gave way to a showery afternoon on St Agnes, Isles of Scilly. It was enough to encourage Rod McCann and me to venture out to make the most of the clearance, despite little evidence of new arrivals of birds. We walked over Wingletang, the open, gorse-grown area at the south of the island.

We returned by different routes from Horse Point at the southern tip and, as I skirted a line of gorse bushes on the Northeast edge of Wingletang, a bird suddenly flew up from under my feet. It dropped into a tangle of gorse a few metres farther on. The incident was so unexpected and brief that I hardly had time to raise my binoculars, but, as the bird flew up, I glimpsed a flash of foxy-rufous which, combined with a thrush-like shape, made me think that it might be a Veery *Catharus fuscescens*. Almost to step on an American thrush on such a birdless day seemed like an hallucination, but the strong rufous colour could not have been imagined: I shouted to Rod to come over. We cautiously approached the gorse bush, but at first nothing appeared. Suddenly, the bird flew out from under the bush, travelling low and fast for 100 m or so, before diving for cover again. We both managed to obtain flight views and agreed that several features looked wrong for Veery. The rufous continued over the head and mantle, but shaded into a Song Thrush *Turdus philomelos* olive-brown on the rump and tail, giving a distinctly two-tone effect to the upperparts. It was also clear that it was somewhat larger than the 'usual' American thrushes – Grey-cheeked *C. minimus* or Swainson's *C. ustulatus* – albeit slim. We considered the possibility of Wood Thrush *Hylocichla mustelina* and with this realisation came a feeling of panic: the adjacent gorse was an impenetrable thicket.

While trying to persuade it to move back into the original isolated bushes, I flushed the thrush once more and the bird passed very close to RM before pitching into a tangle of brambles and gorse. Rod's view revealed white underparts heavily blotched with black and a prominent white orbital area, adding confirmation to our original tentative identification. It seemed prudent to withdraw, to let the Wood Thrush feed and to get other observers to the spot by rushing to the Post Office blackboard. Most of the birdwatchers on St Agnes quickly assembled and the news was transmitted to St Mary's.

We tried to get the bird to move to the original bushes where it could perhaps be watched feeding, so we moved through the area where it had last been seen. Francis Hicks obtained an excellent view at this stage, with the bird on the ground in front of him, but the rest of us had to settle for brief flight views. Eventually, we succeeded in our objective and, from a discreet distance, settled down to await the bird's appearance. Observation was difficult, but several people managed a glimpse of the bird under the bushes. Then some 40 people from St Mary's arrived to double the crowd, but the thrush remained hidden.

In an attempt to limit the amount of disturbance, we decided that a couple of people would try gently to persuade the thrush to emerge into view, but the result was not what we desired. The bird suddenly flew low, towards the crowd, then veered left and pitched into more dense cover. There followed a frustrating hour with some more brief flight views, which at least enabled everyone to appreciate the 'two-tone' upperparts, and a fortunate few saw it perched on an open gorse branch before it dived out of sight.

At this stage, we felt that the thrush had been subjected to enough stress, so we all withdrew from the area to leave it in peace. It looked strong and healthy, but was clearly a new arrival and needed to find a more hospitable location than the bleak, windswept expanse of Wingletang. Strong winds continued for the next 24 hours, but, on 9th, calm weather permitted a mass invasion of hundreds of birdwatchers. Regrettably, nothing more was seen of the Wood Thrush, the first record for Britain.

Dukes, P. 1995. Wood Thrush in Scilly: new to Britain and Ireland. *British Birds* 88, 133–135.

Wood Thrush is a widespread breeding bird in North America; it winters in Central America.

There have been no subsequent records.

OCTOBER 1987

EASTERN BONELLI'S WARBLER ON SCILLY

Tim Wilson and Charles Fentiman

On 8th October 1987, the Isles of Scilly were still being battered by the remnants of a westerly gale associated with a front that had passed the previous day. For the majority of birders on St Mary's, it was a day spent close to the quayside, hoping in vain for calmer seas and positive news of the Wood Thrush *Hylocichla mustelina* that had been seen on St Agnes the previous evening. Having been part of the small but spectacular and successful twitch on 7th, we were still on a high, and were, together with Martin Reid, determined to scour the larger island for other fresh North American arrivals.

At around 11.00 GMT, we arrived at Salakee Farm and found that the line of elms *Ulmus* was protected from the wind. Very few birds were in evidence, however, except for several Goldcrests *Regulus regulus* and an accompanying lone warbler high in the canopy of one tree. It was difficult to see this warbler clearly, but TJW's first impression was of a *Phylloscopus* with rather featureless greyish upperparts and silvery grey underparts. This combination set alarm bells ringing, so he called CF and MR over to look at 'an interesting warbler'.

The bird had now moved somewhat lower and was feeding actively on small insects, both in the canopy and in a hedge that bordered the lane. The warbler was usually obscured by foliage and occasionally perched, out of view, for several minutes at a time. During the next 20 minutes or so, it showed rather poorly. Between us, however, we tried to note all its salient features. CF, on finally obtaining a brief view of the rump, proclaimed the bird to be Bonelli's Warbler *Phylloscopus bonelli*, a conclusion to which MR and TJW were also coming, except for one puzzling feature.

During most of this initial observation period, the bird was seen and heard to utter a distinct, sharp 'chip' note, quite at odds both with any past experience we could remember of the species and with the only field guide which we had with us. The bird was so vocal that it could usually be tracked when out of view and even caused us to think of a possible North American wood-warbler (Parulidae). As a result of this 'wrong' call, we all felt uncomfortable with our initial identification, so, although the plumage features did not seem to fit anything else, TJW put the news out on CB radio as only 'a possible Bonelli's'.

Something then happened that has muddied the waters for many years, until we reviewed the record fairly recently. While we were waiting for reinforcements, the bird moved out of sight along the lane. It had been out of view and silent for some time when we heard a strident, disyllabic 'hooeet' call nearby. Having failed to see any other migrants whilst we had been standing there, we assumed that this call must have come from the Bonelli's, especially since the sound fitted our expectations. Happier now with our identification, TJW put out the news of 'a definite Bonelli's'.

A few birders had appeared by this time, and the bird was in view again, frequently uttering the now-familiar 'chip' call. No dissenting voices were raised as to the identification, so we left to celebrate with a mug of hot chocolate and a slab of cake.

Some time later that day, other observers, including C. D. R. Heard, saw the warbler and ascribed it to the eastern race *orientalis*, on the basis of the diagnostic 'chip' call. The bird was seen by many other observers on 9th and 10th, although it was sometimes elusive. During this time, only the 'chip' note was heard. With hindsight, greater experience and the knowledge that no subsequent observers heard anything other than the 'chip' note, we have decided that the 'hooeet' call which the three of us heard is not proven to have come from the bird under observation.

Description

The following is a summary of the original notes supplied to the Rarities Committee:

Plumage Head and upperparts very greyish, and underparts very pale and almost white in certain lights. General impression from the wings and tail was of a more greyish brown; at certain angles, the greenish panel on the closed wing could be seen, but most of the time, even when the bird was perched in an exposed position (ten yards [9 m] for about 30 seconds), this feature was not obvious. I looked for but could not see the rump patch.

Bill and Legs Bill looked particularly fine in comparison with Chiffchaff *Phylloscopus collybita* and Willow Warbler *P. trochilus*, appearing to be of a yellowish/flesh colour. The bill struck me as being a particularly noticeable feature (I must admit to never having noticed this before on Bonelli's Warbler). I could not clearly see the leg colour, but it was obviously darker than the colour of the bill.

Size and Action Slightly larger possibly than Willow Warbler or Chiffchaff, but in general action and behaviour rather reminiscent of Wood Warbler *P. sibilatrix*.

Call Notes At the time, we were surprised to hear the bird frequently make an American wood-warbler-like 'ptsit' contact note – especially in flight (I did not know of the call of the eastern race at the time). Also, we heard on two occasions the more typical 'hoohheet' call, which was more musical and better pronounced than that of Willow Warbler. Unfortunately, I did not see the bird actually make this call, but from the sound direction I am fairly certain that it came from this bird [but see above].

Wilson, T. J. & Fentiman, C. 1999. Eastern Bonelli's Warbler in Scilly: new to Britain and Ireland. *British Birds* 92, 519–523.

*Eastern Bonelli's Warbler (*Phylloscopus orientalis*) was subsequently split from Bonelli's Warbler (*P. bonelli*) and this record was accepted as the First in 1997. The species breeds in southeastern Europe and winters south of the Sahara.*

There have been three subsequent records:

Northumberland Whitley Bay, 20th–29th September 1995

Shetland Sumburgh and Grutness, 27th August–5th September 1998

Devon Lundy, 27th April 2004 (BBRC decision awaited)

OCTOBER 1987

PHILADELPHIA VIREO ON SCILLY

John Brodie Good

At about 16.00 GMT on 10th October 1987, with the farmer's permission, Dick Filby and I entered the fields on Borough Farm on the northeastern side of Tresco, Isles of Scilly, and began to walk down the main track towards the pines at the bottom, flanked on our right-hand side by a hedge of Sycamore *Acer pseudoplatanus*. As we moved slowly downhill, checking the small fields and their hedges, I noticed a small bird hovering low by the main hedge about 75 m ahead. I raised my binoculars to identify the expected Goldcrest *Regulus regulus* when another bird appeared in my field of view, again in the main hedge, but much closer. Refocusing, I immediately realised that I was looking at a member of the North American family Vireonidae, and exclaimed 'Vireo!' twice. DF joined me for brief views before the bird moved into the hedge. 'Philadelphia?', he said. We then obtained prolonged views at a range of about 30 m, the bird feeding along the edge of a small orchard bathed in direct sunlight. Having built up a description of its salient features, we were able to confirm its identity as a Philadelphia Vireo *Vireo philadelphicus* with the aid of *The National Geographic Society Field Guide to the Birds of North America* (1983), which we happened to have with us. The bird was eventually seen by over 1,000 people during its four-day stay, and was last seen at about 16.00 GMT on 13th October, by me, in the same spot in which Dick Filby and I had found it.

Behaviour Stayed mostly in Sycamore hedges and, occasionally, trees. Moved 'purposefully' when feeding, similar to *Sylvia* warblers, rather than actively like *Phylloscopus* warblers, picking food (mainly caterpillars) from branches and leaves. Hung upside down fairly frequently, picking off prey below itself. Occasionally 'flycatched'. In common with many North American birds, it was approachable and unperturbed by close human presence. No calls heard.

Size and Structure Slightly longer than a Chiffchaff *P. collybita*, but with quite different jizz from any European warbler. Rather robust, deep-bellied and short-tailed, with stout, shortish, broad-based, dark, pointed bill (grey with a black tip: P. G. Lansdown *in litt.*). Relatively 'strong' bluish legs and feet. Tail short in relation to body length, noticeably notched.

Plumage General appearance: green upperparts, yellowish underparts, with relatively bold head pattern and contrastingly dark flight feathers. Crown and forehead matt greyish-blue (darker and greyer at the sides: P. G. Lansdown in *litt.*). Short dark line through bold dark eye. Supercilium white, thicker behind eye. White line below dark eye-stripe, thickest below eye itself, giving rise to unique face pattern. Lower cheeks, mantle, rump, basal two-thirds of uppertail and wing-coverts cold green (with greyish-olive tone: P. G. Lansdown *in litt.*). Primaries, primary coverts and secondaries almost matt black, with very fine pale edgings, more prominent on secondaries. Lower third of uppertail almost as dark. Tail feathers very finely pale edged and tipped, forming very fine, pale tip. Undertail dark. Throat and upper breast deep yellow, with lower breast and flanks much paler yellow/off-white, and belly white. Vent pale lemon yellow, brighter than flanks and lower breast, but not so bright or deep as throat and upper breast.

The bird seemed to be in good health and appeared to have settled into a daily routine. We presume that it had arrived on Tresco before 10th October, since several other Nearctic vagrants had been discovered in southwest England during the previous week, after a number of fast-moving weather systems had crossed the Atlantic.

Pyle *et al.* (1987, *Identification Guide to North American Passerines*) stated 'Juv. (Jun-Aug) is generally drabber with a brownish wash to the plumage and more distinct wing bars. Otherwise, no reliable plumage criteria known.' We have, therefore, been unable to determine whether the Tresco individual was an adult or in first-winter plumage.

Good, J. B. 1991. Philadelphia Vireo: new to Britain.
British Birds 84, 572–574.

Philadelphia Vireo breeds in southern Canada and northern USA; it winters in Central America and northernmost South America.

There have been no subsequent records.

The First for Ireland was at Galley Head, Co. Cork on 12th–17th October 1985.

PLATE 1

1. *Yellow-browed Bunting. Fair Isle, Shetland, October 1980 (Iain Robertson).*

2. *Sandhill Crane. Mainland, Shetland, September 1991 (Robin Chittenden).*

PLATE 2

3. *Little Swift. Skewjack, Cornwall, May 1981 (Rod Hirst).*

4. *Pacific Swift. Cley, Norfolk, May 1993 (Jack Levene).*

5. *Chimney Swift. Porthgwarra, Cornwall, October 1982 (Stuart Hutchings).*

6. *Varied Thrush. Nanquidno, Cornwall, November 1982 (Stuart Hutchings).*

PLATE 3

7. *Oriental Pratincole. Dunwich,*
Suffolk, June 1981 (David W. Burns).

8. *Marmora's Warbler. Langsett, South*
Yorkshire, May 1982 (John Belsey).

9. *Hudsonian Godwit (right).*
Countess Wear, Devon, November
1981 (John Belsey).

10. *Grey-tailed Tattler.*
Burghead, Moray, November
1994 (Steve Young).

PLATE 4

11. *Lark Sparrow. Landguard, Suffolk, July 1981 (Trevor Charlton).*

12. *Savannah Sparrow. Portland, Dorset, April 1982 (David Cottridge).*

PLATE 5

13. *White-crowned Black Wheatear. Kessingland, Suffolk, June 1982 (Brian Brown).*

14. *Lesser Crested Tern. Farne Islands, Northumberland, June 1997 (Dante Munns).*

PLATE 6

15. *Long-toed Stint. Saltholme, Cleveland, August 1982 (John Dunnett).*

16. *Little Whimbrel. Sker, Mid Glamorgan, September 1982 (Richard G. Smith).*

17. *Northern Mockingbird. Horsey Island, Essex, May 1988 (Pete Loud).*

PLATE 7

18. *Cliff Swallow. St Mary's, Isles of Scilly, October 1983 (Robin Chittenden).*

19. *Blue Rock Thrush. St Mary's, Isles of Scilly, October 1999 (George Reszeter).*

20. *Brown Shrike. Mainland, Shetland, October 1985 (Dennis Coutts).*

21. *Wilson's Warbler. Rame, Cornwall, October 1985 (Keith Pellow).*

PLATE 8

22. *Cedar Waxwing. Noss, Shetland, June 1985 (Clive McKay).*

23. *Red-necked Stint. Blacktoft, East Yorkshire, July 1986 (David Cottridge).*

24. *Lesser Scaup (left). Chasewater, Staffordshire, March 1987 (David Cottridge).*

PLATE 9

25. *Eastern Bonelli's Warbler. Whitley Bay, Tyne & Wear, September 1995 (Tony Collinson).*

26. *Philadelphia Vireo. Tresco, Isles of Scilly, October 1987 (David Cottridge).*

27. *Moussier's Redstart. Dinas Head, Dyfed, April 1988 (Mike Barrett).*

28. *Crag Martin. Swithland Reservoir, Leicestershire, April 1999 (Iain Leach).*

PLATE 10

29. *Blackburnian Warbler. Skomer, Dyfed, October 1961 (Peter Fullagar).*

30. *Double-crested Cormorant. Billingham, Cleveland, February 1989 (David Cottridge).*

31. *Swinhoe's Petrel. Tynemouth, Tyne & Wear, July 1994 (Don Page).*

32. *Great Knot (right). Mainland, Shetland, September 1989 (Dennis Coutts).*

PLATE 11

33. *Golden-winged Warbler. Larkfield, Kent, February 1989 (David Cottridge).*

34. *Red-breasted Nuthatch. Holkham, Norfolk, March 1990 (David Cottridge).*

PLATE 12

35. *White-throated Robin. Skokholm, Dyfed, May 1990 (Margaret Potts).*

36. *Ancient Murrelet (left). Off Lundy, Devon, May 1990 (Dave Atkinson).*

37. *Tree Swallow. St Mary's, Isles of Scilly, June 1990 (Jack Levene).*

38. *Barrow's Goldeneye. Irvine, Strathclyde, December 1979 (Pete Wheeler).*

PLATE 13

39. *Yellow-throated Vireo. Kenidjack, Cornwall, September 1990 (Tim Loseby).*

40. *Spectacled Warbler. Filey, North Yorkshire, May 1992 (Mark Coller).*

PLATE 14

41. *Black-faced Bunting. Pennington Flash, Greater Manchester, March 1994 (Steve Young).*

42. *Bay-breasted Warbler. Land's End, Cornwall, October 1995 (David Ferguson).*

43. *Redhead (right). Bleasby, Nottinghamshire, March 1996 (Steve Young).*

PLATE 15

44. *American Coot. Stodmarsh, Kent, April 1996 (Steve Young)*

45. *Indigo Bunting. Ramsey, Pembrokeshire, October 1996 (Alan Tate)*

46. *Canvasback. Welney, Norfolk, January 1997 (Steve Young).*

47. *Steppe Grey Shrike. Swindon, Wiltshire, September 1993 (Mark Coller).*

PLATE 16

48. *Lesser Sand Plover (right). Pagham Harbour, West Sussex, August 1997 (Iain Leach).*

49. *Hume's Warbler. Caernarfon, Gwynedd, December 2003 (Steve Young).*

50. *Slender-billed Curlew (both pictures). Druridge Bay, Northumberland, May 1998 (Justin Carr).*

PLATE 17

51. *Short-billed Dowitcher. Rosehearty, Aberdeenshire, September 1999 (Steve Young).*

52. *Short-toed Eagle. Great Ganilly, Isles of Scilly, October 1999 (Phil Palmer).*

53. *Mourning Dove. North Uist, Outer Hebrides, November 1999 (Nic Hallam).*

PLATE 18

54. *Iberian Chiffchaff. Portland, Dorset, April 1999 (Gary Bellingham).*

55. *Long-tailed Shrike. South Uist, Outer Hebrides, November 2000 (Gwen Evans).*

56. *Siberian Blue Robin. North Ronaldsay, Orkney, October 2001 (John Kinsey).*

57. *Red-billed Tropicbird. Sea area Sole, June 2001 (Roger Barnes).*

PLATE 19

58. *Fea's Petrel. Off Scilly, July 2001 (Ashley Fisher).*

59. *Taiga Flycatcher. Flamborough Head, East Yorkshire, April 2003 (Nigel Blake)*

60. *Snowy Egret. Balvicar, Argyll & Bute, November 2001 (Iain Leach).*

PLATE 20

61. *Ascension Frigatebird. Tiree, Inner Hebrides, July 1953 (Nat. Museums of Scotland).*

62. *Black Lark. South Stack, Anglesey, June 2003 (Nigel Blake).*

PLATE 21

63. *Audouin's Gull. Dungeness, Kent, May 2003 (Nigel Blake).*

64. *Sykes's Warbler. Mainland, Shetland, October 1993 (Kevin Osborn).*

65. *Purple Martin. Lewis, Outer Hebrides, September 2004 (Martin Scott).*

Plate 22

66. *Masked Shrike. Kilrenny, Fife, October 2004 (Steve Young).*

67. *Chestnut-eared Bunting. Fair Isle, Shetland, October 2004 (Rebecca Nason).*

PLATE 23

68. *Rufous-tailed Robin. Fair Isle, Shetland, October 2004 (Rebecca Nason).*

69. *'Two-barred' Greenish Warbler. Gugh, Isles of Scilly, October 1987
(David Cottridge).*

PLATE 24

70. *'Red-throated' Thrush. The Naze, Essex, September 1994 (Robin Chittenden).*

71. *'Brown Skua'. St Mary's, Isles of Scilly, October 2001 (Martin Scott).*

72. *Putative Elegant Tern. Criccieth, Gwynedd, July 2002 (Steve Young).*

1988

THE BIRDER'S YEAR

Adrian Pitches

The year 1987 was a hard act to follow but 1988 served up some excellent birding. There were four Firsts (two of which turned up on the same April day in western Britain), three seconds for Britain, two **Caspian Plovers**, the same number of **Bridled Terns** – and twitchable **Needle-tailed Swift** and **American Robin**.

An adult **Ross's Gull** at Seaforth, Merseyside, on 3rd January was a great start to the new year. On the same day, an unprecedented January **Olive-backed Pipit** was on Shetland, probably a lingerer from the record influx in the autumn of 1987.

A **White-billed Diver** was way down south in St Ives Bay, Cornwall, in February – another was off north Devon in April. And another Ross's Gull headed down south too: a first-winter bird was in Devon and Cornwall in mid-March.

The 24th of April 1988 delivered near-simultaneous Firsts from quite different points of the compass. A **Brown-headed Cowbird** from North America was discovered on Islay, in the Inner Hebrides, by Clive McKay (who found the First Cedar Waxwing on another Scottish island, Noss, in 1985). And a male **Moussier's Redstart** was on Dinas Head, Dyfed, the same afternoon. But this had come from North Africa on a warm southerly wind.

One out-of-range redstart was amazing but two was incredible. So the male **Daurian Redstart** from southeastern Siberia found five days later on the Isle of May, Fife, was sadly regarded as an escape. What is it about Daurian birds? Both Daurian Starling and Daurian Redstart failed to gain acceptance. Will Daurian Jackdaw face the same fate if and when it arrives? The Moussier's Redstart was preceded by a **Rock Thrush** – a male on Portland, Dorset, from 16th-24th April. A surge of *Sylvia* warblers (30+ **Subalpine Warblers** and four **Sardinian Warblers**) continued the Mediterranean theme. Then in late May the flow of extreme rarities started.

A male **Caspian Plover** on St Agnes, Scilly, on 21st May was the first since 1890 but heart-breakingly it was a one-day bird. Incredibly, another bird put in a two-day show at Aberlady, East Lothian, in mid-July. On 28th May, a **Needle-tailed Swift** was sighted on Hoy, Orkney. And it stayed 12 days!

The hordes who travelled to Orkney then chartered fishing boats to sail on to North Ronaldsay after another Siberian bird, a **Pallas's Rosefinch**, appeared. Sadly, this did not become a First for Britain as it was deemed to be another escaped cagebird.

But a genuine First was found at the other end of the country on 22nd June – a **Crag Martin** at Stithians Reservoir, Cornwall. This long-awaited First was followed by another Crag Martin just 17 days later at Beachy Head, East Sussex.

June 22nd was a red-letter day in Kent too. Britain's second **Oriental Pratincole** was found alongside a **Black-winged Pratincole** at Harty on the Isle of Sheppey! The First Oriental Pratincole, in 1981, also turned up on June 22nd. And like that bird, this one lingered until October. There were two other June Black-winged Pratincoles – in Avon and Cheshire. Other wader highlights this spring were three **Broad-billed Sandpipers** together at Cliffe, Kent, in late May and two pairs of **Black-winged Stilts** – in Buckinghamshire and Suffolk in June. But neither pair repeated the Holme breeding record of 1987.

There was just one **Squacco Heron** in 1988 – at Cemlyn Bay, Anglesey, on 11th June. Three weeks later, birders were back in force when a **Bridled Tern** arrived in the ternery on 1st July. Among them was Liverpool goalkeeper Mike Hooper who missed a training session for the twitch and was spotted on the local TV news by his coach! Ten days later another Bridled Tern was on the Northeast coast, in Northumberland; it stayed until late August. Bridled Terns: like buses, you wait for ages and then two come at once.

A **Little Swift** was over Flamborough Head, East Yorkshire, on two dates in late July. And then it was the wader season. The highlights were that Caspian Plover in Midlothian, three **Least Sandpipers** in July/August, with two in landlocked Midlands counties (Derbyshire and Hereford & Worcester), and a troublesome **Greater Sand Plover** on South Walney, Cumbria (another was in Devon and Gwent in May).

Shetland's wader-watchers had an excellent prize on 25th September – Britain's fourth **Western Sandpiper**; this juvenile bird was the first Western Sand since the two in autumn 1973. The next day, Scotland scored again when Britain's second **Hudsonian Godwit** was found at Collieston, Aberdeenshire. It showed itself to only those first fortunate observers.

Fair Isle was back in the headlines on 7th October. A male **Blackburnian Warbler** was a First for Britain, or so it seemed. It later emerged that a record from Skomer, Dyfed, in October 1961 was recirculating the *BB* Rarities Committee as the Fair Isle bird arrived and this was subsequently accepted as the First (see below).

Scilly could not muster a First this year but October did produce only the fifth **Isabelline Wheatear** for Britain, a male **Baltimore Oriole** – and Britain's first **Buff-bellied Pipit** for 35 years. Another excellent find by Chris Heard, this was a 'first' for all concerned as the species had been split from Water and Rock Pipits in 1986. The First was on St Kilda, Western Isles, in September 1910.

Back on Fair Isle there were three **Pallas's Grasshopper Warblers** in October. Elsewhere, a **Red-flanked Bluetail** was trapped in Lincolnshire on 12th October, there were **Pine Buntings** on Flamborough Head and North Ronaldsay – and a multiple arrival of first-winter **Isabelline Shrikes** saw six or seven scattered from Dorset to

Shetland. On 30th October, Britain's fifth **Desert Warbler** was an offshore treat only for its finders on the Isle of Wight.

From the West, **Northern Parulas** arrived in Dorset and Cornwall – where there was a **Blackpoll Warbler** too – and Britain's fourth **Northern Waterthrush** was on the East coast, trapped at Gibraltar Point, Lincolnshire, on 22nd October. Another American was sighted on the East coast the next day – Britain's second **Cliff Swallow** was a great find by Teesmouth birders on South Gare.

The year finished with a flourish – and domestic ructions in many households – when a first-winter male **American Robin** was found at Inverbervie, Aberdeenshire, on Christmas Eve. It stayed until 29th December – the first twitchable American Robin since 1976.

A WHALE OF A TIME

Tim Cleeves

In many ways, 1988 wasn't a particularly memorable year for birds, but it was a settled and happy time for me, a time when I was getting to grips with a great birding scene. In 1987, our family had moved north to Northumberland. From the first cup of tea with our neighbours as we unlocked the door on moving in, to my first seawatch with friends at Seaton Sluice, I knew this was the only place to be. Eight months later, the strong feelings of affection for Northumberland had simply continued to grow.

We lived in Holywell, overlooking a valley which leads to the North Sea. On 1st January 1988, we could watch Short-eared Owls hunting the long grass in the dene below our kitchen. Every morning we woke to the sound of Greylags circling as they flew in to Holywell Pond, just 300 m from our house. This was bliss: a pond just inland from the East coast, a seawatching hide and a valley full of trees and shrubs to attract migrants on our doorstep. Exploring further afield, we could take a shopping trip to North Shields Fish Quay on Saturday morning, pick up something tasty for tea and check over masses of gulls. An Iceland Gull and two Glaucous Gulls on 2nd January were much appreciated. By the following weekend, two Bitterns had taken up residence at Holywell Pond. The same weekend Maurice Hepple, Tim Melling and I went west to look for Black Grouse. It was very cold. We were driving up a steep valley when the car started sliding backwards on the ice, and that was when we connected with the Black Grouse. They were very nervous and took off 400 m from us, looking like landlocked Tufted Ducks in flight with their black-and-white wings.

By early February we had seen predictable winter birds – Snow Buntings, Bramblings, Whooper and Bewick's Swans. Now it was time to search out the first of the 'tubbies'. The 'tubbies' are Hawfinch, Waxwing and Little Auk, my favourite trio of birds. They're not always easy to track down, so we started with Hawfinch at a local stakeout. In Hexham we watched three magnificent bruising bull-necked finches nibbling at forming buds on oaks and ornamental cherry trees.

On 14th February, I was back in Bristol for a visit home. In the late 60s we could see between 5,000 and 7,000 White-fronted Geese at the New Grounds, Slimbridge, but by 1988 numbers were peaking at 3,000. Picking out a smaller goose, with a neat, small bill, thin legs, a square head shape and a bright orange orbital ring should be easy then ... Eventually, we got good, prolonged views of the first-winter Lesser White-fronted Goose and saw my earliest-ever Garganey. Throwing bread for the second-winter Ring-billed Gull at Herriot's Pool, Chew Valley Lake, the next day certainly produced faster results than combing through the geese at New Grounds. To round off the trip to the Southwest we took in the Pied-billed Grebe at Kenfig Pool. The bird was calling like a deranged donkey.

Pied-billed Grebes have a particular place in my affections because I saw the first British bird. The trip to see that was much more bizarre than our Kenfig one. Our family didn't have a car, so I'd wheedled my Nan's friend Ron to drive to Chew Valley Lake so that I could birdwatch over the 1965 August Bank Holiday. With Dusty Springfield's *Stuck in the Middle of Nowhere* blaring out from the car radio, I inched away from the old folks' picnic to join a gaggle of local birders who seemed fixed on a small grebe in Herriot's Green Bay. The late Bernard King – our great mentor and inspiration – told me what it was and that it was from the USA and jolly rare. *Bingo!*

But back to 1988. Early spring was very quiet. In the Northeast, spring is often late and until a Firecrest appeared at Tynemouth on 21st April you would have thought it was still mid-winter. Both male and female Ring-necked Ducks were seen. On 7th May, the 'A team' decided to break the Northumberland 'Big Day' record. Just how many birds could Maurice, Tim, Adam and I find with luck and a fair (but not too strong) wind? We gathered at Holywell at 02.00 hours and kicked off with a calling Tawny Owl opposite our house. During the long day we didn't see anything particularly rare or unusual, but we certainly underlined what a rich avifauna Northumberland has. By 21.45 we had clocked up 138 species, a new county record. Why did we do it? Because we could. Are such activities a useful way to spend your time? Probably not. Have we contributed to climate change problems? Almost certainly. Tricky, isn't it?

This was a quiet time for spring rarities in the Northeast, but a stunning male red-spotted Bluethroat at Whitburn on May 16th provided excellent therapy. Despite being so bright and obvious, it's amazing how skulking Bluethroats can be and this bird was no exception. In June a couple of Cranes at Westmoor, Aislaby, Cleveland, cheered us up, while a Ruddy Shelduck nearby on Teesside threw up the usual dilemma – was it an escape or wasn't it?

Being brought up near Bristol, I was well aware that the Weston-super-Mare 1958 tideline corpse of a Bridled Tern was the only 'modern' record. I had also seen the wing of one found on Lundy in 1977. It seemed that this bird only occurred in kit form! So when a live one arrived at Cemlyn Bay, Anglesey, it was time for a twitch. After a slow spring it was brilliant to take a trip to Wales and with long daylight hours we were watching the bird by 04.05. Indeed, this RSPB site provided a seabird spectacle: at one point six species of tern were gracing the skies.

The 12th July 1988 was a special date in the birding calendar. That evening, there was a large plover at Aberlady, East Lothian and the local birders – including Pete Gordon – had identified it as a Caspian Plover. A short-stayer on St Agnes avoided most would-be admirers and this bird nearly avoided me. Our Northeast team arrived in the dark and in heavy rain. Maurice and I were sheltering in the public toilets watching the rain come down like stair rods, oblivious that outside the Caspian Plover was being watched. Only Tim Melling coming to find us saved the day. I watched the bird through a Questar scope for five minutes until it took off with a small flock of Lapwing at 05.20 … never to be seen again.

There was another new bird for me on 16th July, at Blacktoft Sands RSPB Reserve: a superb, full-adult summer-plumage Broad-billed Sandpiper. I had missed several of these birds before and to get such close views at Blacktoft was a real joy.

August means pelagics. Few people had attempted pelagics around the inshore waters of the River Tyne, so we thought in 1988 that we'd give it a try. For a few days we'd seen the carcass of a small Minke Whale drifting back and forth past the Seaton Sluice watchtower. Eventually the dead whale was washed up on the beach and staff from the Hancock Museum in Newcastle came to collect it. At the museum the animal was de-fleshed so the skeleton could be kept. A friend working near the museum begged the bags of whale meat for chum, although by now the whale had been dead for at least a week…

When we set off from North Shields on 13th August, the skipper's mate looked aghast at the smelly bags and insisted that the meat was put on some four-ply and towed behind the boat instead of fouling the decks of the *New Venture*. It was like a cartoon. A Greater Black-backed Gull approached the boat. When it was 10 m from the blubber, it stuck out its legs, braking in mid-air then, flapping furiously to stop itself mid-flight, it turned and disappeared beyond the far horizon. This gull was the only bird to get even marginally close to the chum and eventually we cut the rope and watched the remains of the whale float out of sight.

The rest of the year was generally quiet, but a period of easterly/northeasterly winds and rain on and off from mid-October until the end of October brought classic east-coast conditions. At Prior's Park, Tynemouth, a Russian-ringed Goldcrest was trapped as a Pallas's Warbler hovered overhead. I'd always wanted to see Radde's Warbler and Adam Hutt found a brilliant one at Prior's on 4th October. Two days later some passing birders showed us a dark juvenile Long-tailed Skua; it was in a cardboard box on its way to the RSPCA. All down the coast, waves of Fieldfares and Redwings crossed the dunes and the seawalls – and the air was full of calling Goldcrests. At Druridge Bay there was a Rustic Bunting. Robins appeared everywhere with late Ring Ouzels, Bramblings and Yellow-browed Warblers. It doesn't get much closer to heaven than this!

Or so we thought, until we missed the short-staying Cliff Swallow on Teesside. That, I guess, is the great leveller that epitomises birding.

APRIL 1988

MOUSSIER'S REDSTART IN DYFED

Mike Barrett

On 24th April 1988, I was one of a party of five following the Pembrokeshire Coast Path northwards at Dinas Head in Dyfed, southwest Wales. Also known as Dinas Island, although it is actually joined to the coast by a low-lying stretch of land, Dinas Head is a high, rocky promontory which separates Fishguard and Newport Bays. Our leader was Graham Walker, the day was fine with some distant haze, and there was a cool but intermittent easterly wind.

By the early part of the afternoon, we were halfway around the headland, not far past the stone triangulation pillar. I had been watching a male Stonechat *Saxicola torquata* darting backwards and forwards across the gorse *Ulex* in what seemed to be some agitation; the other members of the group had moved on, and I was about to follow after a final sweep of the area with my binoculars. The Stonechat again drew my attention with his behaviour, and it was then that I noticed another small bird which had appeared on a rock nearby. My instinctive reaction – that it was a male Redstart *Phoenicurus phoenicurus* – was almost immediately revised when I saw that the bird's crown and upperparts were completely black, with a pronounced white eyebrow extending across the forehead, and down the side of its 'face' to its neck, and that there was also a vivid white wing-patch. The body and tail were orange, the wings black, and the general impression was strongly that of a redstart of some sort. The bird was visible for less than two minutes before the Stonechat – accompanied by his mate – put it to flight. By now, I had called the other members of the party back, but only two of them had seen the bird. After what seemed an interminable few minutes, however, it obligingly reappeared and we were all then able to obtain fine views for much of the next hour, during which time I obtained a series of photographs. Although there was some uncertainty as to identification – a tentative assessment as a male Moussier's Redstart *P. moussieri* was not confirmed until later, with the help of field guides – there was no uncertainty at all that this handsome bird was something very special indeed. These details were noted:

Shape and Size Structure recalled short-tailed Redstart. Compact, about same size as Stonechat, determined in close, direct comparisons, highlighting that it was slightly smaller than Redstart.

General Impression Redstart-like; strikingly black, white and orange; particularly attractive and distinctive.

Plumage Head black, with white supercilia which extended across forehead and
    continued down and around nape, widening to form partial collar; as with
    many male Redstarts, white on head more prominent in field than is suggest-
    ed by many field guides. Underparts orange. Upperparts and wings black,
    with conspicuous white wing-patch. Tail orange, medium-length, and
    notched; no Redstart-like shivering noted.
Bare Parts Bill, eyes, legs and feet dark.
Behaviour Active and lively; alert and wary of any close approach; flight low and
    direct; no call heard.

The bird was quite agile, moving quickly between the ground, rocks and gorse, and
often perching. In the hour or so that it was observed, it did not move far from
the place where I had first seen it, and, although it did sometimes fly from view, its
uniquely contrasting colours enabled us to relocate it fairly easily. It was harassed peri-
odically by the two Stonechats, which were almost certainly nesting in the gorse and
which much resented the presence of the intruder, but it showed a marked reluctance
to stray any great distance, favouring the rocks as perching places. Our last view of the
bird was just before 15.00 GMT, and, despite extensive searches by others later that
afternoon and again during the following day, it was not seen again.

Moussier's Redstart is a Northwest African resident, although *Birds of the Western
Palearctic* (Vol. 5, 1988) does state that it is 'perhaps migratory over relatively short distances, normally staying within North Africa'. Reports of the species in Europe are few
and far between, the only recent records being in Malta (the seventh record was of
three together in April 1982), Italy (the second record was in Sicily in February 1987),
and Greece (the first record was on 30th March 1988) (*Brit. Birds* 76: 275; 82: 21,
349). This Welsh record is the first away from the Mediterranean area.

Interestingly, while we did not see any Redstarts on 24th April, we had seen several
on the previous day, and there were good numbers on 25th in the same general area. The
fact that there had been southerly winds for the week up to 22nd April, coupled with
what may have been a minor Redstart fall, could suggest that the Moussier's Redstart had
somehow got itself involved with a migrating flock crossing its home territory. Whatever
the reasons for its unexpected appearance in Dyfed on that Sunday afternoon, it made
five people very happy.

Barrett, M. 1992. Moussier's Redstart: new to Britain and Ireland.
British Birds 85, 108–111.

*Moussier's Redstart is a resident of northwest Africa.
There have been no subsequent records.*

APRIL 1988

BROWN-HEADED COWBIRD
IN STRATHCLYDE

Clive McKay

Along with my companion, Sue Crosthwaite, I spent the afternoon of 24th April 1988 making observations on the feeding behaviour and movements of Red-billed Choughs *Pyrrhocorax pyrrhocorax* at Ardnave Point, Islay, Strathclyde, as part of my Ph.D project. We were positioned on opposite shores of Loch Gruinart, a sea-loch at the northern end of the island; with the aid of CB radios we were attempting to track birds as they commuted backwards and forwards between two dune systems on either side of the loch (a distance of 1 km as the chough flies, but 26 km by road). The winds had been from the easterly quarter for the previous two days, and we both noted the presence of several 'out-of-habitat' migrant Goldcrests *Regulus regulus*.

Throughout the afternoon, I followed a flock of up to ten choughs as they fed in an extensive area of heavily sheep- and cattle-grazed dune pasture. At one point, I saw a single 'starling *Sturnus*' out of the corner of my eye, and made a mental note to check it later, as I was busy reading chough colour-rings. It seemed a little unusual to see a lone starling just there, as they do not breed nearby and the area is very exposed; when one does meet with them, they are usually in bustling flocks. My pursuit of choughs took me in a different direction, however, and I forgot to check out the 'lone starling' and would have thought nothing more of it, but for subsequent events.

I finished making chough observations at 17.30 and radioed SC to tell her that I would pick her up at 18.00. Walking back through the dune pasture, I noticed a starling-like bird feeding less than 15 m from the track. At this range, with my naked eye, I could see that the bird looked like a very dark 'spotless' starling, and, ever the optimist, thought that I had better check it out, 'just in case'. The bird was in exactly the same place as the lone 'starling' that I had noted there some three hours earlier, and was almost certainly the same bird.

As soon as I looked at the bird through my 10 × 40 binoculars, I knew that it was something odd, and thoughts of Spotless Starling *S. unicolor* flashed through my mind, until I saw that it had a brownish head and short finch-like bill. It was obviously a species with which I was completely unfamiliar – and therefore probably from the Nearctic, which I have never visited. It was strange to be able to communicate the excitement to SC more or less immediately via the CB radio, yet most frustrating that she was half-an-hour away by road – and I had the car. I watched the bird for about 30 minutes, using binoculars and 20–60 × 75 telescope, and took a hasty field description. As there was perhaps only an hour to go before dusk, I then had to decide between fetching SC, and contacting other birders on the island in the process, or getting my camera and 200-mm lens from the car to obtain photographs of the bird. Against SC's advice, I plumped for the former. There was no time to lose: at 18.15 the light was still good, but we were already into that late-afternoon period when everything goes quiet.

I rushed down the road and called on Pete Moore, warden of the RSPB Loch Gruinart reserve. I breathlessly told him about the bird, and knowing that he was not too keen on rarities (unusually for an RSPB warden!) I tried to emphasise how impor-tant it was that a second person at least witnessed the bird, as it might be a first for Europe. Unfortunately, he was just about to have his Sunday dinner, and the bird would have to wait. I asked PM to alert other birders on the island by phone, but he found that no-one else was around. A glance through PM's literature gave no clue as to the bird's identity. I then rushed around Loch Gruinart and picked up SC, a round trip of about 26 km. At 18.50, we arrived back at Ardnave at the same time as PM. Despite the light still being favourable, the dunes had become very quiet, and we failed to find the bird; presumably it had gone to roost. I could not find it the next day, and it was not seen again.

Jizz and feeding behaviour
In general appearance, the bird was like a small starling with a short, black, finch-like bill. It had a metallic bronze-coloured head and throat, the rest of the body plumage being black with a green iridescence. It walked and ran across the pasture in the manner of a Common Starling *S. vulgaris*, with similar back-and-forth movements of the head. Likewise, it associated with grazing cattle, though much more closely (see below). Flight shape was similar to that of Common Starling, but its movements were more erratic, resembling those of Redwing *Turdus iliacus*. It would not have looked out of place in a flock of Common Starlings. There were, however, no other birds in the vicinity, so no interspecific comparisons were possible.

At all times, it associated very closely with the cattle which were grazing in the area. It often walked and fed unconcernedly between the legs of cows, and, if it strayed more than about 10 m from a beast, it would hurriedly fly back to it, as if correcting a mistake. This relationship was so striking that I guessed that the bird might be a cowbird *Molothrus*, though I knew nothing at the time about their appearance or the derivation of their name, only that they were a group of New World brood-parasites. My interpretation of this association with cattle was that the bird used the cows as 'moving cover' in an otherwise featureless environment. The bird did not appear to feed any more successfully when closer to the cattle, nor did it appear to feed on insects disturbed by the animals' hooves. In fact, it fed on grain for much of the time, which was presumably no more available close to the cattle than farther away from them.

The bird employed two feeding methods: (1) picking insects from the pasture surface following a short flight or run (but not sub-surface probing as by Common Starling); and (2) picking seeds (mostly barley/oats from cattle-feed spread in the area) from the pasture surface and dehusking them by rotating them in the bill in a bunting/finch-like manner.

DETAILED DESCRIPTION

Size Though no direct comparisons were possible, it appeared to be a little smaller than a Common Starling, about the size of a Skylark *Alauda arvensis* though not so robust.

Structure Similar proportions to Common Starling in terms of medium leg length, medium-short square-ended tail, and medium-long wings. Unlike Common Starling, bill short, conical and quite pointed, like that of a finch or bunting. Head shape, therefore, more finch-like.

Bare Parts Bill black. Eyes dark, possibly slightly paler than darkish mask surrounding eyes (but could not be certain on this point). Legs brownish-black.

Plumage Head, nape and throat metallic bronze-brown, with hint of a darker mask between bill and eye. Brown head fairly sharply demarcated from the rest of body plumage, which was black with a glossy, bottle-green sheen on both the upperparts and the underparts. Tail black. Close inspection showed the exposed fringes of the primaries to be brownish, and the tips of the greater coverts to be slightly paler than the rest of the wing. The latter appeared to be produced by a (difficult-to-describe) reflection of light from the tips of the feathers rather than by an actual coloration of them. In some lights, a similar type of 'reflection' gave the dark plumage a scaly appearance, particularly around the lower body/vent.

Call None heard.

Identification

The bird's identity remained a mystery until I was able to refer to the Islay Natural History Trust's library with Dr Malcolm Ogilvie a few days later. I first described the bird to MAO, and then looked up the index of the National Geographic Society *Field Guide to the Birds of North America* (1983). Under the heading of 'cowbird' were only two species: Bronzed *Molothrus aeneus* and Brown-headed *M. ater*. Before looking at the illustrations, I suggested that the latter was the more likely candidate, and this was what it proved to be: a male, probably first-year. I was relieved that there were no similar species with which male Brown-headed Cowbird could be confused.

McKay, C. R. 1994. Brown-headed Cowbird in Strathclyde: new to Britain and Ireland. *British Birds* 87, 284–288.

Brown-headed Cowbird is widespread in North America; northern breeders winter in the southern USA and Mexico.

There have been no subsequent records.

The other Western Palearctic record was an adult female found dead in Norway on 1st June 1987.

JUNE 1988

CRAG MARTIN IN CORNWALL

Paul Higson

On the afternoon of 22nd June 1988, I had driven to the Golden Lion causeway at the northwestern end of Stithians Reservoir, Cornwall, to check for waders. As the water level was too high, I decided to stay in the car and eat my lunch. I was aware of a group of 10–15 House Martins *Delichon urbicum* feeding in the area, and a particularly loud burst of twittering from the group caused me to glance casually upwards. I was astonished to see a large, chunky, all-brown martin, with what appeared to be two huge white spots in its tail, gliding about 1 m above the car, in amongst the House Martins. The bird was momentarily lost from sight whilst I tried frantically to grab my binoculars and get out of the car at the same time.

The House Martins had by now moved to the southern shore of the pool, to the West of the causeway. Though mostly silhouetted against the bright sunlight, the bird was easily relocated amongst the other martins by its size, shape and distinctive flight. Convinced that it was a Crag Martin, but unable to believe that it was one, I moved to the southern end of the causeway, and watched the bird for a further 10–15 minutes, broken by a short dash to the pub to try to phone other birdwatchers.

I had noted the following details:

Size and Structure At least ¹/₂ to 1 inch (1¹/₄ –2¹/₂ cm) longer than accompanying House Martins, obviously heavier, bulkier, and more thick-set, wings broader, particularly at base. Tail slightly forked when closed.

General Impression Dark, sandy brown bird, with no white plumage.

Upperparts Darker, greyer brown than underparts, with body at times appearing paler than upperwing. Tail spots sometimes apparent when tail spread, but spots always looked smaller and less significant than when seen from below. Colour paler than that of Sand Martin *Riparia riparia*, although none present for comparison.

Underparts Uniform grey buffy brown. At close range, throat paler, and breast and centre of belly paler, warmer brown, darkening on sides of belly and flanks. No white on underside, apart from tail spots.

Wings Underwing-coverts strikingly dark, almost black, contrasting very markedly with pale primaries and secondaries, and very noticeable when the bird raised its wings when drinking.

Tail Very slightly forked when folded. When spread, white tail spots (four on each side) always apparent, feature most striking when seen against strong sunlight; spots occasionally appeared to blend into each other to become two large spots.

Behaviour Fed in loose association with resident House Martins, but kept to a more distinct and regular circuit. At all times, kept very low, just clearing hedges, fences, etc., and never 'towered' with accompanying House Martins. Twice, it followed the martins over the causeway to the main reservoir, but never went farther than 5–10 m out over the open water before returning to resume feeding over the grass bank at the edge of the pool. Both times it passed within 1–2 m of me, seemingly unconcerned by my presence. Flight very distinctive, and was used to relocate the bird whenever it was lost from sight: a few easy flaps followed by a lot of steady, resolute, regular gliding. It hardly ever 'flicked' from side to side, as the House Martins were constantly doing. The bird drank twice, hanging almost stationary into the wind with its wings held straight up.

I left the bird, which seemed well settled, at 13.30 GMT to spread the news, but, on my return, it had vanished and was never seen again, despite extensive searching.

Higson, P. & Urquhart, E. D. 1990. Crag Martins in Cornwall and East Sussex: new to Britain and Ireland. *British Birds* 83, 155–159.

Crag Martin breeds from southern Europe and northwest Africa through central Asia to southwest Manchuria. The northern populations are partially migratory and winter as far south as Senegal, Ethiopia and central India.

There have been five subsequent records:

East Sussex Beachy Head, 9th July 1988

Gwynedd Llanfairfechan, 3rd September 1989

East Sussex Beachy Head, 8th October 1995

Leicestershire Swithland Reservoir, 17th April 1999 then

West Yorkshire Pugney's Country Park, 18th April 1999

Orkney Finstown, 3rd May 1999

OCTOBER 1988

BLACKBURNIAN WARBLER ON FAIR ISLE
Jack Willmott

Friday 7th October 1988 dawned a wet, grey, and blustery morning on Fair Isle, Shetland. Having been kept awake during the night with very strong northwesterly winds and rain and having already 'ticked' Lanceolated Warbler, Pallas's Grasshopper Warbler and Pechora Pipit in the south of the island earlier in the week, we decided we would walk north in the hope of catching up with a Rough–legged Buzzard reported in that area the previous day.

After breakfast our group of five set off at about 9.15 am, suitably attired in wellingtons, waterproofs etc, as the weather was still pretty foul. About three-quarters of a mile from the bird observatory, Gordon Avery and I left the road to check out the cliff faces of the many 'geos' that dominate the Fair Isle coastline. I was thus looking into North Restensgeo when a flash of yellow, quickly going out of view behind a fold in the rock, caught my eye. Thinking it might be a Great or Blue Tit and realising even that would be a good bird on Fair Isle, I decided to check further. I had just trained my binoculars on the spot when a bird emerged and flew away from me giving excellent rear views; it was basically black and white. Expletives rained as I shouted to Gordon, almost certain that I had discovered a Black-and-white Warbler.

Almost immediately the bird then flew to the other side of the geo and displayed a golden-yellow breast and face, broken only by dark marks through the eye and on the ear-coverts. We called the other three in our party, and Pete Massey, my son Matthew and Gordon's wife Margaret quickly joined us on the clifftop. We were all virtually dumbstruck by the sheer beauty of the bird which was now hopping around on the cliff face. We realised it was an American *Dendroica* warbler, but which one? My mind raced through the pages of the *National Geographic Guide to the Birds of North America*. The bird appeared so bright we assumed it must be an adult male. No yellow rump was visible so that ruled out several species. We thought of Yellow-throated Warbler or even Blackburnian Warbler.

Realising that we needed advice quickly, we dispatched Matthew back to the 'obs' to raise the alarm. I will never forget the sight of him taking off, weighted down with all his waterproofs billowing in the wind, with a speed of which an Olympic medallist would have been proud. Meanwhile, Gordon raced ahead to alert a couple of birders who had been in front of us when we had set out earlier. Pete, Margaret and I stayed on the bird. Unfortunately, after a few minutes, it made its way to the seaward face of the crevasse and disappeared around the headland. I noticed Margaret draw her anorak hood tight over her ears as Pete and I gave vent to our pent-up emotions in very ungentlemanly fashion!

Matthew now reappeared with several birders who had delayed setting out from the observatory until the weather improved (by now the rain had stopped and the sun was trying to break through). Gordon also reappeared with two other birders.

The bird had now disappeared completely. The usual doubting comments were now forthcoming: "Are you sure?" "Was that it?" (pointing to a Red-breasted Flycatcher!) If some people had realised how close they were to having an 'accident' over the cliff edge, they would have been far more believing!

Suddenly, Chris Donald, to whom I will be eternally grateful, gave a shout. He had relocated the bird about 400 yards away from where we had found it. It was now in another crevasse at Furse. At last it could be seen well by everyone present (only two birders on the island dipped) and it was quickly identified as an immature male Blackburnian Warbler *Dendroica fusca*. We all watched the bird on and off for about half an hour, in which time it was very active, moving along the cliff face to Kame O'Furse.

Then suddenly it flew up the cliff face and headed south. It veered east and then back north. For a while we hoped it was coming back to us, but then it gained height and veered east again towards Buness. Although we searched for it throughout the rest of the day, it was never seen again.

Only then did we become aware of how close most of us had been standing to the cliff edges during this excitement, paying scant attention to Liz Riddiford's repeated warnings.

Willmott, J. 1988. Blackburnian Warbler on Fair Isle – a new Western Palearctic bird. *Birding World* 1, 355–356.

An earlier record of Blackburnian Warbler, on Skomer in 1961, was subsequently accepted as the First for Britain and the finders' account appeared in BB in July 1992:

OCTOBER 1961

BLACKBURNIAN WARBLER IN DYFED

David Saunders and Shirley Saunders

On 5th October 1961, DS was nearing the end of his early-morning warden's patrol of the Skomer Island National Nature Reserve, Pembrokeshire (now part of Dyfed). It had been a fruitful walk in overcast conditions, with a number of migrants seen, including Swallows *Hirundo rustica*, Meadow Pipits *Anthus pratensis*, Blackbirds *Turdus merula*, Song Thrushes *T. philomelos*, Blackcaps *Sylvia atricapilla*, Goldcrests *Regulus regulus*, Blue Tits *Parus caeruleus*, Starlings *Sturnus vulgaris* and Chaffinches *Fringilla coelebs*. Pausing to examine the sheltered cliffs above the North Haven landing beach, he observed a strange bird, the first impression of which, at a distance of some 75 m, was of a grey bird about the size of a Pied Flycatcher *Ficedula hypoleuca*, but with the build of a Warbler.

The cliffs are largely covered by ivy *Hedera helix* at this point, and were well sheltered from the wind, which was south to southeast, force 4–5. The bird worked its way among the vegetation and DS was soon able to obtain clearer views, being astonished to see that it had a bright sulphur-yellow breast, and at once realised that it was a bird new to him. SS was quickly summoned from the warden's house, just a few metres away, and together we watched the bird as it moved about the cliff. The path, immediately above, and the main track to the landing beach, below, both provided ideal vantage points from which to watch without disturbance, at ranges down to some 10 m.

The bird remained on the cliff, being active for most of the day, which turned wet as the rain moved in during the afternoon. Mostly, it was easily seen, but on occasions would disappear for short periods among the thicker ivy. Other species present on the cliff were Robins *Erithacus rubecula*, Stonechats *Saxicola torquata*, Blackbirds, a Spotted Flycatcher *Muscicapa striata*, Blue Tits and a Great Tit *P. major*. A search the following morning failed, alas!, to locate the mystery bird, while the Spotted Flycatcher and Great Tit were also missing, and there were generally fewer birds elsewhere on the island. The wind had freshened overnight to force 6–7, and later in the day veered to the Southwest; indeed, it remained stormy until 10th.

None of the books in the small reference library in the warden's house was of assistance in trying to identify the mystery bird. There were no other resident human beings on the island, while the last overnight visitors had left the previous day because of the deteriorating weather conditions (the last day-visitors having landed on 19th September). There was no radio communication with the mainland or with nearby Skokholm, so no means of consulting with anyone who might be able to throw light on the mystery bird.

Description

The following description is based on field notes taken by DS:

Size and Shape About that of Pied Flycatcher, but with longer tail and stance of a *Phylloscopus* warbler.

Head and Neck Crown and nape brownish colour, with yellow stripe running from base of bill to above and a little beyond eye. Small, dull yellow patch on ear-coverts.

Upperparts Mantle, back, rump and upper-side of tail all grey-black. Two some-what pale buffish stripes ran lengthways down mantle. Wings greyish, with two small white wing-bars. When seen at close quarters, wings seemed to be finely lined with white.

Underparts Chin and breast sulphur-yellow, gradually fading to white on flanks and belly. At close quarters, a number of brownish striations were visible on flanks. When seen from below, two small dark marks were noted on outer tail feathers.

Bare Parts Legs dark brown. Bill black or very dark brown.

Behaviour Spent most of the time foraging, presumably for insects, amongst the ivy, making only occasional short flights.

Discussion

The subsequent events surrounding the mysterious bird moved rather slowly. I. J. Ferguson-Lees, then executive editor of *British Birds*, in a letter to the authors dated 15th December 1961, said: 'Your description of the strange bird you saw on 5th October is rather puzzling and I am proposing to send that round the Rarity Records Committee to see if other members of it agree with my suggestions.'

Nearly a year later, in a letter to the authors dated 15th October 1962, the then Secretary of the Rarities Committee, C. M. Swaine, wrote: 'We have at last got your "queer passerine" of 5th October 1961 round this Committee twice; it has been to James Baird in the USA also. The outcome is that we are almost certain the bird was a Blackburnian Warbler *Dendroica fusca*, a bird of the evergreen woodlands of Manitoba, the Gulf of St Lawrence etc. We cannot be quite sure, however, and feel we must agree with James Baird that it is best regarded as a "probable". Congratulations on taking a very thorough description.'

Saunders, D. & Saunders, S. 1992. Blackburnian Warbler: new to the Western Palearctic. *British Birds* 85, 337–343.

Blackburnian Warbler breeds in eastern North America and winters from Guatemala south to central Peru and Venezuela.

There have been no subsequent records.

THE BIRDER'S YEAR

Adrian Pitches

In 1989 there was a brace of Firsts before the year was even six weeks old. A 'funny' cormorant on Teesside from early December 1988 took some working out, but it helpfully stayed on Charlton's Pond in Billingham until it was clinched as a **Double-crested Cormorant** at the end of January.

Another, far more flashy, North American First was found a week later in Kent. That male **Golden-winged Warbler** was famously found by top bird photographer Paul Doherty as he went to post a letter. And it became famous as the stimulus for the biggest-ever twitch in British birding history: an estimated 3,000 people headed round the M25 to Maidstone on the first Saturday of its stay.

Just 25 km away, a male **Common Yellowthroat** (Britain's fourth) was near Sittingbourne from early January until late April. A third overwintering American passerine, a female **Baltimore Oriole**, was in Dyfed, also from early January to late April. And a fourth was the **Dark-eyed Junco** in Hampshire in February – probably the bird that overwintered in 1987/88; it reappeared in December to stay into 1990. Another junco was on the Isle of Wight in early April.

A male **Black-throated Thrush** turned up in Knaresborough, North Yorkshire, in early January, echoing the Sheffield, South Yorkshire, bird in January 1987. And another January first-winter **Ross's Gull** in Cornwall (following last year's bird) was in Newlyn harbour at the end of the month. There were also overwintering **White-tailed Eagles** in Kent and Suffolk, while four or five **Gyrfalcons** were on Scottish isles in March/April with three or four in the Uists, Western Isles.

The American theme to the year resumed in April with a male **Song Sparrow** on Fair Isle for two weeks from the 11th; this was Fair Isle's third April Song Sparrow! And on Mainland Shetland there was a **White-throated Sparrow** at the end of May.

Late April and May brought eight **Black Storks**, with birds from Cornwall to County Durham. Arguably the most bizarre rarity of 1989 – but gratefully received nevertheless – was the **Baillon's Crake** that pottered around the pond in Mowbray

145

Park, Sunderland, for four days in mid-May. Binoculars were unnecessary as it walked unconcernedly past. Two May **Semipalmated Sandpipers**, in Cleveland and Norfolk, were the first spring records for Britain. On 23rd May, a male **Little Bustard** was on North Ronaldsay, Orkney.

A summering **Brünnich's Guillemot** on Sumburgh Head, Shetland, from mid-June was a tempting twitch – a great find by Martin Heubeck on his annual seabird census. And last year's **Bridled Tern** in Northumberland made a repeat showing on 16th July. It's a shame that Northumberland's Aleutian Tern didn't 're-tern' after its only visit in 1979.

Perhaps THE birds of the year were the three **Blue-cheeked Bee-eaters** in June and July. There were one-day birds in Cornwall and Kent but the best of the bunch was a three-day bird at Cowden, East Yorkshire, from 8th July. These beauties were the fifth, sixth and seventh for Britain, following the suppressed fourth record in Devon in June 1987. Autumn started on 2nd July with an adult **Stilt Sandpiper** on Flamborough Head, East Yorkshire. A month before there was a **Great Snipe** in Essex – spring or autumn migrant?

Birders attending a petrel ringing session at the mouth of the Tyne in late July took part in the opening act of an ornithological mystery play that ran for another five years. A larger, dark-rumped petrel tape-lured into the ringers' net alongside the expected Storm Petrels could not be identified. Another was trapped six days later. And a third bird was trapped eight times over the following five seasons! It was to be a further three years before the 'Tyne Petrels' first trapped in 1989 were conclusively identified as **Swinhoe's Storm Petrels**, from the Northeast Asian coast of the Pacific Ocean. Until then, it seemed that a seaside village in northeast England could have its own endemic petrel!

Back to the autumn wader season. A **Solitary Sandpiper** was in the seemingly unlikely county of Hertfordshire in mid-August. But THE wader of the year was a one-day wonder on Shetland on 15th September – Britain's First **Great Knot**, found by Pete Ellis. Britain's third **Crag Martin** came hot on the heels of the first two in 1988 – it was in Gwynedd on 3rd September.

The Scilly season started early with a **Northern Waterthrush** on St Agnes on 29th August a good find for Will Wagstaff as he led summer holidaymakers on a wildlife tour. And on 16th September, Will was 'in on' the next good bird – a juvenile **Common Nighthawk** on Tresco which stayed a week. (He also found a Scops Owl on Tresco in 1989, on the very early date of 3rd April.)

Scilly had a quiet autumn after these early birds. And it was to be Norfolk that would deliver the top-drawer American bird of the autumn – a **Red-breasted Nuthatch** in the pines at Holkham. It stayed for six months. The only other Americans of note were a **Grey-cheeked Thrush** in the Western Isles on 29th October – and simultaneous **Yellow-billed Cuckoos** on Lundy, Devon, and at Landguard, Suffolk, on 25th October.

There were two male **Pied Wheatears**: the earliest ever, in Norfolk on 13th September, and another on Fair Isle on 10th October. Three November **Desert Wheatears** took the year's haul to a record five birds after spring males in Kent and at Barn Elms Reservoir,

Greater London. A total of 13 **Penduline Tits** was logged, including adults with juveniles in Suffolk and West Sussex in late autumn. More emphatic evidence of breeding in Britain came in April 1990, with nesting in Kent and a pair with a juvenile on Tresco, Scilly, in October. An overwintering **Terek Sandpiper** took up residence on the Blyth estuary, Northumberland, on 22nd November. The only previous occurrence of overwintering was in Devon in 1973/74.

And then it was back to American birds at the year's end – that returning junco in Hampshire and another on Portland, Dorset. And the Red-breasted Nuthatch continued to blow its own trumpet in Holkham pines.

MIGRATING NORTH

Adrian Pitches

'Who can say what we'll find, what lies waiting down the line in the end of '89…'

(ABBA, *Happy New Year*)

As ever, ABBA were spot on: when 1989 dawned, I had no inkling that it would be one of the most important years of my life. By the year's end I had changed jobs, relocated 300 miles from London to the Northeast and seen some wonderful birds.

The previous year I had landed a job with BBC Radio News at Broadcasting House writing bulletins for Radio 4. I was living in Harrow-on-the-Hill, northwest London, with my girlfriend (now wife), a newspaper journalist. The only local birds of note were a wintering flock of Common Gulls which I religiously counted and aged – not too tricky with a three-year gull.

My wife is from Teesside. Her home town is Billingham, notable mainly for its enormous chemicals complex and annual Folklore Festival. But in February 1989, Billingham was about to appear on the birding map – with a First for the Western Palearctic! The Double-crested Cormorant on Charlton's Pond had been present for a month before birders seeing a Shag and other birders seeing a Cormorant realised that they were watching neither. I drove up from London to Teesside and took Harold, my 80-year-old father-in-law-to-be, to see the cormorant. He wasn't impressed.

But within a week, arguably the least impressive North American vagrant had been supplanted by probably the most impressive. This time it was a suburban housing estate in Kent and the bird … Golden-winged Warbler. At least I was living in the right part of the country but by the time I arrived on Day 1 of the twitch (having had to hire a car), the bird had gone. The lone Waxwing in the famous Tesco carpark bushes was scant compensation. On a return visit I finally saw the dandy highwayman with its black mask and gaudy yellow wing flash as it flitted over a rooftop.

In March I made my first visit to Israel on a Sunbirder package led by Killian Mullarney and Peter Grant. A week in the sun with two excellent birders – and some superb birds: eight wheatears, eight larks, a Black Bush Robin chased out of an army compound by Hadoram Shirihai – and the second Grey-headed Gull for the Western Palearctic. It seemed wholly appropriate to see such a special gull with the gull man himself. Tragically, Peter Grant died of abdominal cancer the following spring; a huge loss to birding.

Back in the UK, my home life was about to change. My girlfriend's homing instinct made her apply for a job on Teesside's evening paper. Perhaps it was the promise of Double-crested Cormorant on the doorstep (it lingered until the end of April). I promised to relocate too – if I could get a job at the regional BBC. Within three months I had and I moved north in July.

We'd rented a house in Darlington and on that first (Sunday) morning in the Northeast I phoned Birdline to see what my new region had to offer.

"On Humberside, the Blue-cheeked Bee-eater is still at Cowden…"

I had to move quickly.

Loud voice: "I'm just going out for the papers…"

Low voice: "… and a Blue-cheeked Bee-eater… three counties away."

I was back by lunchtime – and I'd remembered the papers. The Northeast seemed like a VERY good place to live.

Of course, there is one Northeast bird which stands out in the memory of most birders from the spring of 1989: the ludicrously tame Baillon's Crake in a Sunderland park in May. But, for a variety of reasons, I had to stay in southern England that week. On my arrival at BBC Look North two months later, I sat down in the video library and watched the news package about the funny bird in Sun'lun town centre over and over again. It was pure masochism. But I had to pull myself together – I was training to be a TV journalist AND I had a new region in which to go birding.

Teesmouth, the Durham Dales, the Northumberland coast – northeast England has some of the best birding in Britain. Seabirds, waders, wildfowl, raptors – and roadside Black Grouse. And a resident Lesser Crested Tern on the Farne Islands.

In October I tore myself away for a week on Scilly: after a wonderful fortnight on the islands in 1987, I'd missed 1988 and was keen to return. When I landed on October 14th, there was just one bird chalked up on the blackboard outside the Porthcressa cafe: Red-breasted Nuthatch … in Norfolk. Many other birders turned on their heel and got back on the boat. But I wanted a week on Scilly – the nuthatch could wait. It wasn't a classic week – Olive-backed Pipit and Pallas's Warbler were the highlights – but at least I hadn't left my girlfriend on the quayside on St Mary's, travelled to Norfolk and dipped (as one of the guys at my B&B did).

Back in the Northeast there was another treat awaiting me as the year wound down. A Terek Sandpiper on the Blyth estuary in Northumberland was a brilliant birthday bird in late November.

I started the year as an adopted Londoner; at the year's end I was an adopted Geordie living in Gateshead. And despite two further attempts to spread my wings beyond the Northeast, I have always returned. My wife's homing instinct seems to have rubbed off on me.

JANUARY 1989

DOUBLE-CRESTED CORMORANT IN CLEVELAND

Terry Williams

As it is usual to see the occasional Great Cormorant *Phalacrocorax carbo* on my patch (Charlton's Pond in Billingham, Cleveland) during the winter months, one present sporadically from early December 1988 into January 1989 received no more than a cursory glance both from me and from several other birders, including several latterly looking for potential 'year ticks'. During this period, however, a birder leaving the pond mentioned to me in passing that there was a Shag *P. aristotelis* perched on the floating island. This piece of information immediately grabbed my attention as I had never seen a Shag on the reserve, of which I was at that time voluntary warden; my notorious interest in Charlton's Pond and my somewhat sedentary nature being the butt of some gentle leg-pulling over the years, I duly raced off to see the bird. On reaching the causeway between the two ponds, I observed the raft from a distance of some 300 m and saw the bird perched on the island. From that range, it was indeed a potential contender for Shag, so I made my way down the path on the East side of the Pond, which brought me to a position only some 100 m from the bird. I then observed it through my 8×40 binoculars and found myself looking at a Cormorant. Either we had both made a mistake or the Shag had flown off. I quickly scanned the Pond and left the area, cursing my bad luck. A few days later, a second birder reported seeing a Shag on the Pond. Thinking that the bird had returned, I again made my way to the East side of the Pond and again found myself looking at a Cormorant. This was getting ridiculous! What was going on? From the causeway, it looked like a Shag, but on closer examination was obviously a Cormorant. Now that I took the time to have a look at it for more than a few seconds, however, it did look small, but still had the jizz of Cormorant. Perhaps it was oiled, or was a small individual? It was only then that I started to scrutinise the bird with any real interest. What struck me immediately was the pattern of dark-and-light coloration on the underparts. While never having studied juvenile Great

Cormorants particularly closely, I did realise that they had a dark upper breast and were paler below, the opposite of this individual. Once again, the oiled-bird theory came into play, or was it perhaps one of the European subspecies? Being by this time mildly interested, I decided to refer to field guides, and subsequently found that the variation in colour was very wide indeed, but pale upper underparts and dark lower underparts did not fit any juvenile variations. I was somewhat confused and decided to bring my 'scope the following day and peruse the bird more closely. It was then that I noticed the rather extensive yellowish coloration on the bill and gular pouch.

Having made some crude field sketches, I went home and referred to the European field guides, looking specifically at all plumages of Great Cormorant and Shag, paying particular attention to flesh configuration on face, and head shape. I ended up even more confused. The shape and extent of bare parts made it a Great Cormorant, but the absence of white (apart from a thin line bordering the gular pouch) was more like Shag. One idea I entertained was 'Shagorant': literally a Shag × Great Cormorant hybrid. I pored through my books, but could find no evidence of this ever occurring. If it *was* a hybrid, what would it look like? This bird was almost certainly nearer to Shag in general size, but more thickset, with a stout neck; the rump was more rounded in shape and like Shag, this being accentuated by the bird being in tail moult. In flight it had a distinct kink in the neck, more obvious when coming in to land (on taking off, the effort seemed to iron out this feature somewhat); the head was held above the level of the body in relaxed flight but the neck drooped. The underparts were blotchy brown, paler on the upper breast; on the closed wing, the wing-coverts were large compared with those of Great Cormorant and fewer in number; a pale centre to each feather gave a very scaly appearance; there was a secondary missing from the right wing. I was able to count eight outer tail feathers, but only four inners, which I estimated to be some 2$\frac{1}{2}$ inches (6 cm) shorter. The bill shape was that of a Great Cormorant, but looked more elongated owing to the long, orange gular pouch of this bird. This effect was further accentuated by a thin orange stripe from the base of the upper mandible to the eye. The head shape appeared to be intermediate between Great Cormorant and Shag, rising fairly steeply from the base of the upper mandible and then sloping back to the crown. The eyes appeared bluish when seen head-on, the coloration and distribution of bare flesh gave a spectacled appearance, and everything seemed to be pointing to Double-crested Cormorant *P. auritus*. The gular pouch was, however, bordered with a thin white line of feathers, which led me to consider the possibility of Neotropic (Olivaceous) Cormorant *P. olivaceus*. The gape appeared to be white with a hint of pink. Feet and legs were black. When swimming with a Great Cormorant, it looked like a scaled-down version of that species, both in body shape and in angle of bill.

While I was watching the bird swimming with a Great Cormorant on 30th January, it adopted a strange diving pattern, following the Great Cormorant some 4 or 5 feet (1.2–1.5 m) behind, and slightly offset. Every time that the Great Cormorant dived, it would also dive, about two seconds later. This synchronised diving lasted about a minute and was so precise that the two birds appeared to be tied together.

On the evening of 30th January 1989, I telephoned M. A. Blick and we discussed the day's observations. During this discussion he informed me that one distinctive feature of Double-crested Cormorant was the feeding pattern we had observed that day. I was by now personally convinced that the bird was a Double-crested Cormorant, by virtue of both my previous observations and the information from MAB about the feeding behaviour. We jointly agreed to release news of the bird's identity. The following day, a number of birders duly arrived, including T. Francis, R. Little, D. J. Britton and M. Hallom, who all had previous experience of this species in North America. They concluded that the bird was indeed a Double-crested Cormorant. The bird was subsequently seen by at least 1,400 other birders and photographed by many, including Robin Chittenden, David Cottridge, Brian Little, David Tipling, Steve Young, Jeff Youngs and Pete Wheeler (*Brit. Birds* 82: plates 180–182; 89: plates 72–76). I made almost daily observations until it was last seen on 26th April 1989; it may have reappeared briefly on the morning of 16th June 1989.

The bird was often reluctant to fly on windless days, and, on the few occasions when these conditions prevailed, it became very agitated, swimming up and down, apparently casting about for some wind into which to take off.

Williams, T. J. 1996. Double-crested Cormorant in Cleveland: new to the Western Palearctic.
British Birds 89, 162–170.

Double-crested Cormorant is a widespread bird in North America; some northern breeders winter south to Guatemala and the Caribbean.

There have been no subsequent records.

The First for Ireland was at Nimmo's Pier, Co. Galway from 18th November 1995–6th January 1996.

FEBRUARY 1989
GOLDEN-WINGED WARBLER IN KENT
Paul Doherty

On 24th January 1989, Mrs C. Miller noticed a colourful bird feeding in the garden of her house at Larkfield, Kent. Though not a bird-watcher, she realised that it was unusual, and made a drawing of it. Three days later, it reappeared, and Mr Miller managed to take some photographs of it. Enquiries were begun as to the identity of this strange bird. In the meantime, on 7th February, whilst on my way to post a letter at the opposite end of the Lunsford Park Estate, I chanced upon the same bird. It was very striking. There were obvious lemon-yellow patches on the crown and greater coverts, a black patch running back from the bill and around the eye, and a broad black bib. The remainder of the upperparts were basically greyish, and the underparts were whitish. I judged the size as similar to that of a Wood Warbler *Phylloscopus sibilatrix*.

I did not have any binoculars with me, but the bird was remarkably tame and I was able to watch it for about three minutes at ranges down to 2 m before it flew off.

My first reaction was that it was an American wood-warbler (Parulidae). After only a few seconds' thought, however, I dismissed that possibility as far too fanciful. The date and place were all wrong; also, I do have a basic knowledge of the American warblers on the British List and this bird did not fit any of them. If it was an American wood-warbler, it had to be a species new to Britain and Ireland, and that seemed to take it into the realms of fantasy.

I returned home and, lacking any books on cagebirds, the first reference that I checked was the *Field Guide to the Birds of North America* (National Geographic Society 1983). I flicked idly through the Warbler plates with no great expectations, but then stopped at page 354, stunned. The bird I had been watching was clearly a male Golden-winged Warbler *Vermivora chrysoptera*.

Over the next few hours, I considered various other options and went through all my field guides. In the end, though, the only conclusion that I could reach was that I had indeed seen a Golden-winged Warbler.

I spoke to S. J. M. Gantlett, who agreed that, in the circumstances (a single observer with no binoculars), confirmation of my sighting was required. The next morning, with the help of Bill Jones, Terry Laws, Tim Loseby and Alan Woodcock, an unsuccessful search was carried out in rather murky weather, the sole bright spot being a Waxwing *Bombycilla garrulus* discovered in the large number of ornamental bushes surrounding the carpark of the nearby Tesco supermarket. In the early afternoon, the weather improved and I returned to check the bushes around Tesco's again. To my great relief, one of the first birds that I saw was the Golden-winged Warbler, and I was able to confirm all the main plumage points before it flew off across the carpark. I obtained the following detailed description:

Size and Shape Size about that of Wood Warbler, but with more robust appearance.

Upperparts Lemon-yellow patch on forehead, extending back onto crown. Black mask running back from lores and around eye. Borders of these patches whitish-grey, paler than rest of upperparts, which were greyish.

Tail Average length. Uppertail and the undertail-coverts grey. Undertail feathers paler, contrasting with the darker undertail-coverts.

Wings Most obvious feature was another lemon-yellow patch, on greater coverts. Primaries, tertials, median and lesser coverts greyish, but tertials were suffused with greenish wash.

Underparts Uniform grey, paler than upperparts. Only noticeable feature was broad, black bib.

Bare Parts Eye, legs and bill blackish. Bill longer than that of any similarly proportioned Palearctic Warbler.

Later in the afternoon, the bird was relocated nearby and was last seen heading towards a patch of rough ground leading down to the River Medway. It had been heading in the same direction when I had last seen it on the previous day. As the riverside vegetation often held wintering Chiffchaffs *P. collybita*, I guessed that the Golden-winged Warbler was spending most of its time in the same area, only occasionally straying to the fringes of the housing estate. Blithely assuming, therefore, that the Golden-winged Warbler was resident in an area of open ground with public access, I felt that it was safe to release the news, and a message was put on 'Birdline'.

Over the next two days, contrary to my expectations, the Golden-winged Warbler was seen in the bushes surrounding Tesco's carpark and the gardens of the housing estate. With such an extreme and beautiful rarity, in the densely populated southeast of England, with convenient motorway access, and at a quiet time of year with little else competing for birdwatchers' attention, it seemed certain that the weekend would bring large numbers of birdwatchers. Even so, I was surprised by the horde which descended on the estate. The actual number will of course never be known, but, from a rough count carried out on the Sunday, I believe there were about 1,200 people present then, with a minimum of 3,000 people on the Saturday (*Brit. Birds* 82: plate 187; 85: plate 271).

Although the Golden-winged Warbler was a tame and distinctive bird (and was photographed: *Brit. Birds* 82: plates 186 & 188; 83: plate 271; 85: plates 268–270), keeping track of it was often difficult, particularly after the initial crowds had melted away. It would occasionally settle in a garden, but more typically it moved quickly from garden to garden and so was easily lost. Relocating it could then be difficult, as it travelled widely.

With large numbers of birdwatchers roaming around a housing estate, there was obvious potential for friction with local people. Indeed, had I known that the Golden-winged Warbler would spend all of its time on the estate, I would probably have felt that it was unwise to release the news. In the event, that would have been a mistake, as most local people seemed to enjoy hosting an avian celebrity. Some minor problems did occur, but most birdwatchers behaved very responsibly, and I am not aware of any serious incidents. (Local radio reported that a wall had been pushed over in the melee, but my attempts to track down this alleged damage met with a blank, and I suspect that the incident never happened.) There is, however, no room for complacency. This 'event' was widely reported on television and in the press (and even made the front page of the *Daily Telegraph*). Public opinion tends to generalise, and if one unpleasant incident had been filmed, there could have been unfortunate consequences for the public perception of birdwatchers. Clearly, at events such as this, birdwatchers' behaviour must be impeccable.

After the initial excitement had died down, the Golden-winged Warbler remained, but, with much smaller numbers of birdwatchers looking, it sometimes went unreported for days at a time. Luckily, it benefited from unusually mild weather, which enabled it to survive.

As spring approached, there were reports of it singing. So far as I am aware, the last sighting was on 10th April, when I saw it in the bushes surrounding Tesco's carpark (where else!). It seems a reasonable assumption that it then began a northward migration.

A rumour reached me the following winter that it had returned, but nothing came of this, so it was doubtless incorrect.

The date when the Golden-winged Warbler arrived in Britain will never be known. The most likely explanation for its occurrence, however, is that it made landfall in the Southwest in the autumn, made its way east to Kent, and found the mild climate of the Medway valley to its liking. It may not be too far-fetched to suggest that it went from Tresco to Tesco. (Sorry!)

By what seemed an amazing coincidence, another American Warbler, a Common Yellowthroat *Geothlypis trichas*, was present just 25 km away on very similar dates: 6th January to 23rd April 1989. Unfortunately, it was on private land with no access for general birdwatching. The third American passerine of this period was a Northern Oriole *Icterus galbula* at Roch, Dyfed, from 2nd January to 23rd April. The dates of all three birds were remarkably similar, perhaps suggesting something more than simple coincidence.

In the case of the Northern Oriole, a collection for the Dyfed Wildlife Trust raised a substantial sum of money. My one regret of the Golden-winged Warbler episode is that no similar collection was made for one of the Kentish conservation bodies. I do not think donations would have been begrudged by the thousands who obviously obtained such enjoyment from this wonderful bird.

Doherty, P. 1992. Golden-winged Warbler: new to the Western Palearctic.
British Birds 85, 595–600.

Golden-winged Warbler breeds south of the Great Lakes in the USA; it winters in Central America and northernmost South America.

There have been no subsequent records.

JULY 1989

SWINHOE'S STORM PETREL ON TYNESIDE

Mark Cubitt

The possibility of catching a vagrant species during a ringing session at a site on the Northumberland coast is never far from the back of one's mind during October, particularly when there is an easterly wind blowing. The concept that anything remotely similar could happen when tape-luring small numbers of European Storm-petrels *Hydrobates pelagicus* would have been considered, at best, fanciful prior to 23rd July 1989.

Since that date, there has been an incredible series of captures of what we now know to be Swinhoe's Storm-petrels *Oceanodroma monorhis*. Three individuals have been involved. The first two were on 23rd and 26th July 1989. The third has, quite amazingly, been caught eight times in five consecutive years: on 6th July 1990, 30th July 1991, 29th July 1992, 21st, 28th and 29th July 1993, and 23rd and 25th July 1994.

Members of our small team take it in turns to watch the nets on the rocky beach at the base of Tynemouth's north pier. Mary Carruthers had noted, with some excitement, a larger bird, stiffer-winged than the familiar European Storm-petrels, circling the nets briefly on 18th July 1989. I immediately switched the tape to that of the presumed Leach's Storm-petrel *O. leucorhoa*, but the bird was not seen again, at least not that night.

On our next outing, on 23rd July, Adam Hutt and I also saw a larger petrel, but this time it circled the nets once and was then caught. Having rushed over to the net, I was astounded to find that the bird did not have any white on its rump and, even in the darkness of the beach, that its outer wing feathers had white shafts.

At our ringing base, in discussion with Les Hall and Keith Regan, it was clear that the bird was of the genus *Oceanodroma*. We recalled that a Matsudaira's Storm-petrel *O. matsudairae* had been claimed on a pelagic trip in the Southwest Approaches, but we had no documented measurements with which to compare those taken from our bird.

All of our captures were of birds attracted to the call of European Storm-petrel rather than that of Leach's. Photographs were taken of all of them. They were quite vocal, both prior to being caught and in the hand; we recorded the call. A blood sample was taken from the one captured in 1991.

Description

The following notes summarise the appearance of all three individuals:

General appearance Sooty-brown *Oceanodroma* storm-petrels.

Upperparts Head and, to a lesser extent, nape, back, rump and upperside of tail distinctly smoky-grey. Small apparently darker area in front of each eye. Bases of outer six primaries with white shafts. Pale wing-bar from scapulars and inner greater coverts through outer median coverts, formed by pale-fringed feathers, to pale brown carpal covert. Alula and primary coverts blackish-brown, as remiges.

Underparts Uniformly sooty-brown, tinged grey. Underwing-coverts rusty-brown. Axillaries faintly barred buff.

Bare parts Bill, legs and feet black. Eye dark.

Measurements The measurements taken for each of the birds caught are shown in table 1.

Table 1. Measurements (in mm) of the three Swinhoe's Storm-petrels *Oceanodroma monorhis* caught at Tynemouth in 1989, 1989 and 1990–94, respectively.

Feature	Bird 1	Bird 2	Bird 3
Wing length	167	166	164
Outer tail length	79	83	78
Inner tail length	61	66	63
Bill length	14.9	14.5	14.5
Bill depth	6.4	–	6.4
Tarsus length	–	–	24.4

The identification

It took over three years to identify these birds positively as Swinhoe's Storm-petrels (Bretagnolle *et al.* 1991; Cubitt *et al.* 1992; Dawson 1992). We split the research into three main areas. The first area was plumage and measurements, upon which we based our first published note shortly after the first capture (Carruthers *et al.* 1989). This stated that they 'were either Swinhoe's Storm-petrels or a close relative'. It was the latter possibility that forced us into looking into vocalisations and DNA sequencing, which have been the other main areas of research.

Our birds are very similar in size and structure to the large races of Leach's Storm-petrel, such as the British population. There are some minor size differences, such as tarsus length being greater and bill length and tail length being shorter in proportion to the size of the bird.

The two most significant differences are the all-dark rump and the white on the outer six primary-feather shafts. Some races of Leach's do have dark rumps, but these races are much smaller than Swinhoe's. Individuals of the British population can have significant variation in rump coloration, but always exhibit some white. The presence of white primary shafts showing beyond the coverts is restricted within this family to

Swinhoe's and Matsudaira's Storm-petrels. The latter is significantly larger, as are the other Pacific dark-rumped storm-petrels.

Our birds' biometrics gave good support to the identification as Swinhoe's, but my measurements of wing length appeared to be at or beyond the extreme of those documented for Swinhoe's, thus causing some concern initially. This, though, appears to be due to differences among recorders in experience and technique of measuring maximum-chord wing lengths.

The second area of research, which took the longest time, was the analysis of cytochrome-b mitochondrial-DNA sequences. Through this, we discovered that species within the family, such as Leach's and Swinhoe's, are quite distinct. The analyses also showed that our birds had identical sequences to those of Swinhoe's from Korea and Russia (Dawson 1992).

It is likely that vocalisations provide an important mechanism for storm-petrels to identify the species and sex of another individual in the darkness of a colony. This was the third area of research. We were fortunate that workers in Japan had recently been looking at the vocalisations of both Swinhoe's and Leach's Storm-petrels. This gave us access to recordings that were previously unavailable in the West. More importantly, they had shown significant differences between the calls of the two species and even between sexes. This enabled them to match a recording that we had made to a sonogram of a female Korean Swinhoe's Storm Petrel.

Origins

Swinhoe's Storm-petrels are known to breed on islands mainly off Korea and Japan, but also west to China and north to Russia. They migrate westwards, with the monsoons, into the western Pacific. Some move into the northern Indian Ocean and even into the Red Sea, where the first Western Palearctic record occurred in 1958. This was, perhaps, the route taken by the individual caught on Islote de Benidorm, Spain, in July 1994 (King & Minguez 1994).

In order to account for the captures of seven Swinhoe's Storm-petrels in the North Atlantic since 1983, it has been suggested that there may be a small breeding population in the North Atlantic. Our returning bird, however, now certainly of breeding age – but apparently still wandering – may make this theory less likely. Vagrancy is perhaps the more probable source of these birds, although the lack of records in the Western Indian Ocean makes this far from certain.

Cubitt, M. G. 1995. Swinhoe's Storm Petrels at Tynemouth: new to Britain and Ireland.
British Birds 88, 342–348.

Swinhoe's Storm-petrel breeds on islands off Korea and Japan, migrating to the western Pacific.

There has been one subsequent record following the series of Tynemouth records:

Aberdeenshire Cove, female, trapped 5th August 2000

The First for Ireland was a bird trapped on Great Skellig Rock, Co. Kerry, on 1st July 2000.

SEPTEMBER 1989

GREAT KNOT ON SHETLAND

Peter Ellis

On 15th September 1989, at about 11.20 GMT, I was walking south at Scatness, Shetland, looking for waders roosting at high tide. I saw a small group of waders about 150 m ahead, so I stopped near an old ruined building to examine them. There were three Grey Plovers *Pluvialis squatarola*, two Dunlins *Calidris alpina*, a Knot *C. canutus* and, just beyond them, a wader of a species I had never seen before. I excitedly reached for my telescope to examine it more closely. The size, structure and the striking black breast-band and black mantle with a pale band across the lower scapulars immediately suggested an adult Great Knot *C. tenuirostris* in worn summer plumage. I watched it for about five minutes before, to my horror, the group of waders took off. Fortunately, they flew towards me and landed at the edge of a small pool about 60 m away. The whiter rump and almost total lack of a wing-bar were very obvious as the Great Knot flew in. I was then able to watch it walk past the Knot and out of the pool, where it began feeding on the short turf. After a couple of minutes, a Redshank *Tringa totanus* flew close over the Great Knot and it flew off with the Redshank to the north, disappearing from sight.

I walked the kilometre back to my car in a state of total euphoria and drove to a phone box in Toab, where I telephoned Martin Heubeck. I told him I had found a Great Knot and asked him to bring 'Shorebirds' (Hayman *et al.* 1986) down to the phone box, as I wanted to make certain that I had remembered the identification features of the species correctly, before I put the word out on the local grapevine. About ten minutes later, Martin arrived in Toab, together with Paul V. Harvey, and, after one brief look at the relevant plate in 'Shorebirds', I was able to confirm the initial identification. PVH and I returned to Scatness, where we failed to relocate the bird. We desperately hoped that, as the tide fell, the Great Knot would reappear on the mudflats on the Pool of Virkie. We went to the pool and, after about 15 minutes, PVH relocated the bird on the far side next to a Knot. Most of the local birders managed to get good views of the Great Knot in the next hour or so. It was photographed by Dennis Coutts.

The bird remained on the pool until 14.40 hours, when it flew off north, but, luckily for several visiting birders, it returned about an hour later, and remained until about 17.30 hours, when it flew off north again with two Curlews *Numenius arquata*. Shortly afterwards, a weather front arrived in Shetland, bringing southwesterly gales and rain for the next few days. About 30 birders flew into Shetland the following morning, but, despite much searching, the Great Knot was never relocated.

DESCRIPTION

Size and Shape Similar in body size to Redshank, but much shorter-legged. Considerably larger than Knot, and much slimmer and more attenuated in the body. In structure, reminiscent of a giant, deep-breasted White-rumped Sandpiper *C. fuscicollis* with a long Dunlin-like bill. Head proportionately smaller and more rounded than that of Knot, but with steeper forehead. Wings very long, primaries extending beyond tertials for about half length of exposed tertials and beyond tip of the tail for about one-quarter of length of exposed tertials. Tertial tips fell at base of tail. In flight, wings looked exceedingly long. Bill was proportionately longer (about 1.3× head-length) and slimmer than that of Knot, particularly over distal two-thirds, with fine tip and gentle downward curve towards tip, although at times there appeared to be distinct downward kink at tip. Leg length proportionately similar to that of Knot. The whole plumage appeared to be very heavily worn and, as the bird did not allow a close approach, it was impossible to obtain individual feather detail.

Head and Neck Crown finely but clearly streaked blackish, forming capped effect. 'Face' pale brownish, but very plain, with only very faint dark eye-stripe, and very indistinct supercilium, which extended from bill to eye, but for less than that distance behind eye. 'Cheeks' considerably paler than ear-coverts. Chin and throat blackish. Nape finely streaked dark brownish-grey, paler than crown on upper part, but darker on lower part, where almost same colour as mantle.

Upperparts Mantle heavily blotched with black. Upper three rows of scapulars also very heavily blotched with black, so that, at a distance, upperparts appeared to be almost uniform black. Fourth row of scapulars creamy-buff on basal two-thirds, with black semicircular markings towards tip of each feather and with faint chestnut tinge on bases of rear ones. Exact patterning of these feathers difficult to make out as feathers appeared to be quite worn and faded. Lowest row of scapulars black, with worn, narrow, creamy fringes. Pale areas on two lowest rows of scapulars forming conspicuous pale bar. Rump white, contrasting with tail, which was mid grey at sides and darker grey in centre, whole tail being darker than on Knot.

Wings Tertials brownish-grey with paler fringes. Greater coverts had dark grey, lanceolate centres, with dark grey shaft streaks and pale grey-brown fringes, with median and lesser coverts similarly marked. Primary coverts dark grey, almost black, contrasting with rest of upperwing. Secondaries grey and primaries dark grey, with no obvious wing-bar in flight. Underwing coverts white.

Underparts Breast densely mottled black, mottles coalescing on lower breast to form complete breast-band, and with a few more-isolated black spots on lower breast. Flanks white, with large, heart-shaped black spots, extending from sides of breast to rear of flanks. Belly and undertail-coverts white.

Bare Parts Bill dark grey, probably slightly paler on proximal quarter. Legs greenish-grey. Eye dark.

Behaviour Feeding action very like that of Knot. Flight very buoyant, with very slow wing beats and almost a rowing action. Glided a lot, particularly as descending to land. Very flighty and often took off and flew around pool for no apparent reason, and did not allow particularly close approach.

Ellis, P. M. 1992. Great Knot: new to Britain and Ireland. *British Birds* 85, 426–428.

Great Knot breeds in northeastern Siberia and winters from southern China south to Australia.

There have been two subsequent records:

Cleveland Seal Sands, 13th October–5th November 1996

Lancashire Wyre Estuary, adult, 31st July and 16th–17th August 2004 (BBRC decision awaited)

The Lancashire bird was presumed to be the same individual as the First for Ireland, which had been on the Swords Estuary, Co. Dublin, on 25th July 2004.

OCTOBER 1989

RED-BREASTED NUTHATCH IN NORFOLK

Jean Aley and Roy Aley

At 13.30 GMT on 13th October 1989, at Holkham Meals, Norfolk, we were watching a group of tits *Parus* and Goldcrests *Regulus regulus* when we noticed an unusual nuthatch *Sitta* feeding on a grassy footpath some 6 m  ahead of us. We watched it for several seconds before it flew into an adjacent pine for a moment, and then away through the trees.

The bird was the shape of a European Nuthatch *Sitta europaea*, with a short tail and fine bill, but was clearly smaller: at the time we estimated it to be 4½ inches (11 cm) long. The upperparts, excluding the head, were blue-grey and all the underparts pinky-buff. The head showed a black eye-stripe with a clear white supercilium and a black crown. The shape and plumage were clearly those of a nuthatch, but *europaea* was ruled out by the size and head pattern. We had no means of identifying the bird at the time, although, subsequently, we looked at a European field guide and had to consider Corsican Nuthatch *S. whiteheadi*; our bird, however, was pinker below, and did not seem to fit in other respects, either.

We looked for it again, with a local birder, but could not relocate it; we soon found out, of course, that it was identified the next day as a Red-breasted Nuthatch *S. canadensis*. It stayed until at least 6th May 1990 (*Brit. Birds* 84: 495).

EDITORIAL COMMENT
Rob Hume, Chairman of the BBRC, and Dr David Parkin, Chairman of the BOURC, have added the following comments: 'The identification of this individual was no problem once the slightly larger, paler Corsican Nuthatch and the superficially similar Krüper's Nuthatch *S. krueperi* (which has a discrete red-brown chest patch) were excluded. Mr and Mrs Aley sent sufficiently detailed notes and a sketch to make identification possible, but Paul Varney and Dave Hatton, both of Cambridge, saw the bird on 14th, locating and identifying it independently, but simultaneously. Their account added more detail, and further descriptions were rendered unnecessary as, after initial incredulity, people descended on Holkham Meals in their hundreds to see the bird. Indeed, it developed into one of the largest gatherings of birdwatchers so far seen in the UK, a situation not helped by the narrowness of the paths, the elusive nature of the bird and the desperation of a few observers literally fighting for a better vantage point. Some people visited eight or more times without seeing it at all, and many needed a second or third attempt before catching a glimpse. For others, however, it performed remarkably well. By listening for its distinctive call, or by following the tit flocks, or by simply waiting in a favoured spot for the nuthatch to appear, many people were able to see and photograph it during its stay of several months (*Brit. Birds* 83: 154, plates 92–94, 323, plate 196; 88: plates 36 & 37).

'Close examination showed the bird to be a well-marked individual, but whether it was a male or a bright female is uncertain. The forehead and crown were jet-black (although some observers noted a faint grey tinge to the crown), extending to the nape. The supercilium was striking and bold, pure white from just behind the bill to the sides of the nape; below this was a long, broad, black eye-stripe, flaring out at the rear and slightly irregular on the lower edge. The chin, throat and lower ear-coverts were off-white, merging into dull, pale rufous on the neck and upper breast, with a slightly blotchy effect. The breast, central belly and undertail-coverts were pale rufous, becoming a slightly richer, more orange colour on the flanks. The upperparts were blue-grey with darker tips to the alula and primary coverts and centres to the tertials, secondaries and exposed primary tips; the uppertail-coverts were blue-grey, and the tail blackish with small white patches near the tips of the outer feathers. The bill was straight along the culmen, while the lower edge curved upwards slightly towards the tip; it appeared bluish-grey with a whiter base and an extensive blackish tip to the lower mandible. The legs and feet were slightly pinkish-grey.

'A distinctive (and helpful) feature of the bird was its call: a quiet, nasal "neh-neh" usually repeated four to five times (sometimes in bursts of up to 15 calls) and an occasional louder, strident, more trumpet-like version which carried for 50 m or more. It responded quickly to a tape-recording and called in flight as it approached.'

Aley, J. & Aley, R. 1995. Red-breasted Nuthatch: new to Britain and Ireland. *British Birds* 88, 150–153.

Red-breasted Nuthatch is a common bird in eastern North America and is occasionally irruptive.

There have been no subsequent records.

THE BIRDER'S YEAR

Adrian Pitches

The 1990s would begin and end in spectacular style. 1990 saw four Firsts for Britain, three of which occurred during a purple patch for rarities in late May and early June. Birders had to take to the water or take to the air to enjoy this spring bonanza as all of these 'most wanted' birds turned up on offshore islands. Another offshore treat in Spring 1990 was the mythical **Pallas's Sandgrouse**, the irruptive enigma from Central Asia. By no means a First – there were hundreds in two major nineteenth-century invasions – the bird on Shetland in May will, for many birders, be the best memory of a memorable year.

The year started with a bang – a male **'Naumann's Thrush'** (Dusky Thrush of the race *naumanni*) in Greater London! 'Norman' was a gift to birders and media alike as it turned up in Tory MP Norman Tebbit's Chingford constituency. It was the first Dusky Thrush of this race to be found in Britain and stayed from mid-January until early March. Meanwhile, another North Yorkshire **Black-throated Thrush** was at Kellington in late January.

The first new **Black Duck** for several years was a male at Loch of Spiggie, Shetland, on 4th February. And another new American duck was Britain's second **Lesser Scaup** – like the First, a Midlands bird. This one was in Nottinghamshire on 22nd April. After going AWOL in 1988 and 1989, 'Albert' the lonesome **Black-browed Albatross** returned to Unst, Shetland, at the end of March.

A wonderful spring started very early with a **Great Spotted Cuckoo** on Lundy on 24th February, the earliest ever. Another bird, at Shoreham, West Sussex, which stayed for a month from early April, was more accessible.

A **Yellow-headed Blackbird** on Fair Isle in late April was a striking bird but with little chance of staking a claim on the British List. However, Shetland birders would shortly have some compensation… The floodgates opened on 19th May when a male **Pallas's Sandgrouse** was discovered by one of Shetland's top teams at Loch of Hillwell. They selflessly abandoned their annual bird race to spread the news! The first since 1975, when there were two on 11th May on the Isle of May, Fife, this longed-for 'blocker' stayed until 4th June. A week later – on 27th May – three fabulous birds were discovered at different offshore locations in southwest Britain. Of these, an **Alpine Accentor** on the Isle of Wight was the first since 1978 – and it stayed for nearly two weeks. The other two birds were both Firsts for Britain, one expected and one totally unexpected. The female **White-throated Robin** on Skokholm, Dyfed, followed a male on the Calf of Man, Isle of Man, in 1983. Birders were asked to stay away, however, rather than invade Skokholm with its vulnerable Manx Shearwater nesting burrows. How many slipped across regardless?

Skokholm's guardians were given some assistance by the simultaneous appearance on Lundy of an auk from the northern Pacific Ocean – **Ancient Murrelet**! Lundy's guardians thought their Puffins could take the pressure of a mass pilgrimage and boat-loads of birders made the crossing from Ilfracombe. The murrelet stayed for a month and evidently liked Lundy so much that it returned in 1991 and 1992! It was an extraordinary example of vagrancy from the same distant part of the world as 1979's Aleutian Tern.

Not to be outdone, that other rarity hotspot, Scilly, also served up a First. In time-honoured fashion, it was a North American passerine – a **Tree Swallow**, on 6th June. The heroic hirundine hawked over Porth Hellick pool until 10th June. Meanwhile, the **Red-breasted Nuthatch** in Norfolk tooted its toy trumpet for the last time on 6th May. Summer 1990 was a time to recover from the excessive expenditure on travel in the spring – and save up for the autumn journeys to come.

Long-legged birds continued their resurgence – there were five **Squacco Herons** in spring/summer 1990 and another eight **Black Storks** in summer/autumn – the same total as in 1989. And following the previous year's record influx of **Little Egrets** there were a further 100 birds logged in 1990. The bulk of them were in southwest England but stragglers got as far north as Orkney. This elegant heron's rapid rise in fortunes saw it cease to be a '*BB* rarity' from the end of 1990.

Autumn kicked off in late July with **Pacific Golden Plovers** in Lancashire and Dorset followed by another at Cley, Norfolk, in early August. The latter bird coincid-ed with an adult **Stilt Sandpiper** in Suffolk – the returning east-coast bird? The **Terek Sandpiper** that arrived in Northumberland in November 1989 not only overwintered; it oversummered too, remaining around the Blyth estuary through the summer and autumn and into 1991.

Birders only had to wait until September for the fourth and final First of the year. Andy Birch's morning stroll down the Kenidjack valley in Cornwall on 20th September was enlivened by a **Yellow-throated Vireo**. Britain's third species of vireo, this golden-spectacled beauty stayed for a week.

And attention stayed focused on southwest England for the next month before Shetland delivered two very special birds as autumn waned. Before that, however, a Shetland speciality – **Pechora Pipit** – was found in both Cornwall and Dorset on 20th October.

October on Scilly produced an **Upland Sandpiper**; a **Black-billed Cuckoo** that died within a day; two **Swainson's Thrushes** and two **Grey-cheeked Thrushes** (another Grey-cheeked was found dead at Slimbridge, Gloucestershire); an **Eyebrowed**

Thrush; an **Isabelline Wheatear** (another was in East Yorkshire); a **Blackpoll Warbler**; and up to ten **Olive-backed Pipits**. It was another record year for 'OBPs' in 1990, with more than 40 logged from Scilly to Shetland – twice the previous record total in 1987.

Shetland's contributions were Britain's third **Rüppell's Warbler**, a male, on Whalsay from 3rd–19th October, and Britain's second **Yellow Warbler**, also a male, but just a two-day bird, in Lerwick in early November. The First was on Bardsey, Gwynedd, in August 1964.

Northumberland had a male **Pine Bunting** at Bamburgh on 21st October – the county also had that fiendishly tricky female at Big Waters in February. And the county's first **Booted Warbler** (the only British record this year) was on Inner Farne on 19th October. A **Bridled Tern** flew past Scarborough, North Yorkshire, on 18th October. And a second **Alpine Accentor** for the year was a very late bird, in Cornwall on 4th November.

On 6th December there was a very odd record: a freshly dead **Yellow-billed Cuckoo** found at Sandy, Bedfordshire. Perhaps the victim of an RSPB hit squad from The Lodge?! The year ended on a high for many birders with a long-staying English mainland **Snowy Owl**. The first-winter male first seen in East Yorkshire on 13th December relocated across the county boundary into Lincolnshire and stayed into 1991.

BUNTING HUNTING
Colin Bradshaw

It was to be my year, I decided, having spent much of 1989 in Canada and missing three Swinhoe's Storm Petrels trapped at my local patch at Tynemouth. Nothing like that was going to happen in 1990. I would concentrate on the North and not travel much; I would even forsake my annual October trip to Scilly. Most particularly, I wouldn't miss a night at home during the petrel season.

New Year's Day got me off to a flying start with Iceland, Glaucous and Med Gulls at North Shields Fish Quay; a Snow Bunting flock being fed up the coast at Cambois also included a Shore Lark; while the Terek Sandpiper continued its winter stay at Blyth. And before the end of January a female Ring-necked Duck had arrived on my local park lake to be joined later in the spring by a male.

The 'Naumann's Thrush' in Chingford seriously weakened my resolve. I hadn't seen this form or the closely related Dusky in any of my trips through Siberia. One night away couldn't do that much harm. After a very long drive and a day tramping around people's back gardens and a school playing field, I remembered why I wasn't going to travel far. Even the bird's eventual appearance produced a feeling of relief rather than elation, and not a little worry that this bird was within three miles of the UK's biggest bird importer. I resolved to stay local and, to celebrate my birthday the following weekend, took my family to look for frogs at Big Waters Nature Reserve. Whilst there I noticed a very frosty-looking 'Yellowhammer' which set alarm bells ringing. I cut short my birthday lunch at the local pub and returned to take copious notes, but was still unsure. After I got home that evening, I was almost convinced that it was a Pine Bunting but wasn't prepared to release the news without a chance to check some features again. (Yes, people did that even as recently as 1990 – no mobile phones, no pagers.) I made several calls suggesting that people should be on standby while I checked something out. I shouldn't have bothered – the queue to the hide was 30 yards long the next morning and all the people I had spoken to were in front of me!

I was out of Britain for much of May so the next major event for me was the return of 'Elsie' to Inner Farne. Even though it had been around the Northeast since 1984, it had taken me till the previous year to see 'our' Lesser Crested Tern. In 'my year' it proved much easier to connect with, taking up residence on Inner Farne for all to see.

Late summer/early autumn produced lots of Storm Petrels trapped at Tynemouth and some great waders: Pacific Golden Plover on the Ribble and both White-rumped and Buff-breasted Sandpipers next to my work in Whitburn.

A classic Northeast autumn is something to savour and this was one of the best. I was lucky enough to get off to a good start finding Scarlet Rosefinch and Yellow-browed Warbler on my local patch at Prior's Park and having Long-tailed and Pomarine Skuas and a Sabine's Gull off Tynemouth in September. By mid-October several falls of hundreds of thrushes (including sprinklings of Ring Ouzels – and Great Spotted Woodpeckers) produced a Dusky Warbler on St Mary's Island, Whitley Bay, and a Rustic Bunting at Newbiggin. The last species caused the most excitement with a strangled phone call from Tim Cleeves: 'I've got a bunting here, haven't seen it well but it's got a yellow supercilium …' Fortunately there were no speed traps on the road that day. The supercilium *was* yellow but it was a Rustic rather than a Yellow-browed. As compensation, on returning to Prior's that day, I found a Pallas's Warbler. Later in the month, Goldcrests had replaced thrushes, with over 1,000 in the park one morning.

My decision to pass over Scilly seemed fully justified when John McLoughlin identified an Isabelline Wheatear at Spurn. Now Spurn isn't exactly close to Tynemouth, but it was the North. I'd never seen one in Britain and always thought they would be tricky to identify – this bird made me realise how right I was. I took Brian Bates down with me and he repaid my kindness less than a week later by finding a Red-eyed Vireo in Mere Knolls Cemetery, Sunderland. Just when things should have quietened down in mid-November, we had an invasion of Crossbills and a few days later several Parrot Crossbills were identified at Chopwell Wood. I spent the rest of the year searching unsuccessfully for undiscovered individuals in various woods in Northumberland. The year ended much as it began with the return of the Terek Sandpiper to Blyth.

1990 was a landmark year for me. My involvement with the Pine and Rustic Buntings has led to the *Emberiza* genus being one of my major interests. I've continued to be fascinated by Isabelline Wheatear and repelled by the thought of travelling long distances for single birds (although this didn't stop me twitching both Snowy Owl and Harlequin in the early months of 1991).

May 1990 saw my first trip to Beidaihe – other than the small group I took, there were only four birders there and none of us had even heard of Happy Island. Some of you may better remember the year for the birds I missed whilst being in China – Alpine Accentor, Tree Swallow, Pallas's Sandgrouse and Ancient Murrelet – a heavy price to pay for not sticking to my vow on travelling. Perhaps the Yellow Warbler or Yellow-throated Vireo in the autumn bring back memories for you.

For me though, 1990 was my year and it was memorable for lots of reasons but mainly for the night I spent with BBRC at Tring in the middle of the petrel season … the night they retrapped the Swinhoe's at Tynemouth…

Professor Colin Bradshaw lives in Tynemouth, North Tyneside. A general practitioner by profession, he also chairs the British Birds Rarities Committee.

MAY 1990

WHITE-THROATED ROBIN IN DYFED

Michael Betts

No detailed write-up of this First for Britain ever appeared. The following terse paragraph written by the warden of Skokholm, Michael Betts, appeared in *Birding World*: 'A female White-throated Robin *Irania gutturalis* was present on Skokholm, Dyfed on 27th–30th May 1990. A large-scale twitch was ruled out because

of the 35,000-plus pairs of Manx Shearwaters incubating in an island-wide burrow system made exceptionally fragile by two consecutive seasons without rain.'

Betts, M. 1990. White-throated Robin on Skokholm. *Birding World* 3, 208.

White-throated Robin breeds from Turkey east into Central Asia; it winters in East Africa.

There have been no subsequent records.

The First for the Isle of Man, a male, was on the Calf of Man on 22nd June 1983.

MAY 1990
ANCIENT MURRELET ON LUNDY
John Waldon

While Fair Isle or the Isles of Scilly in autumn are undeniably exciting, gross rarities sometimes appear at the least expected times and in the most unlikely places and are all the more memorable for that.

The RSPB South West office organised a trip to Lundy, Devon, to see Puffins *Fratercula arctica* on 27th May 1990. Most of the people who took the trip were delighted to be able to see Puffins and showed little or no interest in the finding of a small, 'auk-like' bird: but it was this that was to become the centre of attraction for the rest of that summer and the following one for hundreds of visiting birders.

At 14.15 BST, I was watching Common Guillemots *Uria aalge* and Razorbills *Alca torda* on the water in Jenny's Cove. Two Puffins were also seen. Keith Mortimer and Richard Campey were watching from farther south and I was surprised to see Keith heading quickly my way, as he ran up to report that they had been watching a small, auk-like bird in the bay. He said that it had a pale bill and was smaller than all the other auks. By 14.25, I had walked to the spot where Richard and Keith were watching, and they had relocated

the bird in question, flying far out to sea. I watched through Richard's telescope and saw the mystery bird flying with two Common Guillemots.

It was obviously smaller, not much more than half the size of the Common Guillemots; it looked long-winged, with plain upperwings except for darker primaries, and was basically dark above and pale below. It flew strongly, low over the water, usually ahead of the Common Guillemots, until all three landed together on the water. It swam low in the water, and looked small-headed, with the general appearance of a dark head and a dark horizontal line along the paler body. It soon dived and I lost track of it, feeling somewhat bemused.

At 14.45, I spotted a group of auks well out to sea, flying towards the land. One was noticeably smaller than the others, raising my spirits when I realised that the intriguing mystery individual had been relocated. All four – three Common Guillemots and what by now was evidently a murrelet – landed on the water about 200 m from the rocks. It was lost to view at 15.00.

Richard and Keith had gone to find a reference book, so I watched the bird, using a 20 × telescope, and made a drawing and the following notes:

Back grey; very dark – black – edge to folded wing; pale below. Wings and tail similar length. Head smallish, black, with prominent white stripe [from above eye] meeting in V at nape. Bill small and pale (horn-coloured). Legs trailed behind and could be seen clearly. They were dark – almost black – and looked long and thin in the water.

The bird dived a few times and then flew out to sea accompanied by one Razorbill and a Guillemot. It was clearly only half the size of either. It was slender-looking, a 'long' bird, wings plain grey with markedly darker primaries. Its upper body was plain and it was paler below.

The lack of a good reference guide made positive identification difficult at the time: no-one had expected to find a murrelet on a summer visit to Lundy. When we borrowed and consulted Harrison's *Seabirds: an identification guide* (1983), the illustrations suggested the possibility of Japanese Murrelet *Synthliboramphus wumizusume* ('Crested Murrelet' in that book), because of the marked white V on the nape. It was only on the boat on the way home, when we were feeling somewhat mixed emotions of elation and confusion, that we looked at Tuck & Heinzel's *A Field Guide to the Seabirds of Britain and the World* (1978) and found, somewhat to our surprise, that the illustration of Ancient Murrelet *S. antiquus* clearly matched the bird we had seen. We were, then, confident that what we had seen was, incredibly, an Ancient Murrelet.

When we had returned to Exeter, Richard Campey sought the agreement of the Lundy Island Administration and then began the process of alerting the telephone bird-lines. Most people's reaction was one of incredulity: even a suspicion that the whole thing was a hoax. One birder, who should perhaps remain anonymous, refused to believe the story at all until he came to my house, made me get my six-year-old daughter out of bed and quizzed her: once she had answered all his questions with the right replies and without evident prompting, he dashed off to book his boat trip for the next morning.

The Ancient Murrelet remained on the island until 26th June 1990, and returned in subsequent years from 4th April to at least 20th June 1991 and from 30th March to 29th April 1992. It was, for the most part, elusive and best seen very early in the mornings before it flew off to sea to feed. Although there were many who made more than one trip without success, most people, nevertheless, were eventually able to see the bird, which was surely one of the least expected additions to the West Palearctic list for many years.

Waldon, J. 1994. Ancient Murrelet in Devon: new to the Western Palearctic. *British Birds* 87, 307–310.

Ancient Murrelet breeds on both coasts of the northern Pacific Ocean and winters in the same area.

There have been no subsequent records since the Lundy bird's three seasons in 1990, 1991 and 1992.

JUNE 1990
TREE SWALLOW ON SCILLY
Jeremy Hickman

The Isles of Scilly are renowned as a haven for displaced migrant birds, and the autumn pilgrimage of observers in September and October is famous in ornithological circles. June is usually a quiet month for numbers of visiting birdwatchers, as are the other months outside the autumn, but June 1990 was the exception. In one five-day period, between 800 and 1,000 people came to see one bird: the first record for Britain & Ireland, Europe and the Western Palearctic of a North American species, Tree Swallow *Tachycineta bicolor*.

On Wednesday 6th June 1990, having finished my shift behind the bar in the Mermaid Inn, I decided to go to Porth Hellick. I watched from the main hide for a while and could hardly believe how devoid of bird life it was. I could not even console myself by counting the Moorhens *Gallinula chloropus*.

At about 19.00 BST, five hirundines approached low over the pool: one House Martin *Delichon urbicum*, three Barn Swallows *Hirundo rustica* and another bird. This fifth bird gave the impression of a martin, but with no white rump and a glossy blue-green mantle and crown, and pure white underparts. My heart sank as the bird then flew to the back of the pool and began hawking around the pines and surrounding fields. I rushed to Sluice to obtain closer views and to note its plumage in detail.

It appeared slightly bigger and bulkier in the body than a House Martin, with broader-based wings and more powerful flight. Its underparts were all pure snowy white, from its chin to its undertail-coverts, with only a very tiny extension of white from the flanks to the upperside of the body at the base of the wing. Its upperparts were the most amazing bright, glossy blue-green. The wings and tail were matt-black, and the underwing and undertail off-white to silvery grey. The colour of the crown extended well below the level of the eye and squared off into the ear-coverts. The shape of the tail was similar to that of House Martin, being short, but less forked when closed.

The next few minutes were total panic. Would it go? Would it stay? What was it? I was not calm! As it was June, there was no-one anywhere. At about 20.00 BST, I ran back to my car and drove to Old Town to phone the other resident birders on St Mary's (all two of them). At this stage, I was still unsure of exactly what I had found. I was not expecting to see American birds in June, and I had no knowledge of any eastern species of this nature.

I phoned Carl Downing and Adrian Hickman to discuss the possibilities. CD and AH explained that Violet-green Swallow *T. thalassina* had large white sides to the rump and a bare facial expression, with the only green gloss being on the cap, and white cheeks. It was also unlikely as a vagrant, being found in the Western States of North America. It was, however, the week of the Ancient Murrelet *Synthliboramphus antiquus* on Lundy, Devon, so anything was possible. Bahama Swallow *T. cyaneoviridis*, another unlikely vagrant, is much more like a Barn Swallow, with a deeply forked tail, so was easily eliminated. CD and AH, using *A Handbook to the Swallows and Martins of the World* (Turner & Rose 1989), were able to help me to rule out species originating in the East as well, and to identify the bird that I had found as a North American Tree Swallow.

On driving back to Porth Hellick, my panic had turned into elation. I re-entered the hide like a polaris missile to find, to my embarrassment, three visitors quietly and patiently birdwatching. They enquired as to my disposition and I told them of my earlier sighting. Luckily the bird was still present, but was in amongst a larger group of hirundines. We watched it until dusk, confident that it would be around the following day. Thankfully, it did stay in the Porth Hellick area until the morning of 10th June 1990, when it departed with the same group of hirundines with which it had arrived.

Hickman, D. J. D. 1995. Tree Swallow in Scilly: new to the Western Palearctic. *British Birds* 88, 381–384.

Tree Swallow is a widespread breeding bird in North America; it winters from the Gulf of Mexico to northern South America.

There have been two subsequent records:

Shetland Burrafirth, Unst, 29th May 2002

Dorset Christchurch, 31st October 2004 (BBRC decision awaited)

SEPTEMBER 1990

YELLOW-THROATED VIREO IN CORNWALL

Andrew Birch

I was birding in Kenidjack valley, north of St Just, Cornwall, during the morning of 20th September 1990. I had watched the area regularly during the previous seven years. Mentally, I tossed a coin and decided to check the bushes at the bottom of the valley just one more time. This paid off.

The valley seemed very quiet, but, at the last bush, around 09.00 GMT, I noticed a movement at the back and focused on the wings of what I thought could be a Pied Flycatcher *Ficedula hypoleuca*. When it flitted around to the front of the bush, however, it showed a gleaming yellow throat. It proceeded to flycatch in the open. I was so excited and shaking that I had to sit down and study the bird with my telescope.

I quickly ruled out the American wood-warblers *Dendroica* already on the British List, as I was impressed by the remarkable yellow throat and face, unstreaked, bright green upperparts, broad white wing-bars and the heavyish blue-grey bill and legs. After making mental notes I rushed back to the house to consult the *National Geographic Society Field Guide to the Birds of North America* (1983). To my surprise, none of the wood-warblers seemed to fit. Only two, the Pine Warbler *D. pinus* and the Cerulean Warbler *D. cerulea*, seemed even remotely close. I tried unsuccessfully to phone several local people, but eventually succeeded in speaking to Richard Millington and described the bird to him. He telephoned some other people to try to confirm the sighting. In the meantime, I went back for another look and, after 45 minutes' searching, I had brief, but good, views. I was reminded of Red-eyed Vireo *Vireo olivaceus*, by the jizz and the bluish bill and legs. Quickly turning my mind to vireos, I realised that it was, of course, a Yellow-throated Vireo *V. flavifrons*, a first for the Western Palearctic.

I left a friend, R. Ingham, at the site while I went back to the telephone. The first local birders arrived about midday, when the vireo was not showing. After an agonising two-hour wait, it reappeared and showed well to the few of us present that evening. Although quite elusive, the bird was seen by many hundreds of people during the weekend, was photographed (*Brit. Birds* 84: plate 253; 87: plates 96–101), and stayed until 27th September.

DESCRIPTION

Size Roughly that of a Robin *Erithacus rubecula*. Quite sturdy and long-winged, with a medium-length, slightly notched tail and a thick bill.

Plumage: Head Forehead, crown and nape bright olive-green. Bright yellow eye-ring continued forward to the base of the upper mandible, giving a spectacled effect. Thin green loral stripe and slightly darker eyebrow above the yellow stripe in front of the eye. Ear-coverts washed-out green, merging into yellow throat; *Upperparts* Most of mantle bright olive-green; lower back, scapulars and rump uniform blue-grey. Tail blackish, with white outer feathers; *Wings* Lesser coverts blue-grey, as scapulars; median coverts tipped white to form a clear wing-bar. Greater coverts also tipped white, forming a second, broad white bar. Inner greater coverts blue-grey. Tertials blackish, with clear white fringes. Secondaries blackish, with white fringes and a diffuse green wash. Alula and primary coverts black, with pale fringes. Primaries black, with clear white tips; *Underparts* Throat and breast bright daffodil-yellow, ending quite abruptly against white lower breast; belly and undertail-coverts silky white.

Bare Parts Eyes black. Bill and legs blue-grey.

The vireo foraged rather sluggishly and deliberately in bushes and also in Bracken *Pteridium aquilinum* and knotweed *Polygonum*. When it found an insect, it would often fly up to a bush to eat it. It sometimes flew up to 200 m to a new feeding area and could be elusive, often sitting motionless for several minutes at a time.

Birch, A. 1994. Yellow-throated Vireo: new to Britain and Ireland. *British Birds* 87, 362–365.

Yellow-throated Vireo breeds in the eastern USA and southeastern Canada; it winters in Central America and northern South America.

There have been no subsequent records.

1991

THE BIRDER'S YEAR

Adrian Pitches

1991 could be described as the year of the 'grip back' – birder's parlance for seeing a bird that others had previously seen and gloated about. Second helpings of **American Bittern, Sandhill Crane** and **Lark Sparrow** a decade after their last appearances were highlights of a year that yielded no Firsts for Britain apart from a belated acceptance onto the British List in December of **Barrow's Goldeneye** (see below).

For aficionados of *Aythya* ducks, January offered side-by-side **Lesser Scaup** and **Ring-necked Duck** on Milton Loch, Dumfries & Galloway, where Britain's third Lesser Scaup (another male) had taken up residence on 29th December 1990. And after the two birds in 1987 came third helpings of another duck – **Harlequin** – with a female at Wick, Highland, from 6th February to mid-May.

The male **Snowy Owl** in Lincolnshire found its way to north Norfolk in late March and was then seen for the final time at Spurn, East Yorkshire, on 30th March. The adult **American Bittern** which arrived at Marton Mere, Lancashire, in late January was another long-stayer, remaining until May. It was joyfully received by younger birders who missed the two long-stayers in 1981/82. Another long-stayer, the Northumberland **Terek Sandpiper**, first seen in November 1989, was last seen on 5th January. Orkney recorded its first live **Brünnich's Guillemot**, at Sule Skerry on 25th January. Another auk offered second helpings for the laggards who failed to see it in 1990: the **Ancient Murrelet** returned to Lundy on 14th April and stayed until late June. There were third helpings in 1992. More repeat offerings came from not one but three **Needle-tailed Swifts** which zoomed over Kent, Staffordshire and Shetland from late May to mid-June. Or it could have been one very energetic bird.

There was an 'armchair tick' in April when the BOU Records Committee split the Mediterranean forms of Manx Shearwater from Manx – and both these forms (Balearic and Yelkouan) were given specific status in October 2000, so we now have three shearwaters where once there was one.

A male **Citrine Wagtail** at Eyebrook Reservoir, Leicestershire, on 18th May was an excellent record for this landlocked county. And a female was at Hauxley on the

Northumberland coast three days earlier. A **Lark Sparrow** at Waxham, Norfolk, during 15th–17th May was an excellent 'grip back' for birders who failed to see the 1981 Suffolk bird. Again, it was a late-spring East Anglian record – but this bird had a shorter stay than its predecessor.

Three adult **Franklin's Gulls** was an excellent haul. The first was on Shetland in late May, followed by a long-stayer on Teesside from late June to September; another was in Norfolk on 30th June. Was it three or was it another well-travelled singleton? There were two **Bridled Terns** – a bird that commuted between Essex and Kent on 2nd June and a bird that hung around Scilly in July and August.

Two adult **Least Sandpipers** – in East Yorkshire in late July and Cornwall in late August – were the highlights of an indifferent autumn for waders. However, as seems highly likely, the **Greater Sand Plover** on the Don estuary, Aberdeenshire, on 18th–19th August will probably turn out to be a **Lesser Sand Plover** of the race *mongolus* and could actually become the First record of '**Mongolian Plover**' if and when this form is upgraded to species status. Further Mongolian Plovers were July birds in Hampshire in 2003 and in Lothian in 2004.

Shetland was the place to be in September 1991. Britain's second **Sandhill Crane** stayed for ten days on Mainland and then flew off to the Continent, touching down in Friesland in The Netherlands the following day. According to Keith Vinicombe's lucid analysis (Vinicombe & Cottridge 1996), the bird performed a classic reverse migration from northern Canada via Greenland and Iceland. As the crane departed, a **Baillon's Crake** arrived on Fair Isle.

Orkney struck back with Scotland's first **Yellow-billed Cuckoo** since 1970. It was found freshly dead on North Ronaldsay on 25th September. Another was caught and ringed in Surrey (!) on 17th October. Fair Isle's special birds this autumn were a **Blackpoll Warbler** on 30th September – and a **Little Swift** on 1st November.

Down south, there were **Bobolinks** in Devon in mid-September and on Scilly in mid-October. Scilly also had three **Grey-cheeked Thrushes** (the first was early, on 22nd September) and, for the second year running, **Swainson's Thrush, Eyebrowed Thrush** and **Isabelline Wheatear**. Away from Scilly, the October treats were two **Nutcrackers**, in Hampshire and Staffordshire – and three **Desert Warblers**. Like the last bird, in 1988, one was on the Isle of Wight; the others were on Flamborough Head, East Yorkshire, and at Seasalter, Kent. All stayed into November. And another 'grip back' turned up in November: Britain's sixth **Chimney Swift** enrolled at St Andrew's University, Fife, for three days. It was the second for Scotland.

The latest arrival of the autumn, which alas failed to arrive on the British List, was the **Mugimaki Flycatcher** beside the River Humber on 16th–17th November. A first-year male bird that arrived on a foggy northeast coast in late autumn, it seemed to have all the requisite credentials for an authentic 'Sibe' but it languishes on Category D, its origin suspect. A similar fate befell the **Brown Flycatcher** which arrived the following July on Fair Isle. But, just as the Lark Sparrow had to await a second coming to justify its inclusion on the British List ten years later, maybe the Mugimaki Flycatcher will one day be elevated to Category A when another 'flicker' materialises on an east-coast headland in November. What a 'grip back' that would be.

A NEW WIFE – AND SEVERAL GULL FRIENDS

Martin Garner

Major life changes, the pundits advise, should not be done all at once. 1991 was my first year of marriage; I moved house to a new area (Luton, Bedfordshire); and started a new job. Although each was a form of upheaval, the most dramatic of all was the effect on my birding! I married Sharon in August 1990. Thankfully, she did not have my passion for birds. While the idea of finding a fellow enthusiast has crossed my mind in the past, a girl who could share my tolerances of sleeping under hedges and hitchhiking with lorry drivers in the middle of the night might not be the best choice for a life-long companion. Instead my gal had never been camping, or travelled further north than Carlisle. And she didn't know about obsessive birders. Her shocked expletives upon discovering, under the bed, my suppressed suitcase full of bird wings, and later my shorebird carcasses among the Chicken Kiev in the freezer, caused me to reflect that perhaps I had not been quite so disclosing about my passion as I might have been!

The combination of a new partner, a new job and moving (to a landlocked county with no major migration flyway) meant a drastic change in birding opportunities. Fortunately, I am the sort who enjoys a fresh challenge and so 1991 was the year that this worm was forced to turn. I spent January to August based at Blackheath in London, moving to Luton in September.

My memory of the start of the year is Arctic Redpolls. Hilbre devotee and old friend Andy Stoddart had been finding them along the north Norfolk coast from October 1990, leading the pack in resolving the identification of tricky first-winters. Together we had seen our first 'snowball' Arctic, back in 1985. Four, maybe six, with clean white rumps accompanied that '85 bird, but then only classic adult males were considered worthy of any real attention. Following Andy's lead, I was keen to reacquaint myself with a fresh identification challenge. In late January, I headed up to Lincolnshire and had a fabulous day with an immature male Snowy Owl there. Nearby, at the almost snowbound Kirby Moor, while some Parrot Crossbills proved elusive, studying the subtleties of at least two Arctic Redpolls was the real highlight.

February saw me chauffeured through the snow by Frodsham stalwart and best buddy, Billy Morton, up to Marton Mere, Lancashire, to see an American Bittern. I had to plan trips now (a new phenomenon), but being late for twitches brought an opportunity to enjoy the birds away from crowds (a comforting compensation). In such circumstances I even managed to get reasonable shots of the bittern with my cheap camera kit (see *BB* 84 plate 173).

Still enamoured with the Arctic Redpolls, I began to concentrate on the theme of focusing upon identification challenges rather than chasing the rarities. I went to see more Arctics in a fantastic Mealy Redpoll flock at Church Wood in Kent. This flock seemed to contain more than the two obvious candidates I grabbed at. As if to drive the point home, Andy's pioneering example paid off when he discovered no fewer than 20 Arctic Redpolls (a British record) on the small heath behind his house in Norwich in early March.

The spring saw the return of the Ancient Murrelet to Lundy (off my target list), and a bird-filled Elmley saw me arriving after the crowds had departed to collect Marsh Sandpiper, Temminck's Stint and American Wigeon, although the lilac-headed 'Channel Wagtail' on the Elmley floods intrigued me again as it had in the past at Abberton Reservoir.

Unblocked species of May was undoubtedly a Lark Sparrow at Waxham, Norfolk, which I managed to get on its last day, but perhaps a more significant event for my birding occurred a week later on the Swale in Kent. I managed good views of a Broad-billed Sandpiper there, but what fascinated me more was the challenge of separating the two subspecies of Black-tailed Godwits. I feasted on a flock of stunning *islandica* Black-tailed Godwits and what I took to be *tundrae* Ringed Plovers – so swarthy and clean-looking next to the pale and 'moth-eaten plumaged' local breeders. More to be discovered here methinks!

The summer was fairly quiet as Sharon and I finished college courses, then we headed off on my first non-birding holiday, with her family to the middle of France. I only managed to see a few Cirl Buntings and Serins, which were insufficient to draw me away from a swimming pool and reading *Lord of the Rings*.

Autumn in Luton saw me having to knuckle down to my first proper job. Sad but true, I quickly developed a mantra of, upon hearing news of a rarity, "It's OK I don't need it." To be honest, it worked pretty well. The only Bedfordshire rarity which I tried for and dipped on was a Penduline Tit at Priory Country Park, which was already on my smug self-found list.

Other birds in autumn 1991, like the Eyebrowed Thrush on Scilly, the Nutcracker in Staffordshire and three Desert Warblers, were already under my belt. The only bird I would have cherished seeing was the Mugimaki Flycatcher on Humberside – a once-in-a-lifetime experience by my reckoning. So, with the general lack of travel, I had to activate Plan B.

The most interesting avian arrivals in winter in Bedfordshire were the gulls. Some 4,000 of them turned up during November and December of 1991, and Brogborough Lake became my regular haunt. I have always been fascinated with 'Herring Gulls' with yellow legs – and northern *argentatus* Herring Gulls – going back to Rob Hume's 1979 *British Birds* paper on a West Midlands gull roost.

I had claimed all kinds of odd gulls in my native Cheshire, often to deaf ears. So, learning the lessons from mild-mannered Stoddart and his remarkable progress with Arctic Redpolls, I decided to 'dig in' with my own focused investigations, while at the same time enjoying a great married life. Little did I know where it would lead!

Martin Garner lives in Sheffield. A renowned gull enthusiast and identification expert, he is currently working on a book about 'Pioneer Birding'.

NOVEMBER 1979
BARROW'S GOLDENEYE IN STRATHCLYDE

John Knowler

On 4th November 1979, the Glasgow Birdwatchers' Club met shortly after 10.00 GMT in the carpark at the mouth of the River Irvine in Irvine, Strathclyde. There was a strong southwesterly wind (force 6 or 7) and the sea was very rough after a gale the previous day; the sky was cloudy, giving frequent rain.

A little before 10.20, a drake goldeneye *Bucephala* landed in the surf about 100 m from me and then swam into somewhat calmer water about 75 m from the watching party, which included Mrs V. Carrick, D. Watson, R. Lambie, J. Marshall, I. Rintoul and myself. At the time, there was no rain, and visibility was quite good. In the calmer water, the bird was obviously not a Common Goldeneye *B. clangula*, and I identified it as a Barrow's Goldeneye *B. islandica*. The first feature to become obvious was the white facial crescent on an otherwise black head; the crescent was pronounced and easily visible, rounded at the base and pointed at the top. The head was conspicuously bulbous and very dark, although I could not detect the colour of the sheen. In place of the conspicuous white, black-striped scapulars of a Common Goldeneye, there was a row of short, white bars on the very dark back. The flanks, breast and neck were white.

The bird remained close to us for one or two minutes. It was alone, but engaged in spasmodic, half-hearted head-throw displays, perhaps being aware of two female Common Goldeneyes in flight, which it shortly joined. It proved to be considerably larger than the female Common Goldeneyes.

Knowler, J. T. 1995. Barrow's Goldeneye in Strathclyde: new to Britain and Ireland. *British Birds* 88, 104–106.

Barrow's Goldeneye is found in Iceland, Greenland and North America.

There has been one subsequent record.

Aberdeenshire Meikle Loch/Ythan Estuary and Loch of Strathbeg, male, 13th May to at least 14th June 2005 (BBRC decision awaited).

THE BIRDER'S YEAR

Tim Cleeves

It was probably the spring which made 1992 a memorable year. Three species were seen for the first time in Britain but, in the end, only two of them made it onto the British List. Early winter 1992 delivered two **Pine Buntings**. One, at Dagenham Chase, Greater London, proved to be a real crowd puller. The tenth-ever record of **Pine Grosbeak** arrived on Shetland at the end of March and stayed for four weeks, boosting airline profits at a quiet time of the year. On April 9th, the **Ancient Murrelet** returned to Lundy, Devon, for the third time, but it left only 20 days later.

On 2nd May, at Portland Bill in Dorset, a First for Britain was discovered – **Lesser Short-toed Lark**. This bird, expertly described and identified, did not stay long enough to reach the audience it deserved and by the next morning it was gone. At the time, prior to the Irish Rare Birds Committee's review, only Ireland had recorded this species, with four flocks totalling 42 birds at four locations between January 1956 and March 1958.

The most significant event in terms of rare birds during the year was the fantastic movement of **Red-footed Falcons** to the near Continent and into Britain. Between 14th May and 28th June, there were 112 seen in Britain, making this by far the largest-ever influx into Britain. In Denmark and The Netherlands, there were as many as 1,000 in total.

High pressure and warm air built over Britain in the second week of May and then began to develop over Scandinavia, giving a prolonged period of southeast winds particularly useful for drifting birds towards Scotland. By early June, Shetland was bathed in glorious sunshine, and a temperature of 24°C was recorded there on 9th June. Scarce passage migrants on Shetland (including the outer Isles) were extremely impressive, with a record 100 **Icterine Warblers** between 17th May and 12th June, up to 18 **Golden Orioles**, and a minimum of 47 **Marsh Warblers** breaking another species record.

Other eastern birds were in evidence. Even allowing for some duplication, spring 1992 was remarkable for another five species in particular. Up to 17 **Cattle Egrets**

179

were seen, including eight together on 3rd May in Hertfordshire. And there were 17 **White-winged Black Terns**, including some multiple arrivals – three groups of three and two groups of two. Passerines were not forgotten either, with 15 **Greenish Warblers**, the first-ever records (three) of spring **Booted Warblers** and ten **Black-headed Buntings**.

At Filey Brigg, North Yorkshire, a male **Spectacled Warbler** was an excellent find on 24th May. As all previous claims of this species had been found lacking in a review by the records committees, this splendid individual became a First for Britain. So, two Firsts in the back of the net by June – not bad going. Spurn, East Yorkshire, scored heavily on 8th June with Britain's second **Marmora's Warbler**, keeping up a great Yorkshire average for this species. In early June, a **Trumpeter Finch** was photographed near Durness, Highland, only the seventh ever and at a typically unusual far-northern locality.

On 1st July, a third new bird for Britain was found, this time on Fair Isle – a first-summer **Brown Flycatcher**. Paul Harvey describes the discovery and subsequent fate of this bird in his account of his final season on Fair Isle (see below). July continued to surprise when an adult **Red-necked Stint**, only the second British record, was unearthed at Cley – it stayed to delight visiting birders until 3rd August. A **Baillon's Crake** was trapped in Sussex on 11th August and a **Greater Sand Plover** appeared in Essex and Kent for five days.

August still had enough life in it to deliver two cracking warblers in an uncanny echo of the double whammy on Shetland in autumn 1990. A **Yellow Warbler** was trapped on North Ronaldsay, Orkney, on 24th August – only the third British record and on a similar date to the First – on Bardsey on 29th August 1964. Back with Western Palearctic goodies, a first-winter **Rüppell's Warbler** at Holme, Norfolk, from 31st August to 4th September, a British fourth, was a terrific find.

September included some real 'blockers', starting with a **Hooded Warbler** on St Kilda, Western Isles, on 10th September. Then there was a mind-blowing North Ronaldsay hat-trick with Britain's third **Yellow-browed Bunting**, a **Pallas's Grasshopper Warbler** and, to open October, a female **Siberian Thrush**, the fourth for Britain. The 'Sibe Thrush' was the first to stay long enough to be twitched, creating joy amongst all airline charter companies flying into Orkney.

The rest of October 1992, and indeed the rest of the birding year, was fairly quiet but the Isles of Scilly still managed to produce a **Northern Parula** and a **Black-throated Thrush**. An **Eyebrowed Thrush** on Fair Isle was a very good find. The second **White-throated Sparrow** of the year was found at Willingham in Lincolnshire and it overwintered to give everyone a chance to see it.

The spring overshoots, the remarkable warblers from the Mediterranean, Siberia and the United States, the first Lesser Short-toed Lark, Spectacled Warbler and Brown Flycatcher, all made 1992 gripping enough.

MY FINAL SEASON ON FAIR ISLE
Paul Harvey

I had the good fortune to spend the first few months of the year in the Caribbean – a week in Trinidad, a few days chasing endemics in St Lucia and then six weeks doing some ornithological work in Dominica – finding time to take in all the endemics of course! Then it was back to Fair Isle for my final season as Warden and what a season it was to prove to be. The Observatory is very much a team effort and I was incredibly fortunate to have a first-rate ornithological team comprising Roger Riddington, Steve Votier and Roy Taylor.

Imagine my surprise when, on arriving at the P&O ferry terminal in Aberdeen on 3rd April for the journey north to Shetland, I found myself staring at a host of familiar birding faces. I had made no contact, other than with family, so was completely unaware that a Pine Grosbeak was waiting in Lerwick! The rest of April proved to be fairly uneventful, the highlight watching Leeds United's epic romp to the Championship, made all the better because it was Manchester United that finished second!

By early May, desperation was beginning to set in, the wind seemingly stuck in the western quarter. On the 8th, a phone call from Shetland telling of an unprecedented passage of 470 Pomarine Skuas past Watsness did little to raise the spirits!

Determined, and armed with scopes, we headed for Hoini early next morning – surely at least a few would pass within sight of Fair Isle. Drawing a blank, we returned for breakfast assuming that the passage had stopped; how wrong we were – a further 2,093 were logged off Watsness that day! If I needed confirmation that seawatching from Fair Isle truly was a waste of time, then I guess this was it.

At last, on 13th May, a sign of change. The first scattering of true summer migrants and a 'peep' found by Steve Votier that was soon confirmed as Scotland's first Semipalmated Sandpiper. Two days later Fair Isle's third Firecrest appeared, followed on the 17th by the first of no less than nine Red-throated Pipits. As the month continued, so the pace quickened: the first Nightjar since 1976, a Rustic Bunting, a fine male Red-footed Falcon and then on 27th a stunning arrival of Spotted Flycatchers – numbering 350 individuals! These were accompanied by 20 Red-backed Shrikes, eight Bluethroats, 11 Wood, two Marsh and two Subalpine Warblers, four Rosefinches, a Shorelark and a Honey-buzzard. The next fortnight was exhausting. The migrants kept coming and the long daylight hours had to be exploited fully – I had seen Fair Isle when it was quiet all too often and did not want to miss a minute of the action.

The best day of the spring was 9th June. We were trying to relocate a female Black-headed Bunting that I had found near the airstrip (three more were found next day), when Roy came belting across the airstrip telling us of a warbler at Field that he couldn't place to genus. Following in his wake, we were soon able to confirm it as a Paddyfield. Early evening I heard Steve bellowing in the distance and looking across to South Green. There, flying north, was the Isle's first Stone-curlew since 1974. Not to be outdone, Roger was busy finding a Great Reed Warbler at the Hill Dyke. The back-up cast was impressive too, a Quail, single Greenish and Marsh and ten Icterine Warblers, and six Rosefinches. It was almost a relief when the anticyclone responsible for so much enjoyment finally slipped away on the 12th.

By early July we were well into seabird work, a rewarding aspect of Observatory life, and one that many folk are unaware of. Once experienced, the noise, smell and blur of activity in the centre of a seabird colony is never to be forgotten. And 1992 was a rare good year for seabirds, with an abundance of sand eels. In comparison, early morning trap rounds were now something of a chore, to be missed at all costs if someone else was willing to do the legwork. On 1st July it was my turn. A little over an hour later, however, I returned to the Observatory elated having just found and trapped Britain's first Brown Flycatcher. Not least because my only other first had recently been relegated from Category A to Category D! Surely this one would pass the test – after all, a bevy of Arctic Warblers have turned up in early July and most 'eastern' species breeding in Scandinavia are not on territory there until mid- or late June. Furthermore, a Red-backed Shrike, Marsh Warbler and Pacific Golden Plover were present at the same time as the fly-catcher. Alas no, the BOURC in their infinite wisdom stuck this into Category D too, despite the fact that they could not trace a single one in captivity!

And so to autumn. A good start with a quick trip to Shetland for an all-important county tick, a Sardinian Warbler. August produced Ring-billed Gull and Montagu's Harrier (two of six island firsts in 1992!) – along with three Greenish Warblers, Woodchat Shrike and a Great Snipe. September too started well and on the 13th I was delighted at finding Shetland's first Solitary Sandpiper on the small pool at Field. The pleasure was short-lived though. As I signalled to observers, I noticed Roger emerging from the Field croft yelling, 'It is one isn't it?!' The ******* had flushed it from the mid-den some 15 minutes earlier and, in keeping with tradition in the days before mobile phone coverage, had gone into the croft to 'phone it out'! Talk about feeling gutted!

Booted Warbler, Yellow-breasted Bunting and Sprosser soon followed, along with good numbers of scarce migrants. The 27th promised to be one of those magical Fair Isle days – birds were literally dropping out of the sky and by mid-morning seven Yellow-broweds and a Lanceolated Warbler had appeared. Soon though, dense fog shrouded the island and put paid to the proceedings. This cost us dear as the Yellow-browed Bunting stopped some 20 miles short on North Ronaldsay! Next day, to my continuing regret, I turned down an opportunity to join a charter to see the bird. It remains a much-wanted lifer and no matter how determined you are, the old adage of 'staying here and finding something better' never, ever works!

Early October saw continued easterly winds, large numbers of common migrants and more rarities. Single Pechora, Red-throated, and three Olive-backed Pipits, a snowball of an Arctic Redpoll and, best of all, a fine Eyebrowed Thrush. How I wish I could have swapped that for North Ronaldsay's Siberian Thrush, though! Things quietened down considerably in November, with a Woodlark the highlight. Finally, an early Christmas present arrived in the form of a Mute Swan! Only Fair Isle's third but more importantly the 214th species of the year – we had comprehensively beaten the Observatory's best-ever species total. A fitting end to a fantastic year.

Paul Harvey migrated to Shetland from his native Dorset in 1984. He was warden of Fair Isle from 1989 to 1992. He's now manager of the Shetland Biological Records Centre and a member of the BB Rarities Committee.

MAY 1992

LESSER SHORT-TOED LARK IN DORSET

Ian Dickie and Keith Vinicombe

During the morning of 2nd May 1992, IRD left the bird observatory at Portland Bill, Dorset, to search the 'Top Fields' for migrants. He was accompanied by a Young Ornithologists' Club group, of which he was an assistant leader. At about 10.10 GMT, he noticed a small, pale passerine as it flew away over a large barley field in the dry limestone valley opposite the observatory. He followed it through binoculars but moved on after failing to relocate it with a telescope during five minutes of scanning. At 17.40, he returned to the field with the YOC group while the leaders, Anna Hughes and Charles Wilkins, prepared dinner. The odd bird again flew out from near the path. This time, it settled some 40 m away and was viewable on the ground. It was clearly a small, pale lark.

IRD returned to the observatory to report his find and began discussing the identity of the lark with Martin Cade, the assistant warden. Quite sensibly, MC suggested that it might be a pale Skylark *Alauda arvensis*. IRD could not accept this, although he was unable to suggest a conclusive alternative. A number of other birders in the lounge eavesdropped on the conversation, but no-one showed any real interest. IRD returned to the field and, a short while later, was joined by AH, whose first impression was that it was a Short-toed Lark *Calandrella brachydactyla*. At this stage, however, it was first heard to call, and its small size also became apparent when it was compared directly with a Whinchat *Saxicola rubetra*. AH immediately ordered the fastest YOC member to run back to the observatory, where the incumbents at last erupted from their semi-somnambulant state and were soon running breathlessly up the hill. CW, who was already on his way, was the first to suggest that it might be a Lesser Short-toed Lark *C. rufescens*.

Pretty soon, there were some 20 observers gathered on the track, including S. J. Broyd, MC, R. & S. Hibbett, R. Newton, I. Pembroke, R. J. Senior, R. Taylor and KEV. The bird was feeding at a range of perhaps 40–50 m but slightly against the light. After a quick binocular view, KEV pronounced it a Short-toed Lark. Once in the telescopes, however, it soon became apparent that it was 'wrong' for that species. Most obviously, it had a clearly streaked breast band, a small bill, and a crested effect, while it lacked both a prominent supercilium and a strong median-covert bar. Unaware of CW's earlier suggestion, we excitedly began to discuss the realistic possibility that it was a Lesser Short-toed Lark and we edged closer in an attempt to see the all-important primary projection. Inevitably, we flushed it across the field, but it called loudly twice, and those of us who were familiar with the call became convinced that it was indeed a Lesser. As it flew, E. T. Welland arrived from the opposite direction, having been told that there was a 'funny lark' in Top Fields. He was also familiar with both species abroad, and he quite independently recognised the call as being that of Lesser Short-toed and was confident enough to suggest this identification to SJB.

The bird settled on the path, near where it had originally been flushed. Despite close views (down to 30 m), it was still not possible to see the primaries as the lark grovelled in a small hollow or frustratingly contrived to keep them hidden behind vegetation. Eventually, it flew again and proved to be rather flighty until it settled on an area of bare earth in the Northeast corner of the field. There it gave excellent prolonged, unobscured views at about 30 m, and at this point we could all clearly see that it had a good 'half-inch' (1.3-cm) primary projection. Around this time, we were joined by several local observers who had been summoned by a frantic telephone call. These included P. A. Coe, P. Kent, K. Pritchard, I. Prophet and D. & G. Walbridge. The lark was kept under observation until about 20.15, when it flew over to the far side of the field. By this time, it had been seen by perhaps 30 observers, several of whom were very familiar with the species in Spain, the Canary Islands, North Africa or the Middle East, and others with the eastern forms in China.

The following is a synopsis of the five submitted descriptions and GW's BBRC comments.

Description

In general appearance and structure, it was a small, evenly proportioned, compact *Calandrella* lark, rather short-tailed and similar in size to Short-toed Lark. It often appeared somewhat finch-like because of its small, stubby bill and MC stated that, at first glance, it reminded him of a Linnet *Carduelis cannabina*, an effect heightened by its bill. SJB considered it 'noticeably smaller' than nearby Sky Larks, while ETW noted that it was 'much smaller' than a Skylark which he had flushed on his approach. In his initial views, IRD considered it to be slightly shorter than a Whinchat in direct comparison. When feeding, it crept quietly but busily along the ground, sometimes in a low, shuffling manner. The back was rounded and it sometimes appeared hunched, but it was longer-necked and more upright when alert. Initially, the wings were held relaxed, with the primaries drooping below the level of the tail, but later, when more active and alert, they were held on a level with the top of the tail. When disturbed, it would often creep away rather than fly. When flushed, it flew fast and direct, low over the ground in typical *Calandrella* manner, and it would drop straight to the ground from full flight, with no hovering. It was basically pale sandy-brown in appearance, considerably paler than Skylark, and GW considered it to be a fawner or greyer shade of brown than the greyer-type Short-toed Larks which he has seen. In flight, it looked quite strikingly pale and sandy, an effect heightened by the very pale belly and underwing. It showed a darker tail, with contrasting pale outer tail feathers, but it lacked a pale or white trailing edge to the wing.

The following more-detailed notes expand on the above:

Head Short-toed Lark has a head shape and pattern rather reminiscent of female House Sparrow *Passer domesticus*, with a largish bill, a usually rounded crown, a fairly prominent supercilium and a dark line behind the eye. This bird failed to give this impression. Its head usually looked less rounded than that of Short-toed, with a somewhat steeper forehead. It quite often showed a crested effect, with a sharp angle at the crown/nape juncture, this often being caused by the wind catching the rear crown feathers; they were more typically laid flat when feeding in sheltered conditions. It is important to note that the raised crown feathers did not impart such an obviously crested appearance as on Skylark. Compared with Short-toed, it had a rather plain-faced appearance within which the dark eye stood out. The crown was evenly and finely streaked brown on a sandy-brown background, perhaps recalling Skylark. The buffy supercilium was narrow and faint and blended well with the rest of the head. There was only a narrow inconspicuous dark line behind the eye. The eye itself was surrounded by an obvious pale creamy-buff ring which merged with the lores and supercilium around the front of the eye. The most distinctive facial character was a narrow, but quite noticeable, brown line which extended back from the bottom of the lower mandible, curving upwards below the lores and ending approximately level with the rear of the eye, thus forming the lower border to the pale eye-surround. Ear coverts plain and variously described as light sandy or buffish-white. Indistinct dark moustachial stripe merged into dark ear-covert surround (comprised more of streaks than a solid area of colour) which curved up to meet narrow dark eye-stripe, thus giving complete border to ear-coverts. To KEV, whole facial pattern was characteristic of Lesser Short-toed Lark. GW thought that nape was contrastingly paler and unstreaked, but IRD described it as sandy with dark flecks visible only during the best views.

Underparts Throat and lower neck pale buffish-white. Across the breast was a noticeable pectoral band of profuse, even, fine streaking, the general impression recalling Skylark. The band was less deep in the middle, but was continuous right across the breast. At the sides, the streaking became more organised and more heavily lined. The streaking was delicate, profuse and unlike the more random streaking shown by some Short-toed Larks. It failed to show even a hint of dark patches on the breast sides. Underparts variously described as 'pale with a sandy wash', 'pale buff' or 'sandy-grey'. In hindsight, KEV thought them buffer and less white than on most Short-toeds, while GW also considered them buffer than on that species. Flanks faintly streaked.

Upperparts Pale sandy-brown with distinct greyish cast, heavily streaked dark brown (perhaps heaviest on lower mantle). Two heavy blackish streaks down scapulars, these feathers overhanging innermost wing-coverts. Lower back, rump, uppertail-coverts and closed tail sandy with light greyish cast.

Wings Median coverts, greater coverts and tertials brown, noticeably edged buff. Lacked the obvious dark median-covert bar shown by most Short-toed Larks (which recalls that of Tawny Pipit *Anthus campestris*), because centres of median coverts were brown – not dark brown or black – and did not coalesce to form a bar; in fact, individual feathers could be picked out because of their broad, light buffy-brown fringes. Lesser coverts appeared basically sandy-grey, while primary coverts were noticeably blacker than other wing-coverts. IRD noted secondaries and primaries as being slightly paler than rest of upperparts, forming paler wedge back from the alula, under the tertials. MC noted underwing as pale, 'perhaps dirty whitish'.

Primary Projection This was obviously the key feature and the one that caused us the most frustration. At any distance, it was very difficult to determine where the tertials ended and where the primaries began and the evaluation of this was hampered by the lark frequently moving through the newly sprouting barley. At closer ranges, it frustratingly managed to conceal this vital part of its anatomy behind vegetation or in hollows. On many occasions, we were 95% certain that we could see a primary projection, but it took us a good three-quarters of an hour to see it well enough to be 100% certain. The problem was caused by the fact that the primaries themselves were very faded, sandy-brown, and so appeared more-or-less concolorous with the tertials. When seen well, however, it was possible to count down three tertials from the shortest uppermost to the longest lower one and a primary projection of about half an inch (1.3 cm) was clearly visible beyond the lowest tertial. MC considered that the exposed primaries were approximately equal to half the length of the overlying tertials. In a close, semi-back-on view, the primary projection was in fact obvious. Viewing through a 50× *Questar* telescope at 30 m, SJB was able to count three visible primary tips with the space between the tips of the second and third being greatest. RH, GW and ETW were also able to view the primaries through the *Questar*. There was no question of the bird lacking the covering tertials. Although the tertials were also worn (particularly the longest), it was nevertheless quite easy to count them and to see their pale buffy edges. The primary projection was clearly visible on both wings.

Bare Parts: Bill Very distinctive: noticeably small and pointed, and much less conspicuous than the more sparrow-like bill of Short-toed Lark. Structurally similar to that of a Little Bunting *Emberiza pusilla*, but with the mandibles convex, not concave (IRD). Quite conical, with straighter mandibles than Short-toed, more like Linnet's in both shape and proportions (KEV). Small and somewhat stubby, on occasions giving the head a small finch-like appearance; when concentrating on the head, it was the small bill which always stood out (SJB). In colour, it had a dark tip and a greyer base (described by MC as 'grey-horn'); *Legs* Quite noticeably orange or fleshy-orange.

Call Clearly and loudly heard on three occasions, less clearly on others. It fitted exactly KEV's memory of the call of Lesser Short-toed Lark, which he had last heard in Morocco in 1990. Immediately after it called the first time, he wrote it down as: 'a rapid, almost buzzing "ddddr", sounding like four notes concertinaed together'. He added that 'this call was obviously different from the more usual calls of Short-toed Lark', which, in his most recent notes, he had noted as a hard 't-trip trip', 'chip chip' or as a 'hard chirruping'. The call was, in fact, difficult to describe and this accounted for a variety of transcriptions by the various observers. SJB described it as a 'distinctive, buzzy "chrrr", given several times as the bird flew from one spot to another'. ETW considered it 'a loud buzzing churring note', quite dissimilar to the 'hard chirrupy call' which he associates with Short-toed Lark. GW variously transcribed it as 'dddrr', 'ttttr', 'trrrr' or 'drrrr' and as 'a rasping dry rattle, very distinctive and quite different from Short-toed, being lower in pitch and louder'. MC described it as a short, dry, quite buzzing 'dddr'. As an interesting postscript, MC again encountered the species in southern Morocco in November 1992 and he first detected and correctly identified the birds by 'the dry, buzzing call identical to that heard from the Portland bird'.

Dickie, I. R. & Vinicombe, K. E. 1995. Lesser Short-toed Lark in Dorset: new to Britain. British Birds 88, 593–599.

Lesser Short-toed Lark is found from the Canary Islands across North Africa and the Middle East into eastern Asia.

There have been no subsequent records.

MAY 1992

SPECTACLED WARBLER IN NORTH YORKSHIRE

Craig Thomas, Richard Harbird and Peter Dunn

Mid to late May 1992 was dominated by settled anticyclonic conditions with prevailing easterly winds and coastal mist. Conditions at Filey, North Yorkshire, were therefore near perfect when CCT and REH decided to 'work' the Long Hedge towards the Tip at 08.15 GMT on 24th May.

After 400 m with nothing of note, CCT spotted a movement in the hedge 20 m ahead. Although largely obscured, the bird was clearly a warbler with dark lores, but initial thoughts of Lesser Whitethroat *Sylvia curruca* were quashed when it hopped onto an exposed branch. CCT's heartbeat quickened as he immediately switched to the telescope before shouting over to REH that he had found 'an interesting *Sylvia*'. Within seconds, REH had ploughed through a hole in the hedge so small that a Goldcrest *Regulus regulus* would normally have struggled to get through, and together they watched the warbler feeding out in the open. Several features fitted Spectacled Warbler *S. conspicillata*, notably the small body size, blackish lores, bright rufous wings, pale lower mandible, white throat contrasting with salmon-pink underparts, bright legs and small primary projection. After studying the bird for a further five minutes, the suggestion was made, via the CB radio, to PJD, who was ringing in the Country Park, that he should bring the nets to trap 'an interesting *Sylvia*'. He arrived in no time at all.

Within seconds, the bird started to call and sing briefly and, as the initial scepticism of a gathering crowd waned, all present soon agreed, but could not really believe, that it had to be a Spectacled Warbler. PJD put up the net and, with almost military precision, the first attempt netted a Common Whitethroat *S. communis* and then the Spectacled Warbler. As they were extracted and held side by side, the size difference caused euphoria.

Both birds were taken back to the Country Park to be processed; the Spectacled Warbler was held for 30 minutes before being released – unringed – into Arndale, ahead of advancing rain clouds (PJD had concentrated on getting a full in-hand description and biometrics, but forgot to ring it before release). The bird was released well away from crop fields to eliminate potential damage, and Arndale, with its easy access, seemed ideal. The Spectacled Warbler thought otherwise, however, and it was not seen again that day. To everyone's relief, it was relocated in the field hedges the following morning and, despite crowd pressure, was seen well by 1,500 visitors over the next five days, with no crop damage; it was last seen at dusk on 29th May.

DESCRIPTION

Size and Structure A typical *Sylvia* warbler structurally, approximately two-thirds the size of a Common Whitethroat. Distinctly shorter-winged, with a primary projection one-third the length of the exposed tertials. Wing length = 58 mm.

In flight, combination of short wings and relatively long tail produced distinctive appearance, not unlike that of a Long-tailed Tit *Aegithalos caudatus*. Tail length = 52.7 mm.

Head Medium grey in tone, with subtle brownish suffusion on nape contrasting with blackish lores which extended to just above and below eye. White eye-ring broader above, with small break at rear of eye. Chin and throat pure white.

Upperparts Mantle, back and scapulars warm brown, though not so rufous as on wings, with contrasting greyish-brown rump.

Wings Primaries brown with heavily abraded fringes. Two innermost secondaries brown, relieved by bright chestnut edges. Rest of secondaries duller, but nevertheless forming bright chestnut wing-panel in combination with broad-edged greater coverts. Tertials heavily abraded, with sharply demarcated dark centres and chestnut edges. Alula dark brown, edged buff.

Tail Dark brown with conspicuous white centres to outer feathers, decreasing on inner tail feathers.

Underparts Breast, flanks and upper belly salmon-pink contrasting with demarcated white throat. Lower belly and undertail-coverts buff.

Bare Parts Bill appeared thinner and relatively longer than that of Common Whitethroat. Dark horn upper mandible with yellowish cutting edge. Lower mandible yellowish-pink at base, with distal one-third dark horn. Iris rich chestnut and orbital ring dark brown. Legs and feet bright orange-yellow.

Voice Song quieter and more melodic than that of Common Whitethroat, interspersed with sweeter notes. Call a very distinctive, even 'trrr', uttered frequently.

Over the duration of its stay, the Spectacled Warbler gradually became easier to see and, indeed, appeared to have set up territory in one particular stretch of hedge, where it could be watched and photographed. Its departure, on the night of 29th/30th May, coincided with the arrival of a weather front.

Status in the UK

The Spectacled Warbler has had a rough passage onto the British List. The first accepted record, at Spurn, East Yorkshire, during 21st–31st October 1968 (*Brit. Birds* 71: 53–58), was subsequently proved from in-the-hand photographs to have been a first-winter female Subalpine Warbler *S. cantillans*. Subsequent records had been accepted, of a male at Porthgwarra, Cornwall, on 17th October 1969 (*Brit. Birds*

71: 84–85), and a male on Fair Isle, Shetland, on 4th–5th June 1979 (*Brit. Birds* 73: 523), but, following the rejection of the Spurn bird, the burden of proof which fell upon these records increased, since either could now have to stand alone as the first British record. In the event, a review judged that, although it was by no means certain that either bird had been misidentified, the amount of detail supplied in support of the two records was not sufficient for either to remain on the British List, and both were rejected.

Thomas, C. C., Harbird, R. E. & Dunn, P. J. 1998. Spectacled Warbler in North Yorkshire: new to Britain and Ireland. *British Birds* 91, 225–230.

Spectacled Warbler breeds from the Canary Islands across southern Europe to the Middle East. The western populations winter just south of the Sahara.

There have been three subsequent records:

Suffolk Landguard, male, 26th April–2nd May 1997

Devon Roborough Down, first-summer in song, 3rd–6th June 1999

Scilly Tresco, first-winter, 15th–21st October 2000

THE BIRDER'S YEAR

Tim Cleeves

The year 1993 was one of consolidation, rather than one filled with Firsts for Britain. However, the Pacific Swift at Cley was the first record of the species seen over British soil from the outset (the bird recorded in 1981 was caught on a gas-platform 45 km off the Norfolk coast, taken by helicopter to Beccles, Suffolk, and released).

January provided a **White-throated Sparrow** at Willingham, Lincolnshire, which had lingered since December 1992. A dead **Red-billed Tropicbird** was found above the strand line on the shore at Landguard, Suffolk. It was impossible to trace its origin. On March 27th, an exhausted **Brünnich's Guillemot** drifted past Musselburgh Lagoons, East Lothian. At least it was alive – just.

April was a quiet month for extremely rare birds, but a **Sociable Plover** at Egglington, Derbyshire, on 17th April was a real highlight and this individual was probably the one seen later in the spring in Lincolnshire and Norfolk.

On 2nd May, a female **Black-throated Thrush** was found at Lydd, Kent. A second-summer **Pallid Harrier** was seen in Perth & Kinross on 5th May, only the fourth ever and the first for 40 years! An **Alpine Accentor** on Lundy, Devon, on 8th May was an excellent find. Two records of **Bridled Tern** occurred – one at Rye, East Sussex, on 16th May and another at Earl's Barton Gravel Pits, Northamptonshire, on 25th May.

On 18th May, a pratincole was found at Gimingham, Norfolk. The next day, Dave Holman and Dave Nicholson were able to clinch it as Britain's third-ever **Oriental Pratincole**. Remarkably, Dave Holman had identified Britain's First, at Dunwich, Suffolk, in June 1981. May 18th also produced Britain's third-ever **Spanish Sparrow**, at Martin's Haven, Dyfed.

Then there was a glut of warblers. A **Blyth's Reed Warbler** was trapped on North Ronaldsay, Orkney, on 19th May. On 23rd May, Tim Drew found Britain's third-ever **Marmora's Warbler**, at St. Abb's Head, Borders – yet another singing male. And a singing **Desert Warbler** was found by Mark Golley on Blakeney Point, Norfolk, on 27th May, the first-ever British spring record. Fair Isle produced a **River Warbler** and a **Paddyfield Warbler** in the last week of May.

May 1993 was already excellent for top-class rarities; the **Pacific Swift** hurtling across Cley Marshes, Norfolk, on 30th May made it exceptional. This was an exercise in good birding teamwork as Alan Brown, David Bridges, Steve Gantlett and Richard Millington all pitched in to identify this second for Britain.

June produced another first-summer male Pallid Harrier, this one at Holliwell Point, Essex, on 13th. In July 1990, a female **Swinhoe's Storm Petrel** had been trapped and ringed at Tynemouth, Tyne & Wear. This was remarkable enough, but the same bird returned to the ringing site in 1991 and 1992. On 21st July 1993, the bird was retrapped for the fourth year running. Also on 21st July, yet another **Bridled Tern**, the third of the year, was seen on the island of Eigg, Rhum, Inner Hebrides. A **Pallid Swift** was found on 25th July at Burnham Norton, Norfolk.

On North Ronaldsay, on August 11th, Alison Duncan, Steven Stansfield and Jane Reid were checking the observatory nets when they found a male Spanish Sparrow in one of them – the fourth for Britain, and the second in 1993.

A juvenile **Black-winged Pratincole** was found at Blagdon Lake, Somerset, on 28th August. Another was in Suffolk Breckland in early September. And either the Norfolk Oriental Pratincole put in two more appearances elsewhere or, amazingly, two more Oriental Pratincoles turned up: on 29th/30th August at the Pevensey Levels, East Sussex, and in September on Havergate Island, Suffolk.

After the Pallid Harriers in the spring, it seemed incredible when two more turned up on the same day in the autumn. On 15th September, a male was seen at Saddington Reservoir, Leicestershire, and a juvenile at Exnaboe, Shetland Mainland.

September in Shetland was classic. There was a Paddyfield Warbler on Fair Isle on 8th and a River Warbler at the same locality on 26th; an extraordinary reprise of the duo logged in May. And in between, there was a **Red-flanked Bluetail** on the magic isle. A **Sharp-tailed Sandpiper** was found at Scatness, Shetland, on 13th September and a **White's Thrush** was in Lerwick on 21st. Next day, many miles to the south, a **Least Sandpiper** was found on the Hayle estuary, Cornwall.

Swindon doesn't figure too highly in rarity reports, so a **'Steppe' Grey Shrike**, only the seventh record, was a real bonus for Wiltshire birders on 23rd September. It was to prove a 'banker'. In Sheringham, Norfolk, a Paddyfield Warbler was trapped on 24th September and the following day a Blyth's Reed Warbler was trapped at Bamburgh, Northumberland.

October 1993 produced a lot of great birds. On Scilly, St Mary's boasted an **Eyebrowed Thrush** from 7th. Out Skerries, Shetland, was rewarded on 9th with a River Warbler and a Blyth's Reed Warbler. A juvenile Black-winged Pratincole was discovered at Sennen, Cornwall on 10th, the third record for 1993.

Black-throated Thrushes featured strongly in October 1993, with birds found on Fair Isle on 11th; St Martin's, Isles of Scilly, on 13th; on Whalsay, Shetland, on 19th; and finally, a bird trapped at Sheringham, Norfolk, on 31st.

On 11th October, Britain's fourth **Hermit Thrush** was found on Tresco, Isles of Scilly. It's fantastic to birdwatch in Britain, the international crossroads for so many good birds. The next day, a **Rose-breasted Grosbeak** was found on Tresco. On St Mary's, a **Blyth's Pipit** turned up on 20th October.

A **Swainson's Thrush** was trapped at Holm, Orkney Mainland, on 21st October. The next day, Bill Jackson found an unfamiliar Warbler at Seafield, Lerwick, Shetland. Trapped later by Kevin Osborn, the bird was identified as Britain's third **Sykes's Warbler**. A real rarity on the East coast, a **Blackpoll Warbler** was found on Flamborough Head, East Yorkshire, on 23rd October. Perhaps THE bird of autumn 1993 for most birders was an English mainland Red-flanked Bluetail, found at Winspit, Dorset, on 30th October. It was an emotional experience for some. The last day of October, which already had the Sheringham Black-throated Thrush, saw a Blyth's Pipit on Fair Isle which was trapped the following day.

November was generally quiet, but a **Dark-eyed Junco** at Dorchester, Dorset, first discovered on 8th November was a good find. Apart from two **Ivory Gulls** – one in Shetland and the other, an adult, at Balranald, North Uist, Outer Hebrides – December was also quiet. There were long-staying **Pied-billed Grebes**, at Stithians Reservoir, Cornwall, and in the Druridge Bay area, Northumberland.

Bluetails, Oriental Pratincoles and Pallid Harriers – 1993 had them in abundance.

TERN THE OTHER CHEEK!

Susan Hepton

My 1993 birdwatching year began on New Year's Day – following up a report of a Golden Eagle in Colsterdale, one of the most beautiful parts of Yorkshire. Unfortunately, New Year's Day is also the traditional 'blast-a-pheasant-out-of-the-sky day' in Colsterdale, so we thought that any self-respecting eagle would keep a low profile. Fortunately we were wrong. This immature bird gave fantastic views and provided a brilliant start to the year.

January continued with a personal find of ten Waxwings near my home on the 5th, plus Lapland Bunting at Filey and the long-staying Mediterranean Gull at Hornsea with a penchant for fish and chips. The 16th of the month saw me dashing to Willingham Wood, near Market Rasen in Lincolnshire for my first 'lifer' of the year, the White-throated Sparrow.

A trip to Norfolk in March gave me a second lifer, a Common Crane. This species had always eluded me; they are never that common or easy to see in Yorkshire. March also produced a number of other good Yorkshire sightings: Serin and Firecrest at Spurn, plus three Mediterranean Gulls on a house roof in Withernsea. On 25th March, I saw my third lifer: a White-billed Diver at Filey. It was with a Great Northern Diver for a perfect comparison.

April 25th saw us on a twitch to Holkham in Norfolk for a Sociable Plover, a bird which was first seen in Derbyshire the week before. This was my first lifer for the day. Then, as if that wasn't enough, a male Penduline Tit at Titchwell, my second, plus Purple Heron, seven Black Terns and two Montagu's Harriers as back-up. What a day!

On the 9th of May, we were on a local RSPB group trip to Ravenscar and Filey, on the Yorkshire coast. Ravenscar wasn't very productive, so we made our way to Filey. Then it started to rain … it rained Bluethroats, literally. It seemed they were everywhere. I saw five birds, all red-spotted, but the group total was much higher. Another fantastic day.

Britain's third Oriental Pratincole was found on 14th May in a pony paddock at Gimingham in Norfolk. I was unable to get there until 26th May so I had to keep my fingers crossed that it didn't go. I was so happy that I did get to see this lovely bird. I did a little sketch from life in my field notebook and wrote "holds body forward and down, runs quickly to catch insects, then stops and repeats". Well worth the long drive.

The 30th May started badly as we had just dipped on a reported Tawny Pipit at Gibraltar Point. We sat miserably in a café in Skegness until someone popped out to the phone box to call Birdline …"Pacific Swift, Cley"… What?!

Hang on, Cley's a long way from us now and swifts don't usually hang around. We'll ring again in a minute.

"Pacific Swift, Cley, showing well". Excitement taking hold, we all jumped in the car. I had a little red XR3 at the time; I thought it went quite quickly until we got onto the A148, when I was passed by another birder in an RS turbo which made me feel I was standing still. It was like a scene from *Wacky Races*.

We arrived at Cley with not an inch of space to park, what a spectacle. We still arrived in time to see the bird though, wow! The bird departed at 4.10 pm the same day, disappointing a lot of late arrivals.

I had a disappointing day with friends at Spurn Point on 19th June looking for Common Rosefinch and Lesser Crested Tern. We dipped on both birds but found out later that the Lesser Crested Tern returned as soon as we had left. Interestingly, I had written in my notebook that 57 pairs of Little Tern were present breeding this year. None bred at Spurn in 2004.

On 26th June, we were at Filey Dams when we heard that a Sardinian Warbler, a first-summer male, had been found just a mile up the road. It's wonderful when you're in the right place at the right time. We watched this delightful bird for over an hour. A long-staying bird, it left on 16th October.

On 2nd July, Trevor Charlton, Terry McEvoy and myself were on the Humber estuary poring over a bird book, discussing the finer identification points of Pacific Golden Plover. The bird had appeared at Read's Island in with a flock of Golden Plovers. It was a superb breeding-plumaged adult and was a lifer for Terry and me.

A report of a Woodchat Shrike on 11th July saw a few of us heading off to Weybourne in Norfolk. We had good views of this stunning bird, one of 29 this year, a record showing for Woodchat. We then moved on to Brancaster Staithe to catch a boat out to Scolt Head Island to miss yet again a Lesser Crested Tern by ten minutes. We decided to try again later in the day by foot. Arriving back again at

4.00 pm, we found out that the tern was indeed back on the island. The problem now was that the tide was coming in quickly and to get to the island meant crossing a tidal creek against the rising tide.

Two of my friends immediately discarded their trousers and waded across, as did others who were in the same predicament. I decided in my infinite wisdom that I wasn't going to do this. Perhaps as there were no other women present, but also my dignity seemed more important than a Lesser Crested Tern at that time. My friend Fred Carter stayed with me but I wasn't sure whether it was out of a sense of chivalry or if he was preserving his own dignity. Just then, a man came running down the beach.

"Is it still there?" he breathlessly shouted to us. "Yes," we replied, "just one problem, the tide's coming in."

"You'll have to excuse me," he said, "I've no underpants on, had to leave the caravan quickly."

"That's fine," I said. "I won't look," and politely turned away. A few minutes passed by and I couldn't resist, I had to look. At the other side of the water, telescope and pants raised over his head and bare backside emerging from the water, he sped off to see the bird. I collapsed laughing. Anyway, much to our relief and delight, the tern moved position after the others had left and through telescopes we were able to get reasonable views across the creek.

We were yet again in Norfolk on 18th July, at Hickling Broad for a Caspian Tern, always an impressive bird to see. On 7th August, I returned to Read's Island once again, but this time for a White-rumped Sandpiper. Then on the 12th we were back in Norfolk for a Broad-billed Sandpiper at Cley. Unfortunately, we missed the Broad-billed Sand but were amply compensated by three Red-necked Phalaropes!

On 15th September, we visited Spurn to see a forlorn, drenched, Demoiselle Crane in a field at the side of Beacon Lane. As one would expect, this was considered to be an escape, but an attractive bird all the same. The day continued with Wryneck, Icterine Warbler, Red-backed Shrike and Redstarts everywhere.

September 19th was a highly memorable day as I had two lifers before 9.15 am. We were at Filey and our first bird of the day was a Great Snipe, hard to believe, and the second was a Booted Warbler. We then moved down the coast to Spurn, where we had two Red-throated Pipits, yet another Booted Warbler, Red-backed Shrike and lots of common migrants. Another amazing day!

In October I headed south for my first trip to Scilly. I flew from Land's End at 4.20 pm on 9th October, landing in time to see an Eyebrowed Thrush, then dashing for a North American Upland Sandpiper. What a breathtaking introduction to this fabulous place! Over the next few days we saw Firecrest, Yellow-browed Warbler, Barred Warbler, Rustic Bunting and Red-breasted Flycatcher.

A low point was the twitch to see Britain's fourth Hermit Thrush. To my total disgust, I dipped on this rarity because the horrendous rugby scrum forced me to leave. Next day, we saw a first-winter Rose-breasted Grosbeak, with a Melodious Warbler and a Black-throated Thrush the following day. My final lifer for the week was an American Golden Plover on 14th on the airfield. This brought my total for lifers for the week to seven, certainly more than I had expected. As an extra bonus, in Cornwall we saw a

Subalpine Warbler and both Pied-billed and Red-necked Grebes at Stithians Reservoir. What a hectic bird-filled week!

The next treat for me came on 26th October when an American Blackpoll Warbler was found at Danes Dyke near Flamborough. An unexpected lifer for me in the home county of Yorkshire, especially after a full week on Scilly without a sniff of an American wood-warbler. On 6th November, I saw yet another lifer at Flamborough South Landing: a Dusky Warbler. Also, to complement this bird, a Hume's Warbler. Wonderful!

The discovery of a Red-flanked Bluetail at Winspit, Dorset on 30th October set lots of birders' pulses racing. This was one of the most sought-after birds of the year, and the first-ever twitchable individual. We managed to get to see this lovely bird on 7th November, my final lifer in this wonderful year.

Susan Hepton is a bird artist who lives in West Yorkshire. A freelance artist, her work for greetings card companies features a lot of Robins and Blue Tits!

THE BIRDER'S YEAR

Tim Cleeves

Little Buntings have been found in winter and early spring on a number of occasions in Britain, but the bunting found on 8th March 1994 was a First. This was a **Black-faced Bunting**, discovered at Pennington Flash Country Park, Greater Manchester. It was a first-winter male. The locality was tailor-made for a big twitch and the planning and organisation by the finder – Peter Alker – and the local ranger staff was excellent.

In our accounts we have referred to Black-throated Thrush rather than the more cautious way of describing the super-species, as Dark-throated Thrush. The two forms – Black-throated and the nominate Red-throated form – are similar in first-winter plumage, but Red-throated shows red-brown on the tail sides and this is especially conspicuous in flight. In September 1994, the first British record of **Red-throated Thrush** was identified and this bird posed no identification problems. It was a first-winter male; most of its tail was rufous and its breast was mainly brick-red. Over 2,000 twitchers saw the bird during its nine-day stay. By the end of 1994, there had been 28 records of Black-throated Thrush in Britain. By the end of 2004, still only one Red-throated Thrush had been found.

A **Black-throated Thrush** on 7th January in Bournemouth, Dorset, was the first major rarity in 1994, followed by a first-winter **Forster's Tern** at Fishguard, Dyfed, on 10th January. Two **Brünnich's Guillemots** appeared in February: a live one at Seafield, West Lothian, on the 6th and, more usual, a corpse at Wadbister Voe, Shetland, on the 12th. Two **Buffleheads** were seen in 1994, becoming the eighth and ninth British records. One was an adult male found on 17th March at Colwick Country Park, Nottinghamshire, and the second was a first-summer male found on 1st June at Coatham Marsh, Cleveland.

A **Black Duck** was a good find on Tresco, Isles of Scilly, on 1st April. As the first spring migrants were streaming in, a **Short-toed Treecreeper** appeared on 3rd April at Dungeness, Kent. May was relatively quiet this year, but a **Blyth's Reed Warbler** was trapped at Kergord, Shetland, on 23rd.

June was exceptional for **Bridled Terns**. At 7.30 on the morning of 3rd June, a Bridled Tern was seen at Fairburn Ings RSPB Reserve, West Yorkshire. The same bird travelled northwest and was watched off Foulney Island, Cumbria, at midday. It, or another bird, was seen off Tiree, Inner Hebrides, on 30th June. An adult **Franklin's Gull** was at Topsham, Devon, on 25th June.

July was productive. On 10th, an adult **Pacific Golden Plover** was seen at South Ferriby, Lincolnshire. The following evening, a **Swinhoe's Storm Petrel** was heard below the coastguard station at Tynemouth, Tyne & Wear. On 16th July, a singing **River Warbler** was located at Clatto Reservoir, Fife, and a **Paddyfield Warbler** was a good summer find on 18th at Holm on Orkney. The earlier Swinhoe's Storm Petrel record was confirmed when the female trapped in 1993 was retrapped at Tynemouth on 23rd and 25th July.

In recent years, the fact that **Wilson's Petrel** occurs regularly in the Western Approaches has been confirmed by observers on the annual *Scillonian* pelagic and other local pelagics. 1994 was no exception, with four Wilson's Petrels being seen on 13th August. Stanpit Marsh, Dorset, hosted a juvenile male **Little Crake** on 17th August. Further southwest, an adult **Pacific Golden Plover** was at the Hayle estuary, Cornwall, on 26th August.

Adult summer Red-necked Stints are relatively easy to identify, but juveniles and winter adults are much harder. On 31st August, a freshly dead juvenile **Red-necked Stint** was found on Fair Isle, Shetland. It was only the third record for Britain.

On 10th September, a '*Pterodroma* sp.' was seen from Bardsey, Gwynedd. A **'Steppe Grey Shrike'** was on North Ronaldsay, Orkney, on 14th September. It was a first-winter male and was trapped and ringed. Later in the year, three more 'Steppe' Grey Shrikes appeared – on South Walney, Cumbria, on 2nd November; at Boddam, Shetland, on 7th November; and on Papa Westray, Orkney, on 11th November.

From the middle of September, a **Paddyfield Warbler** was trapped at Newbin Bridge, Cleveland, on 17th. Incredibly, another Paddyfield Warbler was trapped the next day in Cleveland, this time at Marske. An **Isabelline Wheatear** was found on Whalsay, Shetland, on 20th. And the fourth **Calandra Lark** for Britain was found on St Kilda, Western Isles, on 21st. The same day produced a **Pallas's Grasshopper Warbler** on Fair Isle. On September 29th, the first Red-throated Thrush in Britain was found at The Naze, Essex.

It was mid-month before serious rarities were discovered in October 1994. The 15th saw a **Song Sparrow** at Seaforth, Merseyside, and a **Greater Yellowlegs** appeared near Rockcliffe on the River Eden, Cumbria.

Two first-winter male Black-throated Thrushes were found on Fair Isle on 16th and 17th October. And two **Red-flanked Bluetails** were found on Fair Isle on the same dates! More Red-flanked Bluetails were discovered – at Great Yarmouth, Norfolk, on 18th October and a male at Landguard, Suffolk, on 26th.

If it seemed that the Isles of Scilly were missing out, that changed on 19th October, when John Wright identified Britain's fourth **Yellow-browed Bunting** on St Agnes. An adult **Franklin's Gull** was found on 21st at the Hayle estuary, Cornwall. And this seemed to be the year of the Paddyfield Warbler – another turned up at South Ronaldsay, Orkney, on 26th. A **Hermit Thrush** at Chipping Ongar, Essex, on 28th had to be taken into care. The end of the month was marked by a **Myrtle Warbler** (Yellow-rumped Warbler) on the RSPB reserve of Ramsey Island, Dyfed, on 31st.

November 1994 was a very good month for rare birds. A first-winter **Blyth's Pipit** found on 4th and later trapped at Landguard, Suffolk, was the third for Britain. It followed the identification of a museum skin of a bird found in the Brighton area, East Sussex, in 1882 and a sight record on 13th October 1988 on Fair Isle. On 5th November, a male **Little Bustard** was discovered on Fair Isle.

In Kent, another Blyth's Pipit was a great find. This was at South Swale Nature Reserve on 7th November. An adult **Alpine Accentor** on 14th November at Saltfleetby, Lincolnshire, was appreciated by many birdwatchers. Another Myrtle Warbler was discovered at Eastville Park, Bristol, on 16th November, proving that anything can turn up anywhere at any time.

Jeff Stenning was present when Britain's first Grey-tailed Tattler was discovered at Ynys-hir RSPB Reserve on 13th October 1981. On 27th November 1994, Jeff was leading a field trip of the Scottish Ornithologists' Club, when they noticed an unusual wader at the Maltings, Burghead, Moray. It was Britain's second **Grey-tailed Tattler**! A magnificent find!

In December, a first-winter **Forster's Tern** was found in the Musselburgh area, East Lothian. And the year ended with an American wood-warbler – a **Blackpoll Warbler** at Bewl Water, East Sussex, from 10th December.

ROSS'S GULLS AND MEGA BUNTINGS

Steve Young

Does every year begin the same for all birders? A list of target species, fresh enthusiasm for travelling to get new birds on the list, maybe even a first for Britain, and a promise to cover the local patch more thoroughly to find your own mega. Little did I know what was in store…

January began well with a wintering Little Bunting near St Helens, seen on 2nd. This is a real rarity on the West coast and is still the only local one I've seen … The rest of the month passed quietly, but a notable event was seeing Lesser Spotted Woodpecker at Tatton Park. The local patch at Seaforth docks had been quiet, with a hybrid 'Fudged' Duck, and three Glaucous Gulls on 12th the highlights. Incidentally, these days, 'Glaucs' and Iceland Gulls are virtually a thing of the past with both species now occurring maybe once a year, presumably owing to many local tips closing.

February had a very local feel to it with Snow Bunting at Crosby Marina, Glaucous again at Seaforth, plus a few Scaup, and Bean Goose at Martin Mere, but it all changed on 28th when a trip to Sunderland resulted in my sixth Ross's Gull. I fell in love with this species after seeing a summer adult at Titchwell, Norfolk, in 1984 and I've been hooked ever since. It is one of the few birds that I will make an effort to see over and over again. This individual kept us waiting a couple of hours before flying in, bathing in a small pool and then flying along the beach before disappearing. I managed a few record shots but still left for the journey home a happy birder! A second visit provided me with much better views and photographs.

The first week of March passed by with little of note until 9th, when the phone rang and I found myself travelling to Pennington Flash, near Leigh. Thirty minutes later I was watching in disbelief as a first for Britain in the shape of a first-year Black-faced Bunting appeared out of the undergrowth about 30 yards away! Caught and ringed earlier in the day by warden Pete Alker, this was *the* highlight of the winter and stayed in the same area until mid-April. As you can imagine, I spent a lot of time at Pennington, eventually managing to take good photos from a converted litter bin used as a hide...

But March was proving to be a mega month and on 13th, while at Pennington, another Ross's Gull was found at Fleetwood. The seventh was soon on the list and I wondered how many other people had seen Black-faced Bunting and Ross's Gull on the same day! A Bufflehead at Colwick was nice and easy, and then yet another Ross's Gull was found, this time at Seaforth when I wasn't there. But I did see it and hoped it would be number eight, but it was accepted as the Fleetwood bird. A breathtaking month was brought to an end with a summer-plumaged Ring-billed Gull at Rhyl in Wales.

So, what would April bring? Regular visits to Seaforth were made with 170 Little Gulls on 23rd being a good count in a poor year for the species locally. With the wind from the southeast and forecast to continue overnight, myself and Tim Vaughan arranged to go again the following day. I picked him up and we entered the hide on a warm and sunny spring morning. With no evidence of any movement, the day suddenly came to life with the arrival of a large raptor over the Freeport fence. I glanced through my bins and said "Marsh Harrier". Then looked through my scope and said "Err, no" ... TV said quietly: "It's a Black Kite ..." And it was ... and it was heading straight towards us. Mass panic! No-one will believe us!! MUST get photos!! It was banking away, gaining height ... Now it had banked again and was heading back towards us ... It was going over the hide ... I raced outside holding a 600-mm lens with a 1.4× converter attached to it, pointed it at the kite as it flew past and took 10–12 shots, then ran after it along the path shouting at it to come back! It didn't ... two other Seaforth regulars managed to see the bird from other parts of the reserve, and the record was accepted by BBRC.

On a high after this, it didn't really matter what else the spring produced, it couldn't beat a tick on my patch! During May I saw: Red-footed Falcon, Corncrake, Squacco Heron, Black-winged Stilt (the Titchwell bird that is still present ...), Great Reed Warbler, Rosy Starling and a Black-headed Bunting that was deemed to be an escape. Now, apart from having a damaged bill and feeding from a plant pot full of seed on top of an aviary, there wasn't that much wrong with it ... And I still need it for my British List … Highlights of the summer were Marsh Sandpiper in Wales and on a family holiday to Norfolk, Barred and Greenish Warblers and a Pec Sand.

September quickly became a nightmare, with dips on Hilbre Island for a Yellow-breasted Bunting and Burnham Overy for a Siberian Thrush. A Baird's Sandpiper on the journey home at Eyebrook Reservoir was poor compensation for the latter, and even Seaforth was going through a quiet stage. Martin Mere provided some excitement with a first-year Cinnamon Teal that seems to have been forgotten or ignored over the years, and also a very tame juvenile Red-necked Phalarope. But with no seawatching weather to give even a hint of a Leach's Petrel the autumn had been pretty uninspiring.

October began in Essex, watching a male Red-throated Thrush on 2nd perching on various caravans, trees and bushes at The Naze. It was a lovely looking bird and still the only British record. And then it was time for the Isles of Scilly … what awaited everybody this year?

Well, not that much really: six Ruddy Shelducks on the Hayle before leaving for Scilly, a Black Duck on Tresco that kept me waiting for five hours, a Rustic Bunting, Common Rosefinch, Richard's Pipit and then a Radde's Warbler on 15th. It was on this day that news came through of birds in the northwest: Pallas's Warbler on the Great Orme, Gwynedd, Greater Yellowlegs in Cumbria and then, to top it all, Song Sparrow at an undisclosed site on Merseyside … I knew immediately it was Seaforth and the delay would be to get permission from the Dock Board to organise access. And I was correct … The two people I had travelled down with left and saw the sparrow the following day. I elected to stay, as to go home would have meant staying there, as today was also my wife's birthday and I had always made the excuse that I couldn't possibly leave Scilly for it…

An air of despondency hung over the remaining birders on the islands but was lifted on the 20th when everyone had superb views of a Yellow-browed Bunting on St Agnes! There hasn't been a twitchable one since, but there hasn't been a Song Sparrow either, and to this day I'm still not sure which one I would have preferred to have seen.

I did catch up with the Greater Yellowlegs when I left Scilly, and November continued to produce great birds: Yellow-rumped Warbler on Ramsey Island, Alpine Accentor at Rimac, Desert Wheatear in Blackpool and then, best of all, a Grey-tailed Tattler at Burghead in Scotland. Of those birds, the tattler was the rarest, but the Yellow-rumped was the best, a great day involving fast boat trips, car sickness and stunning views of an American warbler flitting around on Bracken.

Just when I thought that was the end of the good birds, a Blackpoll Warbler was an amazing December find at Bewl Water in Sussex, and a nice early Christmas present on 20th. The northwest provided the final bird of the year with a first-winter drake Lesser Scaup being a Lancashire tick at Pine Lake in the final week of 1994.

These days I wouldn't travel far again to see those birds, but back then I was very keen and many of them were new. It was a great year and one that I look back on with much enjoyment.

Steve Young lives on Merseyside. A renowned bird photographer, he has a special affection for Ross's Gull – in February 2005 he saw his lucky 13th Ross's in Britain.

MARCH 1994

BLACK-FACED BUNTING IN GREATER MANCHESTER

Peter Alker

On Tuesday 8th March 1994, I went to work at Pennington Flash Country Park early so that I would have time to do some ringing before starting work. I erected a mist-net at my baited site, by one of the reserve ponds, which I frequently use for ringing during the winter months.

The net had been up for about 20 minutes when I peered through the hedge with my binoculars to see if anything had been caught. I could see five birds in the net, but there was something odd-looking about one of them. At first it looked like a Dunnock *Prunella modularis*, but, as it turned slightly, it showed obvious white on its outer tail feathers. Somewhat perplexed and excited, I rushed around to the net. The bird was clearly a bunting, but one quite unfamiliar to me. I made a mental note of some of its features as I extracted it from the net: straight culmen, pink on the bill and greyish-brown lesser coverts. The only bunting that I could recall having any of these features was Pallas's Reed Bunting *Emberiza pallasi*. It was obviously going to be a 'description species', so I quickly extracted the other birds and took the net down. As usual, I went to my office nearby to process the birds and greeted my colleagues, Tony Whittle and Roger Wood, with the news of the bunting. I also quickly phoned my boss, Graham Workman, to tell him that I would be a little late starting work and to suggest that he should come and have a look at this bird. I did not know then that it would be almost seven weeks before normal working would resume for myself and the other staff at Pennington Flash.

I dealt with the other four birds first and then briefly looked through the *Identification Guide to European Passerines* (Svensson 1992), the only passerine reference material that I had with me. I first checked the bird against the details given for Pallas's Reed Bunting: although some features seemed to fit, others obviously excluded that species. Black-faced Bunting *E. spodocephala* was then considered and seemed to be a likely candidate, but, again, some features did not seem to fit. In particular, the colours of some feather tracts and the pattern of the crown feathers (bearing in mind the bird's wing length, which would make it a male) appeared to be at variance with the details given by Svensson. The bird had no olive/olive-green tones on the head, it lacked a blackish face-mask, there was no yellow tinge to any of the underparts, and the crown feathers were tipped with a long, V-shaped, dark-centred brown marking. It was, however, mainly my lack of experience of Black-faced Bunting and my inability to visualise the species in any plumage which hampered the identification. I also did not appreciate just how variable the plumages of this species can be, and, because of the time of year, I mainly compared the bird with the details given for spring males.

Unable to reach a firm conclusion, I nevertheless then processed the bird, taking a full description that included sketches of various individual feathers. The bird was provisionally aged as a first-winter by the shape and degree of wear of the tail feathers (based on my experience of ageing Reed Buntings *E. schoeniclus*), but I could not wait for additional reference material to be obtained to help to confirm its identity. The bird was then photographed in the hand by RW and released where it had been trapped.

Description in the hand

In general, the bird's head strongly recalled Dunnock: a dull grey, with most of the feathers streaked or tipped brown. The most striking feature was a broad, off-white submoustachial stripe, which hooked under the ear-coverts. The mainly pinkish bill and generally dull grey background colour to the head gave it an appearance recalling a junco *Junco*, with the remainder of the plumage being similar to that of a Reed Bunting. Its plumage was in good condition and was moderately worn.

Head Crown, nape, ear-coverts and lores dull grey, tipped brown. Supercilium pale dirty-buff, less distinct in front of the eye, more obvious above and behind the eye (27 mm total length). Thin pale eye crescent below eye. Submoustachial stripe off-white, becoming broader away from bill and hooking under ear-coverts.

Underparts Chin dull grey/ash-grey (no black). Throat and upperbreast ash-grey, dappled off-white. Remainder of breast, belly and undertail-coverts creamy-white. Flanks streaked mainly with two parallel, long, narrow streaks, formed by narrow, blackish-brown feather centres.

Upperparts Mantle and back boldly streaked with black-centred feathers, edged pale chestnut, then fringed buff. Rump pale olive-brown. Uppertail-coverts as rump, but with darker feather-centres forming faint streaks. Lesser coverts greyish-brown. Median coverts blackish, with buff tips, slightly more extensive on outer web. Greater coverts black, edged pale chestnut, fading to buff on tip and along fringe of outer web. Tertials black, with the colours at tip and along fringe of outer web similar to those on greater coverts. Black of tertials indented on outer web, where these feathers overlapped. Alula and primary coverts blackish-brown; large feather of the alula having very narrow, pale edge along outer web. Primaries and secondaries coloured much as primary coverts, but with rusty brown edging to outer web (narrower on primaries).

Tail Central pair of tail feathers blackish-brown with pale brown edges; remainder brownish-black, with extensive white on outer two. Feathers moderately worn and pointed, except left outermost, which was less worn and more rounded, suggesting that it had been replaced relatively recently.

Bare Parts Eye dull dark brown under artificial light. Upper mandible blackish, with small pinkish area at base of cutting edge. Lower mandible pink, with blackish tip. Culmen straight, but appeared very slightly concave just in front of nostrils, where upper mandible narrowed. Legs pinkish, with darker areas to scale edges on toes.

Measurements Wing 75 mm (max. chord). Primary projection 9 mm. Bill to feathers 10 mm; to skull 11.5 mm. Tail length 66 mm; difference 4 mm (2nd & 3rd outermost longest and central pair shortest). Tarsus 20 mm. Hind claw 7 mm.

Subsequent events

Upon release, the bird's pale rump was quite noticeable. The bunting flew straight into some dead grass and was lost from view. After a few minutes, it rapidly scurried through the vegetation and then out of sight again. With only brief field views, we were no nearer an identification. We returned to the office to discuss the bird's identity and I also telephoned the Birdline Northwest Hotline and left a message for Ted Abraham saying that we had a strange bunting at the country park. Later, a few local birders were alerted to look out for the bird while my colleagues and I tried to resume a normal day's work.

When I arrived home in the evening, I immediately raided my bookshelves and came across an in-the-hand photograph of a Black-faced Bunting in the *Hamlyn Photographic Guide to Birds of the World* (1991) which resembled the Pennington bird. Later, after a few telephone calls, I was put in touch with Julian Hough by TA. JH referred me to the paper on the identification of Black-faced Bunting by Dr Colin Bradshaw in *British Birds* (82: 653–665). After reading that paper and, in particular, after comparing the photographs in it with the description of the Pennington bird, I was 100% certain that the bird was a first-winter male Black-faced Bunting, a potential first for Britain and Ireland.

I met TA at the country park early the next morning. After a short wait, TA located the bird feeding in the net-ride where it had been trapped the previous day. TA agreed with the identification and, after a brief discussion about viewing arrangements, headed off to the nearest telephone. JH arrived a little later and concurred with the identification. I then went back to my office to consider the car parking and other potential problems that a 'first' might bring and to contact my colleagues in the ranger service.

The bird fed in the baited net-ride each day throughout its long stay, and thus enabled observers to get reasonable views through and under the hawthorn hedge that bordered the area. At least 5,000 birders came to see the bird, but the true total was probably nearer to 7,000 and many made one or more repeat visits in order to take a more-leisurely look at the bird after the initial large crowds had subsided. It was usually seen foraging on the ground amongst Reed Buntings, a mixed flock of finches and other common species attracted to a seed mixture that was provided on a daily basis. It frequently flicked open its tail and occasionally showed aggression towards other birds feeding nearby by rapidly scurrying towards them. When disturbed, it usually hopped or flew into low cover.

The bird's appearance in the field was similar to that noted in the hand, especially its likeness to a Dunnock. Any slight differences were caused mainly by the light, the range and the angle of view. This seemed to affect the lores and chin in particular, and those areas sometimes had a darker appearance in the field. The bird's nape was not unmarked as suggested by Hough (1994) and appeared the same in the field as it did in the hand, with most of the grey feathers having obvious brown tips.

Routine ringing operations resumed on 26th March, with the numerous Goldfinches *Carduelis carduelis* being the main target species. The Black-faced Bunting was retrapped on 28th March, during an early-morning ringing session. It was then moulting numerous feathers on its head and neck; many feathers were either missing or in pin on the nape, crown, ear-coverts, lores, chin and throat. Most of the off-white submoustachial stripe had been moulted out, and the new feathers growing were all in pin. A few feathers were also being replaced on the breast and belly. There was also some asymmetrical moult of the wing-coverts, with four median coverts in pin on the left wing and one half-grown greater covert on the right wing. The eye colour was checked (this time in good daylight) and was found to be a greyish-brown, thus supporting the original ageing, but the primary coverts were rounded as opposed to pointed, although perhaps intermediate in the range of shapes that the different ages can display (Svensson 1992).

Subsequent observations up to 24th April, following the bunting's quite extensive pre-breeding moult, showed that it did not acquire the generalised 'typical' summer plumage which is often described and illustrated for the species. In general, it had a rather plain, grey-hooded appearance, with only a small and indistinct darker grey face-mask (sometimes looking blackish). There were no greenish tones to the hood, but it sometimes looked blue-grey, depending on the light. Some feathers of the rear crown and nape were tipped brown, giving the back of the head a lightly streaked appearance. It had retained a small part of the submoustachial stripe in the form of a small off-white spot below the ear-coverts, but this could be seen only given good, close views. The appearance of the remainder of its plumage was unchanged from that described in the hand.

The bird's call – a repeated 'tsick' – was heard on a number of occasions (more so towards the end of its stay) and to my ear was similar to the call of Song Thrush *Turdus philomelos*. On 16th April, the bird was heard calling near the net-ride. A colleague and I followed its calls and located it foraging on bare ground under some willows *Salix* with two Reed Buntings. It then flew up and perched on a low branch before flying out and taking an insect on the wing in the manner of a flycatcher (Muscicapidae). This was one of very few sightings away from the net-ride but one of a number which showed an association with Reed Buntings (PJA unpublished obs.).

Alker, P. J. 1997. Black-faced Bunting: new to Britain and Ireland. *British Birds* 90, 549–561.

Black-faced Bunting breeds in central and eastern Asia. It is chiefly a long-distance migrant, wintering in eastern Nepal, northern Indo-China, southern and eastern China, Korea, and central and southern Japan.
There have been three subsequent records:

Northumberland Woodhorn, Newbiggin, female/first-winter, 24th October 1999

Devon Lundy, 12th October 2001

Shetland Fair Isle, 20th–24th October 2001

1995

THE BIRDER'S YEAR

Tim Cleeves

1995 produced one First for Britain – **Bay-breasted Warbler** near Land's End, Cornwall, in October. Against the recent run of play, this was an excellent year for North American landbirds. Also in this year, two records of the North American form of Herring Gull ('American Herring Gull') from 1994 were accepted and in 1995 another was identified, this one at Seaforth, Merseyside, on 26th March.

January opened with long-staying **Pied-billed Grebes** in Cornwall and the Isles of Scilly. An ailing **Brünnich's Guillemot** was taken into care at Gulberwick, Shetland, on 4th January. Bangor Harbour in Gwynedd hosted a **Forster's Tern** from 20th January. **Lesser Scaup** was still a rare bird in 1995; a first-winter male was at Barton-upon-Humber, Lincolnshire, from 13th February.

'Albert' the **Black-browed Albatross** resumed his solitary stay in the Gannet colony at Hermaness, Unst, Shetland, on 3rd April. First seen in 1972, this was his 22nd season (he had two years 'off' in the late 1980s). But this was to be his final season. He gave up his lonely vigil on 7th July. Where is he now?

A popular find, a **Scops Owl** was discovered at Morwenstow, Cornwall, on 9th April. A male **Pallid Harrier** seen in the Durkadale area, Orkney, on 18th April was to stay for months, delighting visitors. On 23rd April, a splendid male **Red-flanked Bluetail** was found on Holy Island, Northumberland. Equally stunning was a male **Black-throated Thrush** on 24th April on Stronsay, Orkney.

Two **Collared Flycatchers**, both males, turned up in 1995, one on 5th May at Cley, Norfolk, and the other on 5th June at Tresta, Shetland.

There were two records of **Baillon's Crake** in May. Could they relate to the same bird? On 6th, a male was found at Stithians Reservoir, Cornwall, and another was on Lundy, Devon, on 15th. The same day, a first-summer **Greater Yellowlegs** started a tour of Essex, Suffolk and Norfolk. Passerines in May included a fine male **Rock Thrush** discovered on 22nd at Hunstanton, Norfolk; a **River Warbler** on Fair Isle on 27th; and an **Eyebrowed Thrush** at Auchmithie, Perth & Kinross, from 28th May.

In June, an **Eastern Olivaceous Warbler** was trapped on Fair Isle on 5th, while Britain's fifth **Rüppell's Warbler** was a one-day wonder at Aberdaron, Gwynedd, on 21st. The adult **Ivory Gull** discovered in Inverness, Highland, from 18th July was a great bird on an unusual date and a brilliant find! An adult **Least Sandpiper** was found the next day at West Sidlesham, West Sussex.

August 12th produced another Eastern Olivaceous Warbler, at Benacre, Suffolk, and in Northumberland, Britain's fourth **Red-necked Stint** – an adult on the Wansbeck Estuary. Offshore, in sea area Sole, a **Wilson's Petrel** was identified on 20th August. Perhaps more noteworthy, another individual was seen off St Ives, Cornwall, on 24th September. Autumn 1995 was a good one for American landbirds. Leaving aside the 13 **Red-eyed Vireos**, there were 34 individuals of 16 species. A **Tennessee Warbler**, the fourth for Britain, on St Kilda, Western Isles, on 20th September was a great start. The same day, an **Eastern Bonelli's Warbler**, Britain's second, was discovered at Whitley Bay cemetery on Tyneside – a certain 'banker', it was elevated to the British List when Bonelli's Warbler was split into two different species two years later.

October 1st produced that First for Britain – **Bay-breasted Warbler** – at Land's End, Cornwall; alas, it didn't linger. Also on the 1st was a Black-throated Thrush at Sumburgh, Shetland. A **White-crowned Sparrow**, only the third ever, was found at Seaforth, Merseyside. A **Crag Martin** at Beachy Head, East Sussex, on 8th October was a great find – it was Britain's fourth (and the second record was also here in July 1988!). A **Swainson's Thrush** was trapped on Lundy on 9th October and the following day there was a **Northern Parula** on St Agnes, Isles of Scilly. The 13th produced a **Myrtle Warbler** (Yellow-rumped Warbler) on North Ronaldsay, Orkney, and the next day one was found on Tresco, Isles of Scilly.

The second-rarest American Warbler of the year was a **Chestnut-sided Warbler**, only the second British record, at Prawle Point, Devon, on 18th October. Fair Isle produced a **Hermit Thrush** on 19th and the next day a **Veery** was discovered on North Uist, Outer Hebrides. Towards the end of the month, the third British record of **Cliff Swallow** was found at Spurn, East Yorkshire, on 22nd, while at Ventnor, Isle of Wight, a **Rose-breasted Grosbeak** was present on 30th.

November's highlight was a Black-throated Thrush on 13th, at Redmires Reservoir, South Yorkshire. Big influxes of **Arctic Redpolls** and **Little Auks** were a feature of the winter and 4th December saw another Cliff Swallow; this time on Tresco, Isles of Scilly. The action for 1995 ended with a Forster's Tern in Dorset on Boxing Day.

PREMIER LEAGUE BIRDING
IN MANCHESTER

Judith Smith

1995 was my first full year of freedom! My husband had got early retirement at 50, so, having no family responsibilities and a great deal of work as county recorder for Greater Manchester, I decided to pack in the library profession and became a full-time birder in May 1994. As it turned out, that was a good decision, as both 1994 and 1995 were excellent years for our urban county – we even had a first for Britain in March 1994 (Black-faced Bunting). 1995 was to bring 203 species to the county – the second-highest total since its formation in 1976, many of them 'quality' birds – and looking back at my notebooks ten years later brings back the excitement of some of them, and, even in such a short time span, illustrates the population changes which have occurred.

January 2nd, and the year started with a Water Pipit at Hope Carr Nature Reserve – a series of freshwater lagoons alongside the only sewage sludge lagoons now left in United Utilities' ownership. This species used to winter here regularly, but there have been none since 2001. Six Whoopers in the Abram Flashes on 13th included a ringed bird seen regularly since 1994; on 15th there were 14 at Walshes in north Bolton. Until the 1998/99 winter, there was a regular small herd at both sites – sadly these have both disappeared, perhaps preferring the more abundant food supply at Martin Mere. Also on 13th, I saw both Slavonian and Red-necked Grebes at nearby Pennington Flash. On 26th, I led a night-time sortie to Salford Quays to see the internationally important numbers of Tufted Duck and Pochard which fed at night there in January and February. Since oxygenation of the Quays in 2001 destroyed the anaerobic inverte-brates, these flocks too have gone, preferring Woolston Eyes and Martin Mere. Warmer winters in the last ten years haven't helped either.

During the early part of the year, I was carrying out an assessment of ornithological sites in the county for English Nature, to consider whether they met the criteria for SSSI designation. Most didn't, but of the two that did, one is in a long drawn-out process of designation, and another's interest has gone (the Quays). A third has since met the criteria and we are trying to interest EN in designation as it is at risk from developers. My notebook shows I spent a lot of time at Salford Quays and Chorlton WP in that early winter, looking at *Aythya* ducks.

On 8th February, I ventured out of the county, to Seaforth to get a tick (Ross's Gull) and see nine other gulls, which included Kumlien's and Glaucous. Mid-March saw me visiting a private lake almost daily, eagerly awaiting the return of the first Black-necked Grebe of the year. After the draining of Woolston Eyes in the winter of 1991/92, the birds had returned to find no water, and scattered all over the Northwest looking for new suitable habitat. This small lake, for which I was the only keyholder, suited them, and breeding had been successful since 1992. I had to wait until 21st before the first bird appeared, still in partial winter plumage, but it was always a red-letter day when they arrived. Breeding was annual till 1997, but over the subsequent years Woolston refilled, and because these birds like to breed colonially they gradually returned to their former stronghold. Fortunately, though, another private water in the county became available from 1993, and today this has a very high success rate, with numbers of fledged young exceeding Woolston's despite having only a few pairs. The secret appears to be double-brooding and lack of predation.

Another notable event in March was the draining of Audenshaw Reservoirs' largest bed in preparation for the construction of the M60. Waders of all kinds quickly found the shallow water that remained, and on 18th March I saw 72+ Dunlin there – an unprecedented number in the county. During the year, 21 wader species were to visit or breed there, and it retained its interest until it was refilled in August 2000. On 29th March, I got a phone call from Jim Nisbet, the Bolton police Wildlife Liaison Officer and a keen twitcher, to say he'd found a drake Long-tailed Duck on Whitehead Lodges in Bury. This unprepossessing site, consisting of three lodges stepped down a hillside, was unknown to birders, but the bird obligingly stayed into April. That day, I'd already been to Shell Carrington NR to look at a Red-necked Grebe which had arrived there at the end of January and was to stay to 4th May, by which time it was calling loudly, trying to attract a mate.

We joined in the Ruddy Shelduck influx in April with several sightings – I watched a drake which was trying to separate a female Common Shelduck from its mate at Hope Carr reserve, having flown there from Lightshaw Hall Flash via Pennington Flash and tracked all the way by birders!

Most of the spring was spent in survey work – at that time I was doing a Common Birds Census, two Waterways Bird Surveys and two Breeding Bird Surveys. I was also following the fortunes of breeding Mute Swans, and had become involved in rescue work. At the same time, I was preparing the county report, so my time was fully occupied. However, we managed to spend the first week of April in Mallorca – lots of nice birds but nothing new for the Western Palearctic list! Back home, both April and May saw an excellent selection of passage migrants, most of which I missed as they were one-day affairs – Red Kite, Osprey, Hobby and Little Egret (both then rare), Marsh Harrier, Dotterel, Quail, Wood Sandpiper and Bean Goose – this last a county first.

June saw the discovery of a singing River Warbler on 11th at the Wigan Flashes, another tick for the county, which fortunately stayed for a month. It hadn't been there on 9th when I'd been round the site with English Nature! We'd walked from Scotman's Flash to Pennington Flash, noting Little Gulls, breeding Common Terns, a late Goldeneye, Lesser Whitethroat and Cuckoo, but not finding the Shelduck brood at Lightshaw. A Black-headed Bunting was another accepted national rarity and county first at Bromley Cross on 14th; it was found by Phil Garnett, another policeman, but again it was a one-day, one-observer sighting.

July, often a quiet month, was anything but, with a Leach's Petrel at Pennington Flash and a Spotted Crake at Chorlton WP, and culminating with a Great White Egret (then rare!) from 31st. I got a phone call from Radcliffe birder Peter Johnson to say he'd found the egret at Shoretop Reservoir in the Irwell valley and thought it had gone to roost there. I was there by 4.40 am the next day, only to find it had decamped to my local patch, the Abram and Wigan Flashes, 15 miles to the west. I should have stayed put! It departed the following day, but was compensated for by a Wood Sandpiper nearby. My memories of the rest of that month are of searing heat and resultant grass fires – 25,000 in total – and my notebook is mostly a record of breeding successes for wildfowl. From 30th, passage Garganey began to arrive in the Abram Flashes, and were intermittently there till the end of November.

Three Choughs, the first for 88 years, were on moors in the north in mid-September. The 22nd of this month brought the usual stranded Manx Shearwater, this time to Saddleworth, and on 16th there was a Wryneck at Watergrove. All these were single-observer sightings, to the frustration of many county listers.

On 9th October, having published the 1994 county report, I set off for Scilly. I first went as a child in 1955, and have been more or less annually ever since. We were fogbound in Cornwall until 12th, which gave me a chance to see Melodious Warbler and Red-eyed Vireo in the Cornish valleys. As soon as I finally reached the islands, it was off to Tresco to see the Yellow-rumped Warbler, Ortolan and another Red-eyed Vireo. Next day, it was Agnes for the Baird's Sandpiper and Dotterel. St Mary's provided Tawny and Red-throated Pipits, Short-toed Lark, yet another Red-eyed Vireo, as well as many lesser rarities. On Agnes again on 17th, my notebook records 'superb' Subalpine Warbler Troy Town, juvenile White-winged Black Tern Periglis, Red-eyed Vireo and Rose-coloured Starling St Warna's Cove, with Barred Warbler nearby – 'an excellent day'. The 18th saw Red-backed Shrike on the Garrison and Yellow-browed Warbler at Old Town, with Richard's Pipit on Peninnis, then to Bryher for Bonelli's Warbler, with Red-necked Grebe and Great Northern Diver off Samson. I was delighted when ex-GM birder Keith Blomley found the Yellow-billed Cuckoo the next day on Harry's Walls; it flew into the woods at Rocky Hill but we all got good views eventually. I'd had Black-billed Cuckoo in 1990 so was very pleased to get the duo. The sketch in my notebook isn't bad (for me) and brings it back so vividly.

Home again, and I noted a spectacular roost of 10,000 Starlings at the Wigan Flashes on 30th October, hunted by Sparrowhawks. There are perhaps 500–1,000 nowadays, when there is any roost at all. Then a rarity I did manage to see – a confiding Little Auk at Pennington Flash, on 4th November. It seems incredible that, only nine years ago, no-one took any footage of this bird, which was down to 10 m – today everyone would be digiscoping it! I also managed to see the Brent Goose at Salford Quays on 20th. There was a new record of 82 Goosanders in the roost at Ashworth Moor Reservoir on 26th, and, on Carrington Moss, a flock of 150 Corn Buntings! It's only looking in retrospect that we can see how quickly this species has gone downhill. Looking at the 2003 report, 50 in the same general area – on a site now lost to housing – was the best count of the year. In 1995, there were considered to be around 60 pairs breeding; this has now declined to around 30.

December brought an oiled Red-throated Diver in Farnworth, which died in care, seven Russian Whitefronts at Elton Reservoir on 18th, and a Waxwing in Summerseat on 20th, before a sudden Arctic spell over the Christmas period forced 1,700 *Aythya*s onto the Salford Quays, the only open water in the area. On 30th, Bittern, Long-eared Owls, Ruff and Mealy Redpolls were at Pennington Flash in the still-freezing weather.

The exceptional weather conditions in 1995, with the hot summer, dry autumn and cold later winter, obviously combined to bring us several species we wouldn't normally see. But in our inland urban county we have a very wide variety of habitats for birds – perhaps just as much as the rural county with acres of fields barren of birds. Lots of people means lots of sewage works, tips and reservoirs – all excellent for birds. Former industries like mining have brought us subsidence flashes – now protected nature reserves. And we do have some countryside – from moors to mosslands. Even our warehouses have huge flocks of Lapwings and Golden Plovers roosting during the day, and our city centre has resident Peregrines, soon to be provided with nesting facilities. Ornamental plantings of berried shrubs bring us Waxwings galore. And of course there are plenty of people to look for birds, so not too much gets missed!

Judith Smith lives in Greater Manchester where she is county recorder. Judith is administrator of the Association of County Recorders in England.

OCTOBER 1995
BAY-BREASTED WARBLER IN CORNWALL
David Ferguson

The morning of 1st October 1995 was sunny, warm and windy, a cheery contrast to the thick mist that had shrouded our arrival at our holiday cottage near Sennen Cove, Cornwall, the previous afternoon. As I had never been to Land's End, Jo Wayte and I decided that the morning would be spent walking along the cliff path from the cottage to Land's End, then walking back. At about 10.00 BST, when we were about 200 m from First and Last House, I noticed a small bird about 10 m away in the short turf on the landward side of the path. It had its back to me, but I could see that it was Warbler-like, had a bright green back, blackish wings with brilliant white double wing-bars and equally bright white edges to its tertials. After a few seconds of complete confusion, when most of the West Palearctic warblers flashed through my brain, I realised that I did not know what it was, which meant that, whatever it was, it was rare.

As well as my 'scope and binoculars, I carry a video-camera when I am birding. This underrated piece of kit can produce a picture under almost any conditions and can be used with a telescope to produce very high-magnification images. Within seconds, I had the telescope set up and was frantically pointing the camcorder through it at the bird. The resulting few seconds of blurred and shaky video were the product of about five minutes' effort. I gave up this idea, frustrated by an erratically moving bird and the force 5, westerly wind. I took a safety shot using the 1.4× converter and then we cautiously followed the bird as it hopped towards the buildings at Land's End.

During this period of relative tranquility, I realised that the bird must be a North American wood-warbler, and that the lack of eye-stripe and supercilium, and the double wing-bars meant that it was a *Dendroica* Warbler. I was on fairly familiar ground here. I have seen almost all the *Dendroica* warblers in North America, although not usually in immature plumage. I realised that I was in fact amongst the 'Confusing Fall Warblers' of Peterson (1934, *A Field Guide to the Birds East of the Rockies*).

The most likely candidate was Blackpoll Warbler *D. striata*, the most frequent North American Warbler on this side of the Atlantic, but this bird did not look right. It was incredibly bright; indeed, it displayed startling colours. Later, Jo, who is unimpressed by rarities, described it as one of the prettiest birds she had ever seen, and as having a plumage that seemed to be from two different birds: the top half one colour-scheme (green, white, and grey-blue) and the bottom half another (buff and pink). Apart from its brightness, the bird had dark legs and buff undertail-coverts, and, when I noticed these features, the awesome possibility that it was a Bay-breasted Warbler *D. castanea* entered my thoughts.

I knew about the Bay-breasted Warbler/Blackpoll Warbler/Pine Warbler *D. pinus* confusion trio and its problems because, 33 years earlier in the Rocky Mountains of Colorado, where all of these warblers are rare, I had found an immature bird which was one of the three, and which I identified to my own satisfaction as a Bay-breasted. So, I knew that dark legs, buff undertail-coverts and bright white wing-bars indicate Bay-breasted, although I now know (after the event) that the first two features are unreliable.

The immediate task, however, was to get a good video of the bird. I know from experience that field notes are no match for a video recording when trying to convince a rarities committee that a bird is what you say it is. We were staying about 30 m behind the bird, so as not to disturb it, but this was too far away for a decent video. I was just hoping that it would stop moving and then let me get closer. The opportunity occurred when it came to the low dry-stone wall that runs inland from First and Last House. The bird hopped to the leeward side of the wall and sheltered at its base from the wind. This was the moment.

Guided by Jo, who had stayed at the end of the wall with both me and the bird in sight, I walked down the opposite side of the wall, sufficiently far from it to be out of sight of the bird, until I was on a level with the bird. Then, camera at the ready, I walked to the wall until I could see a bright green head and a dark eye. The next 20 seconds of video show the bird hopping slowly away from me. I obtained another short sequence when the bird stopped in the lee of a large rock, but it was disturbed by someone walking on the path behind me and it flew to the other side of the wall, the only time that I saw it fly.

While this was happening, the sun disappeared behind menacing clouds, and it began to rain. Within a few minutes it was torrential. The bird had returned to the wall, where it sheltered in a hole. As we were not wearing weather-proof clothing, we decided to shelter at First and Last House, only 100 m away, having been observing the bird for about 45 minutes. We stood outside the building, but out of the rain, watching the spot where we knew that the bird was. After ten minutes, the rain eased off and we returned to the area where the bird had been last seen. To my astonishment and consternation, it had disappeared.

One possibility was that the bird had died. Although it was often quite lively, it also had periods when, finding somewhere out of the wind, it would remain stationary for several minutes with its eyes half-closed. It looked, indeed, as if it had just flown across the Atlantic, making landfall at Land's End that morning. If it had died, the obvious place to look was in the wall, but we found nothing. An extensive and prolonged search of the surrounding area was equally fruitless.

For all this time, although there were plenty of tourists around, we had not seen any other birders. Watching the helicopters flying past on their way to the Isles of Scilly – no doubt full of birders – was an incredibly frustrating experience. Eventually, I decided that the time had come to give up any hope that help would arrive and we ended the search. Although we had money and there was a phone nearby, I did not have any 'Birdline' numbers with me. I also was not entirely sure of the identity of the bird. We trudged back to our cottage at Carn Towan, on the far side of Sennen Cove.

I had two field guides with me: Jonsson (1992, *Birds of Europe with North Africa and the Middle East*) and Lewington *et al.* (1991). Between them, these two books describe every bird to have been recorded in Europe. I had not seriously considered the possibility of finding a first for the Western Palearctic and had left my North American field guides at home. Within seconds, I had dismissed all the North American warblers illustrated, then read the description of Bay-breasted Warbler in Lewington *et al.* It matched exactly the bird I had seen.

I now decided to make the phone call, but I discovered that the phone at the cottages did not work. We returned to Land's End, had another quick search for the bird, then made the call. It seemed prudent to describe the bird as 'a *Dendroica* warbler, probably Bay-breasted', as there was the slight possibility that it was another Warbler species that was also not illustrated in my field guides. We returned home on 7th October, when I immediately grabbed the National Geographic Society (1983) *Field Guide to the Birds of North America* and confirmed the identification.

DESCRIPTION

Size and Structure Size of Garden Warbler *Sylvia borin*; compact; rather large, neckless head; slightly notched tail.

Plumage Head bright green. Narrow yellow-green eye-ring broken by dark patch on front of and behind eye. Faint yellow-green loral stripe. Mantle bright green, with faint streaks towards lower edge, but these usually not visible. Throat pale buff, shading to deeper buff on breast and belly. Flanks washed with pink. Undertail-coverts buff. No streaking on areas of buff. Rump grey. Median coverts blue-grey, with feathers near shoulder with broad white tips, forming short white wing-bar. Greater coverts blackish, with white tips forming a second, longer wing-bar. Tertials blackish, with broad white tips. Secondaries and primaries blackish, with narrow blue-grey margins. Blackish tail, with two or three white spots on outer feathers, but these usually not visible.

Bare Parts Bill fairly thin, pointed, pale grey. Legs dark grey. Eye dark and prominent.

Habitat and Behaviour The bird frequented the clifftop at Land's End, which has short grass, a low stone wall, and outcrops of rocks. It often appeared tired and would remain stationary for periods. Mostly, it fed in the grass, progressing by hopping. It flew only once, when it was disturbed by a walker. It did not call at any time.

Identification

Although Bay-breasted, Blackpoll and Pine Warblers are considered to be confusion species, identification was fairly straightforward, helped by the unusually bright coloration of the bird. Pine Warbler can be eliminated by its dull, streaky appearance, while Blackpoll Warbler is a duller bird in female and immature plumages, is streaky, and has a fairly distinct supercilium. The throat and breast of Blackpoll are yellow-green, and it has no pink on the flanks. It usually has pale legs and white undertail-coverts, although sometimes the legs can be dark and the undertail-coverts buff. The margins of the remiges are yellow-green, not blue-grey. The value of this last feature seems to be underestimated in the literature, as it was quite easy to see on the Bay-breasted Warbler at Land's End.

Age and sex

The bird was obviously a first-winter. The grey rump suggested that it was a male, as first-winter females have an olive rump (Curson *et al.* 1994). The blue-grey median coverts may also suggest that the bird was a male, as does the exceptionally bright colouring.

Ferguson, D. 1997. Bay-breasted Warbler in Cornwall: new to Britain and Ireland. *British Birds* 90, 444–449.

Bay-breasted Warbler is an uncommon breeding bird in northern North America; it winters in Central America and northern South America.

There have been no subsequent records.

THE BIRDER'S YEAR

Tim Cleeves

1996 produced four Firsts for Britain, all from North America – Redhead, American Coot, Indigo Bunting and Canvasback. And 'Steppe' Grey Shrike received recognition as a full species exactly 40 years after the First on Fair Isle.

So you thought an inland county like Nottinghamshire would be bottom of the ace-rarity list? Well not so. In 1996 both the Redhead and Britain's second **Cedar Waxwing**, also from North America, turned up there.

On February 20th, in the Sherwood district of Nottingham, Peter Smith was checking through a flock of 160 Waxwings when he came across a bird with white undertail-coverts – the rest, as they say, is history. The first British record of Cedar Waxwing had been on Noss, Shetland, in June 1985 – and was seen by just four people – so the Nottingham bird, with the swirling flocks of Waxwings, was the subject of mass appreciation. Even the Chancellor of the Exchequer – and local MP – Ken Clarke turned out to see it!

The early winter period was dominated by **Waxwings**, with an estimate of over 10,000 birds in Britain, equalling and possibly exceeding the massive irruption of 1965/66. An influx of **Arctic Redpolls**, which began in the autumn of 1995, resulted in more birds being found in early 1996. A minimum of 236 birds were found in the early winter period. These 'Arctic rolls' were not confined to coastal localities, with many inland sightings among localities in 25 counties.

Four **Black-throated Thrushes** were found, helping to keep the winter blues at bay. Two **Pine Buntings**, one at Halesowen, West Midlands, in February and the other in South Yorkshire in March, provided great opportunities to enjoy one of our rarer buntings. On 8th March, a male **Redhead** was found on the gravel pits at Bleasby near Nottingham, a First for Britain and a bird to give even more hope to landlocked birders in Notts; another great find in the county.

In April you could have burnt many gallons of fossil fuels zooming around Britain to seek the rare birds on offer. Pride of place went to **American Coot** – a First for Britain, found at Stodmarsh, Kent, on 16th April. A **Calandra Lark** stayed for two

215

days on St Agnes, Isles of Scilly, and two first-summer female **Harlequin Ducks** were discovered at Girvan, Ayrshire.

It was early June before the next 'mega' burst on the scene – Britain's fourth **Caspian Plover**, a female found at Skelberry, South Mainland, Shetland. Singing **River Warblers** were found in the summer in Staffordshire and Northumberland, continuing the recent good run for this species in Britain.

Gull-billed Tern is a very difficult bird to catch up with in Britain (those which are not Sandwich Terns!), and they tend to move on swiftly. A long-staying Gull-billed Tern at Penclacwydd, Carmarthenshire, was much appreciated from July into August. July is often a month for really 'off-the-wall' records and a chirping **Spanish Sparrow** serenading the local female House Sparrows at Waterside in the depths of Cumbria was totally unexpected.

There really is not a lot of recognition of the season of 'summer' in the birding calendar. No sooner have all the 'spring' migrants passed through than 'autumn' migration begins. If you are a Green Sandpiper, for example, life must get quite disorientating. One day you are at a sewage farm and being logged as a spring migrant, say on 15th June, and the next day it's autumn, and you might be expected to be migrating south instead of north. No change then in 'autumn' 1996 as the pools and creeks started to fill with migrating waders. Among them a **Sharp-tailed Sandpiper** was found at Foryd Bay, Gwynedd, two **Black-winged Pratincoles** were seen and, on 25th August, a **Solitary Sandpiper** was a star find on St Mary's, Isles of Scilly.

The autumn spilled rare birds from West and East, including 15 **Great Snipes**, five **Blyth's Reed Warblers**, a **Common Yellowthroat** on Bardsey, Gwynedd, and a **Baltimore Oriole** and a **Buff-bellied Pipit** were discovered on Scilly (a repeat of the duo in autumn 1988).

At Landguard, Suffolk, a perverse **Crested Lark** alighted twice – on 2nd October for four hours and on 9th October for 20 minutes. Was it having a laugh? It was also in October that the rarest wader of the year arrived – Britain's second **Great Knot** shuffled around the mudflats of Seal Sands, Teesmouth, from 13th October to 5th November. This bird made an elite band of birdwatchers – the owners of high-power Questar telescopes – very popular indeed. Without them, no-one was getting a decent view of the so-called 'Great Dot' right out on the Seal Sands mudflats. A **'Two-barred' Greenish Warbler** was present at Holkham Meals, Norfolk, on 15th and 16th October. This is an extremely rare bird and at the time only the second ever discovered in Britain.

Autumn 1996 was very good for North American passerines. After the Buff-bellied Pipit and Baltimore Oriole on Scilly, there was a **Northern Waterthrush** at Portland Bill, Dorset, for four days from 14th October.

The third new bird for Britain arrived on Ramsey, Pembrokeshire – a first-winter male **Indigo Bunting** present from 18th to 26th October. Previous records had been adjudged potential escapes but this one passed muster. Other North American passerines seen in the autumn of 1996 were two **Bobolinks** on Scilly, eight **Red-eyed Vireos**, a **Blackpoll Warbler**, a **White-throated Sparrow**, a **Swainson's Thrush** and FOUR **Black-and-white Warblers**, including birds in Sussex and Norfolk.

A **Blyth's Pipit** in Norfolk in October was a skilful find for local patch birders. Another excellent find was a **'Steppe' Grey Shrike** celebrating its new specific status as it tucked into House Sparrows in Essex in November, only the thirteenth British record. This shrike is placed in the Southern Grey Shrike species group but is likely to be another species again – all British records of the sedentary Southern Grey Shrike have been of the migratory Central Asian 'Steppe' Grey Shrike form. There had been four 'normal' **Paddyfield Warbler** records earlier in the autumn, but a bird at Marazion Marsh, Cornwall, from 16th November to December 28th was late in the extreme and a good end to a very lively birding year.

Unbeknown to the wider world, the First **Canvasback** had been seen in Kent on 7th December; happily it – or another – was found in Norfolk in January 1997.

A TURNING POINT

Alistair Crowle

For Arctic Redpoll aficionados, 1996 began where the previous one left off, but on a personal level, I greeted January with no particular plan. The previous year had been difficult for my family with the sudden and unexpected death of my mother and I was just happy to be moving on. As it turned out, this would be an important year for me with new opportunities as well as many new birds.

The morning of 3rd February found me at Redditch in the West Midlands for the Black-throated Thrush. The bird had been there a few days so the main crowd had been and gone. When I arrived, only a few people were watching as it flew around the housing estate. Fortunately, it showed well and I was able to get good views of a bird that I had long wanted to see. The end of the month brought the discovery of a Cedar Waxwing in Nottingham, forcing a reassessment of the 1985 Shetland bird and its subsequent elevation to Category A.

Winter ended with Britain's first Redhead, discovered at Bleasby on 8th March, also in Nottinghamshire, giving hope to all of us living in landlocked counties that maybe residing away from the coast is not all that bad.

April brought the two Harlequin Ducks at Girvan in Ayrshire. I quite fancied seeing them but it was a long way from where I was living in Wigan, Greater Manchester. I had an interview in Newcastle for a job with RSPB on the 17th and, egged on by Tim Melling, I decided to go for the birds afterwards.

I was the second interviewee and practically ran out of the door afterwards much to the surprise of some of the staff, who I learned later had me marked down as obviously having had a nightmare interview. I only had a rough idea of the location of the Harlequins so decided to deliberately hit the coast south of where I thought they were and work my way north. Soon enough, I came across a birder looking down onto the sea. Within moments, I was having my first view of a species with which I have since become extremely familiar. The next day I was offered the job with RSPB and on 21st I finally caught up with the elusive Lesser Yellowlegs at Houghton Pond near Warrington, Cheshire. Further south, at Stodmarsh in Kent, an American Coot had been found by a sharp-eyed observer on 19th and showed well for 14 days.

In June, I took up my new post with RSPB as their Conservation Officer for Cumbria and Yorkshire Dales, although for the first two months I was based at the Regional Office in Newcastle whilst I learnt the organisational ropes. On my first afternoon, we learned that a boat was going out to Coquet Island and there were a few spaces available. It was a fantastic first day as there is always something special about the noise and excitement of a seabird colony. The three birds of the month for me were the Surf Scoter in the channel between Coquet and the mainland, the Spanish Sparrow at Waterside in Cumbria and the River Warbler in Kielder Forest, Northumberland. My abiding memory of the latter is the swarms of mosquitoes and midges that assailed anyone venturing out of their car.

On 1st July, I left work early with my regional manager, Andy Bunten, to have a look at the White-winged Black Tern on the North Tees Marshes. As befitted his status, Andy was wearing a very smart suit which necessitated his having to tiptoe around the muddy track like some bearded ballerina. Nonetheless, we still managed to see the bird well.

It was about this time that I made my first visit to Geltsdale RSPB Reserve in the North Pennines and became personally acquainted with the national disgrace that is the persecution of birds of prey and, in particular, the Hen Harrier. That year a pair had nested close to the edge of the reserve, which allowed the site manager, Malcolm Stott, to organise a watch on the nest relatively easily and Border TV covered the events very successfully. Since then, the numbers of nesting harriers at this, one of the species' former strongholds, have gradually declined to the present situation where there are no breeding birds.

As part of my induction, I was sent with a colleague, Richard Archer, to Dumfries & Galloway to meet a modern-day legend within RSPB. Chris Rollie was then the conservation officer for the area and would be my immediate neighbour to the north. Like Richard and myself, Chris worked from home and had developed a great deal of experience of how to operate without the immediate support of a Regional Office. Chris is one of the most remarkable people I know. He has boundless enthusiasm and knowledge that is not just confined to birds but spans Robbie Burns (on whom he has written two books) through to church architecture and Celtic Football Club. On this occasion, he took us on a seemingly aimless visit to the coast, where, walking along a clifftop, he suggested that we have a seat. It was a beautiful morning and within a few minutes a Chough had appeared on the cliffs below us, one half of the only Scottish mainland nesting pair. Chris had, of course, engineered the trip to give us this excellent surprise.

In August, my father retired so I decided to spend a few days with him in Cambridgeshire to mark the occasion, and whilst there I took the opportunity of seeing the Buff-breasted Sandpiper at Hanningfield Reservoir on 24th. On the day I travelled back to Cumbria, I was faced with some choices: go to North Wales for the Sharp-tailed Sandpiper or go through Derbyshire for the Blue-winged Teal and then on to Leighton Moss, Lancashire, for the Black-winged Pratincole. I chose the teal/pratincole option on the grounds that if I missed the pratincole at what was effectively my local patch, I would never hear the end of it! I was also keen to compare this species with the Collared Pratincole I had seen in May at Earls Barton in Northamptonshire. Although I saw both the teal and the pratincole, with hindsight, I wish I had gone for the Sharp-tailed.

September was another varied month meeting new colleagues and various RSPB members groups. I went out for a trip on the RSPB-run pelagic from Bridlington, East Yorkshire. Not one of the classic days with only a Bonxie and a Sooty Shearwater for our efforts but we also managed to catch up with a Barred Warbler in the afternoon at Flamborough.

In October, I found myself with many others trying to get decent views of the Great Knot at Seal Sands on Teesside, but at least it was not raining. Those with more time and money were able to travel to Ramsey Island to see what would become the first accepted Indigo Bunting for Britain.

On the night of 5th November, I had a telephone conversation with Tim Melling. He had just been talking to one of our colleagues, Nick Mason, who had found a strange shrike by Stocks Reservoir in the Forest of Bowland, Lancashire. We agreed to meet there at dawn to have a look. It was a wild night and I had to stop and pull bits of tree off the road in the early morning darkness, a job made no easier by my head-lights continually cutting out. Having made it to the reservoir and met up with Tim and the others, we quickly located a first-year Isabelline Shrike which stayed for a few days and provided excellent views for those who made the journey to this isolated spot.

On 9th November, I travelled down to Marshside, Lancashire, with Simon Webb to look for the Snow Goose. We had not been there long when one of the best sights in nature appeared in the sky in front of us – geese in their thousands, in this case Pinkfeet, their calls ringing out over the saltmarsh. In their midst, standing out like a beacon was the Snow Goose. It is a shame that so many are tarred with the brush of 'escapes' as there is something magical about them.

On 7th December, some lucky observers found a male Canvasback on North Quarry Pools at Cliffe in Kent. Sadly, as this was a private site, the birding fraternity had to wait until the following year before catching up with this long-expected American duck.

Although still needing Sharp-tailed Sandpiper, I look back to 1996 and realise what a defining year it became. The move to RSPB and Cumbria brought me into contact with many people who have since become good friends and through them I have been able to get to know places like Iceland and Fair Isle intimately. Had I not taken the opportunities that presented themselves in 1996, there is no doubt in my mind that my life would have been much poorer as a result.

Alistair Crowle lives in Northamptonshire. He has worked for the Joint Nature Conservation Committee and RSPB and is currently the Uplands Ecologist for English Nature.

MARCH 1996
REDHEAD IN NOTTINGHAMSHIRE
Mark Dennis

Achance conversation with Simon Roberts on Friday 8th March 1996 resulted in my searching a former gravel pit at Bleasby, Nottinghamshire, for (reported) Bearded Tits *Panurus biarmicus*.

I arrived at around 15.45 GMT and set off to seek the area most likely to hold Bearded Tits, walking the 40-ha complex anti-clockwise. As the footpath skirted the first small (3–4 ha) pool on the circuit, Common Pochards *Aythya ferina* began to emerge from their feeding area under the overhanging vegetation. As they swam away, I casually raised my binoculars and immediately saw a larger, slightly darker but otherwise Common Pochard-like bird which I identified as a drake Redhead *A. americana*. I am very familiar with Common Pochard, as my job as Senior Warden at Colwick Country Park brings me into contact with the species throughout the winter, so I knew that the darker individual was something different; I have seen public collections which held both Canvasback *A. valisineria* and Redhead, so I knew which features to look for.

I quickly returned to the car with mixed emotions: completely sure of my identification, but obviously dubious of the bird's origins. I settled down to take notes and was able to view the bird through 10×42 binoculars at a range of about 100 m. I then compiled as thorough a description as I could, using Common Pochard for direct comparison. After ten minutes or so, I telephoned other local observers, but was able to contact only two: John Hopper, the County Recorder, and Bernie Ellis, who arrived after what seemed to me an interminable wait. We then all enjoyed good views as the Redhead fed, preened and courted a female Common Pochard within the small flock.

During this period of observation, both legs were noted to be without rings, and full perfect wings were seen; further notes were then taken.

Description (from notes taken on 8th & 9th March)
Obviously bigger and sitting higher in the water than Common Pochard. All subsequent comments relate to a direct comparison with Common Pochard.

Same basic plumage and coloration. Bill longish, with fine black line at base (not easy to see). Lower mandible straight, blackish underside. Upper mandible decurved to halfway, but not so much as on Common Pochard, more proportioned. A white band on bill was cut square and not angled, less clear-cut towards the 'face' and grading into the general blue/grey colour of the bill; black 'dipped in ink' tip and nail; slight hook at tip. Nostrils large, blackish inside. Leg colour not properly noted; no rings on legs. Eye colour yellow/orange, but more yellowy; pupil black.

Head shape recalled that of Red-crested Pochard *Netta rufina*, especially in silhouette, having steep forehead and full-looking back of head, quite different from that of Common Pochard. Breast black, fuller than that of Common Pochard, and seemingly ending squarer on sides, not curved as on Common Pochard. Belly whitish. Tail greyish. Rump and undertail blackish, which seemed to be slightly more extensive than on Common Pochard, also slightly different shape. Mantle vermiculated darker grey. Flanks warmer than the steely cold grey of Common Pochard. Wing colour and pattern not clearly seen, but had a full, perfect set of wings.

Behaviour identical to that of Common Pochard. When the birds first moved out from the bank, it swam away in typical Common Pochard manner: unhurried, but purposeful. It fed with them in a similar manner, making short dives and coming up with a bill full of weed. Call 'weeooo', similar to that of Eurasian Wigeon *Anas penelope*, but less whistly.

Unfortunately, the initial site was private and the local Parish Council Chairperson flatly refused en-bloc access, agreeing only to 'local' viewing. Next morning, about 20 'locals' were on site at dawn. Fortunately, the bird was flushed by a dog-walker and flew to the nearby Gibsmere pool, which allowed public viewing. News was broadcast via our own Nottinghamshire Birdnews service and the national lines, and Bleasby braced itself for the invasion.

I was away for the weekend, but I understand that local parking evolved, and Bleasby traders had an excellent day. I was also away when the bird slipped away with the wintering Common Pochards, right on cue, being last seen on 27th March. During its 20-day stay, it provided numerous photo opportunities (*Brit. Birds* 90: plate 164; 91: plates 37–40).

Dennis, M. 1996. The Redhead in Nottingham – a new Western Palearctic bird. *Birding World* 9, 93–97.

Redhead is a widespread breeding species in North America; it winters in coastal lowlands from the Great Lakes south to Mexico and Cuba.

There have been three subsequent records:

Leicestershire Rutland Water, male, 4th–24th February 1997 (the Nottingham bird?)

Glamorgan Kenfig Pool, etc., male, 7th November 2001–5th February 2002; 21st September 2002–23rd February 2003; 29th October 2003–18th March 2004; 13th October–26th December 2004

Outer Hebrides Loch Tangasdail, Barra, female, 20th September 2003–15th April 2004; 8th November 2004

APRIL 1996
AMERICAN COOT IN KENT
Chris Hindle

On 16th April 1996, I was birding at Stodmarsh NNR, Kent, together with my wife Anne and son Matthew. Although migrants were uppermost in my mind, I thought that this would be a timely opportunity to familiarise myself with Common Coots *Fulica atra* prior to a birding trip to northern Morocco, where Red-knobbed Coot *F. cristata* would be a possibility. I was conscious that I needed to be absolutely sure what a Common Coot actually looked like! Upon reaching the Lampen Wall, I paused and scanned the reedbed and pools while the others carried on ahead. Having seen nothing of note, I turned my attention to the Common Coots. I focused my binoculars on the nearest coot, which was feeding actively about 20 m in front of me, and was surprised to find that the bird in question had no indentation where the bill met the shield and, furthermore, had what appeared to be a patch of black skin above the oddly shaped shield. Somewhat bemused, I looked again and noticed a black subterminal band on the bill. Although I was unfamiliar with American Coot *F. americana*, not having been to North America, I recalled the account of the bird at Ballycotton, Co. Cork, in 1981 (Hutchinson *et al.* 1984), which mentioned that it had white undertail-coverts. I looked once more at the bird in front of me and, lo and behold, there they were: conspicuous white undertail-coverts!

Although my wife and son returned in due course, and checked through the features I had observed, there was no-one else to discuss the bird with, and since I had a suspicion that a hybrid Common Coot × Moorhen *Gallinula chloropus* could be confused with American Coot, we decided to return home and compare our notes with published descriptions. These seemed to confirm that the bird I had found was indeed an American Coot! I then phoned various people, most of whom were out, but eventually I managed to track down Brian Short at work, and he agreed to meet me at Stodmarsh 45 minutes later. Brian passed the news on to John Cantelo, and it was in fact John who arrived at Stodmarsh first. John concurred with my identification, as, shortly afterwards, did Brian Short and Don Worsfold. By this time, the bird had swum off into a small stream running into the main dyke, so our views were adequate rather than exceptional, and the bird continued to feed here for the remainder of the evening. By the following morning, it had returned to the main dyke, and the large crowd which had gathered was rewarded with excellent views of this national 'first'. Over the following week, it entertained hundreds, if not thousands, of birders, and continued to be seen regularly until 29th or 30th April (*Brit. Birds* 90: 467).

Description

The bird's overall structure appeared slightly less bulky than that of Common Coot, with a flatter back and a more angular or 'chunky' head on a shorter neck. It was a particularly active bird, constantly diving and pulling up pondweed, which was consumed on the surface. When swimming, it had a head-jerking action similar to that shown by Moorhen.

The entire head and neck were essentially jet black, which merged into the fairly uniform greyish-black body. When up-ending to dive, the lower belly was noted as being pale grey. Only the outer undertail-coverts were white, and these were clearly not as well marked or conspicuous as those of Moorhen.

The bill and the small frontal shield on the forehead were cold white with a slight ivory tint, but the bill tip appeared to show a hint of blue, not pink as often seen in Common Coot. The bill also possessed an obvious dark subterminal band that became diffuse towards the cutting edge and which, at close range, appeared to show a slight reddish tinge. Above the 'U-shaped' upper border to the shield, there was a slightly swollen, oval-shaped patch of bare skin which appeared black through binoculars but was, in fact, dark red when seen through a telescope. The profile formed where the edge of the bill and shield met the black feathering of the head was almost straight, unlike Common Coot, which has a marked indentation of black feathering coming to a point and partially separating the shield and bill. The irides were red, while the legs and feet appeared little different from those of Common Coot.

It was largely silent, but when threatened by territorial Common Coots it uttered a repeated gruff 'kwok'.

Hindle, C. 2004. American Coot in Kent: new to Britain.
British Birds 97, 444–447.

*American Coot is widely distributed in North and Central America; northern popula-
tions winter in the southern USA.*

There have been four, five or six subsequent records:

Cumbria South Walney, first-summer, 17th April 1999

Shetland Loch of Clickimin, Mainland, first-winter, 30th November 2003–5th
April 2004

Outer Hebrides West Loch Ollay, 25th January–7th April 2004

Dumfries & Galloway Castle Loch, February 11th–17th 2004

***Shetland** Loch of Benston, Mainland, 13th November 2004–25th March 2005
(2003 bird?)

***Outer Hebrides** Coot Loch, Benbecula, 25th February 2005–7th April 2005
(2004 bird?)

The First for Ireland was at Ballycotton, Co. Cork from 7th February–4th April
1981.

*Awaiting BBRC decision

SEPTEMBER 1956

'STEPPE' GREY SHRIKE
ON FAIR ISLE

Kenneth Williamson

A first-winter example of *Lanius excubitor pallidirostris*,
variously known as Bogdanoff's Shrike (Dresser
1895), Grimm's Grey Shrike (Dresser 1902), and the
Steppe Shrike (Edberg 1954), was watched, trapped
and examined in the hand at Fair Isle on 21st
September 1956, the first occasion on which this
form has been recognised in the British Isles.

With my daughter Hervör I was maintaining a watch
over a group of Japanese mist-nets in crops and stubble on the
afternoon of 21st September when a large and exceedingly pale grey
shrike flew into the area and alighted on one of the mist-net supports. During the next
hour we had it under constant observation, and were joined successively by R. F. Allison,
M. F. M. Meiklejohn and (after the capture of the bird) H. A. Craw. At the Bird
Observatory it was also seen by Miss Janet M. McLellan, my wife and G. Stansfield.

We found the bird remarkably confiding, and were able to get excellent close-up views and take down observations on plumage and field-characters. At first we tried to ensnare it in one or other of the nets, but it was too intent on making good vantage-points of the bamboo supports and their guys to give much hope of capture by this means. After half-an-hour or so it left the root-crops, to which it had descended from time to time for insects, and flew with deep undulations to the neighbourhood of the Haa, where there is a Heligoland trap. Eventually we were fortunate enough to catch it there – assisted by a small flock of Starling (*Sturnus vulgaris*) which 'mobbed' the bird as it passed in front of the entrance.

It had a superficial resemblance in size, carriage and manner of flight to a Great Grey Shrike (*L. e. excubitor*), but was a much paler and cleaner grey, and far less wild than any Great Grey Shrike I have encountered. The under-parts were suffused with pinkish-buff, but the pale grey of the flank-feathers tended to smother the contrast between upper and underparts. The wing was beautifully variegated and a detailed description is given later, but it is perhaps worth noting here that the amount of white visible was greater than in *excubitor* and more reminiscent of the condition found in Lesser Grey Shrikes (*L. minor*). A white shoulder-patch was present as in *excubitor* (there is none in the Lesser Grey), but the head was very different: firstly, the broad black band behind the eye ended squarely, and was not gently rounded posteriorly as in the Great Grey; secondly, the lores were dusky, not black; and thirdly, the base of the bill was noticeably pale, appearing pale brown at a short distance, whereas the bill of the other is wholly black. The bird was provisionally identified as *pallidirostris* on this character coupled with the very pale coloration, and the identification was later confirmed in the laboratory with the aid of Dresser (1895, 1902), Hartert (1910) and Meinertzhagen (1954).

The shrike may well have been newly arrived as 21st September was a fine day of moderate south-easterly wind, ahead of a weak cold front stretching from north to south of the British Isles.

Description

The whole of the upperparts were pale french-grey, the rump having a slight yellowish tinge; the scapulars were slightly paler with their whitish tips forming a shoulder-band, suffused with yellowish. The chief feature of the head was the broad black band on the ear-coverts, square-cut posteriorly; some of these feathers had slight brownish fringes, the lores were dusky, and there was a narrow white eye-stripe. The malar region, chin and throat were whitish, the breast and upper belly pinkish-buff, and the lower portions off-white with a greyish suffusion on the flanks.

Wing Primaries blackish-brown, their basal halves white, and the three innermost tipped with white. Primary coverts blackish-brown, the innermost with white tips. Secondaries blackish-brown with broad white tips and outer edges. Alula dark brown, the feathers fringed whitish. Greater coverts dark brown mottled buffish towards the tips and fringed with white. Median coverts jet black, forming a bar across the mid-wing: these feathers appeared to be new in comparison with the other coverts, which were more abraded. Lesser coverts french-grey with dark tips obscured by yellowish fringes. Underwing-coverts and axillaries white.

Tail The two outer pairs of feathers were white, the next pair black with white outer webs, white at the base and with broad white tips; the fourth pair was similar but with the white basal patch and tips reduced; the fifth pair was blackish-brown, and the middle pair dark brown.

Bare Parts The bill was horn-coloured, the ridge of the culmen black, and both mandibles darkened perceptibly towards the tip, the underside of the lower mandible becoming black. There was a strong flesh-coloured tinge at the base of the bill, very pronounced in the field. The tarsi were blackish-brown, the claws black.

Field-characters The best field-characters are provided by the very pale grey appearance, without any strong contrast between upper- and under-parts; the abruptly squared termination of the broad black band behind the eye; and the noticeably pale base of the bill, which appears to be pale brown rather than flesh-colour at a short distance.

Williamson, K. 1957. A desert race of the Great Grey Shrike, new to the British Isles. *British Birds* 50, 246–249.

'Steppe' Grey Shrike **Lanius (meridionalis) pallidirostris** *is the migratory Central Asian form of Southern Grey Shrike, a sedentary species of southern Europe. 'Steppe' Grey Shrike winters in Sudan and Ethiopia.*

There have been 16 subsequent records to the end of 2004.

OCTOBER 1996

INDIGO BUNTING IN PEMBROKESHIRE

Ian Bullock

On 18th October, the telephone rang not long after first light. It was a message to say 'Darren's found a bird and it's definitely not a Rosefinch'! It was enough to have me reaching for waterproofs, notebook and car keys.

I had 10 minutes to 'phone round local birders for a couple of companions, and two of the keenest were already at the lifeboat station as I ran down the steps. While we butted across the sound in the Ramsey boat, *Shearwater*, I had time to review Darren's roll of honour: Darren Woodhead, Pembrokeshire's Ramsey Island and October are a heady mix. He had first come to Ramsey as an art student several years before, but staying on the island in October 1993 to prepare some illustrations for our reception displays, he had found a Pied Wheatear which landed on the farmhouse fence beside him. Staying with us in late October 1994, he found a Yellow-rumped Warbler which was to treat over 400 birders to spectacular views.

At 12.30 pm the day before, as he walked down to the farmhouse, a small bird had landed on the stone wall ahead of him. At first glance it had seemed rather rosefinch-like, but it flipped over into the rushes beyond the farmhouse garden to find shelter from the horizontal rain, so Darren stalked it and waited. At last, it came up onto the wire fence and, yes, it had a dark eye in a plain face, no striking features, and a finch-like bill, but only a single wing-bar and apparently *dark* legs. Something was not right!

As the four of us surrounded the garden that next morning, we were all looking for the same details, but Darren had another name with which to tantalise us. After making detailed field sketches and a frantic search through the field guides, he had not been able to shake another name from his head: Indigo Bunting.

After careful stalking, we found it, perched in *Juncus* clumps, feeding on the seed-heads like a Linnet. From a distance, its two-tone impression was reminiscent of a Spotted Flycatcher: silvery grey below and browner above. There was faint streaking on the pale breast, a darker brown back with traces of grey streaks, a distinctly warmer tan head reminiscent of female Blackcap, a dark eye in a plain face, a fine, bunting-like bill, and dark grey legs. As the bird turned and fluffed its plumage, at last the key colours could be seen: a glint of smoky caerulean blue on the tail and wing-coverts. A last check of our notes, a comparison of four different field guides, and a final nail-biting consensus: reach for that 'phone!

The news was on Birdline by lunchtime, and eight bumpstart birders made it across to the island before dark on the Saturday. But at dawn on the Sunday, in a force 7 wind and lashing rain, over 300 sodden figures were waiting patiently on the lifeboat steps, staring longingly across Ramsey Sound. In horrendous conditions, we got across all those who waited. This amazing little bird, stoking up on craneflies and blackberries, remained faithful to the same tiny valley until 26th October, to the delight of a total of 630 birders who made the pilgrimage to see it.

Bullock, I. 1996. The Indigo Bunting on Ramsey.
Birding World 9, 398.

Indigo Bunting breeds in southern North America; it winters in Florida, the West Indies and Central America.

There have been no subsequent records.

DECEMBER 1996
CANVASBACK IN KENT
Paul Larkin and David Mercer

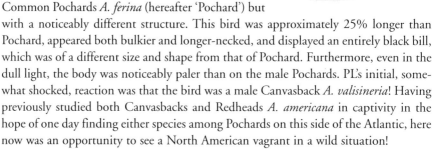

At 14.30 hrs on 7th December 1996, PL was carrying out a recce of the North Quarry pools at Cliffe, Kent, in preparation for a Wetland Bird Survey count there the following weekend. Almost immediately after having begun to count the diving duck present, he came across an *Aythya* duck with a similar plumage pattern to the accompanying Common Pochards *A. ferina* (hereafter 'Pochard') but with a noticeably different structure. This bird was approximately 25% longer than Pochard, appeared both bulkier and longer-necked, and displayed an entirely black bill, which was of a different size and shape from that of Pochard. Furthermore, even in the dull light, the body was noticeably paler than on the male Pochards. PL's initial, somewhat shocked, reaction was that the bird was a male Canvasback *A. valisineria*! Having previously studied both Canvasbacks and Redheads *A. americana* in captivity in the hope of one day finding either species among Pochards on this side of the Atlantic, here now was an opportunity to see a North American vagrant in a wild situation!

About half an hour after the initial discovery, DM arrived and together we made detailed observations of the bird until dusk. We were acutely aware of the pitfalls of a hybrid *Aythya* resembling a pure Canvasback, and thus paid particular attention to the bill. We could detect no suggestion of pale markings, however; indeed, the bill appeared to be that of a classic Canvasback! Despite its distinctive appearance, the bird could at times be difficult to pick out within the Pochard flock, as it frequently tucked its head in and appeared to sleep. We watched it until the light faded completely; subsequent searches of the area over the following days failed to relocate it, and the bird was not seen again.

Despite its rarity, we were unable to release the news to anyone other than the North Kent Recorder, as the site owners had specifically instructed that news of rare birds should not be released. This was primarily because North Quarry is a working quarry and subject to the regulations contained within the Health & Safety at Work Act (1974). Therefore, the presence of large numbers of birdwatchers visiting the site might have resulted in damage, accident or injury, and left the owners liable to prosecution.

Description

Head and neck Head essentially red, but browner in tone than on the accompanying Pochards. A darker area ran over the crown to the rear of the head, round below the cheek to the throat. The feathering between the bill base and the eye became much darker, almost black, making it sometimes difficult to establish where the feathering ended and the bill base began.

The head shape was clearly different from that of Pochard, with the highest point of the head behind the eye, and a steep, but flattish slope down the nape. The forehead merged smoothly into the bill in a long 'ski-slope' curve. The neck was long, perhaps relative to Pochard as Pintail *Anas acuta* is to Mallard *A. platyrhynchos*. This was particularly noticeable when the bird made a neck-stretching display (presumed to be aggressive) to the Pochard. The neck was more evenly thick than on Pochard, which gave it a more muscular appearance, and similar in colour to the paler areas of the head, slightly darker to the rear. When relaxed, the head was held in a more 'swan-like' posture than on Pochard.

Body The body was basically similar in pattern to that of Pochard: breast black, with pale grey mid-body and black stern. It was about 25% larger than Pochard, perhaps approaching the size of a female Mallard, and when seen out of the water, or diving, it was obviously bulkier than Pochard. General body shape was noticeably different from that of Pochard, being deeper in the back and with the centre of gravity appearing further forward. This was particularly obvious when the tail was depressed, giving an attenuated appearance to the rear. The body was also broader-beamed than that of Pochard.

When viewed from the side, the outline of the breast had a noticeable curve, particularly when the head was retracted. In contrast, the Pochards had a straighter, more vertical profile.

Upperparts and flanks greyish-white, paler than on Pochard, and generally appeared concolorous. Occasionally, the upperparts seemed a little darker than the flanks, but this may have been an effect created by the different way the feathers were lying. No vermiculations were visible. The tertials were slightly darker than the rest of the upperparts, forming a darker triangle. The tail, when cocked, was longer and more prominent than that of Pochard, and showed a grey margin, darker than the flanks, similar in tone to the tertials.

When viewed head-on, the black area on the breast was proportionately narrower than on Pochard, with the flanks appearing as prominent pale panels on either side (unlike Pochard). When seen out of the water, the lower breast had a slightly ill-defined edge. The black stern seemed similar in extent and pattern to that of Pochard.

Wings Underwing uniformly pale greyish-white, perhaps paler than the flanks. The upperwing differed from that of Pochard in several ways. The bulk of the forewing was greyish-white, similar in tone to the flanks but darker than the mantle (and paler than on Pochard). The primary coverts appeared darker than the scapulars. The outer primaries appeared darker when the wing was partially open than when the wing was spread, so possibly only the outer webs were darker. The inner primaries showed only darker tips, the darkness of the feather tips gradually fading onto the secondaries. The primary coverts and the remainder of the greater coverts formed a tapering dark line along the mid-wing. The secondaries were basically similar in tone to the rest of the pale wing-coverts. The bird was full-winged.

Bare parts Bill blackish, long and deep based, and slightly reminiscent of Common Eider *Somateria mollissima*. The bill was studied particularly carefully, and from different viewing angles, to confirm that there were no pale areas present. Both legs were seen several times while the bird was preening. They were grey in colour and the bird was unringed. The eye was similar in colour to that of Pochard, although perhaps a little darker.

General behaviour Generally, the Canvasback behaved in a similar fashion to the accompanying Pochards, and dozed between periods of preening and diving. Although associating with the Pochards, it appeared to be dominant over them. At one point, on the close approach of a Pochard, the Canvasback stretched its head forward with bill open in what was assumed to be a show of aggression, and the Pochard gave way. On a separate occasion, it repeated this behaviour towards a Pochard that was preening on a half-submerged branch. As the Pochard retreated, it took over this perch and began to preen itself. While preening, it also raised and stretched its wings, allowing the upperwing and underwing to be inspected. When diving, it jumped out of the water more powerfully than the Pochards, resulting in the head and tail being clear of the water at the same time. In general, the Pochards made much shallower dives.

Discussion

After returning home, PL and DM checked their observations against several references. Of these, the most useful was Madge & Borrow (1991), who noted that one of the distinguishing features is that the grey flank of Canvasback forms a sloping line at the front while that of Pochard is more vertical. This was not noted specifically at the time, but appears on PL's original field sketch.

Although we felt that the identification was not in doubt, the age of the bird had yet to be determined. Consequently, in January 1997, PL visited the WWT at Arundel, West Sussex, to view the captive Canvasbacks held there, and to seek advice on ageing the species. A subsequent visit was made to the WWT at Llanelli, Carmarthenshire (now the National Wetlands Centre Wales), and advice was also sought from the USA via the *ID Frontiers* internet discussion group. The information obtained suggested that, by December, adult males have completed the moult from eclipse and are in full breeding plumage; first-winter males, although variable, generally appear similar to adult males, but the following features may be useful in distinguishing them:

- The body and mantle are a darker shade of grey, with those of adults appearing 'almost white'. This phrase kept appearing when the body and wings of adult drakes were described.
- The tertials are darker on first-winter males than on adults, although some birds can moult these by December. These darker tertials contrast with the paler body plumage.
- The upperparts of adult males, including the mantle, wings and flanks, appear

entirely 'white'. Any male with dark feathering on the upperwing is a first-winter. This feature is variable, however, and first-winters can range from having entirely brownish, female-type wings to just a few retained dark feathers.

We believe that the Cliffe Canvasback was a first-winter male.

Larkin, P. & Mercer, D. 2004. Canvasback in Kent: new to Britain.
British Birds 97, 139–143.

Canvasback breeds in northern USA and Canada; it winters on both coasts of North America south to Mexico.

There have been five subsequent records:

Norfolk Wissington Beet Factory then Welney, male, 18th January–10th March 1997; 3rd December 1997–9th March 1998

Essex Abberton Reservoir, male, 23rd, 24th, 30th November 1997 (Presumed same as Norfolk)

Essex Abberton Reservoir, male, 6th–16th April 1999; 8th November 1999–15th February 2000 (Presumed same as 1997)

Kent Monk's Wall, male, 28th May 1999

Kent Lade, Dungeness, male, 29th January–14th March 2000; 18th November 2000–8th March 2001

Cornwall Par Beach Pool, male, 19th April 2000

Essex Abberton Reservoir, male, 12th November 2000–13th February 2001 (Presumed 1997 bird)

Greater Manchester Pennington Flash, male, 11th–30th July 2002

THE BIRDER'S YEAR

Tim Cleeves

As in 1996, a **Black-throated Thrush** was 'your starter for ten'. This time it was a bird in Hollingwood, Derbyshire, and it brought joy to many. A **'Naumann's Thrush'** (Dusky Thrush of the race *naumanni*) was present at a site in London for six days but, unfortunately, no-one but the finders knew about it. Amazingly, this first-winter bird was just a few kilometres from the site of the 1990 individual.

1997 produced one First for Britain – **Lesser Sand Plover** – and a second which was widely regarded as the First – **Canvasback** – found in January in Norfolk, getting the year off to a cracking start.

In March a confiding male **Little Crake** in Kent provided a great Easter gift for many birders. Britain's second **Spectacled Warbler** was found at Landguard, Suffolk, in April, but it was May before the action really hotted up. **Little Swifts** on the Isle of Wight and on Shetland; a superb, twitchable first-summer male **Collared Flycatcher** at Ethie Mains, Angus; and a **Common Yellowthroat** in Shetland were all great records. Lundy, Devon, had recorded a **Veery** before (in autumn 1987) but a May record in 1997 was outstanding.

A plover first seen during April at Dawlish Warren, Devon, was finally tracked down in June and firmly identified as a first-summer **Semipalmated Plover**, only the second for Britain, following a bird on St Agnes, Scilly, in October 1978. It stayed until 21st September and was very much appreciated. Meanwhile, at the other end of the country, a superb **Blue-cheeked Bee-eater** at the end of June/ early July stayed a fortnight in Shetland, no doubt finding the climate a little harsher than at sites in the Middle East, India or Africa where it might normally be found.

It was August at Pagham Harbour, West Sussex, when local birders belatedly identified Britain's First **Lesser Sand Plover**. The bird was at the same locality as Britain's First Greater Sand Plover, in December 1978.

A **Western Sandpiper** was found on the Musselburgh wader scrape in East Lothian in August. It was never going to be an easy identification – and this bird was in non-breeding plumage – so the finders did exceptionally well to sort this bird out. It was the sixth record for Britain. An adult **Stilt Sandpiper** at Minsmere, Suffolk, in September was the next rare North American wader to turn up; it was the first to be seen in Britain since 1990.

As October loomed, most people were eagerly awaiting some good passerines. This was the year for **Desert Wheatears** with 17 being found between 16th October and 31st December. **Dusky Warblers** also arrived in strength, 16 being found in the autumn. But it was a male **Siberian Rubythroat** at Osmington Mills, Dorset, on 19th October that was undeniably the 'blocker' of the autumn, as it was – sadly – a one-day wonder.

A good solid year without mentioning the **Calandra Lark** on the Isle of Man (do *you* count it on your *British* list?), the twelfth British **'Steppe' Grey Shrike** in Northamptonshire in November, or that huge **Purple Gallinule** stomping around Sandscale Haws, Cumbria, in late October.

A belated addition to the British List was **Hume's Warbler**, which was finally recognised by the BOURC as a separate species from Yellow-browed Warbler in October 1997. The First record had been at Beachy Head, East Sussex, in November 1966.

YEAR LISTING ONE LAST TIME
Alan Davies

It has always been birds. Since a very early age, birds have been the main focus of my life. The reason to get up in the middle of the night, drive hundreds of miles, travel to far-flung parts of the globe, it has always been birds. Way back in 1979, when I was an 18-year-old doing my first contract job for the RSPB in mid-Wales, I clearly remember saying 'To see 300 species would be a lifetime ambition realised and contentment would follow.' I was talking of 300 species in a lifetime – how things have changed!

Less than ten years later, in 1987, Ken Croft and I had set out to see 300 species in a year, in the UK. Sadly, I didn't quite make it and a second attempt in 1989 also resulted in a near miss. Foreign travel then became my main focus for birding resources and the 300 species in a lifetime was beaten in less than a week in Ecuador! For some reason I can't imagine now, I decided to give the 300 in the UK a last try in 1997 and the year turned out to be a great birding adventure.

As always, New Year's Day is a highlight of every birding year, everything counts! I usually start the year close to home and 1997 was no different – just 15 miles away at the Ogwen Estuary, Gwynedd, the first 'good' bird of the year was collected. Careful scanning produced a fine drake American Wigeon. A Little Egret at the same site was still a pretty good bird locally in those days. A Green Sandpiper was watched feeding in a roadside ditch at Llandudno Junction, Conwy, and two Hawfinches were in Beech trees in the Conwy Valley.

In early January, we headed north up the M6 in the small hours. Before dawn we arrived at Waterside, Cumbria. It was a bitterly cold day and we were nervous; the long-staying Spanish Sparrow hadn't been seen the previous day so why had we come? If you're going to get a big list you need to try hard. As dawn broke we reluctantly left the relative warmth of the car and braved the cold. The feeder had plenty of food so that wasn't the problem. A few House Sparrows turned up and went away again; we walked about hoping to strike lucky, nothing. The hours dragged, we were now seriously cold and questioning our sanity, the bird had gone. No it hasn't, it's on the feeder! Suddenly it didn't seem so cold, and what's a couple of hours for a quality bird?

Early in 1997 was a great time to be year listing, with good birds coming thick and fast! A Black-throated Thrush at Hollingwood, Derbyshire, was watched in a suburban back garden. A drake Canvasback, first for Britain no less, was seen on a beet factory pool at Wissington, Norfolk. A Pied-billed Grebe was enjoyed on a park lake, South Norwood, London; the same trip also provided Red-breasted Goose, Ring-necked Duck and Great Grey Shrike!

Local birding also provided plenty of excitement and of course more fuel for the growing year list. Holyhead Harbour, Anglesey, produced Black-throated Diver and Red-necked Grebe, while a Firecrest dazzled at Malltraeth. Conwy RSPB Reserve held a redhead Smew.

Into February and less time spent on the road. However, news of an Olive-backed Pipit wintering in Devon was too good to miss. A long drive through the night had us in Brixham by early morning. We joined the queue and filed through a terrace house to view the tiny back garden complete with its Olive-backed Pipit! How many other hobbies could produce such circumstances? No time for contemplating such things at the time, more birds to see. We tracked down the Little Bunting at South Milton Ley, then blasted north to score with Penduline Tit at Westhay, Somerset. A pretty good day!

Back in North Wales, regular coverage of my local patch, Conwy RSPB, paid off with second-winter Iceland Gull on the 6th and a Mediterranean Gull the very next day. March saw many more motorway miles on the clock for Blue-winged Teal in Derbyshire and a long haul down to Kent for a stunning Little Crake at Bough Beech Reservoir.

April's highlight was Britain's second Spectacled Warbler, at Landguard Bird Observatory, Suffolk, on the 27th. Not one of my favourite twitches of the year. The warbler took a good time to locate and when it was found a crush ensued to view the bird. Eventually, we all enjoyed good views. Other good birds in April included a Black-winged Stilt on the Llyn Peninsula, Caernarfonshire, Glaucous Gull at Seaforth, Liverpool, a Shore Lark on Anglesey, and two Glossy Ibises flying into roost at Pilling, Lancashire.

A great start to May with a male Citrine Wagtail at Maer Lake, Cornwall, on the 6th. A cracking bird and a species that I had long wanted to catch up with. The edge was taken off it a little when Ted Abraham rang to inform me that a Citrine Wagtail was now showing in Lancashire, some two hours from home compared to the seven hours I had just spent driving to Cornwall!

Four days later and I was in north Norfolk watching a Night Heron at Holkham. Of course a trip to Norfolk in May gives a huge boost to any year list! Other goodies included Dotterel, Stone Curlew, Temminck's Stint and a Woodlark.

June was hectic with good birds coming thick and fast. North up the M6 to Dock Acres gravel pits, Lancashire, for a breeding-plumaged Pied-billed Grebe, not a year tick but too good to drive past en route to a Roller at Lochaber, Dumfries & Galloway.

Into the Midlands for singing Great Reed Warbler at Netherfield, Nottinghamshire, and an embarrassing hole on my UK life list plugged.

Hardly time to draw breath and down the M5 to Dawlish Warren, Devon, for Britain's second Semipalmated Plover.

Another long day saw female Red-footed Falcon in Oxfordshire, crippling views! Then down to Gloucestershire for a Squacco Heron at a large ornamental garden pond!

By contrast, July was a month spent birding locally and with few year ticks. A long drive to Kent resulted in rather poor views of a male Black-headed Bunting and a night in a really crummy and weird B&B. The bedroom was done out in lace with numerous dead moths around the room.

August 16th was a hot day and early morning saw us stuck in traffic some six hours into a journey to Pagham Harbour, Sussex. A breeding-plumaged 'Greater Sand Plover' had been found and after a lean July I needed some year ticks. So here I was sat in a traffic jam getting hot and bothered! The traffic was hardly moving and it was this day more than any other that I questioned year listing in the UK. I had seen Greater Sand Plover before, both here and abroad, yet here I was struggling to see another! Finally, we arrived and eventually had distant but reasonable views of the bird and added Curlew Sandpiper to the year list. Then a long tiring drive home. Of course, it was days later that the news broke that the sand plover had been re-identified as a Lesser Sand Plover, the first for Britain and we had seen it!

August 23rd and another rare wader, Western Sandpiper. The bird had been at Aberlady Bay on the 22nd, so we drove through the night and trudged across the dunes to view the bay. No sandpiper. We waited and scanned, no. Then birders were running, so were we, the Western Sand had been relocated at Musselburgh Lagoons. We did a good impression of a Formula One grid as everyone piled into cars and burnt rubber! We soon had the Western Sandpiper in our scopes, whew! Then further north to King's Barn, Fife, for an adult Bonaparte's Gull before the long drive home, well pleased.

No time to rest, next day saw us over the Pennines to Hornsea Mere, Yorkshire, and a White-winged Black Tern. A call from home told of an adult Rose-coloured Starling on Anglesey – can't be everywhere, sadly. Back over the Pennines into Lancashire and a Black-winged Pratincole at Martin Mere WWT Reserve. No sign of the Rosy Starling next day. August finished with a Spotted Crake at Parkgate Marsh, on the Dee Estuary, Cheshire.

It was a long drive to Cornwall for a Lesser Yellowlegs but it had to be done! So the 5th of September saw us on the Hayle estuary watching this elegant wader. Seawatching at Pendeen produced Sooty Shearwater, Balearic Shearwater and

Pomarine Skua. With good seawatching conditions, we stayed down and enjoyed amazing views of juvenile Sabine's Gull on Lyme Regis beach, Dorset. We ended the same day with a Grey Phalarope.

Good birds just kept coming – Stilt Sandpiper at Minsmere, Suffolk. A Spotted Sandpiper in the Northeast. A rare twitch to Bardsey Island, Caernarfonshire, for Isabelline Wheatear ended with chronic sea sickness when the boat broke down and we were adrift for hours, luckily on the way back from the bird!

The year had flown by and suddenly it was October and of course no big year would be complete without a visit to the Isles of Scilly. We arrived on St Mary's on the 13th and quickly dumped the bags in our Hugh Town flat and set off in pursuit of the Common Yellowthroat! Over four hours stood in Porthloo Lane produced just one glimpse of the bird! Not a good start. A Blackcap and a Brown Rat were the other highlights. We gave up and walked to the Garrison where a Yellow-browed Warbler was the only year-tick of the day!

The 14th dawned calm and sunny, and another try to nail the yellowthroat. Finally, we got some views that allowed this Yank to be added to the list, whew! We then took the 10 am boat to Tresco and worked hard for Blackpoll Warbler, also a Firecrest. On the Great Pool poor views of Black Duck – will nothing show well?! A Richard's Pipit flew over us on Castle Down.

The rest of the week was pretty quiet with Red-breasted Flycatcher and Rose-coloured Starling being the highlights. We did eventually have great views of the Common Yellowthroat. I left Scilly on 293 species for the year, surely 300 would be possible?

A Pied Wheatear showed well at Kilnsea, Yorkshire, in late October. By mopping up a few winter birds that eluded me early in the year, November saw the 1997 year list on 299 and I had not seen a Tawny Owl! No way was that going to be 300, so I needed a year tick just in case I accidentally came across a Tawny!

News of a Great White Egret in Northamptonshire was just the job. So we headed off south and tried to find the site. Our directions were vague and the people we asked were less than helpful. Eventually we found a lake but no bird! No other birders around either. We walked about and noticed another lake; at last the Great White Egret was in the scope and I'd seen 300 species in just eleven months. Can't say it felt that good. Surprisingly, it was rather an anticlimax; it was over, the thing that had obsessed me for eleven months was done, finished. I felt a little empty.

Just two more birds were added to my 1997 list; and yes, I did get Tawny Owl. The other was much less expected, Bluethroat at Conwy RSPB Reserve and not one but two birds! An amazing record to finish off a great year of birding. My desire for UK year listing is satisfied, but not for seeing birds. If anything I am keener now than ever to get out in the field and enjoy birds.

Alan Davies lives in North Wales where he is site manager at the RSPB Conwy Reserve. The joint founder of both Birdline Northwest and Birdline Wales, he is now retired from UK twitching but is keen on local patch birding.

AUGUST 1997

LESSER SAND PLOVER IN WEST SUSSEX

Jack Hunt

At 09.00 GMT on Thursday 14th August 1997, Ralph Hollins, accompanied by Alistair Martin, arrived at Church Norton, Pagham Harbour, West Sussex. The first bird to attract his attention was a very pale plover *Charadrius*, clearly a different species from the Ringed Plovers *C. hiaticula* that it accompanied. Just as RH was drawing AM's attention to the bird, they were joined by John W. P. Bacon and Tim Edwards, followed by others, so that eventually the bird was being watched by eight observers.

That afternoon, I received a telephone call from Alan Ford, another regular Pagham birder, to inform me that a bird described by him as being a sand plover was currently at Pagham Harbour. I arrived a little after 15.00 GMT, and joined a throng of birders on the shingle spit. By this time, the bird had been seen by some nationally well-known birders, who had positively identified it as a Greater Sand Plover *C. leschenaultii*, and this opinion was generally accepted.

The bird was far out on the mudflats, slowly making its way towards us, but even at its closest it was still a long way off. The general impression was of a bird not so dumpy as the Ringed Plovers with which it was associating. At times, it was very active, running quickly, sometimes over long distances, almost in the way that Sanderlings *Calidris alba* behave on the tideline.

Being Australian, I had seen numerous Greater Sand Plovers on the coast of southwestern Australia, often in flocks of up to ten birds. In my experience, the Greater Sand Plover is a large, rotund wader, with a distinctive jizz that is quite unmistakable once learnt. The combination of size, length of bill, sloping forehead and distinctively rounded shape makes it easy to identify.

The Pagham sand plover did not fit that image. It was very pale on the mantle and head, almost the colour of milky tea (perhaps as a result of sun-bleaching). Its 'face-mask' was very dark and appeared to have no white areas. Its breast-band was wide. Its bill was short, and its legs were very dark.

The following evening, I went to Pagham Spit at high tide, hoping that the bird would come in to roost on the shingle with the Ringed Plovers, which is exactly what it did. At a range of about 200–300 m, I was able to get reasonably good views through my telescope, at a much closer range than those of the day before at Church Norton.

With the bird surrounded by Ringed Plovers, it was easy to get an accurate estimation of size. There was no appreciable difference between the sand plover and the Ringed Plovers; if anything, it was marginally bigger, but not sufficiently so to notice without paying careful attention. The legs appeared dark from this distance, but were not black, and were long. The dark face-mask showed no sign whatsoever of any white over the bill, which was short and dumpy. Once again, the bird was very active, running repeatedly.

SUMMARY OF KEY FEATURES

Jizz In my experience, Greater Sand Plovers are slow in their reactions, but this bird appeared to be anything but that. It was very active for a great deal of the time, and was repeatedly seen running very fast over distances of up to 20 m. The general shape was also most unlike that of a Greater Sand Plover, being far less rotund, and more upright.

Size When completely surrounded by Ringed Plovers at roost, there appeared to be no appreciable difference in size (if anything, the sand plover was slightly larger, but only just).

Head Shape Rounded, and not at all angular (seen very clearly from my position at the roost).

Head Pattern Face-mask entirely dark, without a hint of white over the bill.

Bill Small, and blunt-ended, but with no sign of a bulbous tip.

Legs Dark, appearing virtually black from a distance, and quite long.

Breast-band Wide, with flank extension.

Discussion

Unfortunately, this bird was declared to be a Greater Sand Plover very quickly, with most observers agreeing. I, however, had seen the bird closer than had most other birders, so found myself in disagreement with almost everybody else who had seen it, including the leading bird luminaries. Although I did not know it at the time, the original finder, Ralph Hollins, and John W. P. Bacon had also, after consulting reference books, both independently concluded that the bird was a Lesser Sand Plover *Charadrius mongolus*.

On Saturday 16th August, I went back to Church Norton and joined a large gathering of birders who were watching the sand plover. I made myself known to them, and asked groups if they could tell me why this bird was a Greater Sand Plover. Not one person could; all said that they were happy to accept the view of 'the experts'. It seemed that, apart from a few very experienced birders, most people would be hard pressed to tell a Greater from a Lesser Sand Plover, there having been only 11 previous British records of the former and none of the latter. At that time, the major identification paper by Hirschfeld *et al.* (2000) was still in preparation and unpublished.

From what I had seen at the roost the previous day, I was convinced that the bird was a Lesser Sand Plover of the race *atrifrons*. Unfortunately, the bird stayed only three days, and I thought that I was alone in my belief, putting me at odds with all my peers. It came as a relief, therefore, to learn later that photographic evidence – especially that provided by a set of 20 photographs supplied to the British Birds Rarities Committee by Dr Iain H. Leach – had proved beyond doubt that the bird had been a Lesser (*Brit. Birds* 92: 534, plates 207, 208 & 236; 93: plates 242–247).

Between them, these two sand plovers have eight recognised races: three of Greater and five of Lesser. The main distinctions between the species are in structure and plumage. The proportions of Lesser Sand Plover suggest a less rotund, more upright bird, which is altogether more active. Plumage can vary, but, in general, Lesser Sand Plover typically has a broader breast-band, which extends onto the flanks and upper belly. The bill length of both species is variable, with Lesser Sand Plover of the race *schaeferi* and Greater Sand Plover of the race *columbinus* being almost identical in bill length. The shape of the Lesser's bill, however, looks much finer, and, together with the rounded head shape, gives that species a distinctive profile, very different from that produced by the sloping forehead of Greater Sand Plover. The leg colour of Lesser Sand Plover is described as 'dark grey ... may look black at a distance', whereas the Greater Sand Plover's legs are described as 'variable', but almost always paler (e.g. Hayman *et al* 1986).

Hunt, J. 2000. Lesser Sand Plover in West Sussex: new to Britain and Ireland. *British Birds* 93, 435–441.

*Lesser Sand Plover has disjunct breeding populations in northeast Siberia (**mongolus**) and Central Asia (**atrifrons**); the former race winters in southeast Asia and Australia while the latter winters around the western shores of the Indian Ocean from Sumatra to South Africa. The different populations seem to be candidates for upgrade to two separate species.*

*There have been three subsequent records (although the 'Greater Sand Plover' on the Don estuary, Aberdeenshire, in August 1991 was most likely a **mongolus** Lesser Sand Plover):*

Lincolnshire Rimac, female *atrifrons*, 11th–15th May 2002

Hampshire Keyhaven Marshes, male *mongolus*, 22nd–26th July 2003

Midlothian Aberlady Bay, male *mongolus*, 8th–9th July 2004 (Awaiting BBRC decision)

NOVEMBER 1966
HUME'S WARBLER IN EAST SUSSEX
Peter Clement and Bob Scott

It was Horace Alexander (1955) who first drew the attention of British birdwatchers, principally observatory workers, to the fact that the (then) Hume's Yellow-browed Warbler *Phylloscopus inornatus humei* was a serious contender for addition to the British List. The 1970s, 1980s and 1990s saw Hume's Warbler *P. humei* travel a rather familiar road to full species status, with several articles on its field identification and the BOURC in its 23rd Report (1997) formally announced that 'it seems appropriate to treat *P. inornatus* (monotypic) and *P. humei* (including *P. h. mandellii*) as separate species'.

The Beachy Head bird was found by PC on 13th November and subsequently seen that day by Roger Charlwood, Barry Cooper, Brian Metcalfe and Tony Quinn. The following morning, Roger Charlwood telephoned RES at Dungeness to inform him of the bird's presence and the two of them spent over an hour watching the individual on 14th November. Throughout its stay (the bird was last seen on 17th November), it frequented the Belle Tout wood at Beachy Head, apparently preferring the canopy, but at times coming almost to ground level, when it presented excellent views.

The bird resembled a Yellow-browed Warbler *P. inornatus* in size, shape, movements and behaviour. The key initial distinguishing features were the generally dull appearance and the presence of just a single wing-bar on each wing. The only yellow present in the plumage was a small mark on the underwing at the carpal joint, and the faintest of yellow suffusion on the breast. The remainder of the plumage lacked any yellow, this being particularly noticeable on the upperparts, which were mainly greyish-olive, the dirty-white supercilium and the buffish-white wing-bar at the tips of the greater coverts. The left wing showed no trace of a second wing-bar, but the right wing showed a barely perceptible bar formed by tips to the median coverts. The voice was described by Roger Charlwood (verbally) as a 'loud ringing note' and by Quinn & Clement

(1971, *The Beachy Head Bird Report* 1960–70) as a 'loud, disyllabic "puit-chu" and "che-ee" '.

The only relevant literature available to us in 1966 was Williamson (1962, *Identification for Ringers. 2. The Genus* Phylloscopus) and Ticehurst (1938, *A Systematic Review of the Genus* Phylloscopus) and, after consulting those two publications, it was considered that the bird was *humei* because of the following features:

(1) greyish-olive (not green) upperparts and lack of striking yellow in fringes of primaries;
(2) lack of yellow on underparts;
(3) lack of yellow in supercilium and wing-bar;
(4) absent or indistinct median-covert wing-bar;
(5) call-note.

In addition, the late date is more typical of far-eastern *Phylloscopus* warblers than of Yellow-browed Warbler, which usually appears in September and early October, although November records, and even overwintering individuals in southern England, are not unknown.

More recently, it has been shown that separation from Greenish Warbler *P. trochiloides* needs to be taken into account, because of the similarity of their call-notes (Madge & Quinn 1997). In fresh plumage, the longer wing-bar and whitish fringes and tips to the tertials are all diagnostic of *humei*. Both Hume's and Yellow-browed generally show a flatter or less domed crown than that of Greenish. In addition, the bill of Hume's lacks the extensive pinkish lower mandible of Greenish. The Beachy Head bird was noted to have a dark bill, with only the base of the lower mandible orangey-flesh-coloured.

Clement, P. & Scott, R. E. 1999. Hume's Warbler in Sussex: new to Britain and Ireland. *British Birds* 92, 96–100.

Hume's Warbler breeds in the mountains of Central Asia and winters in northern India. There have been at least 75 subsequent records.

1998

THE BIRDER'S YEAR

Tim Cleeves

A **Dark-eyed Junco** remaining from December 1997 tempted the faithful to stare into gardens in suburban Chester at the start of 1998 and the **Canvasback** remained in Norfolk. And in Cumbria the male **Spanish Sparrow** continued his residence at the small village of Waterside throughout the year, so a leisurely trip for a year tick was a far cry from the panic that ensued following its discovery in July 1996.

Early in the new year, a starling on St Mary's, Isles of Scilly, caused some confusion. Do any of us spend enough time scrutinising commoner birds? What about the general condition and health of the birds we see? The 'Scilly starling' was a real mixture – as Mike Crewe pointed out in *Birding World*, it appeared to show features of Starling *and* Spotless Starling. This individual had fault bars on its tertials, tail feathers and greater coverts and had retained old scruffy body feathers. With its pale claws, atypical pale pink legs and feathers of differing ages on either wing, this bird was more hopeless than spotless!

A **Short-toed Treecreeper** trapped at Dungeness in late March was a real bonus and only the 19th record. White-phase **Gyrfalcons** are a bit more straightforward. The finder of a bird at Wembury in Devon in April had also found another Devon bird, at Berry Head in 1986.

The previous year's **Semipalmated Plover** returned to Dawlish Warren, Devon, on 31st March and remained until 10th May, allowing a second chance for those who did not venture south to view the second British record in 1997.

May can provide some stunning birds and in 1998 three arrived – the First **Slender-billed Curlew** (a first-summer bird) was at Druridge Bay, Northumberland, from 4th–7th May; the fifth British **Yellow-browed Bunting** was on Hoy, Orkney, from 4th–5th May; and from 14th–18th May a third for Britain, **Cretzschmar's Bunting**, stayed on Stronsay, Orkney. There were also two **Little Swifts**, both discovered on 10th May, one in Cornwall and the other in Cleveland. Later in the summer, a third bird was seen at Barton-upon-Humber, Lincolnshire.

Gulls are long-lived and some individual transatlantic vagrants might have reached western Europe in previous years. On 10th May, an adult **Laughing Gull** was at the same shallow pool at Titchwell, Norfolk, as a first-summer **Franklin's Gull**. By May 15th, the same Franklin's Gull had made it to Shetland, where a first-summer Laughing Gull had been present since March. This time though, the two species were not seen together.

A **Scops Owl**, found injured near Port Glasgow, Renfrewshire, on May 20th was rehabilitated and released on 12th June in front of a crowd of some 300 people. Other spring rarities included two **Pallid Swifts**, two **Terek Sandpipers**, a **River Warbler** in Lincolnshire, a **Lesser-crested Tern** in East Sussex, a '**Black-headed Wagtail**' in Conwy – and a **Hermit Thrush** on Fetlar, Shetland (Britain's First was also a spring bird in Shetland, in 1975).

August produced only the third acceptable British record of an **Eastern Bonelli's Warbler**, at Sumburgh, Shetland. The Isles of Scilly responded in September with two **Common Nighthawks** and an **Eastern Olivaceous Warbler** which stayed on St Agnes from 24th September to 8th October. Three **Red-flanked Bluetails** were found between late September and mid-October, and three **Isabelline Wheatears** between 20th September and 1st October.

It was a quiet autumn for North American passerines but there were two **Red-eyed Vireos** (in Gwynedd and Cornwall), a **Rose-breasted Grosbeak** and an **American Robin** on Scilly, a dead **Grey-cheeked Thrush** in Cornwall and a **Bobolink** on Shetland.

Many of the best birds of the autumn were in either the extreme north or the extreme south of Britain. There was a superb, well-marked juvenile **Western Sandpiper** at Deerness, Orkney, a **Little Bustard** near Sumburgh, Shetland, and TWO **Sociable Plovers** in Kent. As the last species becomes scarcer and scarcer in its native breeding areas, we will have fewer opportunities to see it as a vagrant in western Europe. Four **Pallas's Grasshopper Warblers** were found on Fair Isle between September 30th and October 8th, an island record.

Before the fat lady put her 'scope in the case, it fell to Dorset to come up with some late prizes – two **Blyth's Pipits**, both trapped on 22nd November at Portland Bill. Brilliant!

THE PATCHWATCHER'S REWARD
Russell Slack

With the new year I had made a resolution to become better acquainted with many of my local sites within striking distance of my then adopted city of Sheffield. January started well with two Red-necked Grebes, and plenty of other decent local birding, but best of all was an immature Rough-legged Buzzard that took up residence in Upper Derwentdale in the Peak District. This obliging bird attracted large numbers of observers through its stay until at least the end of March, and I indulged myself with numerous hours of entertainment with this fantastic raptor, gorging myself on every detail during several close encounters.

February for me was spent travelling in Vietnam, a country that I had long wished to visit. The country did not disappoint, the whole travel experience being well worth the wait and the birding tough but rewarding. Personal highlights included Bar-bellied Pitta at Nam Bai Cat Tien, a welcome addition to my Asian pitta collection, and a Cutia although not a 'lifer' continued my run of good fortune with a species that in the past had eluded me on numerous Asian trips. A short visit to Thailand allowed enough time to visit the south and head off to the idyllic island of Ko Similan. The main purpose of the visit to this beautiful location was the bizarre Nicobar Pigeon. Having failed some years previously to see this elusive pigeon, it was more than a relief to find them easy on Similan, to the point of one even walking into the entrance of our tent!

I always find it hard to motivate myself to get out and about after returning from a trip abroad, especially during the winter months. A month of birding in shorts and T-shirts and looking at exotic birds made it difficult to slip back into the reality of a cold British afternoon and a gull roost. It was mid-month before I could venture out, but several visits to local sites and my coastal patch up at Whitby were enough to whet my appetite and three Sand Martins passing underneath the wintering Rough-leg were a sure sign that spring was in the air on the 21st. For me, April continued in the same way, I now had the bit between my teeth and pre- and post-work visits to local reservoirs were keeping me entertained. The highlights were few and far between, but the rhythm of systematic patchwatching on my doorstep had, for the time being at least, captured my attention.

Spring can sometimes be slow in getting going in Yorkshire, but May opened with me on Burbage Moor watching three resplendent Dotterel just after dawn on the 2nd. You can keep birds in lowland pea fields, this is one species that should be seen in the splendour of an upland setting, and time by myself with these birds was a magical moment to savour. As is often the case in my birding calendar, my attention from mid-May onwards switched back to my coastal patch and prayers for easterlies and a fall.

Spring falls are hard to come by and are never as exciting as a good autumn deluge. It was not until the end of the month that such conditions presented themselves and the 30th saw me wandering around a fogbound Whitby with scarcities in mind. It was tough going, with fog hampering viewing, but we were rewarded mid-morning with the dulcet tones of a drab Common Rosefinch, then later a skulking Marsh Warbler.

June was a quiet month for me, much of the month taken up by more World Cup disappointment. July continued in similar vein; I indulged myself in inland wader watching and occasional seawatching, but neither could claim too much space in my notebook.

The pace quickened in September, and for me my attention switched to my Yorkshire coastal patch. I wasn't to be disappointed, bagging several Wrynecks, a Barred Warbler and a Greenish Warbler during a fall in the first few days of the month. An easterly airflow at the end of the month ensured that I was again bashing my coastal patch. The 26th looked full of promise, but much of the day had been an anticlimax until my long-standing Whitby fellow addict John Beaumont and I reached a recently ploughed field. There amongst the Wheatears was a pale bird, and careful scrutiny of each and every feather tract yielded an Isabelline Wheatear.

Finding your own birds is damned hard work, even in locations in which the odds favour a find, but this bird was just reward for many hours of pounding the patch to no avail. The farmer kindly granted access to his private fields if the bird was present the next morning, but whilst John and I celebrated in the pub that night a thick fog enveloped the coast and as our bleary eyes peered out of the tent the next morning, it was clear that little would materialise from such a thick hanging sea fret.

The 'Issie' was one of three that week, with others in Shetland and Suffolk. The easterly airflow lasted into early October, and Whitby received the attention it deserved. A Rustic Bunting led me a tense song and dance before I saw it, some compensation coming with a Marsh Warbler later trapped and ringed.

November can still produce the goods; I reverted to watching locally, enjoying some superb visible-migration movements. December continued to produce surprises; modern-day birding is to expect the unexpected, and an obliging Pied Wheatear in Tynemouth rounded off the year nicely for many birders.

*Russell Slack lives in York. He works for BirdGuides **www.birdguides.com,** managing their news service and undertaking work on various projects, such as BWPi. A member of the Yorkshire Records Committee, he is addicted to local patch birding in the Lower Derwent Valley and Whitby.*

MAY 1998

SLENDER-BILLED CURLEW IN NORTHUMBERLAND

Tim Cleeves

At approximately 17.50 hours on 4th May 1998, my wife Ann and I entered the Budge Hide at the Northumberland Wildlife Trust reserve at Druridge Bay, Northumberland. Shortly before, we had met another birder who told us there were some Eurasian Curlews *Numenius*

arquata and a Whimbrel *N. phaeopus* visible from the hide. As we opened the hide shutters, a light aircraft flew over scaring the curlews, a Black-tailed Godwit *Limosa limosa* and a smaller, curlew-like wader, which I assumed was the Whimbrel. Switching from binoculars to my 'scope, I followed the unidentified bird back down and simply expected to see the stripey crown, darker chest and steeply curved bill of a classic Whimbrel. Not so; although superficially like a small curlew, the most striking features were its very pale wing-coverts, which contrasted sharply with dark-centred scapulars, and a fine, thin bill. I looked at it long and hard, but couldn't work it out. Both puzzled and intrigued, I started to scribble some sketches and take field notes.

Having watched it carefully for a while, I did not think it was a Eurasian Curlew. Admittedly, I had never seen an aberrant Eurasian Curlew, but this bird seemed distinctly different in many ways. As Ann and I sat there chewing over the possibilities, we did mention Slender-billed Curlew *N. tenuirostris*, but mainly in jest, and my money was still on some sort of aberrant Whimbrel. Nonetheless, some extra help seemed a sensible strategy, and I suggested to Ann that she should contact Tom Tams, Colin Bradshaw and Jimmy Steele from the nearest phone box. A little later, when only Tom arrived, Ann confessed that she had 'bottled out' and not contacted Colin or Jimmy! Clearly she thought my imagination was getting the better of me … Tom and I continued to watch the mystery bird, and increasingly (and amid growing excitement) we felt that it had features consistent with Slender-billed Curlew. Using Tom's mobile phone, we summoned Colin and Jimmy and, once they had arrived, the four of us plus Mary Carruthers watched it until 20.25 hours. The following description is based largely on my own field notes and sketches taken on 4th May, with some refinements added following reference to photographs and video material, and notes from other observers.

Size and structure

First seen in flight, with approximately 15 Eurasian Curlews and a single Black-tailed Godwit, when it appeared smaller than the accompanying Eurasian Curlews. This was subsequently well illustrated by Gary Bellingham's photograph of it in flight with Eurasian Curlews on 7th May. It also looked to have thinner wings in flight. As it landed, it was obviously a *Numenius*-type wader, but was clearly smaller than the Eurasian Curlews, and looked quite distinctly thinner-necked.

Behaviour

The Druridge bird appeared to walk more quickly than the Eurasian Curlews. It often adopted a nervous stance, and when it stopped feeding it would stretch its neck up and peer around. It seemed to prefer feeding in quite rank vegetation, mainly taller grasses and rushes *Juncus*, and once it waded thigh-deep in a shallow pool. Later in the week, a number of observers watched it flatten itself in the grass as a Eurasian Sparrowhawk *Accipiter nisus* passed over, while the Eurasian Curlews took flight. When feeding, it probed deeply and vigorously. With rather quick movements and its distinctive, thinner-necked appearance, it recalled an Upland Sandpiper *Bartramia longicauda* at times.

Bare parts

The bill was approximately one and a third times the length of the head, and was distinctly thinner (less deep) than that of any of the Eurasian Curlews nearby. Viewed head-on, the bill was obviously narrower than on Eurasian Curlew, too. The shape also differed from the latter species, being straighter along the basal two-thirds, before gently curving for the distal third. The shape of the bill tip in particular was noticeably different, as it shelved to a very fine point and lacked the droop-tipped appearance, first pinched in then laterally expanded, characteristic of Eurasian Curlew. The bill was black, apart from a dark pink base to the lower mandible.

Most of the time the legs were obscured by vegetation. When they could be seen, they looked shorter than those of Eurasian Curlew. In flight, the toes protruded just beyond the tail tip.

Upperparts

The extreme base of the forehead, adjacent to the bill, was off-white. This joined an off-white supercilium, which was widest just above and behind the eye, became thinner beyond that and faded above the rear ear-coverts. The crown was brown, finely streaked darker, and was darker and browner than the cheeks and nape, which were greyish buff with fine dark streaks. In dull, even light, the 'capped effect' of the darker crown was quite noticeable, but in stronger light this was almost completely lost. At very close range, a thin buff median crown-stripe, which began at the forehead and faded towards the centre of the crown, could be seen. When viewed head-on, the pale supercilium was seen to be bordered by short, dark lateral crown-stripes for about half its length. Below the supercilium, at the base of the bill and in front of the eye, was a dark blackish smudge or spot. A short and wispy, dark eye-stripe extended only just beyond the eye, and the bird showed an indistinct, narrow pale eye-ring.

Below the pale nape, the mantle was very dark, almost black, and this formed an isolated and conspicuous dark triangular area. The upper scapulars were blackish-brown with narrow creamy-buff edges; and the lower scapulars were similarly coloured, with narrow buff edges. The tertials were long and pointed, with dark brown centres, and edges patterned with triangular dark brown and pale whitish-buff indentations. The wing-coverts were obviously worn and faded, being very pale with small, inconspicuous dark subterminal tips. At times, the wing-coverts looked almost silvery, contrasting boldly with the dark mantle and scapulars. This contrast confirmed the age of the bird as a first-summer. The primary projection was relatively short, with approximately three dark primary tips extending beyond the tertails; the primary tips just reached the tail tip. During preening, the rump and undertail-coverts looked pure white. Compared with Eurasian Curlew, the tail always looked whiter with narrower, greyer tail bars, and much more white than dark.

Underparts

The chin and throat were white. The neck and breast were pale buff, quite warm and streaked with blackish-brown lines. These longitudinal, parallel streaks ended abruptly on the lower breast, which gave the impression of a pectoral band when viewed head-on. Below this, there was an irregular patterning of spotting on the flanks, above the thighs and below the folded carpal joint. Because the bird spent much of its time in dense, long grass, it was hard to determine the exact shape of the spotting on the first evening. In better light, on May 5th, Tom Tams reported on the shape of some of the breast spots, which were 'isolated dark brown or blackish-brown spots, roughly oval in shape, and, at least on the left side of the bird, three spots had slight indents at the front and were tapered towards the rear. At least one of these spots had a tiny extension from the indent backup the feather shaft.' The underparts did not show any conspicuous cross-barring or anchor-shaped barring typical of Eurasian Curlew. The thighs were neat, compact and pure white. The lower belly, vent and undertail-coverts were white.

Flight pattern

In flight, the upperwing pattern was quite striking. The outer four or five primaries looked very dark (blackish) and contrasted with the paler, browner inner primaries. The outermost primary showed a conspicuous white shaft. The primary coverts looked black, but the very worn wing-coverts contrasted markedly with the dark outer primaries. Later in the week, at least two observers commented on a very narrow pale trailing edge along some of the flight feathers (Brett Richards and Robin Ward, verbally). On both wings, the bird had apparently dropped the innermost primary (Robin Ward, verbally).

On 4th May, when the bird took a short flight, Tom Tams and I noticed that it raised its wings as it landed, almost like a Common Redshank *Tringa totanus*. The entire underwing-coverts and axillaries were white. In flight, the rump looked white and extended well up the back in a pronounced 'V'. The tail looked very white too, with four or five well-defined, thin bars, these being much narrower than the areas of white in between. The toes extended just beyond the tail tip.

On the evening of 4th May, I had to return to work and inland confinement in Bedfordshire, so was unable to visit Druridge again while the bird was still present. It remained until 7th May, and caused enormous debate among birders throughout Britain, and beyond. The record was widely discussed in many of the birding magazines, and the Internet birding sites were buzzing with conjecture. Strong arguments were put forward about the bird's identity, some supporting Slender-billed Curlew, others not; many of the most forceful opinions came from people who had not seen the bird in question, which is interesting since it is all too easy to undermine the credibility of such a record from a distance.

Later the same month, I visited the Natural History Museum at Tring and examined the collection of 21 Slender-billed Curlew skins there, as well as a number of Eurasian Curlew skins. By that time, I had also been given two videos of the Druridge bird, taken by Peter Colston and Trevor Charlton, and I was able to watch these on the same day as looking at the skins. Most of the Slender-billed Curlew skins at Tring are of birds obtained in the Mediterranean in the nineteenth and early twentieth centuries (between 1857 and 1918). There are 12 males and 9 females, and six of the skins appeared to be of first-years, which looked more streaked than spotted below. Just one skin (ref. 1939.12.9.3666 BMNH) appears to be of a first-summer, a male from Siellbar, near Gotha, Germany, which is dated 12th May (there is dispute about the year it was obtained, but it was before 1864). This specimen looks most like the Druridge bird because it has worn wing-coverts contrasting with dark scapulars. It is also interesting that it was found in northwest Europe in May.

Virtually all illustrations of Slender-billed Curlews, in field guides, in *BWP* and in other reference books, show only adults and/or juveniles, and I could not find an illustration of a first-summer. Eventually, I did find a painting by Christopher Schmidt, which was produced in 1992 and used by the Wildlife Management Department, Forestry Service and the Ministry of Agriculture in Greece to help local fishermen and others recognise and report this globally threatened species at Greek coastal sites. This illustration of a juvenile/first-winter Slender-billed Curlew is, in fact, quite similar to the Druridge bird, but instead of spotting on the breast and flank sides it shows the typical streaks of a juvenile.

In summary, my research confirmed my belief that the Druridge bird showed the key identification features of Slender-billed Curlew. Most importantly, it had a noticeably fine bill, which was thinner in both depth and width compared with Eurasian Curlew. The bill tip in particular was very fine, and lacked any expansion laterally near the tip. The sides of the breast and flanks were spotted, and lacked any cross-barring or arrow-shaped markings, unlike Eurasian Curlew. The tail was strikingly pale-looking, with large areas of white between the neat grey tail bars. This feature may not always be diagnostic of Slender-billed Curlew, but is a useful supplementary feature (see, for example, the line-drawings and description in Glutz *et al.* 1977, *Handbuch der Vögel Mitteleuropas*). The bird did not show the very fine flank streaking associated with the eastern race of Eurasian Curlew *N. a. orientalis*, which is, on average, paler and larger than nominate *arquata*, and thus much larger than even the largest female Slender-billed Curlew. Additional pointers in support of Slender-billed Curlew were the overall size of the bird, and the pattern of the upper-parts, with the bleached, worn wing-coverts contrasting strongly with the dark mantle and scapulars. Each individual aspect of the identification of the Druridge bird is covered more thoroughly in Jimmy Steele's report, with detailed reference to skins and to field descriptions of Slender-billed Curlew.

Cleeves, T. 2002. Slender-billed Curlew in Northumberland: new to Britain and Ireland. *British Birds* 95, 272–278.

Slender-billed Curlew is Critically Endangered. BirdLife International estimated a world population of 50-270 birds in 1994. It breeds – or bred – in Siberia, where the last nest was recorded in 1924 north of Omsk. Wintering birds were regularly seen in Morocco until 1995. The last confirmed sighting anywhere in the world was of four birds in spring 1999 in Greece.

There have been no subsequent records in Britain.

THE BIRDER'S YEAR

Tim Cleeves

Looking back over the decades, there are certain rarity-packed years that stand out. 1975 was the undisputed champion for vagrants from east and west, but others, like 1981, 1982 and 1985, produced both a high total of rarities and a great range of species. 1999 was one of these 'special' years. Three Firsts were discovered: **Short-billed Dowitcher**, **Short-toed Eagle** and **Mourning Dove**.

Kent produced a **Greater Yellowlegs** – always a grade 1 rarity – in mid-March. In April, three species stole the limelight. The first twitchable **Crag Martin** (Britain's fifth) was seen in Leicestershire and West Yorkshire on successive days. In May, it or another individual was seen at Finstown, Orkney.

An **American Coot** (Britain's second) put in an all-too-brief appearance at South Walney, Cumbria, on 17th April. Two **Calandra Larks** were found this spring, one on the Farne Islands, off Northumberland, on 28th April, the other on Fair Isle, Shetland, in mid-May. An **American Bittern** on the Camel estuary, Cornwall, in mid-May was a totally unexpected bonus, as was a male **Pallid Harrier** at Bramford, Suffolk, on 7th May.

It was another good year for **Terek Sandpipers** with birds seen in Conwy, Cheshire, Kent, Suffolk and on Scilly in the spring. Kent played host to an adult **Slender-billed Gull** in early May. Britain's third and fourth **Iberian Chiffchaffs** were identified at Portland Bill, Dorset, and at Start Point, south Devon. And two male **Collared Flycatchers** graced sites in Northeast Scotland and on Unst, Shetland.

On 3rd June, Britain's third **Spectacled Warbler** was found at Roborough Down, Devon; and a male **Myrtle Warbler** (so much nicer-sounding than *Yellow-rumped Warbler*) was discovered on Fair Isle. Kent scored again on 6th June with a showy male **Baillon's Crake**, which sounded like an exotic species of frog as it sped across the surface of the marsh at Grove Ferry; it stayed until 20th July.

A superb summer-plumaged **Greater Sand Plover** in East Lothian in early June was followed by a **Black-winged Pratincole** doing the rounds in north Norfolk in July. Then East Lothian surpassed itself with Britain's fifth **Royal Tern** on 9th August – if only it had stayed a little longer.

Often claimed but rarely accepted, there were no fewer than three **Little Shearwater** records, all in August, which passed scrutiny by BBRC. August and early September were also good for large shearwaters with more than 300 **Great Shearwaters** and 40 **Cory's Shearwaters** seen during the *Scillonian* pelagic on 15th August, along with a minimum of three **Wilson's Petrels** and up to 13 **Sabine's Gulls**. By the end of August, birders seawatching from Cornwall and around the Isles of Scilly had logged at least 2,400 Cory's and 2,840 Greats.

Scotland was really setting the pace for extreme rarities. On 11th September, a juvenile **Short-billed Dowitcher** – a First for Britain – was identified at Rosehearty near Fraserburgh, Aberdeenshire. In an uncanny echo of the Hudsonian Godwit in 1981, the dowitcher was refound hundreds of miles to the south, at Teesmouth on 29th September, and settled down for a lengthy stay. At last, two species of dowitcher had been confirmed in Britain. But will the third (Asiatic) ever arrive?

A **Common Nighthawk** was seen on St Agnes, Isles of Scilly on 22nd September and in October another bird was seen on Bryher. Monarch butterflies began to appear on the islands in early October, encouraging thoughts that it would be a 'western' autumn.

A first-winter **Siberian Thrush** on the Gugh, St Agnes, put paid to that idea. The next day, 6th October, a **White's Thrush** was found by Ren Hathway on St Agnes. The joint was jumping! A shadow over the St Agnes coastguard cottages on 7th October signalled the arrival of Britain's first **Short-toed Eagle**. It toured most of the islands during its five-day stay.

There was no time to relax. No fewer than nine **Radde's Warblers** arrived on Scilly within as many days. An **Eyebrowed Thrush** on Bardsey, Gwynedd, on October 12th was the first for Wales and next day a first-winter **Veery** was found in Cornwall.

Birds from all points of the compass seemed to be converging. There were two **Yellow-billed Cuckoos** – one on Tresco, Isles of Scilly, the other in Cornwall. As October drew on, two **Upland Sandpipers** teamed up on St Mary's, Isles of Scilly, and five **Chimney Swifts** reached Devon, Cornwall and Scilly. Eclipsing even the swifts, two **Blue Rock Thrushes** were found – on St Mary's and in Cot Valley, Cornwall. These were only the second and third British records.

On 24th October, attention finally switched from the Southwest with a major find in Northumberland: a **Black-faced Bunting**, the second for Britain, but it stayed for only one day.

There were so many good birds in 1999 that it's difficult to keep the summary concise. A lot of 'also seens' were of real quality: **Baltimore Oriole**, Bryher, September; **Bobolink**, Skokholm, Dyfed, October (a first for Wales); another Myrtle Warbler, South Uist, Outer Hebrides, October; **Eastern Olivaceous Warbler**, Portland Bill, July. Then there were the 11 **Pallid Swifts** – and a fall of at least 13 **Semipalmated Sandpipers** on North Uist, Outer Hebrides, in September. Another amazing multiple arrival came with the five **Red-flanked Bluetails** discovered between 16th October and 22nd, breaking the record of three in 1998. A near-mythical vagrant had become an almost expected bonus, but still one that everyone wants to find!

And then there was the **Booted Eagle**. A bird seen in Ireland from March until August appeared in Cornwall in late October (it was also reported in Kent in late

September). A second-calendar-year bird, it hung around southwest England into spring 2000 – but the rarities committees remained unconvinced that it was a genuine wild bird.

November can deliver some real stormers and the First British record of **Mourning Dove** mid-month, at Carinish, North Uist, Outer Hebrides, proved the point. At Loch Mor on Benbecula, in the Outer Hebrides, the locals weren't resting on their laurels. On 2nd November they banged in a Greater Yellowlegs which stayed well into the new millennium.

In a year of virtually unparalleled quality, especially for eastern rarities, it was weird that only one **Olive-backed Pipit** arrived – and that was in May in Shetland. Don't let the lack of 'OBPs' fool you though. 1999 was a year never to be forgotten.

FINDING THE BIG ONE

Jimmy Steele

It started with a 'tsik'. Not the year, which started with a head cold, but the realisation that I had found a really rare bird, the rarest that I will ever find, unless that accentor does what it knows it should.

Birding can be as much therapy as pastime: sometimes a counterpoint to real life, sometimes an escape and sometimes an opportunity to reflect. The ups and downs of day-to-day birding are utterly trivial, but the ups can keep a birder mentally stable. I have picked a year that had highs and lows in real life, but where the progress of the birding provided essential therapy for the lows. 1999 was a great year for rare birds, one of the very best, but you will find no further reference to Short-toed Eagle, Blue Rock Thrush, Crag Martin, Short-billed Dowitcher or any of the other legendary birds here, bar one.

To comprehend what makes me tick, you have to understand that I am a commit-ted patch man. For all its innumerable faults – the frequent lack of birds, the litter, the psychotic horses, the psychotic dogs and the psychotic kids – I love my patch. The only list I maintain is my Newbiggin list and for me, birding success is finding birds there. The startling reality of birding in the Royston Vasey of Northumberland is a rare wheatear perched on a burnt-out Ford Escort. But as a patch person, a bad spell gets you down, and 1998 was a very long, very bad spell. A half-share in a Yellow-browed Warbler was a lousy return for a lot of work. Having recently joined BBRC, I was starting to feel the pressure to find birds and credibility. It just wasn't happening. Perhaps 1999 would be better.

The year began inauspiciously, with the occasional Iceland Gull just about enough to maintain consciousness. March brought some relief with a short work trip to Vancouver. There were few new birds to chase, so I spent some time alone with … Thayer's Gulls (for non-birders reading this, I do understand the tragedy of that statement). I was relaxed, concentrated, and there on Clover Point, amongst the black wing-tips, was an Iceland (technically Kumlien's) Gull. Finding rares abroad is almost as good as finding them on your patch. The species that I had opened my patch year with was, in a different continent, my best find for a very long time. Maybe this was early season form.

Back home a Firecrest sang on 1st May and signalled a change of patch fortune. A Little Ringed Plover a few days later was even better. All right, so LRP is not Siberian Rubythroat but it was rarer than Dusky Warbler on my patch. The Woodchat Shrike on the 9th was a patch tick of genuine quality, almost as rare was the Green Woodpecker a few minutes later.

Good things pass. May fizzled out, June was poor, and by July and August there was all sorts of stuff going on. It seemed traumatic, not for birds, just real life. Even the para-reality of BBRC was causing unnecessary pain. The assessment of the Northumberland Slender-billed Curlew was reaching a very heavy stage and I was deeply embroiled in trying to make sense of this most political of records. This was supposed to be fun, an interest, relaxation, but it wasn't.

So, if you want an escape, there is nothing like seawatch therapy, and the seawatching was good. A Cory's Shearwater gliding past the end of the rocks in perfect evening sunshine on the 22nd was the Newbiggin highlight, but a week in West Cork in August was where the real treatment was. Big shearwaters started to 'run' like salmon in a river, but it was the weaving acrobatics of a 'Fea's' Petrel that signalled that real birds were back. Not my first from Mizen Head, but my second 'away' find of the year.

Back east, September arrived in westerly flatness. Wind direction is everything on an east-coast patch. Sometimes, on pointlessly dull visits in February, I think that this is nonsense, but it isn't. On the 19th a change of weather proved the point when a southeasterly gave me Balearic Shearwater and Dotterel in rapid succession, whilst a Yellow-browed Warbler signalled the first 'proper' passerine at the end of the month. Bearing in mind that a half-share of a Yellow-browed was all I got from the whole of 1998, my scarce-bird haul so far marked a major improvement.

And then it all died again. My notebook entry for 10th October reads 'really pretty crap', and I can remember the day now for its shocking hopelessness. You never appreciate them at the time but days like that are a necessary evil, because without them you wouldn't know the definition of good. Good was redefined at the end of October. Flat, overcast and slightly misty days when you hear the 'tseeep' and 'chak' of thrush flocks falling out of the sky into coastal bushes are good. Not because the birds are rare, but because there is hope. Hope arrived on October 15th. Soon hope was confirmed with rares up and down the coast, I even saw a Bluetail at St Abb's. On the 17th, I hoped, gambled, and won a Radde's Warbler. Hallelujah, a *BB* rarity. Credibility, initials in the report, several near arrests (because it was in a Newbiggin garden and I still put the news out), all that stuff, who cares, it was rare. With the pressure off I scored again – a Pallas's Warbler five days later. By Saturday 23rd I couldn't lose. Hope was abundant and justified. At 8.30 am I had a conversation with my co-patcher. It went like this:

Stef (co-patcher): "I fancy a rare bunting."

Me: "There haven't been many…"

Stef: "I reckon there must be a Little or Rustic around."

Me: "I was thinking Black-faced, there was one in Norway last week." (How I knew that is another story.)

By 1 pm, there wasn't. He left. The message on his pager at 4.00 pm read:

"MEGA-ALERT … Northumbs … Black-faced Bunting … Newbiggin-by-the-Sea … Woodhorn Hedge."

It was when it went 'tsik' that I knew it really was a second for Britain. Recovery was complete.

Professor Jimmy Steele lives in Newcastle upon Tyne. A dentist by profession, he has an excellent track record in filling the cavities in other birders' life lists with his rare-bird finds. Jimmy is a member of the BB Rarities Committee.

SEPTEMBER 1999
SHORT-BILLED DOWITCHER IN ABERDEENSHIRE
Dave Pullan

On Saturday 11th September 1999, a Long-billed Dowitcher was reported on the beach at Rosehearty, Aberdeenshire, and it stayed as a 'Long-billed Dowitcher' on *Birdline* and Birdline Scotland for two days.

On the Sunday night, having been away for over a week, I was chatting on the telephone to Paul Baxter about what interesting birds were around in northeast Scotland, when the subject of the dowitcher came up. I was planning to go and see it sometime during the next few days, but what I heard from Paul made me decide to go sooner rather than later. Paul had seen the dowitcher that day and confessed to a 'slight uneasiness' about the identification.

I had been watching juvenile Short-billed Dowitchers in Nova Scotia, Canada, only three weeks earlier, and I noticed that the diagnostic tertial markings on some birds could be quite dull and only apparent at close range, so, when Paul said that this bird appeared to have parallel markings within the borders of the tertials, alarm bells started ringing for me. I asked him about other features of the bird, such as its greater coverts, but the light conditions and distance involved had been unfavourable for him to discern much detail. To counterbalance a surge of optimism at this point, it appeared that other experienced birders had settled for the identification of Long-billed, plus someone knew someone who had heard it call like a Long-billed. Also, some reference books (eg Hayman *et al.* 1986 and Lewington *et al.* 1991) illustrate some variability in the tertial markings of juvenile Long-billed.

On the following morning, Monday 13th September, James Smith and I arrived at Rosehearty at about 11.00 am. Initially there was no sign of the dowitcher, but 30 minutes later I found it about 150 yards away, feeding at the eastern end of the beach. It was breezy, overcast and threatening to rain, so the light conditions were poor, but even so the distinctly capped appearance of the bird looked interesting and we began to gradually edge closer. We halved the distance, and through telescopes it was clear that the tertials were well marked and, importantly, so were the inner greater coverts – we were surely looking at a juvenile Short-billed Dowitcher!

Knowing the enormity of this identification – the first British record – and the effect it would have on the birding community, and also acutely aware that experienced birders had been calling it a Long-billed, we set about putting together a watertight case before calling the news out to local birders and Birdline Scotland mid-afternoon. During this time, the bird was often out of view, either behind rocks or piles of seaweed, or flushed by walkers and dogs, so that it sometimes took long periods to relocate. Most often, it fed around washed up seaweed on the rocky shore or on the tideline. It was often accompanied by Redshanks, and at high tide it roosted with Oystercatchers and Redshanks on rocks at the end of the beach.

The light conditions gradually improved and we gathered the following list of main features in favour of Short-billed Dowitcher:

1. *Tertial pattern* Every tertial was dark brownish-grey, darker towards the tip. Each feather had a narrow, pale, unbroken buff border, with a broader, parallel, slightly richer buff 'sub-border' which extended the whole length of the outer edge of the feather and hooked round to about a third of the inner edge – it was slightly wavy and broken in parts, forming dots on the inner edge and towards the base of the outer edge.

   Two tertials were missing on the right wing, leaving the inner web of the longest tertial exposed – this gave a misleading impression of a large area of pale, plain grey.

2. *Inner greater coverts* The innermost three greater coverts were patterned very similarly to the tertials. An uneven buff 'sub-border' ran parallel to the even narrower outer border and was broken into dots, particularly on the inner edge.

3. *Inner median coverts* The inner median coverts were patterned like the inner greater coverts, but fainter – again showing internal patterning.

4. *Crown* There was a dark, well-defined cap. This looked black, dark brown or dark rufous (reminiscent of Sharp-tailed Sandpiper) depending on the light conditions and distance. It always appeared well defined and never looked grey.

5. *Lower scapulars* The mantle and scapular feathers were dark brown with rich golden-buff borders (none of the scapulars, tertials or wing-coverts had rusty-buff fringes as can be the case in Long-billed). Each scapular in the lower row had a broad buff internal mark on each web. The rearmost scapulars had two marks on each web. (There may be some overlap with Long-billed in the actual markings, but the colour is useful.)

6. *Underparts* The breast, flanks and belly were toned peachy-buff, possibly less grey than on Long-billed. The rear flanks and undertail-coverts were spotted with dark brown, possibly more delicately than on Long-billed: more dots and fewer blotches and bars.

7. *Tail* There was extensive white in the tail. In general, the white bars tended to look broader than, or equal to, the dark bars. This was difficult to judge, but the overall impression was of a lot of white in the tail.

8. *Structure* The bird was perhaps less 'front heavy' and more evenly proportioned than a Long-billed Dowitcher. The bill length was judged to be about $1\frac{1}{2}$ times the head length (it can be nearer 2 times in Long-billed).

The features numbered 6–8 are probably variable, and no doubt open to interpretation, but offer good support to the first five. Some people put an emphasis on needing to hear the call, but in my opinion on a juvenile this is actually not necessary; it is a nice additional feature but not critical.

By late afternoon, some 30 birders had arrived and it was then that the bird decided to fly to the harbour at Rosehearty and pose brilliantly only 15–20 yards away in perfect light conditions – the closest it had been all day. Just before we left, it flew a few yards and gave a trisyllabic call very reminiscent of Turnstone, the classic call of Short-billed Dowitcher – a fine ending to a very special day.

Pullan, D. 1999. The Short-billed Dowitcher in Aberdeenshire – a new British bird. *Birding World* 12, 364–370.

Short-billed Dowitcher breeds in northern North America and winters from the USA to northern South America.

This is the only record. The bird was relocated on the North Tees marshes, Cleveland, on 29th September; it was last seen on 30th October 1999.

The First for Ireland was at Tacumshin, Co. Wexford, from 30th September-2nd October 1985.

OCTOBER 1999

SHORT-TOED EAGLE ON SCILLY

Tim Cleeves, Maurice Hepple and Ken Shaw

Every time you arrive on the Isles of Scilly in October, you hope your fortnight will be part of a classic autumn. Looking back over the past three or four decades, certain rarity-packed years stand out. The autumns of 1975, 1983, 1985 and 1987 were all not to be missed, and that of 1999 certainly bears comparison with these. For aficionados of St Agnes in particular, things had started well, with a fine first-winter male Siberian Thrush *Zoothera sibirica* found on 5th October on the Gugh (a small island linked to St Agnes by a sandbar) by the Bradshaw family (minus Colin). Next day, Ren Hathway saw one of his superb illustrations come to life, when he chanced upon a White's Thrush *Z. dauma* at Troytown. Continuing the eastern theme, while the rest of us were glued to the spot waiting for a glimpse of the White's Thrush, KDS found a Radde's Warbler *Phylloscopus schwarzi*. Many people wait a lifetime to see a vagrant *Zoothera* in Britain; two in two days was simply breathtaking. As a result, it was not surprising that most thoughts were of birds from the east, and what might appear next. Would it be a Yellow-browed Bunting *Emberiza chrysophrys?* Could another Bimaculated Lark *Melanocorypha bimaculata* make an appearance?

On 7th October, TRC, MH, KDS, Ann Cleeves and Sarah Money were chatting near the lighthouse on St Agnes just before 13.00 hrs. Turning to look back towards the Coastguards, TRC noticed a large raptor flying towards us from the Southwest. The bird had pale underparts and he instinctively yelled 'Osprey!' KDS and MH locked onto the raptor, and took a couple of seconds longer to take in the bird's appearance. At that point, we all suffered momentary deafness as KDS screamed like a banshee, 'Short-toed Eagle!' *Circaetus gallicus.* The sound could probably have been heard on St Mary's! As the bird flew overhead, we were able to focus on its brown head; buff breast-band; pale lower breast and flanks spotted and marked with warm brown; barred tail; and pale, grey-brown upperwing-coverts, contrasting with very dark primaries, primary coverts, greater coverts and secondaries.

After clearing St Agnes's airspace, the bird flew across to St Mary's, travelled on to St Martin's and White Island and then settled down on the Eastern Isles, where it favoured Great Ganilly. On 11th October, in clearing skies, the eagle left the Eastern Isles, circled up to a height of around 350 m over Tresco, crossed to the skies above St Mary's and headed off towards the south or southeast.

Description

During that initial sighting, our total observation time was less than 60 seconds, the bird coming as close as *c.* 80 m. From these views, the three of us compiled the following description:

The bird looked large, although there were no other birds around for comparison. It looked much longer- and thicker-winged than a Common Buzzard *Buteo buteo*; it also seemed a stronger, more powerful bird than Common Buzzard. The flight was powerful but relaxed, consisting of two or three flaps then a glide with the wings held flat and the wing-tips depressed, giving it an appearance somewhat recalling a giant Honey-buzzard *Pernis apivorus*. The head looked broad and thickset, and was beige in colour, as were the chin and throat. There was a brighter breast-band, composed of an orange-buff background with darker, smudgy spots. Below this, the breast and belly were white, with obvious orange/brown spots and smudges. The underwing-coverts were white, with rows of brown/grey spots and blotches, and the carpal joints were pale. From below, the secondaries had grey tips and paler bases, while the primaries were darker than the 'wing-linings', and six 'fingered' primaries were visible at the wing-tip. The upperparts showed much contrast between the pale grey/brown upper-wing-coverts and the darker blackish-brown primaries and secondaries. The wings showed no missing flight feathers or any obvious signs of feather wear or damage. The mantle was brown, darker than the upperwing-coverts. The tail was broad when spread, pale beige in colour and with four evenly spaced, darker brown bars across its width.

Age

Later, after examining photographs and video footage of the bird, we were able to age it as a juvenile, based on the following points: the uniformly beige head; pale upperwing-coverts; the presence of pale tips to the greater upperwing-coverts, forming a thin pale band along the middle of the upperwing; the fact that it was not in moult, with no worn or missing flight feathers; and the warm, orange-buff breast-band and scattered orange/brown spotting on the underparts.

Possible origins of the Scilly Short-toed Eagle

It appears that those Short-toed Eagles breeding closest to Scilly may not be increasing as breeding birds, but there is a regular summer staging area in Brittany, which may have been the source of the British record. If not, the bird might have wandered west from The Netherlands or Germany, or it may have come from farther east. With Siberian and White's Thrushes, the first of nine Radde's Warblers to appear in 11 days on Scilly, a 'Siberian Stonechat' *Saxicola torquatus maurus* on St Agnes on 7th–12th October and a Blue Rock Thrush *Monticola solitarius* appearing on St Mary's on 14th October, the 'supporting cast' for the eagle certainly had a markedly eastern feel to it rather than being one of displaced birds from southern Europe, such as Hoopoes *Upupa epops,* Alpine Swifts *Apus melba* and Red-rumped Swallows *Hirundo daurica.*

The discovery of the Blue Rock Thrush is also of interest when trying to look at the possible origins of the Short-toed Eagle. The Blue Rock Thrush could not be ascribed to any particular race, but the bird occurred during an arrival of eastern rarities on the island. The first accepted British record of Blue Rock Thrush – a first-summer male at Skerryvore Lighthouse, Strathclyde, on 4th–7th June 1985 – was found dead on 8th June (Hume 1995). This bird also could not be ascribed to a particular race with certainty, but the biometrics (wing length and bill length) of the specimen 'appeared closest to those of birds from the Middle East, and was unlikely to have come from western Europe'.

There are no hard facts which allow us to attribute the source of the Short-toed Eagle to the eastern part of the species' range rather than the closer, more obvious origins of southern France or Spain, and, indeed, the weather data appear to suggest that an origin in western France is most likely. Nonetheless, the assemblage of eastern vagrants (*i.e.* east of the Mediterranean basin) on Scilly during the first two weeks of October 1999, together with the paucity of migrants from an obvious southwest European origin, does give us food for thought.

Cleeves, T. R., Hepple, M. & Shaw, K. D. 2004. Short-toed Eagle: new to Britain. *British Birds* 97, 27–32.

Short-toed Eagle breeds in southern and eastern Europe and Central Asia; this Palearctic population winters in sub-Saharan Africa. Another, sedentary, population is found in the Indian subcontinent.

There have been no subsequent records.

NOVEMBER 1999

MOURNING DOVE ON THE OUTER HEBRIDES

Brian Rabbitts

On Sunday 14th November 1999, I received a telephone message from Mairi MacPhail, a neighbour at Carinish, at the south end of North Uist, Outer Hebrides, reporting that there was an unusual dove in her garden. As it was fast approaching dusk, I quickly walked to her garden where she pointed it out sitting on the top of a fence: I was more than surprised to find that it was a Mourning Dove!

The bird was very confiding and seemed very tired, but its plumage was in good condition and it fed well on the chicken food that Mairi provided for it. Angus, Mairi's husband, had seen the bird briefly the previous day and it was still present the following day, 15th, when it was seen by 25 of the keenest twitchers from the mainland. Unfortunately, it had disappeared by the next morning.

Identification of the American Mourning Dove is quite straightforward. It is the most abundant and widespread dove in North America, breeding from southeast Alaska and southern Canada to central Panama and the West Indies. Northern populations are migratory within this range, with some moving south as far as Panama. Some also wander significant distances to the north and east in autumn. As well as two previous Western Palearctic records, there are two records from Greenland, while small numbers regularly winter north to northern Ontario, British Columbia, Nova Scotia and Newfoundland.

The sole previous record in the British Isles is of a first-winter found in a Heligoland trap at the Calf of Man Bird Observatory, Isle of Man, on 31st October 1989. At 83 g this bird appeared to be very underweight (123 g is given as the mean weight for males, 115 g for females), indicating that it had just arrived, and it was found dead the next morning. The specimen is now in the Manx Museum. This species might seem a likely candidate for ship-assisted vagrancy, but both David Parkin (in Sapsford 1996) and Keith Vinicombe (Vinicombe & Cottridge 1996) considered that the emaciated state of the Calf of Man bird indicated that it was quite likely to have made the crossing unaided.

The only other Western Palearctic record is of a first-winter female collected (illegally) on Heimaey, Iceland, on 19th October 1995, although there has also been an accidental import: one was found in London Heathrow Airport Cargo Depot on 9th February 1998, having arrived in the hold of an aeroplane from Chicago, USA, earlier that day.

Rabbitts, B. 1999. The Mourning Dove on the Outer Hebrides. *Birding World* 12, 453.

Mourning Dove breeds from Southeast Alaska to Panama and the West Indies.
There have been no subsequent records.

2000

THE BIRDER'S YEAR

Tim Cleeves

2000 was a steadier, less hectic year for rare birds in Britain than 1999 but two Firsts were found – a **Long-tailed Shrike** on the Outer Hebrides and **Siberian Blue Robin** at Minsmere, Suffolk. And then there was the female **Hooded Merganser** on North Uist, also in the Outer Hebrides, in October which, although consigned to Category D, will hopefully be promoted to Category A before long. But there were two other 'armchair ticks' on offer: the BOURC split the Redpoll into two species: Common (Mealy) Redpoll and Lesser Redpoll. And the American Green-winged Teal was split from Teal.

The year opened well with an approachable **Sora** at Stover Country Park, in Devon in January. The Southwest scored again when a white-phase **Gyrfalcon** spent nearly three weeks touring a number of sites in Cornwall.

An **Iberian Chiffchaff** was recorded singing at Great Tew in Oxfordshire in late April (the First record, in 1972, was officially admitted to the British List in October – see below). And, after an absence of 23 years, not one but two **Fan-tailed Warblers** were seen in Dorset in May. Also in May, a **Little Crake** was at Dungeness, Kent; and, in Gwent, a Whimbrel of the North American form, '**Hudsonian Whimbrel**' (a potential split to bank for the future), was present for two days.

The seventh to ninth **Slender-billed Gulls** for Britain were seen in 2000, with two at Cley, Norfolk (an extraordinary repeat of the May 1987 event), and one at Dungeness. A **Calandra Lark** on Fair Isle, Shetland, was, amazingly, the third record for the island. Two **Alpine Accentors** (one in Suffolk and one in Kent), a female **Blue Rock Thrush** and an **Iberian Chiffchaff** in Cornwall, and a confiding **Desert Warbler** at Easington, East Yorkshire, made up the supporting cast for a very good May.

On 2nd June, a superb breeding-plumaged male **Blackpoll Warbler** was found at Seaforth Nature Reserve, Merseyside. Two days later, a **Little Swift** was found in the New Forest, Hampshire. Seaforth was back in the news on 9th June when a **Terek Sandpiper** was discovered there.

In July, the Pool of Virkie produced a summer-plumaged adult **Red-necked Stint**, wader of the year for most of the Shetland birders. After finding an Eastern

Olivaceous Warbler at Portland Bill in early July 1999, Martin Cade at Portland Bird Observatory lifted another *Hippolais* Warbler out of a mist-net on 1st July 2000. This was another good 'banker' as the two forms of Booted Warbler were about to be 'split' – this bird was identified as *Hippolais (caligata) rama* – known as **Sykes's Warbler**.

Ringers at Cove, Aberdeen, struck gold on 5th August, trapping the fourth-ever **Swinhoe's Storm Petrel**. In late August, the Pool of Virkie delivered its second great wader of the year – an adult **Sharp-tailed Sandpiper**.

September was an excellent month, with an unprecedented passage of over 1,900 **Honey-buzzards** in Britain, the majority in the last ten days of the month. The largest numbers were (in decreasing order) in Sussex, Essex, Kent, Yorkshire, Hampshire and Dorset. An adult female **Isabelline Shrike** at the Nene Washes RSPB Reserve, Cambridgeshire, was assigned to the form *isabellinus*, known as 'Daurian Shrike' – another potential 'banker'? An **Eastern Olivaceous Warbler** was present at Collieston, Aberdeenshire, from 13th.

Now it was the turn of transatlantic vagrants, with a **Bobolink** on the Out Skerries, Shetland, and four **Red-eyed Vireos** at localities in Cornwall and the Isles of Scilly. A **Solitary Sandpiper** found on 22nd on St Mary's stayed on Scilly for nearly a month. Two **Cliff Swallows** – one at Portland and one on St Mary's – turned up over 29th/30th. A **'Steppe' Grey Shrike** on 22nd cheered up a fairly quiet Orkney autumn. A juvenile Little Crake was a good find in Conwy on 28th. The month ended with a 'fall' of **Radde's Warblers** – eight of which were at Spurn between 30th September and 1st October.

There was a more western influence in October with a **Yellow-billed Cuckoo** at St Levan, Cornwall, and two **Swainson's Thrushes** – one in Shetland, one on St Mary's. And Scilly had the next big find (by Steve Broyd on Tresco): a first-winter **Spectacled Warbler** on 15th. At the other end of the country, Fair Isle woke from its slumbers and turned up Britain's second-ever **Brown Shrike** for the lucky few observers on 21st. On 23rd, a First for Britain was found – a **Siberian Blue Robin** at Minsmere, Suffolk – a much-longed-for 'Sibe' which, sadly, was a one-day wonder.

November provided the next First in the shape of a **Long-tailed Shrike**. Look at the distribution of this species and you can see why the people who found and identified it were so shocked! The bird was at Howmore, South Uist, in the Outer Hebrides. At the South Gare in Cleveland one of the eastern forms of Lesser Whitethroat was trapped and ringed by Damian Money. The bird was identified as *Sylvia (curruca) minula* – known as **'Desert Lesser Whitethroat'**. There had been four previous records of this form, which is just one of probably five recognised forms of Lesser Whitethroat. Yet another 'banker' for the future?

A **Spanish Sparrow** in Cornwall was an excellent find on 12th November; and a female **Steller's Eider** at Hopeman, Moray, on 16th November presented the first chance anyone had had for 16 years to see this species in Britain.

The year ended fairly quietly. Many of the rarest birds in 2000 had been short-stayers, but the quality was certainly high.

IN THE RECOVERY WARD WITH A RED-NECKED STINT

Roger Riddington

What is it, exactly, that makes any one year's birding particularly memorable? Is it new species, extreme rarities, good birds that you find yourself, a big list or a long-dreamed-of foreign trip? Is it the unexpected, or a reward that had to be really worked for? When AP asked me to write this account, I had no clear idea of the answer. Perversely, what I did know was that if I was going to write about a memorable year, I wanted to do 2000. Why exactly did it stand out so much in my mind? I took my logbook for that year off the shelf and started to read…

The first six weeks of the new millennium were largely uneventful, which is pretty much the norm for Shetland winter birding. On 11th February, however, the first twitch of the year came unexpectedly early: to Fair Isle, for Gyrfalcon. Not an exceptional rarity, but a Shetland tick for me. That bird remains, arguably, my best twitch ever. It involved a day tramping round my all-time favourite birding island (and former home), largely on my own, in spectacularly clear, cold winter weather and, finally, with the help of Del, the observatory warden, connecting with the bird. It will be a long time before I forget watching this king of falcons disputing a rabbit kill with two of the local Ravens (themselves accustomed to bossing the airspace, and irritated by the intruder). Eventually, the Gyr had had enough of snapping at the corbies on the ground and a quite stunning aerial display by the three birds ensued. It remains one of my most thrilling Fair Isle memories.

Spring 2000 wasn't exceptional in Shetland, but another Fair Isle trip, this time for Shetland's first Dartford Warbler, on 30th April, was noteworthy. Two good finds in early May stick in my mind rather more: American Wigeon at Loch of Spiggie and Red-rumped Swallow at Scatness; like the Gyr, not particularly rare although both were new for Shetland for me, and were species I hadn't found before. What's more, both birds were within five miles of home, seemingly vindicating the purchase of my first house the previous September.

Seabird ringing trips in late June effectively mark the onset of 'high summer' in Shetland, but the results of the extraordinary storm of 13th June, with its gusts of up to 90 mph, were all too evident at Sumburgh Head and it was not a vintage season.

Midsummer it may be, but I've always rather enjoyed July as a birding month. Early July 2000 was best remembered for a fine Black-headed Bunting on Unst, finally laying to rest an eight-year ghost. I missed five (or was it six?) on Fair Isle in spring 1992, despite working at the observatory (and still don't want to talk about it). As the month wore on, the numbers of migrant waders at the Pool of Virkie, the closest we come in Shetland to 'estuarine habitat', were a constant attraction. Two Pectoral Sandpipers together on

10th preceded a White-rumped Sandpiper on 13th, found by my old mate Steve Votier, and which I had a very small input into helping to identify. On the evening of 17th, I arrived earlier than usual. I had spent most of the day in hospital, undergoing some highly unpleasant tests to investigate an ailing stomach (which ultimately revealed an allergy to wheat). Having been heavily sedated, I wasn't even supposed to be driving, but I had to escape, and they would never find me at Virkie … When I first saw the bird, I thought the chemicals still had a hold of me, but after a nerve-jangling half hour of lost-and-found I was certain it was no drug-induced apparition – it really was an adult Red-necked Stint! Having played some part in the identification of Shetland's first RNS, a freshly dead juvenile on Fair Isle in 1994, this fifth for Britain was an especially satisfying bird.

That stint kicked off a quite remarkable autumn for me personally, in terms of finding good birds. Some of them, like the stint, were solo finds, but rather more were joint efforts with one or both of two regular birding companions, Paul Harvey (PVH) and Pete Ellis (PME). The highlights were, in brief: Greenish Warbler, 26th August (with PVH); Sharp-tailed Sandpiper, 27th August (PVH); Citrine Wagtail, 30th August (solo); Lanceolated Warbler, 1st September, (PME, PVH); Yellow-breasted Bunting and Temminck's Stint, 2nd September (solo/PVH); another Citrine Wagtail and Honey-buzzard, 13th September (solo); Black-headed Bunting and a third Citrine Wagtail, 15th September (PME, PVH); American Wigeon, 16th September (PVH); Pied Wheatear, 17th September (PVH); Lesser Grey Shrike and Booted Warbler and 'Ehrenberg's Redstart' (*Phoenicurus phoenicurus samamisicus*), 23rd September (PVH); and, finally, another Yellow-breasted Bunting on 3rd October, this one with Tony Blake.

A truly sparkling period, with admittedly nothing to get the nation's twitchers mobilised, no firsts for Britain never mind Europe. But to be in on the action on such a regular basis made this an unforgettable, perhaps even unrepeatable spell. With the exception of the Lancey and the Black-headed Bunting/Citrine Wagtail double, all of which were on Out Skerries, all these birds were within a few miles of home too, which sharpened the sense of enjoyment. On 3rd October I left Shetland, not without mis-givings, for a long-planned three-week spell in China, the delights of which are far too numerous to mention, but which culminated with a magical day on the Lotus Hills in Beidaihe, watching the first day of significant crane migration that autumn. Back in Shetland at the end of October, the birding year was virtually spent, although late 2000 will be remembered as the time I put pen to paper on a contract to work as the editor of *British Birds*.

So, what is the answer to that initial question? Unsurprisingly, perhaps, I think it is not one but a combination of things. For me, the adrenalin surge which comes with finding good birds is probably the single most important reason why 2000 was partic-ularly memorable. Nonetheless, the quality of the birds set in the context of the whole birding/outdoor experience is significant. For me, a big part of that is weather and landscape, and (without wishing to come over all arty) the aesthetics of the birds them-selves – like the Gyr and the Ravens sparring over Malcolm's Head.

I think people are important too – the fact that I can count on one or two trusted companions most of the time, whose approach is at least broadly similar to mine and whose company I enjoy, all adds 'value' to the game. Subconsciously, I think I knew all that anyway, but writing it all down and thinking about it has helped to crystallise my thoughts. But, to use a Ken Shaw mantra, you're only as good as your last *BB*. I'd better get out there…

Dr Roger Riddington lives on Shetland. A former warden of Fair Isle, he is the editor of the journal British Birds.

JUNE 1972

IBERIAN CHIFFCHAFF IN GREATER LONDON

Leo Batten

While carrying out a Common Birds Census at the Brent Reservoir, Greater London, on 3rd June 1972, J. H. Wood heard an unfamiliar, loud, clear song coming from the top of a group of willows *Salix*. It was somewhat reminiscent of the song of a Cetti's Warbler *Cettia cetti*, but lacked the power of delivery of that species. After several minutes, the bird was seen by JHW, who was a little surprised to find that it was a  *Phylloscopus* warbler. His first thought was that it was, perhaps, a Willow Warbler *P. trochilus* with an aberrant song; but the legs appeared blackish. After taking a brief description, JHW returned to his car to consult the 'Peterson' field guide. This suggested that the bird might be a Greenish Warbler *P. trochiloides*, on account of its song. JHW had not noted any wing-bar, but he was aware that some Greenish Warblers could lack a wing-bar, as a result of wear. At this stage, JHW telephoned me and reported his observations. Unfortunately, although we tried to contact them, none of the other birdwatchers who regularly visited the reservoir was available at the time. We therefore arranged to meet at the Brent Reservoir, where, luckily, the bird was still singing when I arrived.

I made a long series of recordings with a cassette tape recorder, and noted the following description of the bird:

Head and upperparts olive-brown. Distinct creamy-white supercilium, which terminated well beyond the eye. Dark line through the eye, broader behind than in front. From certain angles, an indistinct yellow bar visible, produced by pale tips to primary coverts. (JHW could not detect any bar on the greater coverts, although I detected a slight indication of one and felt that it was possibly caused by wear to the tips of the greater coverts; in any case, it was no more distinct than the wing-bar shown by a small proportion of Chiffchaffs *P. collybita*.) Underparts washed greyish, with a light, ill-defined, yellow band across the breast, and, slightly, onto the lower sides of the neck. Undertail-coverts light yellow, contrasting with light creamy-grey lower belly. Legs appeared dark brown in good light. General appearance was dumpier than that of either Willow Warbler or Chiffchaff.

The bird sang and called frequently. The call was quite unlike the 'hooeet' call of Willow Warbler or Chiffchaff, being more reminiscent of a young chicken's anxiety call. It was uttered several times in a disconnected sequence before the song, and sounded rather similar to the one repeated in the full song. It was also not unlike the 'chiff' in a Chiffchaff's song. A 'tic-tic-tic' call, heard on one occasion, may have been an alarm note.

The song consisted of about ten to 12 'chip' notes, the first five or six of which were delivered at a slower rate than the remaining ones, with the whole song lasting two to two-and-a-half seconds.

The habitat that the bird frequented was a narrow strip of land forming the reservoir bank between some factories and the reservoir itself. This area included many medium-sized willows, with some Elder *Sambucus nigra* and hawthorn *Crataegus*. There was a lush growth of Common Nettle *Urtica dioica* and Bramble *Rubus fruticosus* in the clearings. The bird fed solely in the willows, and remained at a height of at least 6 m, coming lower only once, when flying across an open space. Despite subsequent searches of the area on the following days, the bird was not heard or seen again.

Identification

At this stage, we were not able to identify the bird and were not even aware of the existence of a distinctively different Iberian form (*brehmii*) of what was then 'the Chiffchaff'. We were favouring the idea that the bird had been a Greenish Warbler, and this impression was reinforced later, on hearing recordings of the song of that species. Although the song of 'our' bird had lacked the high-frequency trill, the speed of delivery and the variety of the Greenish Warbler's song, that was the closest match that we could get to it, and this was the view of a number of other people to whom we played the recordings. We remained uneasy, however, and continued to look for more recordings. It was not until several weeks later, when I met I. J. Ferguson-Lees on the stairs of the BTO's headquarters at Beech Grove, Tring, Hertfordshire, where I worked at the time, that we were able finally to identify the bird. I played the tape to him and he immediately identified the song as that of Iberian Chiffchaff, a bird with which he was familiar in Spain.

Soon afterwards, I found a set of recordings by Jean-Claude Roché that included Iberian Chiffchaff. The song sounded identical to that of the Brent Reservoir bird, and left no doubt as to the latter's identity. Sonograms of the Brent Reservoir bird and parts of the Roché tape showed very similar patterns.

Status

This Brent Reservoir observation seemed to represent the first occurrence of this form to be reported in the UK. The record was submitted to the London Natural History Society, which accepted it and published an account of the occurrence in the *London Bird Report* (Batten & Wood 1974). Since Iberian Chiffchaff was considered to be 'only a race' in those days, the record attracted little further interest, although it was mentioned in several books (Batten *et al.* 1973, *Birdwatcher's Year*; Simms 1985, *British Warblers*; Clement 1995, *The Chiffchaff*).

Interest was resurrected when phylogenetic analyses of mitochondrial-DNA sequences indicated that the Iberian form was sufficiently distinct from Chiffchaff *P. collybita* to merit being considered a separate species, the Iberian Chiffchaff *P. brehmii* (Helbig *et al.* 1996). Other accounts of the rationale behind the spilt can be found in Clement *et al.* (1998) and Richards (1999).

Batten, L. A. 2000. Iberian Chiffchaff in Greater London: new to Britain and Ireland.
British Birds 93, 329–332.

Iberian Chiffchaff, now known as **Phylloscopus ibericus***, breeds in the Iberian Peninsula and northwest Africa. It apparently winters mainly within Iberia, at low altitudes, although there are winter records from as far south as Mali and Burkina Faso.*

There have been nine subsequent records:

Scilly St Mary's, in song, 14th April–21st May 1992

Dorset Verne Common, Portland, in song, 25th April–8th July 1999

Devon Start Point, in song, 6th–14th May 1999

Kent Dungeness, in song, 14th–17th April 2000

Oxfordshire Great Tew, in song, 27th April–15th May 2000

Cornwall Dunmere Woods, Bodmin, 13th–31st May 2000

Devon Kingswear, in song, 19th May–17th June 2003

*****Northumberland** Woodhorn, Newbiggin, in song, 18th–19th April 2004

*****East Yorkshire** Kilnsea, in song, 17th May 2004

*BBRC decision awaited

OCTOBER 2000

SIBERIAN BLUE ROBIN IN SUFFOLK

Kieran Foster

On Monday 23rd October 2000, I decided to go to Suffolk, to look for the Sociable Plover and Pallas's Warbler that had been seen at Minsmere. Due to heavy traffic on the way, I arrived later in the afternoon than I expected, but I hurried along the beach towards the Levels, where the plover had been seen.

When I arrived at the Sluice Bushes, birders there told me that the Pallas's Warbler was being elusive, so I quickly carried on down to see the Sociable Plover. Just before I reached the Levels at about 4.50 pm, I noticed a bush which offered a convenient spot to have a discreet 'pee' and, upon reaching it, I flushed a small brown passerine. It was not immediately obvious what the bird was, but its broad tail somehow gave me the impression of a *Locustella* warbler. It dropped into the marram grass a short distance away. I soon refound it and immediately noticed that it was unstreaked and had strikingly pale pink legs. It flew again and I lost it in the marram, so I hurried over to the single birder who was watching the Sociable Plover and, after having a quick look at it, asked him if he would help me to relocate the bird I had just seen. After a bit of persuasion, he agreed, but we failed to find it.

I returned to the Sluice Bushes and was told that the Pallas's Warbler was still being elusive. I told the birders there what I had seen and tried again to get people interested in helping to relocate my mystery bird. Eventually Mark Cornish and another birder said they would look with me as they were on their way back past the spot heading towards Sizewell.

Mark soon flushed the bird from the seaward edge of the dunes. It flew again, but this time I refound it, skulking in view at the base of a marram clump. This time we noted that the bird had a prominent pale buff eye-ring, but none of us could put a name to it. I ran to attract the attention of the birders that were still waiting for a view of the Pallas's Warbler, and this time they came over quickly.

To my horror, the bird flew from the dunes, across the beach and out over the waves, but thankfully it quickly doubled back and landed in view on the shingle. One of the birders announced 'It's a Swainson's!' But I had seen Swainson's Thrush in America and knew that this was no Swainson's Thrush. It was tiny. With its pale eye-ring and warm, yellowish-brown breast it did give the impression of a Swainson's Thrush, however.

Mobile telephones then really proved their worth. Paul Varney, who had come over to see the bird, tentatively suggested that it might be a Siberian Blue Robin and telephoned Richard Millington at Birdline to discuss the identification, while I described what we could see to Chris Batty and Andrew Raine at Rare Bird Alert. I was asked if it had any blue in the tail. Due to the angle of the bird and the obviously very short tail this was difficult to ascertain. I moved along the dune to get a better angle to view the tail, but the bird turned to face me again and at this point it was seen to quiver its tail. One observer thought that he did see a blue tinge to the tail, but I did not see this myself. Due to the helpful discussion of the features with Richard Millington and the RBA team, the bird was soon confidently identified as a first-winter female Siberian Blue Robin – the first for Britain.

The bird was on view on the beach for about 15 minutes. It appeared exhausted – sitting motionless with its head hunched in and pointing skywards at about 45°. The bird eventually returned into the marram, but it was then only seen again in flight about three or four times before it was last seen flying over the marram ridge and was lost to view. Daylight was fading fast and a brief search failed to produce any other sightings. It was considered that no further plumage features would be noted due to the light conditions, and a more extensive search of the area was not only unfair on the bird, but also on the birders who would be arriving in the morning. The bird was therefore left in peace, and so only about 10 lucky people saw it. Even people that were still on the reserve when the news broke failed to see the bird before it was lost to view at about 5.55 pm.

Description summary

A small, quite slender bird about the size of a Dunnock, with a short, broad tail. Contrasting brown upperparts and pale underparts – this particularly noticeable in flight when it gave the bird a very obviously two-toned appearance. It was seen to quiver its tail, as well as adopt an upright stance.

Breast warm honey-yellowish-brown, reminiscent of Swainson's Thrush. A band of slightly darker feathering came into the main breast colour, but did not extend completely across the breast. Crescentic markings on the upper breast. Belly and undertail-coverts white.

Legs strikingly pale pink (one of the first features noticed). Disproportionately large-looking dark eye surrounded by a very obvious pale buff eye-ring. Bill long and dark, with a pale grey base to the lower mandible.

Next morning, some 800 birders assembled in the hope that the bird was still going to be present, but unfortunately it could not be found despite extensive searching. The crowd had to be content with the supporting cast of Sociable Plover, Great White Egret and Pallas's Warbler. I was given a present from one of my friends at the site: a piece of the bush that had previously contained the bird that had created all the fuss.

My thanks go to Chris Batty, Andrew Raine and Richard Millington who all helped in resolving the bird's identification, as well as to those who helped in relocating and describing the bird. It just goes to show that even late in the day rare birds can be found and that, no matter what is going on, if someone tells you that they have got a bird that looks unusual, you should have a look just in case. I only hope that the birders who did not respond to my request for help in relocating the bird did not kick themselves too hard when they heard the news!

The only other Western Palearctic records of this species are one trapped on Sark, Channel Islands, on the 27th October 1975 and one trapped in the Ebro Delta, Spain, on the 18th October 2000 – just five days before the Minsmere bird.

Foster, K. 2000. The Siberian Blue Robin in Suffolk – a new British bird. *Birding World* 13, 412–414.

Siberian Blue Robin breeds in Siberia, China and Japan and winters in southeast Asia. There has been one subsequent record:

Orkney North Ronaldsay, immature/female, 2nd October 2001

OCTOBER 2000
LONG-TAILED SHRIKE ON THE OUTER HEBRIDES

Andrew Stevenson

The autumn of 2000, particularly October, brought an exciting mixture of vagrants and scarce migrants to northern and western Scotland. In Shetland, these included a Brown Shrike *Lanius cristatus* on Fair Isle on 21st October, while on the Outer Hebrides we had enjoyed vagrants of predominantly Nearctic origin, with an influx of American waders in the Uists, a Red-eyed Vireo *Vireo olivaceus* on Lewis, and a hotly debated female Hooded Merganser *Lophodytes cucullatus* on North Uist which, ultimately, was accepted onto Category D of the British List.

As local birders contemplated what could be next to turn up, Jon Brain reported seeing what he thought was a male Red-backed Shrike *Lanius collurio* fly into a garden at the Howbeg road junction, South Uist, on 27th October. He saw it only briefly, at dusk, when returning home from a day's fishing, and his views were far from conclusive.

Red-backed Shrike is a genuinely scarce migrant on the Outer Hebrides, with fewer than 25 records at the time of writing. As most of these have been autumn records of juveniles, an adult male in late October seemed a little odd.

I was due to leave the islands the following day but, as Howbeg is close to my home, I thought I would check it out. Unfortunately, I could not find the bird and I left South Uist for the ferry, stopping en route to watch the Hooded Merganser, where I mentioned the possible Red-backed Shrike to some visiting birders when they asked the age-old question of 'anything about?' When I returned to South Uist on 1st November, there had been no further reports of the shrike.

At 12.45 hrs on 3rd November, I was driving home from the office at lunchtime and, as I was passing a small deer-fenced plantation at Howmore, I noticed a large number of Redwings *Turdus iliacus* sunning themselves on the wires. As I slowed a little on my way past, another pale-fronted bird caught my eye. It clearly was not a thrush, so I pulled in just past the plantation for a second look. It was obviously a large shrike, but none of the obvious candidates fitted. The grey head with characteristic 'highwayman's mask' was fine, but the almost apricot tone to the underparts and rufous back caused panic. I quickly phoned Gwen Evans, who at the time was RSPB officer for the Uists and lived close to Howmore, saying that I had found Jon's shrike, that I was not sure what species it was, and that she should come and see it as soon as possible! As I tried phoning other local birders, the shrike flew into some Gorse *Ulex europaeus* bushes, revealing a long, narrow tail, which had previously been hidden behind the fencing. This confirmed my previous, seemingly ludicrous thoughts that it could be a Long-tailed Shrike *Lanius schach*, which I vaguely recalled was mentioned in Lewington *et al.* (1991). What followed was almost surreal. As I described the bird over the phone to a somewhat incredulous Angus Murray at Birdline Scotland, he confirmed the features of Long-tailed Shrike from Lewington *et al.* as the bird fed on beetles by the roadside, within a few metres of where I sat, totally oblivious to the panic it was causing. Worse was to follow, as a Merlin *Falco columbarius* shot through and caught a bird close to where the shrike was feeding. At this point, only Gwen and I had seen the bird, and we had an agonising 10–15-minute wait, which seemed far longer at the time, before the shrike reappeared.

Later in the afternoon, the shrike moved to the area around the Howmore Post Office and nearby garage, where it remained through the following day, 4th November. Being a Saturday, that day saw the largest-ever one-day twitch to the Outer Hebrides, with over 130 people managing to see the bird, plus a number of locals (including the two local estate gamekeepers) who came along to twitch the twitchers as well as the bird! The shrike spent much of the day in just one willow *Salix*, eating mice from a larder, before becoming quite active in the late afternoon. It was looked for again the following and subsequent days but was not seen again, and probably left the island on the clear frosty night of 4th/5th November.

Description

My initial description and sketches were taken on 3rd November, with the bird performing well on a calm, crisp, sunny afternoon, within the first hour of the sighting. During this time, the bird was also photographed. With hindsight and the opportunity to look at various photographs of the bird under different light conditions, I consider that bright, sunny weather heightened the plumage tones a little, perhaps leading me to over-emphasise the bright coloration of the bird in my description.

Size and structure

A large shrike, about the same size as a Blackbird *T. merula*, with a long, graduated tail, and a stout, deep-based, slightly hooked bill.

Plumage

The crown, nape and mantle were medium/pale grey with a lilac tinge, especially noticeable in bright light. The face showed the typical 'highwayman's mask', which was blackish on the lores but dark brownish on the ear-coverts. There was a thin whitish line between the mask and the crown, starting above the eye and fading out along the upper edge of the ear-coverts. A pencil-thin line of black extended across the forehead above the base of the bill. Although the throat was white, the rest of the underparts were warm, pale buff, deepening to a deep apricot or peach colour towards the flanks and breast-sides. One or two juvenile, crescent-edged feathers were retained on the breast-sides, but these were typically obscured under the bend of the wing.

On the upperparts, the grey mantle merged with the rich rufous colour of the scapulars. The rump and uppertail-coverts were also a rich rufous. The wings were dark brown, with broad, faded-buff edges to most feathers, producing a faint bar across the tips of the greater coverts. At rest, a poorly defined, thin, pale buffish-white crescent was visible at the base of the primaries, but this was more obvious in flight. All these features suggested that the wing feathers were retained (unmoulted) juvenile feathering. The long, dark brown tail showed buff edging, and appeared rather narrow owing to the feathers being tightly held together.

Bare parts

The bill-tip was blackish, while the bill base was paler grey, most obvious on the lower mandible. The eye was dark, and the legs dark grey in colour.

Age

Ageing the bird in the field proved straightforward, as it clearly showed the retained juvenile greater-coverts and remiges and some vestiges of dark barring on the sides of the breast. I was, however, slightly surprised to discover, when checking various reference sources, that some illustrations showed first-winter birds still in largely juvenile plumage. Initially, this caused some confusion as the Howmore bird was considerably more advanced. Subsequent checking revealed that, in fact, the moult from juvenile to first-winter plumage is often complete by autumn (Beaman & Madge 1999). Lefranc & Worfolk (1997) expanded upon this, stating that birds of the western form, *erythronotus*, undertake post-juvenile moult shortly after fledging, and this can be completed as early as the end of July, although most juveniles are still moulting in the second half of August, with some continuing to do so until early October. This fits much better with the appearance of the Howmore bird, and would suggest that it belonged to *erythronotus*, although there is an absence of data on the moults of other subspecies.

Behaviour
During 3rd–4th November the bird was often quite confiding and unconcerned by the crowd that had gathered to enjoy it. It was observed catching beetles as well as a Wood Mouse *Apodemus sylvaticus* and Short-tailed Vole *Microtus agrestis*. It also appeared to be quite settled in the area, with three larders discovered at sites up to 400 m apart, and was reported to have visited gardens in Howbeg, some 800 m away from the Howmore Post Office. All this suggests that it had been present for long enough to have established a territory.

Stevenson, A. 2005. Long-tailed Shrike: new to Britain.
British Birds 98, 26–31.

Long-tailed Shrike is found across south and southeast Asia. The race erythronotus *is highly migratory and breeds from Turkmenistan, Afghanistan and Kazakhstan southeastwards into India.*

There have been no subsequent records.

THE BIRDER'S YEAR

Tim Cleeves

2001 was a quality year, although some of the best birds didn't stay around long. The three confirmed Firsts were **Snowy Egret, Red-billed Tropicbird** (at sea) and **Grey Catbird**. And in this high-scoring year, there was good back-up material too.

Besides the confirmed Firsts, there were records of two potential Firsts in 2001. Two records of **Fea's Petrel** may well prove to be the first bird(s) specifically accepted as *Pterodroma feae*. One was seen *c.* 12 km south of St Mary's, Isles of Scilly, on 8th July and it – or another – was also seen on the *Scillonian* pelagic on 12th August. The second potential First was a *Catharacta* skua found in poor condition on St Agnes, Isles of Scilly, on October 7th, which could be ascribed to one of the southern hemisphere '**Brown Skua'** species.

The first winter period of 2001 was lively, with two **Canvasbacks** – one in Essex, one in Kent – in January and February. On 29th January, a dead **Brünnich's Guillemot** was found on North Ronaldsay, Orkney. The reputation Dungeness, Kent, has for **Short-toed Treecreeper** was enhanced again as one spent four days there at the end of March.

In April, Fair Isle, Shetland, had a **Black-throated Thrush** and Dungeness continued a good spring with an **Iberian Chiffchaff**, seen and sound-recorded. On 4th May, Dungeness was still *the* place to be when seawatchers' patience was truly rewarded – a **Black-browed Albatross** was on view for nearly an hour. In Shetland, a **Scops Owl** at Cunningsburgh was on show for only one day, 14th May.

Other top-class rarities found in May were a **Little Swift** at Netherfield Lagoons, Nottingham, on view from 26th–29th May, and two **Marmora's Warblers**, one in Norfolk and one in Suffolk (only the fourth and fifth for Britain).

Without doubt, the star bird in June was the adult **Red-billed Tropicbird** seen from a boat in sea area Sole, some 32 km SSE of the Isles of Scilly on the 7th. We wonder how much the skipper of the sailing vessel *Marg a Rita* could have charged for tickets if he'd known of the record in advance! This was a First for Britain well out of reach.

On land, history was repeating itself. A male **Baillon's Crake** had been seen and heard at Grove Ferry, Kent, in June/July 1999 and this year a bird was singing at Oare Marshes, also in Kent, from 16th June to 6th July.

Back at sea, on 8th July, this time 12 km south of the Isles of Scilly, a *Pterodroma* petrel was watched, photographed and videoed by Ashley Fisher, Bob Flood and others on a local pelagic trip. *Pterodroma feae* (Fea's Petrel), *Pterodroma madeira* (Zino's or Madeira Petrel) and the slightly more distinctive *Pterodroma mollis* (Soft-plumaged Petrel) are not easy to distinguish and good, close photographic evidence has to be a major bonus. 2001 produced at least five records of *Pterodroma* petrels: the two putative **Fea's Petrels**; a bird off Walney Island, Cumbria, on 17th July; and one off the south Devon coast on the same date; and one off Flamborough Head on 23rd September. The most widely appreciated, at least by the birders who were on the *Scillonian* pelagic, was the Fea's Petrel seen *c.* 96 km southwest of the Isles of Scilly on 12th August. This latter bird was also video-recorded and photographed.

Two **Black-winged Pratincoles** were seen in Wales during the summer: one at Goldcliff Pools, Gwent on 25th June and one at Mona, Anglesey, on 4th July. In August, an adult **Sharp-tailed Sandpiper** was at Grove Ferry at the end of the month.

September was very productive, particularly for vagrants from the East. A **Pallid Harrier** found on 8th at Brow Marsh, Shetland, opened the bidding. On 14th, while the harrier was still present, perhaps the most experienced field team in Britain – Pete Ellis, Paul Harvey, Roger Riddington and Ken Shaw – unearthed a **Thick-billed Warbler** on Out Skerries, Shetland's most easterly group of islands. It was only the third British record. Those of us on Shetland Mainland, joyous after seeing the harrier, heard the news from the Skerries and could only stand in the rain and cry!

Also on 14th September, just north of the Out Skerries, an **Isabelline Wheatear** was on Fetlar; another was at Landguard, Suffolk, on 21st. The last date was also significant for birders forced to live inland. The adult **Red-necked Stint** at Somersham gravel pits, Cambridgeshire, was a real scene stealer and gave hope that anything can turn up anywhere. On 22nd September, a **Pallas's Grasshopper Warbler** found at Blakeney Point, Norfolk, gave southern birders a chance to see what is normally a Shetland speciality.

The value of video and digital cameras was realised on Bryher on 24th September when images of a shrike previously overlooked as a Red-backed allowed it to be re-identified as a **Brown Shrike**. If you saw it when it was a Red-backed, did you tick it when it was re-identified? It was only the third British record.

September 24th also produced the fourth record – but only the second found alive – of **Green Heron**, at Messingham Sand Quarry, Lincolnshire, almost 20 years after the 1982 bird. A **Red-flanked Bluetail** was found at Skinningrove, Cleveland, on 25th. The month closed with a **Sociable Plover** at Pett Levels, East Sussex, and, on 29th, another English mainland Pallas's Grasshopper Warbler; a great find by Jimmy Steele and Stef McElwee at Newbiggin, Northumberland.

October began with an **Eyebrowed Thrush** on St Kilda, Western Isles. The next day, 2nd October, Britain's second-ever **Siberian Blue Robin** emerged on North Ronaldsay, Orkney, just a year after the First record. On Fair Isle, Shetland, the first of at least eight **Pallid Swifts** was found. The others were seen from Kent to Northumberland until the month's end. A very elusive **Grey Catbird**, a First for Britain, was found by Ken Croft on his local patch at South Stack, Anglesey, on 4th October and stayed another day.

Lundy, Devon, followed the trend for American passerines with a **Rose-breasted Grosbeak** on 6th. On 9th, a **Bobolink** was found at Prawle Point, South Devon. Rare enough in the Southwest, but unheard of in Yorkshire, another Bobolink was found on 27th October, at Long Bank, Easington, East Yorkshire. Two **Black-faced Buntings** were found in October, one on Lundy (on 12th) and the other on Fair Isle (on 21st). These were only the third and fourth British records.

The places to be were the Isles of Scilly and the Northern Isles from mid-October. The second Rose-breasted Grosbeak of the year was found on 13th on St Martin's, Isles of Scilly. A **Grey-cheeked Thrush** was at Stromness, Orkney, on 14th. The Pallas's Grasshopper Warbler on Fair Isle on 19th turned up rather late, but at least it was in the 'right' place! Also on Shetland, at Maywick on 18th, was an exhausted first-winter **Baillon's Crake**. October 25th was a day of mourning on Shetland when a freshly dead male **Siberian Rubythroat** was found on the road near Bixter. The next day was happier with a **Cliff Swallow** on the Isles of Scilly. The month ended with a **Chimney Swift**, also on the Isles of Scilly.

November saw four birds of note, three clear-cut, the fourth less so. The first of these was another First for Britain – a superb long-staying **Snowy Egret** – discovered by Bill Jackson at Balvicar, Seil Island, Argyll, on 5th. Another good find, still following the North American theme, was a drake **Redhead** at Kenfig NNR on 7th November, only the second British record. A long-staying **Gull-billed Tern** was watched by many at Titchwell from 16th November. Then the tricky one. Still on Category D of the British List, the **Baikal Teal** at Minsmere RSPB Reserve, Suffolk, from 18th November–29th December had solid identification but debatable status.

The year ended quietly, with many birders still travelling on a pilgrimage to see the Snowy Egret and others catching up with **Ivory Gull**. There were birds in Shetland, Caithness and at the Montrose Basin, Angus & Dundee.

TOUCH AND GO ON NORTH RONALDSAY

Malcolm Roxby

The difficulty with being asked to give an account of a birding year is deciding what to include and what to leave out. Would anyone really be interested in my record count of four Wood Sandpipers at Hurworth Burn Reservoir or the male Blackcap which wintered in my garden for the second year running? Probably not, so I will concentrate on events with a broader appeal and, given the scope of this book, those that deal with rarer species.

The year was blighted by foot-and-mouth disease rendering large tracts of countryside inaccessible; in fact, for several months I wasn't able to visit any of my local patches. I sought solace for five weeks during January and February with a trip to Venezuela and again in March with a trip to Vietnam. The spring was quiet but Teesmouth had a run of good birds with a beautifully summer-plumaged White-winged Black Tern followed by a Great White Egret and a Spoonbill, the last two sharing the same clump of vegetation.

I spent part of the summer visiting Sweden and western Scotland. The countryside began to open up in August and there was a taste of autumn with a fine male Red-backed Shrike at Whitburn. September produced some classic fall conditions on the Northeast coast with a minimum of six Red-breasted Flycatchers on the headland at Hartlepool, a Hoopoe in Seaton Carew and a Radde's Warbler at South Gare.

Coatham Marsh played host to a Wilson's Phalarope and, not to be outdone, the north side of the estuary boasted a White-rumped Sandpiper. The highlight of the month was the first twitchable Green Heron in Britain for 19 years, at Messingham Sand Quarry in Lincolnshire. Fortunately it was found early enough in the day to allow me to see it after work. It showed brilliantly in late-evening sunshine, my first new bird in Britain for ten months and a pleasant surprise.

October began with the proverbial bang. A Siberian Blue Robin was found on North Ronaldsay on the morning of the 2nd. Three hours later I had left work and organised a private light aircraft to take three friends and myself to Orkney. We took off in a stiff southwesterly wind, the whole flight north was troubled by severe turbulence and the wind was even stronger as we approached the tiny airfield on North Ronaldsay, increasing to around 35 knots.

Our little craft was operating at its very limit and our approach would have to be perfect. Unfortunately it wasn't, and just as we came in to land we clipped a wire fence bordering the runway. The plane crashed into the ground before bouncing back into the air and colliding with the earth a second time. Amid a tirade of expletives, the pilot managed to get us back into the air but despite my frantic pleadings was not prepared to attempt another landing. There were anxious moments as we made a fly-past of the control tower at Kirkwall Airport, where ground staff made a visual check for damage. Fortunately there was none and we landed safely much to the relief of ourselves and the assembled emergency vehicles.

With little daylight remaining, our collective mood was grim; we had come so close to seeing a fantastic bird only to be thwarted at the very last moment. Dejectedly walking into the terminal building, I was surprised to be met by Ron Johns, who was essentially in the same predicament as us, unable to land on the island. However, he had secured the services of an Islander aircraft, capable of landing in extreme conditions, and 20 minutes later we were airborne again. This time the landing was trouble-free and the warden was waiting to whisk us to the bird in his battered Land Rover.

There was more anxiety when we arrived to find the Robin out of view but all the stress of a difficult day melted away when it ran out from the cover of a drystone wall and showed brilliantly. It was just a fantastic moment; a beautiful, charismatic eastern vagrant on a windswept Scottish island sheltering in scant vegetation and being enjoyed by a 'crowd' of about a dozen people. Our relief was tangible and we enjoyed a celebratory drink or two in the Kirkwall Hotel that evening.

Just two days later, I experienced the downside of twitching when a Grey Catbird was found near South Stack, Anglesey. I dashed to the site after work only to find the bird had disappeared into thick cover where it remained hidden for the rest of the day.

I had to return home that night and, predictably, the bird was seen again the following day, eliciting another drive into North Wales. Again, no further sign of the bird and I also spent the whole of the next day in a fruitless and increasingly desperate search. After the high of the Siberian Blue Robin, I had been brought crashing back to earth. But just think how enjoyable the next Grey Catbird will be.

Local birds included a Great Grey Shrike and a Pectoral Sandpiper as October drifted into November. Early in the month, a Ross's Goose was found amongst Pink-footed Geese in Norfolk. It was judged to be a first-winter bird and therefore a reasonable candidate for vagrancy. I saw it on a crisp winter afternoon, the fields a swarming mass of cackling geese. A party of five Common Cranes flew overhead to complete the day.

The next surprise was the Snowy Egret, the first British record, at Balvicar in Argyll. This is a beautiful part of the world and a successful trip to see the Egret made for a great day out.

After the Ross's Goose, controversy continued with a Baikal Teal at Minsmere, Suffolk. Again a first-winter bird, again the possibility of genuine vagrancy. I saw it the following morning, then called in at Titchwell, Norfolk, on the way home to enjoy a lingering Gull-billed Tern and the now-resident Black-winged Stilt.

There was just time for a quick visit to Nepal before another mild, wet winter settled over the UK. The year ended as it began, with a trip to Hurworth Burn Reservoir where, surprise surprise, bird species were much the same on 31st December as they had been on 1st January.

2002 – now there's a story…

Malcolm Roxby lives in County Durham. One of Britain's most intrepid twitchers, he is also a very keen world birder.

JUNE 2001

RED-BILLED TROPICBIRD OFF SCILLY

Sheila Blamire

One afternoon in July 2001, I received a phone call from Roger Barnes, whom I had got to know at the Knutsford Ornithological Society (KOS) and more recently as a member of the Cheshire and Wirral Ornithological Society (CAWOS). This was no ordinary 'catching up on the news' call, however; I could immediately hear the excitement in his voice. He had just returned from a five-week cruise in his yacht *Marg a Rita*, a 32-foot Westerly Fulmar, a bilge-keeled sailing yacht. He had left New Quay, in Ceredigion, on Saturday 2nd June to travel to Belle-Île, in the Bay of Biscay, and back – a journey of some 1,900 km. Roger was, in his own words, 'the nearest thing on board to a birdwatcher'. As usual, he had taken photographs documenting his trip, which had now been developed. Among these prints he was very pleased to see that several 'grab' shots of a mystery 'tern-like' bird seen on the trip had come out reasonably well.

His first thought was to ring Jeff Clarke from CAWOS, who had recently run a 'Tern Identification Workshop'. Jeff thought that the bird sounded like a Red-billed Tropicbird *Phaethon aethereus* from the description, but suggested that Roger show me the photographs to confirm the identification, since he knew that I had seen tropicbirds from various holiday destinations. I had first seen Red-billed Tropicbirds in the Galapagos, where it is not uncommon to see them soaring over the cliffs of islands such as South Plaza, Espanola, Genovesa, and North Seymour, and had also seen this species in Trinidad & Tobago. I had seen Red-tailed Tropicbirds *P. rubricauda* on Nosy Ve, off the Southwest coast of Madagascar, but White-tailed Tropicbird *P. lepturus* has so far eluded me. I must admit that I was expecting a few distant and probably blurred but, hopefully, 'record' shots of the bird in question. You can imagine my reaction when Roger brought them round, and there, staring me in the face, was a brilliant image of a stunning Red-billed Tropicbird!

I tried to convey the importance of the event to Roger, in that it was, potentially, the first proven record of a Red-billed Tropicbird in Britain and that, as such, the record would need to be fully documented and submitted to both the BBRC and the BOU Records Committee for their assessment. Initially, Roger found it difficult to grasp that his word would not be sufficient and that he would need to provide evidence to backup his claims so that the record would stand the test of time and any future reviews. He was then subjected to the third degree: Exactly where was the bird seen? Could he prove the exact location? What entries were made in the *Yacht Log Book* (it is a requirement of the skipper to keep this up to date)? Furthermore, we needed to know the distance from land that was currently adopted as the outer limit for UK waters in terms of admission to the British List. I had no idea at the time. Finally, were there any doubts at all as to the identification? I would need to be absolutely 100% certain before we went any further. First of all, I asked Roger to describe in detail the events of that day in June 2001.

Thursday 7th June 2001

It was 10.00 hrs on 7th June when the *Marg a Rita* left St Mary's, Scilly, for the passage through the Chenal de la Helle to Dournenez, in Brittany. George Legg from New Quay was at the helm, Paul Fraser from Northwich was on look-out, Martin White from Manchester was below decks preparing lunch and Roger Barnes from Knutsford, the skipper, was sitting at the chart table trying to work out where they were and what the tide was doing to them. RB describes what happened next:

'We were about 20 miles SSE of the Scillies when GL called us on deck to view an unusual-looking bird, the like of which he had never seen in all his years at sea. It hovered and flew in large circles around the boat. We thought on more than one occasion that it was contemplating landing on the boat; we have in the past had tired birds land on top of the mast, rest for a few hours, and then fly on. This one didn't, however, but it stayed with us for about five minutes, coming close enough for us to get a good look and take some photographs.

'The bird had the appearance and mannerisms of a large tern. I knew that it was not a European bird, or, to be more precise, it was not in my 1983 edition *Peterson's Field Guide to the Birds of Britain and Europe*. It flew between sea level and 100 feet in the air, hovering occasionally. What we immediately noticed was the very long tail (longer than the body), but we could not decide whether it comprised of one or two streamers. In brief, it was predominantly white with a large, blood-red bill, a conspicuous black eye-stripe, black on the wings towards the wing-tips and black feet.

'While the others were watching the bird, I rushed below to change the lens on my camera. As I have only two, a 35-mm and 90-mm, the choice was not difficult! I put on the 90-mm lens, hoping that the bird would come close enough for me to get a good shot. I set the shutter speed at l/1000th of a second, aperture to f2.8 and pre-set the distance at 30 feet. At the time, I was using up some old Kodak 200 ASA film. Fortunately the bird obliged and I managed to get one good shot. I use a Leica M6, which helps in these circumstances as the viewfinder has a larger field of view than the lens, and this made it easier to track the bird in flight.'

Establishing the location

An index print of the film showed images of the Isles of Scilly before and France after the photographs taken of the mystery bird. These, along with the *Yacht Log Book*, confirmed the locality of the sighting. Entries are updated in the log book approximately every hour and include time, course steered, barometer reading, latitude and longitude, distance to go to the next waypoint, and a narrative log. The important narrative entry made by

MW against 13.00 hrs reads: 'Sea bird. Ternish – long tail, b/r [bright- or blood-red?] beak.' At the top of the page, RB subsequently added: 'Tern – v. long tail single streamer, black wing-tips, black feet, red bill, black eye-stripe.' There are various other scribbles added at a later date to this page, including 'Red-billed Tropicbird' once the bird was identified. The latitude and longitude at 13.00 hrs were recorded as 49°40′05″N 06°09′62″W, then 49°36′01″N 06°05′32″W at 14.00 hrs, so the approximate position at the time of the sighting was estimated to be 49°38′N 6°08′W. This placed the sighting in sea area Sole, about 32 km SSE of Scilly. The British List includes birds seen 'at sea' within the British Economic Zone, which now extends to 200 nautical miles (370 km) from the nearest point of land, so the sighting was well within this zone.

Identification

Even though I was quite sure of the identification, Red-billed Tropicbird is one of three closely related species in the genus *Phaethon*, so I still did my homework thoroughly, using the internet and various field guides as key reference sources. I also looked through photographs I had taken of tropicbirds over several holidays.

Tropicbirds are medium-sized seabirds, with a body roughly the size of a domestic pigeon, and a wedge-shaped tail with exceptionally long central tail feathers, or streamers, when adult; all three are essentially white, with a more or less conspicuous black mask through the eye. When seen well, however, each species has diagnostic characters which make identification reasonably straightforward.

The upperparts and wing pattern in particular are usually diagnostic, even from a distance. On Red-billed Tropicbird, fine, blackish-grey barring on the mantle, back and rump extends onto the wing-coverts, with the innermost secondaries being solidly dark with white fringes. The outermost primaries and primary coverts are black, forming an obvious dark wedge on the leading edge of the outer wing, while the inner primaries and most of the secondaries are white. The upperwing of White-tailed Tropicbird also shows a black wedge on the outer primaries (although this does not extend onto the primary coverts), but differs markedly from that of the former species in having a striking black diagonal band across the inner wing (from the inner median coverts to the tertials). Finally, Red-tailed Tropicbird has the upperwing completely white except for black shafts to the outer primaries, and looks entirely white-winged in the field. All adult tropicbirds have elongated central tail feathers, which are lacking in juveniles, and the colour of the central tail-streamers in adults is an important character for identification. These feathers, which form half the total length of the bird, are white in Red-billed and White-tailed Tropicbirds, and red in Red-tailed (although the red can sometimes be difficult to see, for example in bright light against a blue sky, making this species appear short-tailed). Bill colour is another key feature, being bright red in Red-billed (dull yellow in juveniles), yellow in White-tailed (dull yellow in juveniles), and red in Red-tailed adults (blackish in juveniles).

RB's photographs reveal a bird with a white head, conspicuous black mask and white body, and black in the outer primaries and the innermost secondaries or tertials. As there were no shots of the bird from above, the pattern of the upperwings, and the degree of barring on the upperparts could not be judged. Nonetheless, the combination of long, white tail-streamers and blood-red bill establish the identity of the bird without any doubt as an adult Red-billed Tropicbird. The length of the two central tail feathers (they look as one in the field – explaining the initial confusion) looks particularly long compared with the length of the body, so the bird was possibly a male.

Blamire, S. 2004. Red-billed Tropicbird: new to Britain.
British Birds 97, 231–237.

*Red-billed Tropicbird breeds in tropical and subtropical regions of the Atlantic, the eastern Pacific and the northwest Indian Oceans and is pelagic outside the breeding season. Within the Western Palearctic, it breeds regularly only in the Red Sea and on the Cape Verde Islands (ssp. **mesonauta**); this bird was considered to be probably of that race.*

There have been two subsequent records:

Sea area Sole About 6.5 km SE of Scilly from the *Scillonian III*, 29th March 2002

Cornwall About 1.5 km off The Lizard, 21st April 2002

JULY 2001

FEA'S PETREL OFF SCILLY

Ashley Fisher and Bob Flood

On 8th July 2001 we were at sea again, about seven miles south of the Isles of Scilly. This was the twelfth pelagic of the season. Early in the season we had seen single Wilson's Petrels (on 5th and 7th June), as well as the usual Storm Petrels, Manx Shearwaters and occasional skua. These were all nice, but not quite what we had in mind for over 60 hours of rocking and rolling! The weather conditions on 8th July were fair. The wind was a moderate northwesterly, force 3–4, and there was a slight swell. The sky was overcast, but not heavily so and thus viewing conditions were good.

A couple of hours into the trip, at about 5.50 pm, all was quiet and we started to think that it was going to be another disappointing evening. We scanned the chumslick off the port side for the umpteenth time, AF from the deck and BF from the cabin, but there were no birds in attendance. Silence ensued once more, save for the sound of small waves lapping against the *Kingfisher,* and the skipper, Alec Hicks, reeling in his fishing line.

Then, breaking the silence from the starboard side, came Nigel Wheatley's distinctive voice, 'What's that?', and then again, flavoured with a touch of panic, 'What's that?!' AF turned round, saw the bird at point-blank range and immediately yelled, 'It's a Fea's! It's a Fea's! It's a Fea's!' We all got the message!

Pandemonium ensued as the seven birders on board scrambled from their positions to get the best views as the bird continued on its way, just like the ones seen off the *Kingfisher* in 1996 and 1999 – or so we thought.

It had approached the bow from the east, passed the starboard side of the boat at a distance of about 30 feet, and then headed off from the stern, roughly to the Southwest. Nobody expected that this dream bird would turn back on itself and pass the boat again, but it did, not just once more, but four or five times, and down to 60 feet! The total duration of the event was some 12 minutes. The exact location was 049°48.573', 006°11.370'.

At each pass we were able to look in detail at the bill structure, wing structure, body bulk and plumage. Never before have birders in Britain or Ireland had the chance to see this species at such close range over such an extended period of time.

There was no bird photographer on board, but we both had video cameras. We both experienced immense dissonance in thought, however, wanting to experience every second of the bird, but at the same time wanting to put some of this experience onto video footage. As the Fea's approached for its fourth or fifth pass, which turned out to be its last, we both 'cracked' and dived for our video cameras. On AF's video footage there are several gems in Alec Hick's near-scripted commentary, one of them being, 'Look at Bob's ******* hand shaking!', followed by raucous laughter. Fortunately, AF captured one excellent sequence of the bird as it swept by at about 70 feet, before heading off for the last time to the Southwest.

Description
Size and general appearance Roughly the body length of Manx Shearwater (seen that evening), but longer-winged and considerably stockier-bodied. At a distance, looked almost monochrome. The crown was dark, with a panda-like smudge through the eye. The throat and underparts were white. The mantle was clean grey. At closer range, one of the most eye-catching features was the deep, heavy bill (seen very clearly at down to 30 feet range).

Flight action Flight action distinctive. It glided effortlessly, low over the sea on bowed wings, with occasional punctuations of two to six wing-beats. Sometimes it gained momentum with a run of faster wing-beats, then rose effortlessly up to 10–15 feet, turning and completing a full circle on a downward glide before tilting the other way and peeling off in the opposite direction. We found Madge's (1990) and Gantlett's (1995) pratincole analogy useful in describing the flight action. Gantlett (1995) describes our bird well: 'pratincole-like, buoyant with quick wing-beats and circling glides'. Furthermore, Enticott (1991) describes the flight action of the 'soft-plumaged' complex in calm, intermediate and windy conditions. Our field description of the flight action above is well supported by Enticott's description for relatively calm conditions.

Structure Large head with thick neck and stocky body with full chest attenuating and tapering at rear end to pointed tail. Long, slim pointed wings with both arm and hand relatively long. Bill, deep and heavy.

Head, neck and underparts Crown darker than neck and mantle, but not quite as dark as panda-like facial mask. Clear white gap between neck smudges, thus lacking full breast band. Rest of underbody pure white.

Upperparts Mantle grey, clearly darker than tail.

Wings A subtle 'M' was visible across the greyish-brown (more brown than grey) upperwing. This was created by a dark area across primaries and wing-coverts to the carpal joint, then to the inner area of the hindwing, this feature on each wing being joined by a relatively narrow dark band across the lower back. As stated, this was subtle and several observers commented that they found it difficult to detect. Underwings appeared all black at long range. At mid–range, a small extension of white onto the base of under-forewing was apparent. At close range, the underwing showed complex shades of grey. A broad dark bar ran alongside the white extension onto the base of the forewing, apparently in the region of the median underwing-coverts. This faded at the carpal joint. A greyer central area to the underwing arm and hand accentuated the dark bar. The trailing edge of the underwing was darker than the greyer central area.

Tail Tail and uppertail-coverts uniformly pale grey, paler than mantle.

Bare parts Bill black, large, heavy and deep. This was clearly seen, identical to those in published photographs of Fea's and quite unlike those of Zino's (*eg* in Fisher 1989).

Fisher, A. & Flood, B. 2001. The Fea's Petrel off the Isles of Scilly. *Birding World* 14, 289–292.

Fea's Petrel breeds on Madeira and the Cape Verde Islands. It is pelagic outside the breeding season. The very similar Zino's Petrel breeds on Madeira. It is a much rarer bird than Fea's – the estimated maximum world population is just 80 pairs and it is classified as Critically Endangered.

Fea's/Zino's Petrels have been reported in British waters more than 30 times since 1983 (Dungeness, Kent on 15th October) to the end of 2003, with the majority off northeast England. The 2001 Scilly bird was the first referable to species. This record awaits acceptance by BOURC.

OCTOBER 2001

GREY CATBIRD ON ANGLESEY

Ken Croft

The morning of 4th October 2001 dawned cloudy with a southwesterly wind blowing, much as it had done for the previous week, and I began the day seawatching from the steps of the South Stack lighthouse at the western tip of Holy Island, Anglesey. After 30 minutes, during which time I had seen only a single Manx Shearwater *Puffinus puffinus*, my enthusiasm for seawatching had waned and my thoughts turned to passerine migrants – this was October after all – and I made my way inland a few hundred metres to the 'Plantation', a small stand of conifers interspersed with a few hawthorns *Crataegus* and elders *Sambucus*. This is an area which I check regularly each spring and autumn, and in the past I have discovered Barred Warbler *Sylvia nisoria*, Pallas's Leaf Warbler *Phylloscopus proregulus* and Red-breasted Flycatcher *Ficedula parva* here.

While walking up from the carpark, slowly working my way to the waterworks compound adjacent to the Plantation, I failed to see a single bird. Finally, around 09.00 hrs, I glimpsed a movement in the hawthorns at the top end of the Plantation. In hope rather than expectation, I focused my telescope on the bird and saw that it was a Goldcrest *Regulus regulus*, but while I was watching it, another bird emerged from some ivy *Hedera* and appeared in the same field of view. It looked almost entirely blue-grey, except for the black crown and eye, and a long black tail. I stood there, quite stunned, as I realised that it could only be a Grey Catbird *Dumetella carolinensis*! Agonisingly, it then began to play cat-and-mouse with me, disappearing into the vegetation but then quickly emerging again. It continued to show on and off like this for five minutes or so, as it hopped about through the bushes. Unfortunately, a Eurasian Sparrowhawk *Accipiter nisus* then flashed past and behind it, not particularly close but sufficient for the catbird to dive deep into the cover of an elder bush. I waited a further ten minutes for it to reappear, but there was no sign.

At that point, I decided that I had better get to a telephone and put the news out. Having done so, I returned to the site, where five members of the South Stack RSPB staff had already raced across from their office and seen the bird in the elder. As they watched, it had flown across the adjacent field and into dense cover. Other birders soon began to arrive but the bird proved to be extremely elusive. Remarkably, given that the catbird was the first American passerine recorded on Anglesey, a Red-eyed Vireo *Vireo olivaceus* was found that afternoon, but was of little consolation to most!

Although still present the following day, the Grey Catbird remained extremely uncooperative, spending much of the morning skulking in an area of thick gorse *Ulex*, being glimpsed just occasionally before diving back into cover, and calling infrequently. During the afternoon, it gradually became more obliging and was eventually seen by numerous birders.

Description

The Grey Catbird was of similar size to a Redwing *Turdus iliacus* (the two species were seen briefly, side by side, on the first morning), but with a slimmer, more elongated body shape and long, rounded tail. Its plumage was entirely uniform blue-grey except for its black tail and crown, and a distinctive chestnut-red patch on the vent (seen occasionally as the bird moved through the scrub with its tail raised). The bill was black, the iris and legs dark.

Weather conditions and associated species

October 2001 was not a good month for Nearctic landbirds in Britain, although the number and variety of species improved significantly in the second half of the month, and particularly so towards the end. Although the South Stack Red-eyed Vireo was the only other Nearctic landbird reported in Britain during the two-day period that the Grey Catbird was present, there was a Rose-breasted Grosbeak *Pheucticus ludovicianus* on Lundy, Devon, on 6th–9th October and a Red-eyed Vireo at Porthgwarra, Cornwall, on 7th–18th October (with two seen there on 13th only).

In the days leading up to 4th October 2001, an area of low pressure formed in the western North Atlantic. This gradually deepened as it moved northeast into the mid Atlantic, with associated strong southwesterly winds along its southern flank. The airstream in which the catbird was embedded indicates that the strong southwesterly winds could have taken the bird swiftly through the frontal system and into western Ireland by the night of 3rd October, and then on to Anglesey the following day. Subsequent arrivals, on 6th and 7th October, of American passerines sharing a similar breeding range with Grey Catbird may have also been associated with this system.

Croft, K. 2004. Grey Catbird on Anglesey: new to Britain.
British Birds 97, 630–632.

Grey Catbird is a widespread breeding bird in North America; it winters in southeastern USA south to Panama and the West Indies.

There have been no subsequent records.

The First for Ireland was on Cape Clear Island, Co. Cork, on 4th November 1986.

SNOWY EGRET IN ARGYLL & BUTE

Bill Jackson

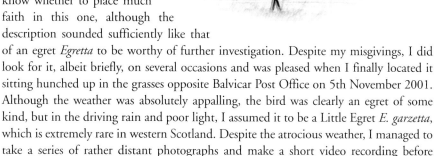

Rumours of the presence of an unusual white bird feeding on the shore, and occasionally in water-logged gardens, at Balvicar, Argyll & Bute, had been circulating through the local community since about 30th October 2001. As with so many rumours, it was difficult to know whether to place much faith in this one, although the description sounded sufficiently like that of an egret *Egretta* to be worthy of further investigation. Despite my misgivings, I did look for it, albeit briefly, on several occasions and was pleased when I finally located it sitting hunched up in the grasses opposite Balvicar Post Office on 5th November 2001. Although the weather was absolutely appalling, the bird was clearly an egret of some kind, but in the driving rain and poor light, I assumed it to be a Little Egret *E. garzetta*, which is extremely rare in western Scotland. Despite the atrocious weather, I managed to take a series of rather distant photographs and make a short video recording before returning home to telephone Jim Dickson (JD), my neighbouring birder, who is based at Lochgilphead, some 50 minutes' drive away.

JD arrived in the early afternoon and we settled down to watch the egret feeding in the tidal pools on the rocky shoreline. By now, the weather conditions had slowly improved, so we decided to approach the bird more closely and try to obtain better photographs. As we did this, I began to note several features that I thought unusual for Little Egret, including its strikingly yellow legs, marked with a black stripe up the front, and the yellow facial skin around the eye and bill base. Then the penny dropped! We were watching Britain's first Snowy Egret *E. thula*, and the enormity of the find began to sink in. Before releasing the news to the outside world, we compared my photographs with those in reference books at my home and I also downloaded photographs of Snowy Egret from the internet. This removed all doubt from our minds. Confident of our identification, I e-mailed photographs of the bird far and wide and, by late afternoon, John Holloway's words were ringing in my ears over the phone as we looked at our photos: 'check the legs and the lores'. Furthermore, Jim Duncan had e-mailed me a page from Kenn Kaufman's book with the accompanying message: 'Here's your bird Bill, Snowy Egret!'

The following morning (6th November) brought the hard core of British twitchers to the golf course, some 50 to 60 in all, and this was the start of the largest gathering of birders ever to be seen in Argyll, and probably Scotland. It was good to see a few old friends whom I had met while living in Shetland, along with several of Britain's top bird photographers. Over the next few days a regular pattern of behaviour emerged. At first light, about 08.30 hrs, the egret would arrive from its nearby roost in the pine trees at Balvicar Farm and settle into a feeding routine depending upon the state of the tide. Food was no problem for it, with several 'flatties' and other fish being caught using a combination of foot-paddling and a swift strike with its dagger-like bill. Continually feeding, the bird was obviously in excellent health, suggesting that it had made a speedy recovery from its transatlantic flight.

During the egret's tour of western Scotland, an estimated 4,500 birders managed to catch up with it. This included a rough estimate of some 2,500 at Balvicar lagoons alone, where all were rewarded with outstanding views, some down to just a few metres, as it fed quite unconcerned and seemingly oblivious to the hordes of photographers. During its three periodic visits to Balvicar, it became a popular attraction, with many locals, including school children, taking an interest.

Description

The following description was submitted to BBRC:

Size and structure   A small egret, very similar in size and structure to Little Egret, although perhaps slightly smaller and more compact, with shorter legs (no direct comparison possible, obviously!). Bill long and pointed, but appeared slightly shorter than that of Little Egret, length approximately 1.25 times longer than the head length, and slightly kinked downwards towards the tip. At rest, the closed wings reached to end of tail.

Plumage   Entirely white, with very short, fine plumes on the nape and loose feathering on the breast.

Bare parts   Bill appeared entirely black at a distance, but at close range the base of the upper mandible was noted as bright yellow, and inner two-thirds of lower mandible pale horn. Small area of bare skin around eye, lores and corners of gape bright yellow. Legs and feet yellow with greenish tinge, with black line on front of tarsus just above feet extending above knee and onto lower part of tibia. Iris bright yellow.

Behaviour   Similar to Little Egret in feeding behaviour and jizz, but often more approachable than is typical for that species.

Jackson, B. 2004. Snowy Egret in Argyll and Bute: new to Britain.
British Birds 97, 270–275.

Snowy Egret breeds from the Northeast USA south to Chile; northern North American birds winter south to the Gulf of Mexico.
This individual wandered across southwest Scotland until the last sighting on the Solway in Dumfries and Galloway on 17th September 2002.
There have been no subsequent records.

THE BIRDER'S YEAR

Tim Cleeves

Strictly speaking, there were no new birds for Britain in 2002, although the moribund juvenile/first-winter **Allen's Gallinule** on Portland in February came very close; it was the second record ever. The First was a bird caught on a fishing boat off the Norfolk/Suffolk coast 100 years previously, on 1st January 1902. However, in time, a large skua and an orange-billed tern might yet prove to be Firsts for Britain, but the jury is still out on both.

One rare bird remaining from 2001 was an **Ovenbird**. This was only Britain's second live record and was present in a garden in Herefordshire for 59 days from 20th December 2001. Sadly, access was denied.

A **Hume's Warbler** found on January 20th near Newbiggin, Northumberland, stayed through until early April. **Ivory Gulls** were giving great views early in the year. In January, the first-winter individual from December 2001 was still present in the Montrose Basin; and in February, a full adult was seen munching a dead Harbour Porpoise at Criccieth, Gwynedd, while another adult was at Fairhaven, Lancashire.

A *Catharacta* skua was found exhausted at Aberafon, Glamorgan, on 1st February. It appeared to belong to the '**Brown Skua**' species group from the southern hemisphere and resembled the *Catharacta* skua found on 7th October 2001 on St Agnes, Isles of Scilly. Both birds may yet prove to be ascribed to a new species for Britain. An inland **Olive-backed Pipit** at Lynford Aboretum, Norfolk, was a good February find.

Three good birds were discovered in March – an **Alpine Accentor** at Minsmere, Suffolk, on 16th; a male **Little Bustard** on St Agnes, Isles of Scilly, on 22nd; and a **Scops Owl** at Porthgwarra, Cornwall on 24th.

April was relatively quiet but May, as so often happens, provided a rarity feast. A whimbrel found at Goldcliff Pools, Gwent, on 3rd was of the dark-rumped, buff-looking North American race **'Hudsonian Whimbrel'**. Could this be a potential 'banker'?

North Ronaldsay, Orkney, furthered its reputation for excellent birds with a **Calandra Lark** found on 10th May. On 11th, the foreshore at Rimac, Lincolnshire, hosted a **Lesser Sand Plover**, only the second for Britain. Of no 'Lesser' significance was a first-summer male **Lesser Kestrel** discovered on 13th May on St Mary's, Isles of Scilly – the seventh record since 1958. This extremely rare bird stayed for nine days, giving many people a chance to enjoy it. **Greater Yellowlegs** were seen on St Kilda, Western Isles, and Islay, Argyll & Bute. And a **Little Swift** was found on St Mary's, Isles of Scilly; another was at Gibraltar Point, Lincolnshire, at the end of June.

On 18th May, an orange-billed tern was sighted at Dawlish Warren, Devon. It is possible that the same individual ranged around our coasts throughout the summer, with sightings in Norfolk, Yorkshire, Gwynedd, Essex and Cornwall. The bird may well have been a First for Britain – an **Elegant Tern** – but identification isn't easy. It is also possible that a number of different individuals were involved, but we may never know. On 29th May, Wendy Dickson had a superb find: a **Tree Swallow** on Unst, Shetland. This was only the second record for Britain.

The summer provided England's second-ever breeding attempt by **Bee-eaters**. Two young fledged successfully in a quarry in County Durham and 15,000 people came to see them. A record invasion of **Rose-coloured Starlings** was another remarkable feature of 2002. There were 128 adults and first-summer birds during the summer.

In August, a male **Pallid Harrier** at Elmley RSPB Reserve, Kent, was very much appreciated, as was an **Eastern Olivaceous Warbler** at Sandwick, Shetland. There were two confirmed records of **Sykes's Warbler** in the same month – one at Sheringham, Norfolk, on 23rd and the other at Beachy Head, Sussex, on 31st.

In September, the star birds were a **Solitary Sandpiper** at Rye Meads, Hertfordshire, from 13th and a **Veery**, trapped and ringed on North Ronaldsay on 30th. A minimum of four *Pterodroma* petrels were seen around the coast.

In October, the prize birds were both American passerines – a **White-throated Sparrow** at Flamborough Head, East Yorkshire, from 22nd and a **Grey-cheeked Thrush** on St Agnes, Isles of Scilly, from 26th. No fewer than three **Black-throated Thrushes** also turned up, with birds in Cornwall, Scilly and Shetland.

November's star birds were two **Oriental Turtle Doves** – one in Highland on the 9th and the other from the 20th at Stromness, Orkney, which was a much appreciated long-stayer. A **Killdeer** was found on the Isles of Scilly, a **Bobolink** was in Dorset and an obliging **Red-flanked Bluetail** was in Lincolnshire.

The year did not die quietly; two excellent birds saw off 2002 in style. A juvenile Pallid Harrier was discovered in the Stiffkey and Warham Greens area of north Norfolk from 24th December. On 28th, in Nottinghamshire, Lance Degnan produced the birding equivalent of scoring the winning goal in the last seconds of injury time in a European Cup Final: he found a **Blyth's Pipit** on call at Gringley Carr; bird identification par excellence!

MIGRATION WATCH AND WEDDING MARCH

Dawn Balmer

For me, 2002 was a memorable and exciting year at work, in the field and personally. Living in the Brecks on the Norfolk/Suffolk border gives easy access to some excellent birding areas and the opportunity to see and find a wide range of species throughout the year. Like most years, 2002 would see a few trips out of East Anglia to see sought-after species, although it was birding close to home that brought the greatest rewards.

The year got off to a good start with a Red-breasted Goose amongst the huge flock of Pink-feet on the north Norfolk coast, a small-race Canada Goose (perhaps of the race *interior*) and a King Eider in Holkham Gap mid-month. Gulls have been a passion since my student days in Plymouth in the late 1980s, and the Brecks has a couple of good sites that I regularly check with my partner Peter Wilson. We were lucky enough to find an adult Ring-billed Gull at Livermere Lake on 13th January, the fifth record for Suffolk. News of an Olive-backed Pipit at Lynford Arboretum on 1st February was most unexpected and another superb local bird to see. The lure of gulls pulled me to Killybegs, Co. Donegal, in early February for my third visit to this gull mecca. Four days in Killybegs produced at least 19 Iceland Gulls, 6 Glaucous Gulls and an adult Kumlien's Gull. You might remember February 2002 for the Ivory Gulls at Black Rock Sands and Lytham St Anne's or the Allen's Gallinule picked up at Portland Bill.

March 1st saw the launch of *Migration Watch*, an online project organised by the BTO and BirdWatch Ireland to track the timing and pattern of arrival of spring migrants. As the national organiser, this was a really exciting initiative to be involved with and it produced some fascinating results during its first year. With few migrants in evidence, a trip to Plymouth to see the Ross's Gull, just one of an impressive influx, and the Bonaparte's Gull at nearby Millbrook seemed a good idea. An Iceland Gull, a couple of Mediterranean Gulls and the Ring-billed Gull at Michael Wood Service Station on the M5 added to the weekend's gull total.

An after-work trip to Hockwold Washes in early May to show a couple of new work colleagues this local birding site was better than expected as we found two Black-winged Stilts feeding gracefully along the far shore. A few days later, I saw the Lesser Sand Plover at Rimac, which was an extremely instructive experience; the fly-over Crane was a bonus! Luck was certainly with me in May as I found a Bee-eater in the Cambridgeshire Fens whilst carrying out fieldwork on Yellow Wagtails for the BTO. After several failed attempts to see Bee-eater in Britain, it was pleasing to find my own. Sadly, it didn't hang around for local birders to connect with this third record for the county.

June was a busy month in all respects. I led my first trip for Naturetrek to the Spanish Pyrenees, which produced some great birding and was a thoroughly enjoyable experience. During a visit to Shropshire to sort out some last-minute wedding plans, I received a call from a friend in the county who had seen a strange-looking bird in his uncle's garden. Having taken many similar calls at work, my expectations weren't too high. He was surprised to learn I was in Shropshire, so I offered to pop round and have a look. To my amazement, in the back garden was a pristine adult Rose-coloured Starling! This proved to be the first accepted record for Shropshire and occurred during a large influx of this species into Britain. Peter and I 'tied the knot' on 22nd June and spent the following week in Madeira.

It's funny how birding goes sometimes; after my first British Bee-eater in May, I heard a group of Bee-eaters calling over Hickling Reserve in the Broads in mid-July. Summer 2002 will be remembered for the breeding pair at Bishop Middleham in County Durham. A Red-footed Falcon graced the skies of Hickling and nearby a White-headed Duck was at Hardley Flood.

Late summer is always a good time for waders so it was good to catch up with the two juvenile Broad-billed Sandpipers at Cley in early August.

The International Ornithological Congress was held in Beijing in August and I was lucky enough to go with a small number of colleagues from BTO to present our latest work at this prestigious conference. After taking in the well-known sights in Beijing, I spent a few days on Happy Island; the mix of the new species and rarely encountered Western Palearctic vagrants was magical. What a great place to spend a birthday! Some of you might remember the male Pallid Harrier at Sheppey during this time; a rare chance to encounter four species of harrier in one day.

Autumn in East Anglia offers plenty of birding opportunities and during September I saw a couple of Red-backed Shrikes, Red-breasted Flycatcher, Icterine Warbler and White-rumped Sandpiper along the north Norfolk coast but the four Glossy Ibises gave birders the run around. I'm not a Scilly regular so I was pleased to catch up with a Solitary Sandpiper at Rye Meads in Hertfordshire.

Early October saw me attending the Spurn Ringing Course and I was excited by the easterly winds that were blowing. Visible migration was spectacular with hundreds of thrushes arriving 'in-off'. I managed to find a Yellow-browed Warbler between the net rounds and was overwhelmed to catch five Firecrests in one morning! Typically, a Pallas's Warbler was found in the net the day after I left…

Back in Norfolk, an obliging Radde's Warbler was at Wells Wood and a Sardinian Warbler at Hunstanton, plus the usual supporting cast of Yellow-browed and Pallas's Warblers nearby. Two fly-over Richard's Pipits was our best find.

The Southwest is a great attraction for me in the autumn with the chance to meet up with old friends and perhaps the odd good bird. The highlight of a week birding 'the valleys' of west Cornwall was a very confiding Arctic Warbler but nearby Drift Reservoir produced a Lesser Scaup. Those on Scilly might remember the Black-throated Thrush, Grey-cheeked Thrush or Blyth's Reed Warbler. Although I had previously seen the Fagbury Cliff bird in 1992, a day out to Flamborough at the end of October to see the obliging White-throated Sparrow was enjoyable.

November and December can often bring surprises, and a Bobolink at Hengistbury Head was just too hard to resist. Those that made the trip to Stromness to see the Oriental Turtle Dove in December or the Blyth's Pipit at Gringley Carr will not forget this year. On the Norfolk coast, a Yellow-browed Warbler overwintered at Stiffkey Woods. There was just one last surprise in store for me before the year was out: a Pallid Harrier was discovered at Warham Greens giving me the opportunity to get this one back.

*Dawn Balmer lives in Norfolk, close to the British Trust for Ornithology HQ in Thetford where she runs the online bird recording scheme BirdTrack **www.birdtrack.net**.*

THE BIRDER'S YEAR

Tim Cleeves

Three new birds for Britain occurred in 2003, beside a good number of other rare birds. And there was a rave from the grave that took one species off the British List – and added another, far more obscure species in its place.

The Firsts that arrived in 2003 were **Taiga Flycatcher** (two records), **Audouin's Gull** and **Black Lark**. The latter was then usurped when the record of a male Black Lark at Spurn, East Yorkshire, on 27th April 1984 was belatedly accepted. Black Lark was one of the six species purged from the British List after the fraud of the Hastings Rarities was exposed – but it's back with a vengeance!

In 2003 the arrival of a Black Lark on the Isle of Anglesey was greeted with amazement: a magnificent bird from the wild steppes of central Asia running around on a Welsh clifftop. But it was a **'Magnificent Frigatebird'** from half a century ago that grabbed the headlines in February. Assiduous museum work by Grahame Walbridge and Robert McGowan revealed that the skin of the frigatebird that expired on Tiree, Inner Hebrides, in July 1953 was actually that of an **Ascension Frigatebird**, a seabird with a tiny population in the South Atlantic, rather than of the far more widespread Magnificent Frigatebird. The re-identification meant subtract one from the British List – and add one. See the account below. The Isle of Man now has Magnificent on *its* List while Britain awaits its first authentic arrival. (The Manx bird was taken into care in December 1998 and expired in October 1999.)

The early winter period of 2003 included birds remaining from 2002 – the juvenile female **Pallid Harrier** in Norfolk and **Blyth's Pipit** in Nottinghamshire. Other good birds included the returning male **'Black Scoter'** at Llanfairfechan, Gwynedd – a definite 'banker' for the future and only the seventh record – and the male **Redhead** at Kenfig Pool, Glamorgan, for its third winter. At the end of March another Pallid Harrier appeared, this time a male at Sennen, Cornwall. It seems that the same bird crossed the country and was in the Spurn area in early April.

April provided the first new bird for Britain. A first-summer male **Taiga Flycatcher** (newly split from Red-breasted Flycatcher) was trapped, ringed and released at South

Landing, Flamborough Head, East Yorkshire. It was there from 26th–29th April. On 28th, a **Little Swift** was seen on St Mary's, Isles of Scilly.

Long service was truly rewarded on 5th May when Dave Walker, the Dungeness Bird Observatory warden, found a second-summer **Audouin's Gull** from the seawatching hide. Remarkably, the bird was also seen four days earlier at Neeltje Jans, Zeeland, The Netherlands – a Dutch First too!

On 16th May, the first spring **Thick-billed Warbler** was found on Fair Isle. Only the fourth British record, this cemented the Shetland monopoly of this long-tailed, short-winged *Acrocephalus*. May also produced a **Dark-eyed Junco** on Out Skerries, Shetland, and two **White-throated Sparrows**, one on Fetlar, Shetland, from 10th and one at Caldy, Cheshire, from 21st. In May and June, an **Iberian Chiffchaff** was singing at Kingswear, Devon, for over four weeks. This was the eighth British record.

On 1st June, South Stack RSPB Reserve played host to the **Black Lark**. The sight of this bird methodically feeding in the spring flowers on the coastal heathland was the experience of a lifetime. The fact that the First for Britain had been seen by a few observers at Spurn almost 20 years previously did nothing to detract from the glory of the Anglesey bird. It doesn't get much better than that!

And two other black birds provided an 'armchair tick' for British birders in June 2003 – the BOURC acknowledged that **Carrion** and **Hooded Crows** were separate species. But, as we'd have to go back to just after the last Ice Age to find the First, there's no write-up in this book!

On 3rd June, an **Isabelline Shrike** of the form *Lanius isabellinus phoenicuroides* was found at Porlock Marsh, Somerset. This form, popularly referred to as 'Turkestan Shrike', may be a future 'banker'.

A **Lesser Sand Plover**, only Britain's third, was discovered at Keyhaven Marshes, Hampshire, on 22nd July. The bird was an adult male and the plumage features identified it as belonging to one of the two sub-forms in the *mongolus* group. The following day, a **Solitary Sandpiper** was discovered on St Mary's, Isles of Scilly. In early August, another western wader, an adult **Least Sandpiper**, was seen for a week at Startops End Reservoir in Hertfordshire.

On 31st August, an **Eastern Olivaceous Warbler** was trapped at Portland Bill, making Portland top contender for best *Hippolais* Bird Observatory (after another Eastern Olivaceous in 1999, a Sykes's Warbler in 2000 and a Booted in 2002).

In September two *Catharus* thrushes were in Shetland – a **Grey-cheeked Thrush** on Foula and a **Swainson's Thrush** on Unst; both were first seen on 27th. Also in Shetland, a **Red-flanked Bluetail** was found on Fetlar on 28th September. Had it arrived on the same weather system as the two American thrushes?

Meanwhile, on the Isles of Scilly, the East Asian form of Greenish Warbler – **'Two-barred' Greenish Warbler** – was found on Bryher. This was the third record of this form – and the second for Scilly. The seventh **Sykes's Warbler** was trapped on North Ronaldsay, Orkney, on 29th September.

October 2003 was a good one, with vagrants from a wide geographical spread. On the 4th, another Sykes's Warbler was discovered, this time on Unst, Shetland. On Tresco, Isles of Scilly, another Grey-cheeked Thrush turned up on 11th.

The second **Taiga Flycatcher** came hot on the heels of the First, and was discovered by Mark Chapman on 12th October at Sandgarth, Dales Voe, in Shetland. Two days later, the third British **Savannah Sparrow** was discovered on the magic Fair Isle, but more was to follow...

Another Swainson's Thrush in Shetland – two in one autumn and both on Unst! This one was at Burrafirth on 15th October. In Fife, at Denburn Wood, a Red-flanked Bluetail appeared, also on the 15th. On Bryher, Isles of Scilly, a **Bobolink** was a good find on 16th. With the Savannah Sparrow still present, Fair Isle was already doing well, but when a **Siberian Rubythroat** caught the eye of Alan Bull on 17th October, it looked as if Fair Isle was reclaiming its place as the top British rarity site. Two class birds meant plenty of money for the air-charter operators. Let's hope Fair Isle Bird Observatory made some well-deserved cash from the influx of birders too.

By way of a change from the passerines, birders on St Mary's, Isles of Scilly, were delighted by a juvenile **Little Crake** on 20th October. The third Swainson's Thrush of the autumn was found on Bryher, Isles of Scilly, on 21st.

A **Solitary Sandpiper** found on Lewis, Outer Hebrides, on 23rd October was by far the best wader of the autumn. On the last day of the month, a **Myrtle Warbler** was a good find at Evie, Orkney Mainland.

In November the third British record of **Redhead** was convincingly decided. This was the first female identified in the Western Palearctic, and had been present on Barra, Outer Hebrides, since 20th September. Bardsey, Gwynedd, hosted an **American Robin** from 11th November and the last day of that month produced a first-winter **American Coot** on the Loch of Clickimin, Shetland Mainland. This was only the third British record and an excellent discovery by Steve Duffield.

December saw the discovery of Britain's seventh **Oriental Turtle Dove**, by Neil Money way up in Dunnet, Hill of Ratter, Caithness. The bird was of the form *meena*, like the Orkney bird of 2002. Two American passerines closed the year – an **American Robin** at Godrevy, Cornwall, and a **Baltimore Oriole** at Headington, Oxford; both were first-winter birds. The oriole probably saw the only time that birders have willingly given money to the Cats Protection League! A kind owner took the collection in return for allowing people into her garden to see the stunning American visitor.

A FINE YEAR IN FIFE

Ken Shaw

It is difficult to choose a year – so many good years, so many good birds! My best two years, 1987 and 1999, were already taken. I considered 1985, 1992 and 2001 but finally plumped for 2003 ... one of my favourite all-round birdwatching years.

On 1st February, arriving at work at the RSPB Vane Farm Reserve, Loch Leven, I noted 2,000 diving ducks in the bay. Going through them, I found a Lesser Scaup. I phoned Birdline only to find that Dave Abraham had found it independently. I would find another before the winter was over!

Early March saw Kathy and me in northwest Scotland, on a raptor weekend with Brian and Annie Cosnette, Jon and Lorna Hardey and Logan Steele. The highlight was a pair of displaying White-tailed Eagles. Jim Steele and I spent most of March looking for Goshawks and on the 26th we had one of our best days ever, watching three males in the Borders, one for 30 minutes on the top of a Larch! Two days later, I was on Islay with Alan Lauder watching a variety of rare geese and Golden Eagles displaying.

Much of April and May is taken up with survey work on Vane Farm, and 2003 was an excellent year for Snipe and Skylark, with a pair of Garganey breeding. At the end of May, I visited the Carolinas in the Eastern States. Richard Schofield, Rod Miller, Angus Murray and I had planned three pelagics. We went on only two, mainly because the boat caught fire on the second! Most target species were seen, the highlights being Fea's Petrel and Black Rail.

Arriving back in Glasgow, I received a text from Jeremy Squire. 'Black Lark on Anglesey!' This was too good to miss – I had seen them on the Steppes but this was Britain, this was the Western Palearctic! The next day, Jem and I headed for Anglesey; seeing this beautiful bird amongst the clifftop flowers was a highlight of the year. A 'black' month became 'blacker' when Jem and I drove up to Kinbrace after work on 18th June, kipped in the car, and the next morning saw our first Scottish Black Kite.

Midsummer was a blur of duck broods; a good year on Loch Leven. However, in the hills, one of my favourite species was not doing so well – I found a dead adult Long-eared Owl at one of my sites. Another favourite, the Whinchat, was doing better, both pairs had young. The breeding-bird theme continued in mid-July when Kathy and I travelled north to work on the North East Scotland Breeding Bird Atlas.

On 19th July, Jem and I were at Leven when we got a call – 'Bridled Tern, Arbroath!' We swung round and headed north. Fifteen birders were gathered when Gordon Addison called the bird; I was slow, but assisted by mainland Scotland's finest young rarity finder, Keith Gillon, I finally got on it. The finder, Stuart Green, deserves mention – everyone likes to find county firsts but Stuart's record is enviable – Angus's first Eyebrowed Thrush, Collared Flycatcher and Bridled Tern.

However, our turn was to come. Late July is a great time for finding rarities. On the 30th, Jem, Davy Ogilvie, Dave Fotheringham and I headed for the Fife Bird Club AGM. Stopping at Loch Gelly, we went through the ducks. I could feel Jem tensing and the conversation slow down. 'What's up, got something?' I said.

'You'd better look at this duck,' he replied. The four of us 'dug in' – it looked good for Fife's first Ferruginous Duck. It was a long way off and we weren't certain by the time we had to leave. I hate 'defensive birding' but it is all part of the game these days if you want to retain your reputation so we kept quiet that night.

The next morning, Dave Fotheringham picked up the bird again and we got excellent views – Fife's first Ferruginous Duck! It stayed into August and was seen by 200 birders. I refound it at Vane Farm in Perth & Kinross on 1st September.

September also began with an influx of Ring-necked Ducks. Loch Leven is internationally important for diving ducks and a flock of 3,000 in Vane Bay is worth checking. On 6th September, we had one Ring-necked Duck and, with the help of Alan Lauder, John Nadin and Jem, it built up to four by mid-month. A few days later, the Pink-footed Geese returned.

The Isle of May week, in late September, is a highlight for me. I love staying at the Observatory, sitting in the same room as Baxter and Rintoul, writing up the same Log as Meiklejohn. You get the whole island to yourself, as brilliantly portrayed by Keith Brockie in *One Man's Island*. A strong crew helps of course and as Jonathan and Jeremy Osborne, Alan Lauder, Keith Morton and I unpacked, I wondered what this visit would bring.

The week started slowly with some seawatching; a Balearic on 29th September was the fifth record for the Isle of May. By then a high was building into Siberia. They were coming! By 1st October, it was misty and drifting from the east. In the morning a few birds appeared – Redstart, Long-eared Owl, and a Rosefinch – not a lot, but enough. I walked south, building up my concentration levels. Jonathan and Alan were at the south light and they had a bird. 'Unstreaked Acro, Ken, you'd better have a look at this,' Alan said pointedly.

As soon as I saw the bird in the nettle patch, I thought 'Aha'. Alan and I began to talk; we both knew where we were heading … 'This looks really good for Blyth's Reed,' one of us said. 'Get the nets and get descriptions. We can do this in the field if we have to.'

The rest of the team arrived. Alan took charge and with some nifty work from Keef we had caught it within minutes. A few minutes after that Alan had processed it. There wasn't even a murmur of surprise or celebration when Alan gave the thumbs up through the ringing-hut window. However, that night we had a few beers!

My next stop was Coll to cover for the warden – Sarah Money – for a week in October while she was working in New Zealand.

I saw this as an opportunity to find a vireo and spent two hours every day at the best migrant spots without success. News from my beloved Fife was bittersweet … Red-flanked Bluetail at Fife Ness! A drunken phone call from Jem summarised it – apparently, it was more beautiful than any woman he had ever seen. Obviously, he just hasn't seen enough women … or Bluetails?

As I drove to Fife Ness the next Saturday, I knew it would not stay for a fourth day. Denburn Wood was full of middle-distance travellers and Edinburgh weekenders. It would have been easy to waste the morning chatting and hoping. However, there was no hope. Fife Ness has been my local patch for nine years and there is one rule – if in doubt, start walking. Later I meet Rab Shand and Gerry Owens – always out, always finding birds. As we chatted at Kilminning, a few birds flew into a Sycamore. Without thinking, I raised my bins; I saw the features but it took a second to add them up – Ortolan Bunting! Gerry refound the bird and 15 Bluetail dippers saw it. It was a county third. Did it make up for the Bluetail? Of course it didn't!

In 1987, I made a compromise. I had been visiting St Mary's, Isles of Scilly, most Octobers since the late '70s. Kathy had been visiting St Agnes. We got married in July '87, so one of us had to change – a 'Mary's man' was joining the 'Golf Club'.

St Agnes has been good to me – I love the island and I feel lucky to be part of the same birding scene as Paul Dukes, Alan Dean, Doug Page, Francis Hicks and others. Here, more than Shetland, I feel I can find birds. It is a sport, and if you feel you can do it, you can do it!

We arrived on St Agnes on 24th October, seeing Olive-backed Pipit and Isabelline Shrike on the way. I settled into my regular routes. On 27th October, I found an Olive-backed Pipit in Chapel fields – a beautiful bird in a lovely setting. The days passed quickly. Kathy found a late Red-backed Shrike, there was a sprinkling of Yellow-browed Warblers and Red-breasted Flycatchers – but sadly another autumn was ending.

Ken Shaw lives in Kinross. He worked for the RSPB for nearly 30 years, latterly as the manager of the RSPB Vane Farm Reserve. He has found or co-found countless rare birds in Britain, including the first Short-toed Eagle in 1999. His ambitions are to see 400 species in Scotland – and to reach a British self-found list of 350.

JULY 1953

ASCENSION FRIGATEBIRD ON THE INNER HEBRIDES

Grahame Walbridge, Brian Small and Robert McGowan

An exhausted frigatebird *Fregata* captured in a net on Tiree, Inner Hebrides, Scotland, on 10th July 1953 was identified at the time as Magnificent Frigatebird *F. magnificens*, and this identification has gone unquestioned for almost 50 years. In an account by John Graham, who captured the bird in a landing net at Loch a' Phuill, in the Southwest of the island, it is described as 'a big bird with an all-white head and an albatross beak'. He noted that the whole of the back and tail were brown and the tail was deeply forked. There was 'quite a lot of white on the underparts, and freckled black-and-white feathers down the legs to the toes'. Having been found exhausted at 10.30 hrs, the bird unfortunately died at 20.00 hrs the same day. Originally reported as an immature female, with a wingspan of '6 feet 6 inches' (*c.* 1,980 mm) and a length of '33 inches' (*c.* 840 mm), the corpse was sent to the then Royal Scottish Museum, Edinburgh (now part of the National Museums of Scotland (NMS)), for preparation as a cabinet skin.

It was identified as a Magnificent Frigatebird (of the race *rothschildi*) by Sir Norman Kinnear at the British Museum (Natural History), now Natural History Museum (NHM). The specimen is retained in the NMS, Edinburgh (current taxonomic thinking suggests that *F. magnificens* is, in fact, monotypic).

Having occurred before 1958, the year that the British Birds Rarities Committee was established, the Tiree frigatebird subsequently became part of BBRC's on-going review of 1950–58 records. Reassessment of the record, principally by Grahame Walbridge (GW), and a close examination of the skin by Robert McGowan (RMcG) have shown that plumage, morphological features and biometrics of the Tiree bird are incompatible with *F. magnificens*. In this paper we describe the Tiree specimen in detail and present arguments to substantiate our assertion that the original identification as Magnificent Frigatebird was incorrect. After reviewing the characters associated with each of the world's five species of frigatebird, we conclude that the features of the Tiree bird are compatible with one species only, Ascension Frigatebird *F. aquila*.

Discussion

In 1953, the occurrence of any frigatebird in the British Isles must have seemed highly improbable. Instinctively, thoughts about the identity and origin of such a bird would focus on the nearest breeding colonies. With *magnificens* being widespread in the tropical Atlantic Ocean and also the species breeding closest to the British Isles, with colonies in southern Florida, USA, the Caribbean and the Cape Verde archipelago, it is understandable that the 'reasonable assumption' was that it was a Magnificent Frigatebird. This assumption, coupled with the lack of suitable comparative material and information about immature plumages, was presumably enough to set the original reviewers off on the wrong track. Although the Tiree frigatebird occurred when the population of *aquila* may have been greater than it is today, there were no records outside the Afrotropical region in 1953, and no reason to suppose it could occur here. Once accepted as a Magnificent Frigatebird, the identification went unquestioned for almost 50 years.

Conclusion/Summary

The identification of juvenile frigatebirds is fraught with problems, particularly in the field, and these should not be underestimated. We do, however, feel confident that the identification of the Tiree bird as Ascension Frigatebird has been fully established. Having confirmed its age as first-stage juvenile, the characters proving its identity as Ascension Frigatebird are as follows: the head is clean white, well demarcated from the mantle and breast-band, with no cinnamon or rufous wash; the brown breast-band, with some dark feathers, is virtually complete, of even depth and high on the chest (this is the most important, and probably the only truly diagnostic feature); and the presence of the axillar spur, which has been established through detailed museum analysis but is not, unfortunately, obvious on the images of the partly relaxed wing. The measurements are insufficient to confirm identity, but do at least establish that it is not Magnificent Frigatebird. Finally, and in some ways most importantly, we have confirmation by perhaps the world's leading authority on the identification of frigatebirds, Steve Howell, that, in his opinion, the Tiree bird could only have been Ascension Frigatebird, and we are extremely grateful for this testimony.

Walbridge, G., Small, B. & McGowan, R. Y. 2003. From the Rarities Committee's files: Ascension Frigatebird on Tiree – new to the Western Palearctic. *British Birds* 96, 58–73.

Ascension Frigatebird nests on Boatswainbird Islet, Ascension in the South Atlantic and rarely strays more than 150 km from the island. The population is c. 10,000 birds. There have been no subsequent records.

APRIL 2003

TAIGA FLYCATCHER IN EAST YORKSHIRE

Andrew Lassey

The early morning of 26th April 2003 brought hope of fresh migrants at Flamborough Head, East Yorkshire, as there had been overnight rain and the wind had been light southeasterly. The morning began with strong sunlight as I took my regular morning walk checking the hedgerows on the southern part of the headland.

At 6.55 am, I glimpsed a small, brown-capped bird which, seconds later, to my astonishment, turned out to be an apparent adult male Red-breasted Flycatcher *Ficedula parva*. I took several photographs of it with my digital camera, but became increasingly concerned as several aspects of the bird did not seem quite correct! In spring, Red-breasted Flycatcher is a scarce migrant to Yorkshire, and all the previous nine birds I had seen in the county had been in late May, and none of them had shown any red on the throat – the assumption being that the majority of first-summer male

Red-breasted Flycatchers do not develop the adult characteristics. I was struck by the bird's brown cap, but why was the red throat so restricted and yet so intense in colour? And why did the underparts look so 'cold' in tone? Additionally, the narrow but obvious pale edges to the greater coverts and tertials were not consistent with adult Red-breasted Flycatcher.

After some 20 minutes, Ian Marshall approached me to see what I was photographing, and I asked him to telephone Mike Pearson to bring mist nets. This was soon done and the bird was quickly caught. In the hand, it revealed the full extent of the grey surround to the throat, which was not that apparent in the field. I suggested to my colleagues that we had a Taiga Flycatcher *F. albicilla* – a species that breeds no nearer than the Urals in Russia!

Brett Richards was then informed at the Head. At first, he admitted that he could not really be troubled to interrupt his morning seawatch, even to see a male Red-breasted Flycatcher in the hand, but he changed his attitude when the name *albicilla* was mentioned! Brett agreed with my identification and then began to shake – and this phenomenon continued with him for over half an hour!

The flycatcher was photographed in the hand and biometrics taken. Paul Butterworth, the observatory's ringer-in-charge, was informed and we all agreed that the bird should be released into the cover and shelter of nearby South Landing. Brett promptly telephoned the details of the find to the various pagers and birdlines. Upon release, the flycatcher flew strongly into thick cover. It was frustratingly elusive for over three hours as visiting birders began gathering but, by early afternoon, it began feeding more actively and it showed well to the assembled crowd in the late afternoon and evening. It remained in South Landing ravine until 29th April and was enjoyed by hundreds of visiting birders, although it was often elusive for long periods.

Description

Structure A distinct impression of being stouter than *parva* and overall more substantial, lacking the delicate appearance so often noticed in *parva*.

Upperparts Forehead, crown and nape medium brown, in sunlight suggesting the colour of female Blackcap. An eye-stripe effect was caused by the extension of the blue-grey sides to the breast and sides of the neck. The ear-coverts were pale brown and encircled by the grey. The mantle and back were a colder brown than the cap and merged into a pale brown-grey rump. The greater coverts were tipped pale, giving the effect of an indistinct wing-bar, which was visible at considerable distance. The flight feathers were dark brown with paler fringes, and the tertials were blackish-brown with neat pale grey fringes to the outer webs. The uppertail-coverts were black (even blacker than the uppertail), with several feathers showing a very small pale tip. The central and distal portion of the tail was blackish with paler tips. The basal area of the outer four tail feathers was white, with this extending to just over half the length of the tail.

Underparts Chin and throat deep, rich orange-red, narrowly bordered dark grey, with the whole throat area being encircled by a broad blue-grey area, broadest at the centre of the lower throat and extending onto the breast, equivalent in length at this point to the length of the orange-red throat. The blue-grey gave way to 'cold' pale grey-white belly, flanks and undertail-coverts.

Bare parts Both mandibles blackish, with scarcely any paler area discernible on the sides of the base of the lower mandible, even in the hand. Legs dark.

Ageing

Based on some familiarity with *parva*, the bright throat colour and its grey surround suggested that the bird was an adult male, but the pale tips to the greater coverts and the pale edging to the tertials suggested that it was an immature. The sharply pointed central tail feathers also suggested that the bird was an immature (the tips to the outer tail feathers were slightly broken). This apparent ageing anomaly was soon explained, however, when Dave Britton drew my attention to literature indicating that *albicilla* assumes advanced plumage more quickly than *parva* and that, unlike *parva*, male *albicilla* are in superficially adult appearance in their second calendar-year (Cederroth *et al.* 1999). It can therefore be safely concluded that the Flamborough bird was a first-summer male.

Lassey, A. 2003. The Taiga Flycatcher in East Yorkshire – a new British bird. *Birding World* 16, 153–155.

Taiga Flycatcher is the Eastern Palearctic counterpart of Red-breasted Flycatcher. It breeds from the Urals east to northeast Siberia and winters in southeast Asia.

There has been one subsequent record:

Shetland Sandgarth, Dales Voe, Mainland, first-winter, 12th–15th October 2003

MAY 2003

AUDOUIN'S GULL IN KENT

David Walker

On the morning of 5th May 2003, I had gone to the seawatch hide at Dungeness, Kent, but after staring out to sea for about 45 minutes, the only bird of interest I had seen was a passing Arctic Skua *Stercorarius*

parasiticus. In desperation, I began scanning through a large gathering of gulls *Larus* feeding along the surf line, which included several Mediterranean Gulls *L. melanocephalus*. At about 12.00 hrs, as I continued to look for 'Caspian Gulls' *L. (c.) cachinnans* and 'Yellow-legged Gulls' *L. (c.) michahellis*, I noticed an unfamiliar gull flying along the beach towards me from the east, initially some 250–300 m away. It had an upperwing pattern somewhat similar to that of a first-summer Mediterranean Gull, but this was clearly something quite different, and considerably larger. As it flew by, I was convinced that it had a red base to the bill and I recognised the bird almost instantly as an Audouin's Gull *L. audouinii*! I yelled to the one person nearby to 'Get on this bird!!' I knew that there had been a second-summer Audouin's Gull in The Netherlands a few days earlier, and had even joked about it appearing at Dungeness, but surely this would not really happen? In stunned silence the two of us watched the bird as it circled around the hide and then over the top of the power station before flying back east and, worryingly, out of sight.

Once over the initial shock, I was still sure that it had to be an Audouin's Gull, and most likely the same bird as the one seen in The Netherlands. I was well aware that it would be the first for Britain, but who would believe me given such brief views? After all, there is a widespread assumption that a 'first' for Britain should, ideally, be seen by many observers, and, furthermore, that a seabird record such as this must be photographed. Clearly, I needed some help to relocate the bird and I phoned my assistant, Andy Wraithmell (AW). Thankfully, some 15 minutes later, AW relocated the gull near 'the Patch' (the outflow from the power station), flying along the beach, then over the power station and inland towards the RSPB reserve. Mightily reassured that I had not gone completely mad, I called Ray Turley (RT) at home and explained the situation, suggesting that he go to the RSPB reserve to check the gulls, while we maintained a vigil at the Patch. RT, Anna Hughes and Charles Wilkins rushed to the reserve and, with his first scan of the islands from the Firth Hide, RT picked out the bird among the roosting Herring *L. argentatus* and Great Black-backed Gulls *L. marinus*. A flurry of radio and telephone calls were made and the hide rapidly filled with reserve staff and local birders.

At 13.10 hrs, the bird flew off, again in the direction of the power station. It was assumed to have gone back towards the Patch, and many of the Dungeness regulars spread out in an effort to relocate it. For over half an hour there was no further sign of it but, at about 13.45 hrs, it was again seen flying over the power station and back towards the reserve. During this time I had remained in the Firth Hide, and a phone call alerted me to its imminent arrival. This time, the critical photographs and video recordings were obtained at last, as it flew back onto the island.

Present throughout the remainder of that day, and much of the following day (6th May), the Audouin's Gull gave often brilliant views to an estimated 1,400 birders who travelled to see it, and huge numbers of photographs and many hours of video footage were taken. It was not seen on 7th May until the evening, when it came in to roost on the RSPB reserve for what proved to be its final sighting.

Description

The bird was seen extremely well at times, in a variety of light conditions, both at rest and in flight. The first views of the bird were in flight as it came towards me, more or less at eye level. At this stage it looked like a large first-summer Mediterranean Gull, but lacking any significant head markings. The mantle was uniform light grey and the wings appeared to have obvious, unmarked, black primaries. As it passed me, I noted a black secondary bar and a white tail with a narrow black subterminal band. The head was white and the underparts appeared white but with a smoky-grey wash around the sides of the breast. The bill looked large, with extensive bright red at the base and tipped black, while the eye appeared large and dark. As the bird circled and climbed above me, I could see that the underwings were mainly white but with obvious contrasting black wing-tips.

My next views of the bird were on the reserve, at a range of about 270 m. Here, it was possible to confirm most of the features seen in flight. In comparison with Herring Gulls, it was distinctly smaller but with noticeably long wings, giving an elegant, elongated shape. The tertials were dark brown with broad, uneven white fringes, and the bend of the wing was also dark brown, formed by dark centres to many of the lesser coverts. The legs were relatively short and dark grey. The bill pattern was striking, with a rich scarlet base and a solidly black tip.

When the bird left the reserve and went to roost on the beach at the Point, more features were noted. The bill was short and stout, lacked an obvious gonydeal angle and was quite blunt-tipped. Although the head shape seemed to vary somewhat, it generally appeared to have a long, sloping forehead and a slightly peaked crown behind the eye, which combined to give a 'snouty' appearance not unlike the head shape of some Caspian Gulls. The gape was long and extended almost to the eye, and the feathering at the base of the bill was extensive. The lower nape showed a few faint, dark brown spots and streaks, which at times produced a 'necklace effect' to the head. The head was mostly white except for a subtle pale grey shadow around the eye. The eye was dark with no hint of a paler iris and the orbital ring was white. The colour of the underparts varied with the angle and intensity of the light, but is best described as a beautiful, satin grey which contrasted with the pure white head. When the bird stretched its wing, the broad black secondary bar was visible and it was apparent that the secondaries were broadly tipped white. The primary tips on the closed wing were uniformly black and there was no hint of any white mirrors on the underside of the primaries.

On 6th May, the bird spent most of the day roosting on the shingle beach at Dungeness. On at least one occasion, however, it disappeared out to sea, returning about an hour later. In the late afternoon, it gave brilliant flight views as it patrolled along the beach and at this point it was possible to see fairly precise details of the wing and tail patterns. The outer five primaries were black and the inner primaries were medium grey, with black tongues along the outer webs, decreasing in extent inwards. All the primary coverts, and the alula, were black. The lesser coverts contained a mixture of recently moulted grey feathers and unmoulted dull brown feathers. The secondaries were black with broad white tips, giving a white trailing edge to the inner wing. The rump was white and squarely cut off from the grey mantle. The uppertail-coverts were white. The rectrices were white with a broad black subterminal band and inward extension of black along the feather shafts. There was no sign of any active wing or tail moult.

Behaviour
Although the bird was often seen roosting with other gulls, it would frequently fly off or stand alone on the beach. It was rarely seen to feed, but on the afternoon of 6th May, it was watched as it picked small food items from the sea surface. It was always graceful in flight, often gliding long distances on slightly arched wings with very few wingbeats. I did not hear it call.

Walker, D. 2004. Audouin's Gull: new to Britain.
British Birds 97, 537–541.

Audouin's Gull breeds in the western Mediterranean. In winter, birds disperse along the Atlantic coast of Africa as far south as Senegal.

There has been one subsequent record:

East Yorkshire Beacon Ponds, Spurn, second summer, 1st June 2005 (BBRC decision awaited).

JUNE 2003

BLACK LARKS IN EAST YORKSHIRE AND ON ANGLESEY

Lance Degnan and Ken Croft

The Spurn bird

Following three days of light easterly winds with clear conditions at Spurn, East Yorkshire, the afternoon of 26th April 1984 brought a freshening northeasterly wind with associated low cloud and sea fret. On 27th April, a cold, light north-easterly breeze with thick sea fog persisted for most of the day, until the sun finally broke through at 19.00 hrs, leaving clear conditions for the remainder of the evening. A thin scattering of grounded migrants had been seen during the week, including small numbers of Northern Wheatears *Oenanthe oenanthe*, a few thrushes *Turdus*, one or two Black Redstarts *Phoenicurus ochruros* and a Whinchat *Saxicola rubetra*.

At 08.45 hrs on 27th April, Nick Bell (NAB) found an unusual passerine feeding on the short turf of the Parade Ground at the Point which he was unable to identify. He returned with B. R. Spence (BRS) and G. Thomas, who were equally puzzled by its identity. A single-panel mist-net was erected in order to attempt to catch and establish the bird's identity but, unfortunately, this proved unsuccessful. After flying over the net on the first attempt, the bird returned and, after a short wait, it was once again ushered towards the net. This time it flew above the net and kept going, flying over the nearby Heligoland trap, out across the Humber estuary and on towards Lincolnshire. It was never seen again.

The remarkable plumage and confiding nature of the bird led the observers to believe that it must be an escaped cagebird, albeit an unusual one. Although various books on cagebirds were consulted at the time, the observers were unable to put a name to the bird. The general size and gait reminded NAB of a cowbird *Molothrus*, although clearly not one with which he was familiar. Nonetheless, after considering the options available, the observers decided that it must be an escape from captivity, perhaps a species of cowbird from Central or South America, or one of the African weavers (Ploceidae).

The bird was described briefly in a short note in the Spurn Bird Observatory (SBO) log, but this made no mention of the only other birder to see the bird, Alex Cruickshanks (AC), who had watched the attempts to trap it from afar. To his credit, AC did suggest that the bird could be a Black Lark *Melanocorypha yeltoniensis*, a suggestion that did not find favour with the more experienced NAB and BRS at the time. Sadly, the bird was dismissed and quickly forgotten, with the details hidden away in the depths of the SBO log.

In the early 1990s, NAB saw the plate of Black Lark in Volume 5 of *BWP*, and this revived old memories of the mystery bird at Spurn. Unfortunately, he was unable to find his old notebook which contained his notes of the bird, and it was not until 1996 that this was discovered in the attic of his mother's house in Hull, East Yorkshire. The notebook included a description and sketch of the bird. At about the same time, NAB also became aware of a photograph of a Black Lark that had occurred recently in Sweden, and it was at this point that NAB and BRS realised that they had probably made an error. Regrettably, BRS had, by this time, discarded his old notebook with details of the bird. With only one source of evidence, the record was thought unlikely to find favour with BBRC, so, despite an initial rush of renewed enthusiasm, interest in the sighting was once again destined to languish. Nothing further happened with the record until early in 2000. At that time, the old SBO logs were retained by John Cudworth, chairman of SBO, but following his retirement in 1999, they were transferred back to Spurn. Intrigued by NAB's tale, Dave Boyle, then SBO warden, looked back through the old logs and rediscovered the account of the mysterious 'escaped' passerine. He was surprised to discover that the nightly log for 27th April 1984 had been written by NAB himself, an action that he had long since forgotten about! With two primary sources of information now available, and with further encouragement from Spurn regulars, NAB once again retrieved his old notebook and this, coupled with the account in the SBO log, formed the basis of a formal submission to BBRC in spring 2000.

Description

The following notes were taken, based largely on NAB's sketch and handwritten notes, as the observers watched the bird at ranges down to 15 m:

It was a large, plump passerine, a little larger than a Starling *Sturnus vulgaris*, but strikingly marked and quite purposeful in its actions. In size, it was similar to a chunky, short-tailed Starling, but with a large, finch-like head. Its actions as it walked and ran around on the short grass were also reminiscent of those of Common Starling.

Throat, breast, belly and remainder of underparts were black, with a panel of greyish-white feathering along the flanks below the closed wing. Crown, nape and mantle to uppertail-coverts were pale grey, with some dark brown edgings to the mantle feathers. Wings blackish with dark brown primaries. Tail blackish, short and forked. Legs blackish with 'trouser' feathering.

One of the most distinctive features was the large, finch-like bill, which was pale ivory in colour and of similar proportions to that of Corn Bunting *Emberiza calandra*.

No call was heard.

In flight, NAB noted the wing action to be unusual, the ample wings being broad yet pointed, and the flight was quite clipped, reminiscent of that of Fieldfare *Turdus pilaris* or Jackdaw *Corvus monedula*. The bird was noted to hover before landing. BRS considered the wings to be pointed and almost lark-like.

Assessment by BBRC

During the first circulation, BBRC asked for more details, but there seemed to be little likelihood of achieving this. Serendipitously, a chance conversation between NAB and AC, who was visiting Spurn in late May 2000, led to AC submitting his own independent notes from 1984, which were added to the BBRC file. The events and circumstances of the occurrence were now corroborated by a second, independent source, and also benefited from some additional notes supplied by BRS. Together, these notes confirmed the distinctive appearance of the bird, as well as its approachability and the prevailing misty conditions. They also established that the confusion over the bird's identity was caused largely by broad grey fringes to the mantle and head feathering, creating an impression quite different from that expected of Black Lark.

During circulation, all likely confusion species were discussed. The four most likely species were considered to be Shiny Cowbird *Molothrus bonariensis*, Bronzed Cowbird *M. aeneus*, Lark Bunting *Calamospiza melanocorys* and White-billed Buffalo Weaver *Bubalornis albirostris*. The first two have entirely dark bills, are long-tailed, and apparently never show such pale tips to the plumage. Lark Bunting also has a dark bill, but displays a white patch on the wing similar to that of Snow Bunting *Plectrophenax nivalis*. White-billed Buffalo Weaver shows greater resemblance to Black Lark, with a deep-based, white bill and largely black plumage, apart from diffuse greyish-white patches on the flanks. The sketches rule out these possibilities, leaving Black Lark as the only species to match the features shown by the mystery bird.

Acknowledgments

Without the support of Nick Bell, who generously shared the details of this record with many Spurn regulars, including myself, this record is unlikely ever to have been accepted. Sadly, Nick died in 2001 and was unable to enjoy the formal acceptance of his Black Lark as the first for Britain. My thanks also go to Barry Spence and Pete Crowther for their help in pulling the details together.

The South Stack bird

The days leading up to 1st June 2003 had been warm and settled across North Wales, with light east to southeasterly winds and frequent sea mist resulting in reduced visibility. Although the winds were coming from a promising direction, they had produced little of interest at my local patch, South Stack, on Holy Island, Anglesey, other than a large movement of Collared Doves *Streptopelia decaocto* and a single Turtle Dove *S. turtur*. I ventured out again on the morning of the 1st, still hopeful of finding some good migrants, but by early afternoon I had not found anything of note, so I decided to go home to watch some sport on television. I was well settled when the telephone rang. It was Dave Bateson (DB), one of the RSPB wardens at South Stack, who told me that earlier that morning a volunteer warden, Stephen Rosser, had seen an unusual bird which he could not identify. As DB had been working away from his office, he had not heard about the mystery bird until his return, and although he had had a quick look for it, he was unable to refind it. It sounded sufficiently interesting for him to ask me if I would try to relocate and identify the bird.

I arrived at South Stack at about 16.00 hrs and walked the area where the bird had been seen but, like DB, I was unable to find it. I returned to the carpark and was showing a visiting birder a pair of Red-billed Choughs *Pyrrhocorax pyrrhocorax*, when I noticed a dumpy, short-tailed, black bird flying out of a grassy field bordering the reserve. It flew low across the heath and appeared to land near the cliff edge. I do not remember what I said to the visitor as I left him standing there, and quickly made my way across the heath. Initially, I did not see anything, but as I walked slowly onto the clifftop path, a male Black Lark suddenly ran out in front of me!

Scarcely believing my own eyes, I gradually got my breath back as I watched yet another amazing bird on my local patch (following the Grey Catbird of October 2001). It then flew back towards the grassy field and landed on the wall but, thankfully, dropped back down onto the path instead of into the field. It was now 16.50 hrs. With nobody around and the bird apparently settled in an area sufficiently far from the main tourist paths not to be disturbed, I decided to make a run for the RSPB office. Fortunately, DB was still there. I told him the news, picked him up off the floor, and telephoned the news out.

I returned with DB and we quickly relocated the bird, feeding happily on the path. Local birders began arriving shortly afterwards and soon a steady stream of visitors appeared and all enjoyed outstanding views until dusk. The following morning, with birders massed in the carpark before dawn, the bird was quickly relocated and, thanks to excellent crowd control by Alan Davies and DB, was seen well by all. It continued to give excellent views to an estimated 4,000 admirers over the following week and was last seen on the evening of 8th June.

Description

A large, dumpy lark with long wings that reached almost to the tail tip. Head relatively large, rounded and black, but with scattered narrow and indistinct greyish-white fringes. Mantle and scapulars showed slightly more conspicuous, but still narrow and fairly indistinct, greyish-white fringes. Rump much paler, appearing greyish-white and mottled, although this area was usually hidden by the long wings. Underparts black and unmarked. Tertials and primary tips showed narrow white tips. Primaries and secondaries distinctly browner than body contour plumage and appeared abraded. Bill conical in shape, pale ivory-white. Legs dark brownish.

Ageing

Both adult and juvenile Black Larks undergo a complete moult in the summer, between July and October, although juveniles can retain outer primaries as late as December (Svensson 1992). Following this moult, age classes become inseparable. Although the Anglesey bird showed obviously worn and faded primaries, which appeared browner than the body, these cannot be used to establish the age of this individual.

Degnan, L. & Croft, K. 2005. Black Lark: new to Britain.
British Birds 98, 306–313.

Black Lark breeds on the steppes of Kazakhstan and winters to the Black Sea coast of Ukraine.

These are the only records to date.

2004

THE BIRDER'S YEAR

Tim Cleeves

2004 was seriously rich in Firsts for Britain. There were four in total – **Purple Martin, Chestnut-eared Bunting, Rufous-tailed Robin** and **Masked Shrike** – and all occurred in Scotland in the autumn, all bar the martin in October.

January started well with the **American Robin** in Cornwall still present from 2003. Another American Robin was discovered in Grimsby on New Year's Day. And the **Baltimore Oriole** was still in Oxford. Two **American Coots** were present: the wintering bird at the Loch of Clickimin, Shetland, and one at West Loch Ollay on the Outer Hebrides from 25th January.

Notable wildfowl in the period included the male **Redhead** in Glamorgan, the female Redhead on Barra in the Outer Hebrides and, also in the Western Isles, a female **Harlequin Duck** on Lewis. Drake **Buffleheads** were found in Greater Manchester in April (the same bird was seen in West Yorkshire) and in the Midlands in May and June. A drake was also seen in May in the Outer Hebrides, supporting cast for a drake **Cinnamon Teal** at Loch Thamister, Lewis that may struggle to find its way onto the British List as rare wildfowl are usually suspect, particularly potential Firsts.

Pallid Harriers continued to be found in numbers in 2004, with an adult male flying south at Scalby Mills, North Yorkshire, on 8th April. Later in the year, juveniles were seen on Shetland and on Scilly in September.

Spring 2004 was relatively uneventful, although good birds were located, including **Iberian Chiffchaffs** on 18th–19th April at Woodhorn churchyard, Northumberland, and on 17th May at Kilnsea, East Yorkshire. An **Alpine Accentor** was found at Overstrand, Norfolk, on 20th April.

One of the rarest birds of the spring was an **Eastern Bonelli's Warbler** on Lundy, Devon, on 27th April. Two male **Collared Flycatchers** were found in Shetland, on 9th May on Fair Isle and on 2nd June on Unst. Meanwhile, a splendid male **Rock Thrush** was discovered in the Erme Valley, Dartmoor, Devon, on 25th May by a diligent bird-census volunteer.

311

On 8th July, for one day only, a **Lesser Sand Plover** of the nominate form *mongolus* was found at Aberlady Bay, East Lothian. On the last day of July, another extremely rare wader was discovered, this time on the Wyre Estuary, Lancashire – Britain's third **Great Knot**.

Six miles south of St Mary's, Isles of Scilly, on 2nd August, a potential 'banker' was seen and seven digital images were taken. The bird? The Mediterranean form of Cory's Shearwater known as **'Scopoli's Shearwater'**. Another potential First for Britain. An adult **Sharp-tailed Sandpiper** at Drift Reservoir on 6th August was Cornwall's first. Still in Cornwall, a potential 'banker' was a **Hudsonian Whimbrel** flying past Pendeen on 20th August.

A juvenile **Purple Martin**, the First for Britain, was found on the Butt of Lewis, Outer Hebrides, on 5th September. A great discovery and the third North American hirundine to be found in Britain. A *Pterodroma* petrel, another likely **Fea's Petrel**, was seen and photographed from a pelagic off the Isles of Scilly on 6th September. The 19th September saw the fourth British record of **Brown Shrike**, on Whalsay, Shetland.

A juvenile **Cream-coloured Courser**, one of the most popular birds of the autumn, was seen flying in off the sea and landing on St Agnes, Isles of Scilly, on 28th September. This was the first British record since 1984. Next day, a juvenile **Western Sandpiper** was discovered on Brownsea Island, Dorset, only the seventh British record.

October is often a great month for extreme rarities and October 2004 was certainly no exception with a fantastic cast of rare birds. The fourth **Yellow Warbler** was on the new rarity hotspot of Barra, Outer Hebrides, on 2nd. The next North American warbler was a **Common Yellowthroat** on Foula, Shetland, on 9th.

On Foula, no fewer than three **Pallas's Grasshopper Warblers** were found between 1st and 15th. In poor weather conditions, a skulking 'Little Bunting' was watched on neighbouring Fair Isle on 12th October. As weather conditions improved, it was clear that the bunting was something quite unfamiliar and, after examination in the hand, the bird was re-identified as Britain's First **Chestnut-eared Bunting**, a blistering find.

So what were the odds on Fair Isle striking gold twice in just over a week? On 23rd October, Britain's First **Rufous-tailed Robin** (or Swinhoe's Robin) was found. The wonder of such eastern vagrants finding landfall on this small island is beyond comprehension. When Fair Isle is on form it really is the number one location. Another Fair Isle First was confirmed at the year's end – **Sykes's Warbler**. The bird recorded in August 1959 was given the official nod by the BOURC as Britain's First (see below).

At Sumburgh, Shetland, an **Isabelline Wheatear** was discovered on 23rd October. Then, just as all the action seemed concentrated in the Northern Isles, the Isles of Scilly struck back with Britain's fourth **Ovenbird**, on St Mary's on 25th. And it was alive! At least for a few days ... Backup was provided by a **Swainson's Thrush** on the Gugh, St Agnes.

Back in Scotland, on 29th October, another bird struck off the British List after the review of the Hastings Rarities was found at Kilrenny Common, Fife – a juvenile

Masked Shrike. A fantastic and very obliging bird, this was another authentic First for Britain, the third of the month! This remarkable October ended with a **Tree Swallow** reported flying over Christchurch, Dorset.

November began well with a **'Steppe' Grey Shrike** at Westmarsh, Kent, on 5th November. A **Pine Grosbeak** at Easington, East Yorkshire, was, unfortunately, a short-stayer on 8th November. It was England's first since 1975. A summer-plumaged **Chinese Pond Heron** that turned up on garden ponds in Norfolk and Hampshire in late October and early November was of dubious provenance – a hothouse aviary probably accounted for its unseasonal attire.

At Land's End, Cornwall, a **Blyth's Pipit**, which remained into late December, was discovered on 15th November. On December 5th, another 'banker' for the future – a **'Desert Lesser Whitethroat'** (*Sylvia curruca minula* or possibly *Sylvia curruca halimodendri*) was trapped in Aberdeen. Inland birders have a tough time, so it was fitting that patience and persistence paid off in Nottinghamshire. On 12th December, the thirteenth British **Sora** was discovered at Attenborough Nottinghamshire Wildlife Trust Nature Reserve. The confiding Sora brought to a close a year – and a quarter century – packed with rare birds. What will 2005–2030 bring?

FABULOUS FAIR ISLE

Rebecca Nason

Being Assistant Warden on such a birding Mecca as Fair Isle was a dream for me. I had never visited Shetland before taking up my post in March 2003, only having heard about this distant and magical place through birders' tales bandied about enthusiastically over pints in the student bar during university days.

The post had everything I wanted other than perhaps more money! It combined my birding passion with intense seabird monitoring and ringing in the summer, and daily migrant censusing of the island in the spring and autumn. Censusing involved splitting the island into three with the Warden and other Assistant Warden and then working 'my' third before pooling all our records together in the daily 'evening log'. How incredible it was to be out on one of the remotest – and arguably the best – birding spots in Britain, and have a third of it to myself each day. There was never a dull day and always the optimistic excitement as we left the boot room and headed out into the unknown, for here, anything was possible!

After the events of 2003, it was with little hesitation that I accepted the invitation to return for a second year in 2004. My birding highlights in 2003 had been the Thick-billed Warbler in May and the Scops Owl in July, as well as finding my own first BBRC rarities: a Yellow-breasted Bunting and Citrine Wagtail, both on the morning of the 7th September. However, convinced that we had had the best of 2003 in the spring, I had continued with plans to finish my contract on Fair Isle three weeks early and head down to the Scilly Isles where I was to take and sell rarity shots with good friend and inspirational bird photographer, Steve Young. This decision to relocate south turned out to be the worst I could have made, as Scilly was relatively quiet and I missed out on the best birds on Fair Isle that autumn: Savannah Sparrow and Siberian Rubythroat!

What a mistake! I was kneeling in mud and wet vegetation getting glimpses of an elusive Grey-cheeked Thrush when I got the first (of many) jubilant calls from Rubythroat-finder Alan Bull and other staff that morning. I will never forget it.

Over the winter, I wrote up my thesis at my parents' home in Cambridgeshire, thus completing my MSc in Conservation Management. A consuming passion of mine is bird photography, so I also spent many happy hours in the winter months snapping common and rarer birds. I also invested in a superb new 500-mm Nikon auto-focus lens. Together with keen birder and firefighter Phil Harris, who I'd met on Fair Isle in October (when he got me onto a Pechora Pipit he had just found), I enjoyed several twitches, including American Robin, Penduline Tit and Baltimore Oriole, before heading back north.

As New Year 2004 dawned, a mammoth trip up to Shetland followed, with friend Martin Culshaw from Glasgow, for the American Coot. Later, the Pine Bunting in Norfolk and Franklin's Gull in Dorset combined to make the start of the year a very memorable one. On my return to Fair Isle in March, there seemed to be extra pressure to find 'big' birds after the megas the year before. However, the spring was relatively quiet, with the major bird of note being a stunning Collared Flycatcher in May, and a Red-throated Pipit I found one May afternoon whilst returning to the Observatory from seabird monitoring.

The summer was marred by the devastating seabird situation which was unfolding before our eyes. 2003 had been the worst breeding season on record, but the 2004 season was by far the most dramatically unproductive season ever known on Fair Isle. Fair Isle, Shetland and northeast Scotland all experienced sudden and devastating losses, with indications that Fair Isle had been the worst hit. Species such as Arctic Tern, Arctic Skua and Kittiwake all saw 100% breeding failure, with Great Skua not far behind, fledging only one chick. The auks did not fare much better.

On roping down the cliffs into the boulder-beach colonies on Fair Isle where, in previous times, ringing staff have been met with the frenzied calling of adult birds and buoyant sounds of lively chicks amongst the boulders, we were met instead by an eerie silence, an unforgettable quiet – and overpowering sense of failure.

The few underweight Razorbill and Guillemot chicks that were present were barely alive, starving and unbrooded as both parents had been forced out to sea in search of food. Even the Shags, which seemed at first to be faring relatively well this year, failed a day or so short of fledging; the large chicks, having been suddenly starved, lay lifeless and strewn across the boulders, our only task to retrieve the rings we had put on them on our previous visits. It was an awful event to witness, even more so I'm sure for others who had witnessed the comparative thriving and successful seabird years Fair Isle has boasted in the past.

As with most years of poor productivity, it appears to be a lack of Lesser Sandeel, the main diet of most of the seabirds, that is the root cause of the problem, with an absence of a particular required 'age' of sandeel. Only very small sandeels were observed out in the field and in desperation, seabirds such as the Puffin were forced to bring in food items such as Snake Pipefish to their starving chicks, which were often unpalatable and discarded.

It seems, at least in part, that as a result of global warming, changes in sea temperature and shifting ocean currents are causing plankton and therefore sandeels to move further northwards, making them unavailable to Britain's breeding seabirds. Only time will tell what will be the outcome of this redistribution of food source, together with the continued pollution and unsustainable harvesting of our seas.

As summer gave way to autumn, everywhere, even places we could see from the island, appeared to be producing rarities, apart from us. It was a long and desperate wait throughout September (was it to be the worst autumn on Fair Isle – ever?!), finally broken by light southeasterlies and a cracking Red-flanked Bluetail at North Gunnawark. At the time, I couldn't have been further away: it was a gruelling, stressful run but soon I was precariously placed along with many others enjoying good views of this blue beauty against the dark sandstone cliffs below us. The date was 29th September, and the bird was at exactly the same location as the Red-flanked Bluetail in 2003 (one I missed!). A superb end to a very slow September!

On my morning trap round on 5th October, Phil Harris, Martin Culshaw and I found and trapped a Booted Warbler in Single Dyke trap! Well over a week later, on the 16th October, I was asked to check if the 'strange-looking', elusive Little Bunting was still in the Skadan Crop on my morning census in the southwest of the island. I reported that it was and later that day we trapped the bird and brought it back for processing. After much deliberation and frantic searching of texts, we clinched its identification; we had a first for the Western Palearctic in our hands! A Chestnut-eared Bunting! Wow, we finally had a real 'mega', the pressure was off, though the elation was soon to be doubled!

Saturday 23rd October was Rufous-tailed Robin day. I will never forget the debate over identification of what was thought (with good reason at the time) to be a North American *Catharus* thrush, either Hermit Thrush or Veery. It was agreed that it was possibly the former, although somehow none of us seemed totally convinced!

Over lunch, and inspired by Nick Dymond's comments on Asian 'Rufous-tailed Robins', I hunted out the *Birds of Southeast Asia*, still in the ringing room after the last eastern find! After seeing the small illustration of the bird for the first time, it was then a manic search to find other pictorial sources of the species. Alan and Deryk sourced a *Birding World* article and an internet site with wonderful photographs and descriptions of the species and temperatures in the office rose dramatically! Fair Isle had done it again! Managing to get good photographs of this bird out in the field before it was trapped will, I think, be one of the most pleasurable moments in my life, let alone 2004…

Rebecca Nason divides her time between England and Shetland. An assistant warden on Fair Isle in 2003 and 2004, she is an accomplished photographer and wildlife tour leader.

SEPTEMBER 2004

PURPLE MARTIN ON THE OUTER HEBRIDES

Shaun Coyle, Torcuil Grant & Mark Witherall

On the Isle of Lewis, Outer Hebrides, Sunday 5th September 2004 was cloudy and dull, with a light southerly wind. After a rather unproductive morning's birding around Stornoway, we decided to try the Butt of Lewis, at the northern tip of the island, perhaps in the hope of finding an American wader.

Upon our arrival at the Butt lighthouse at about 2.30 pm, we immediately noticed a large martin flying around the cliffs. Straight away, it was clear that it was something different!

It was obviously larger than any European hirundine, and we noted dark brown upperparts with a pale collar, and a greyish-brown breast and flanks contrasting with a pale belly. After a few minutes, it alighted on an overhead wire in the lighthouse compound. We studied it through telescopes and soon realised that we were watching a juvenile Purple Martin – a species new to the Western Palearctic!

We did not have a North American field guide with us, but we made a quick mobile telephone call to Tom McKinney and, from our description, he was able to check references and confirm our identification. We had already alerted Martin Scott and, soon after this, he arrived on site, and quickly came to the same conclusion. The exciting news was now out and a few other local birders arrived.

The Purple Martin remained faithful to the vicinity of the lighthouse and the nearby cliffs. In the rather dull and grey conditions, it was flying low to feed, and often came within a few metres of the few assembled observers, and gave several prolonged views when it perched on the overhead wires. On one occasion, it headed northeast out to sea, until it was almost lost from sight, before it headed back again and fed over a nearby pool. It continued to fly around the headland until dusk, when it presumably roosted on the cliffs or lighthouse buildings. Due to the remoteness of the site, just ten people had seen the bird. On our way home, we called in at Martin and Jackie Scott's house to celebrate and discuss the events of the day, which still had not quite sunk in.

Despite the celebrations, we managed to return to the Butt at dawn the next morning, which was dull and misty. The bird was missing for the first half an hour or so of the day but, as the morning brightened, we refound it on the lighthouse wires at 7.30 am. We 'phoned out the news immediately, to ensure that those who were already on their way, or who were on standby, knew that the bird was still present.

At 8.50 am, a Sparrowhawk flew through the area and flushed the bird, which then went missing; it seemed to fly off south at this time, just ten minutes before the first mainland birders arrived. There was no sign of the bird for over an hour; it seemed to have gone, but much to everybody's relief, just after 10 am, it was relocated flying around over Eoropie village, about a mile south of the Butt. By now, the morning was warm and sunny with a light easterly breeze, and the bird was feeding overhead, at an estimated height of mostly about 50 feet.

Birders travelled from all over Britain, with some chartering aircraft and others arriving on scheduled flights and ferries. The bird remained feeding over Eoropie and the surrounding fields for almost three hours (also perching on electricity wires for just a few seconds) but, at 12.45 pm, it climbed to about 100 feet in the now clear blue sky and headed off to the south. It was not seen again. Fewer than 50 birders had made it from the mainland in time. Another 50 or so arrived just too late.

Description

General appearance and jizz Clearly a martin, but noticeably large and dark above, with a conspicuous pale collar. Flight strong, with rather slow wing beats, often gliding for relatively long distances before 'stooping' and flying close to the ground, when occasionally even reminiscent of a small female Merlin. When perched, often showed a peaked crown (which reminded one of the observers of certain Nearctic *Myiarchus* and *Contopus* flycatchers) and the wing tips extended just beyond the tail. The tail was shallow-forked and dark brown, although it appeared black most of the time, especially in flight.

Head and neck Brown forehead contrasting with thick blackish eye-stripe and sooty-brown crown. Blue sheen noticeable along lower edge of crown when bird face-on only in good light. Nape sooty-brown. Chin and throat greyish-brown with fine darker streaking.

Upperparts Mantle, rump and uppertail-coverts dark brown. Blue sheen noted on upper mantle occasionally. Pale edges to uppertail-coverts near to base of tail. Upperwings dark brown, with buff-brown tips to coverts, pale tips to secondaries and very fine pale tips to primaries. On one occasion, blue tinge noted on shoulder when bird perched, but this was very faint.

Underparts Dirty white, with extensive brown blotches and streaks forming band on upper breast, which contrasted with pale collar, and dark brown streaks on breast becoming finer on belly, and brown blotches along flanks. Undertail-coverts finely streaked with small dark brown 'arrowheads', and a pale brown band noticeable across vent area. Underwings dark sooty-brown, with blackish axillaries.

Bare parts Eye dark. Bill relatively long, black, thick and broad-based, with upper mandible distinctively curved. Legs and feet brown.

Coyle, S., Grant, T. & Witherall, M. 2004. The Purple Martin on the Outer Hebrides – a new Western Palearctic bird. *Birding World* 17, 381–383.

Purple Martin breeds from Canada south to Mexico; it winters in central South America. This is the only record to date. It awaits acceptance by BOURC.

OCTOBER 2004

CHESTNUT-EARED BUNTING ON FAIR ISLE

Deryk Shaw

Autumn 2004 was looking set to be the worst on record for birds on Fair Isle and, to make matters worse, Foula (another of the Shetland Isles, which has even been labelled 'the new Fair Isle') had been scoring well, even with multiple Pallas's Grasshopper Warblers – the ultimate Fair Isle speciality! But Fair Isle was about to strike back…

On 12th and 14th October, a Little Bunting had been seen in the Meadow Burn, and what was assumed to be the same bird was reported again at lunchtime on 15th, in the specially planted bird-cover oat crop at the Skadan, but with a comment that 'it looked a bit odd'. I first saw this bird late that afternoon and, in the fading light, I too thought that it looked a bit odd. Its tail seemed too long for Little Bunting, it appeared to lack the black ear-covert surround of that species, and I thought I saw a chestnut rump (but decided I must have been mistaken). I considered all the European buntings, but could not find a better fit than Little Bunting. I decided that it must be that species: the 'long' tail was perhaps just a trick of the light, as was the apparent chestnut rump, and I explained the lack of black in the face on perhaps it being very fresh and having buff tips to the feathers concealing the black.

However, the identification troubled me all that night, so next morning I asked assistant warden Rebecca Nason to let me know if she found the bird still present on her migrant census of that southernmost part of the island. She reported that it was still in the oat crop, so after lunch I headed down for better views.

The bird was quite elusive, mostly keeping out of the stiff wind by hiding down in the oats and giving only brief flight views when flushed before dropping back down into the crop (usually hovering for a second before it did so). However, from the views available, it was clear that it was not a Little Bunting. But what was it?

It had an Ortolan Bunting look about it, with a grey-toned nape, pale buff sub-moustachial stripes and throat, obvious whitish eye-ring and a pale orange-brown wash across the underparts, but also obvious chestnut ear-coverts, with a pale spot at the rear, like Little Bunting. It was not being very co-operative and, from the views we had, we were little nearer to an identification, so I decided we should trap it. A net was erected in the crop and the bird gently coaxed into it and caught with ease.

Once in the hand, the questions really began. It did have a chestnut rump! Was it a Yellowhammer? No; there were no yellow tones and it had a pink lower mandible (which also ruled out Pine Bunting), but the obvious eye-ring (amongst other features) immediately disqualified some other species with a chestnut rump, such as Yellow-breasted Bunting and Chestnut Bunting. Rustic Bunting was another possibility, but again the distinct eye-ring and lack of white wing-bars ruled that out too. We were none the wiser.

We took the bird back to the ringing room at the observatory and, whilst I quietly proceeded to take a detailed description and some measurements (and tried to ignore the shouts of 'Hybrid! It must be a hybrid!' in the background), my two assistant wardens (Alan Bull and Rebecca Nason), Mark Newell and Phil Harris consulted the literature. Various questions were fired at me about features to check and each reply crossed another species off the list of possibilities. Phil then remembered an article on vagrant eastern buntings by Steve Votier he had been perusing recently in a back issue of *Birding World* (Vol. 14 No. 9) and went off to retrieve it. He returned a few minutes later and slapped it down in front of me. There it was! A rear-view photograph of a Chestnut-eared Bunting *Emberiza fucata*.

'That's it!' The excitement levels rose! Chestnut-eared Bunting was looked up in the various books to hand. The description, measurements and wing formula all fitted a first-winter male Chestnut-eared Bunting. We could hardly believe it. We had a first for the Western Palearctic and reading the caption beneath the *Birding World* photograph 'Chestnut-eared Buntings breed in northeast China and Korea and are middle- to long-distance migrants to their wintering grounds in southeast Asia. This species has not been recorded in western Europe, but a bit of blind optimism never hurts!' had us leaping around the room! Funnily, Foula was mentioned a few times at this point!

The news was announced to the small, patient crowd assembled outside, and quickly broadcast to the local Shetland Grapevine, Birdline Scotland and several interested islanders. Photographs were taken and the bird was then returned to the oat crop at Skadan and released.

The bird observatory telephone suddenly became red hot and, although the BirdGuides website had the audacity to label it as an escape on its news pages, about 120 birders made the trip north to see it over the next four days before it was last seen on 20th (and more would have travelled had it stayed longer).

The bird was aged as a first-winter by the fact that it had a retained juvenile alula feather (the largest), very pointed tail feathers (although this was difficult to judge as adults of this species also have pointed tail feathers) and a dark grey-brown iris (adults have a chestnut iris), and sexed as a male on wing and tail lengths (*Buntings and Sparrows*, Byers *et al.* 1995).

Shaw, D. 2004. The Chestnut-eared Bunting on Fair Isle – a new Western Palearctic bird. *Birding World* 17, 415–419.

Chestnut-eared Bunting breeds in the western Himalayas, China, southeast Siberia, Mongolia and Japan; it winters south to northern Indo-China.

This is the only record to date. It awaits acceptance by BOURC.

OCTOBER 2004

RUFOUS-TAILED ROBIN ON FAIR ISLE

Deryk Shaw

On Saturday 23rd October 2004, Fair Isle Bird Observatory staff were still basking in the glory of the first Chestnut-eared Bunting for the Western Palearctic, which was last seen three days before. The day dawned with a light northeasterly wind and a good few thrushes and Blackcaps around the traps, and so it was with typical enthusiasm and optimism that we headed out on our daily migrant census of the isle. I was censusing the north of the island that morning and, by 11.00 am, when I had reached the top of Ward Hill, my highlight had been a handful of stunningly bright male Northern Bullfinches. As I descended towards the communications mast, my mobile phone rang. It was my assistant warden, Alan Bull. He was panting and, from the distorted noise, obviously still running: 'Mark Newell has just described to me a bird found by Mike Wood at Bull's Park. It sounds like it could be a Veery – well a *Catharus* thrush anyway – but there's no point you coming down yet. I'll keep you informed!' 'Okay!' I replied – and immediately started hurrying down the hill. Mark then phoned me and I told him I had just spoken to Alan and was on my way.

I arrived at the observatory, somewhat out of breath, rounded up all who were there (the kitchen staff and Hollie, my wife and Administrator, and the children) and jumped into the van.

Upon my arrival at the site, there were a few people present and I asked if it was a Veery. I was answered in the affirmative and was directed to look behind a broken gate leaning against the drystone wall. A small chat with a heavily mottled breast, olive-brown upperparts, a rufous tail and pink legs could be seen. I have never seen any of the *Catharus* thrushes, but expected a Veery to be rufous all over the upperparts and not to have a distinctly brighter tail. I was asked my opinion and I said that I thought it looked more like a Hermit Thrush in colouration, but agreed that the breast markings were more like a Veery.

A consultation of *Collins Bird Guide* followed. Nobody had seen the underwing, but that did not seem to matter as all the *Catharus* thrushes have the same distinctive pattern. The bird did not have the bold black breast spots of the Hermit Thrush shown in the guide – the breast pattern was more like that illustrated for Veery, but it did have a rufous tail offset against colder olive-brown upperparts – just like the Hermit Thrush and unlike the Veery! No other species were considered at this time. The camp was split. I canvassed the dozen or so people present for anyone with experience of either species. One person had seen both and said it was definitely a Hermit Thrush! I decided to put the news out to the Shetland birders and Birdline Scotland that we had a possible Hermit Thrush – to give people time to organise a charter across to the island. (If only I had called it as a Veery, then poor Roger Riddington would have braved the five-hour round boat trip and would not have minded being sick all the way!)

The bird was keeping close to the wall and often disappeared into it for several minutes at a time. It would frequently raise its tail to about 75° and slowly 'bounce' it down again with a little shiver at the end. The discussion as to its identity continued until we had to head back to the observatory for lunch. Mark had a packed lunch with him and therefore was unanimously voted as the one to stay with the bird.

Nick Dymond (whose last October visit to Fair Isle had produced Britain's second Brown Shrike) casually mentioned that it looked a bit like a Rufous-tailed Robin, a species he had seen in Thailand about 15 years ago, 'but they are quite small and the jizz doesn't look right. It can't be that because they are from South East Asia!'

'What?!' We reminded him where last week's Chestnut-eared Bunting was from and set off to find a reference to Rufous-tailed Robin.

Alan Bull checked some books and back copies of *Birding World* and I went onto the internet. Alan arrived in my office with a copy of *Birding World* showing the species (Vol. 16 page 345; it also features in Vol. 9 pages 354–355) as I was looking at a picture on my computer screen. We looked at each other in disbelief. That was it! Incredibly, it looked like we had another first for the Western Palearctic!

Not wishing to start a stampede to Fair Isle for nothing, we all headed back down the road for more views to confirm our suspicions. Alas, Mark had not seen the bird since we had left. To our immense relief, a walk along the wall soon found it again and we were then in no doubt that it was, indeed, a Rufous-tailed Robin! That moment will live long in the memory of all that were there. A moment of shock, followed by shouts of delight and much punching of the air and backslapping.

I phoned Paul Harvey who was on a boat heading across from Shetland Mainland with other Shetland birders, not knowing if they were coming to see a Veery or a Hermit Thrush. The phone signal was poor, but I managed to get the words 'Rufous-tailed Robin' across. 'You what!?' came the stunned reply. The tension on that boat must have been intense; they were only half an hour away by now, but seemed a great deal longer! Hollie met them on the pier with the observatory van and brought them to us. The sight of them all striding towards us, brandishing telescopes, with Dave Okill at the helm, was rather reminiscent of a scene from some Spaghetti Western and a photo-opportunity not to be missed!

Once all had obtained good views of the bird, I decided that it could be easily trapped and that it should be to make absolutely sure of the identification and to check for signs of captivity. A net was erected next to the wall and the bird was easily coaxed into it. I glanced at the underwing to check that we were not making some horrendous *faux pas*, but it was plain buffish-white (not striped as in the *Catharus* thrushes). In the hand, I was amazed at how small it felt – even smaller than a European Robin!

We took the bird back to the observatory's ringing room and took some measurements and a brief description. The bird was in good condition, with no feather, claw or bill damage. It was aged as a first-winter due to it having retained nearly all of its brown juvenile greater coverts, which had obvious small deep buff tips (the innermost two had been moulted and were more olive and lacked buff tips), and to it having pointed tail feathers.

The bird had good fat and muscle scores and had obviously not arrived from very far away – perhaps just a short hop from Mainland Shetland. It was photographed and then released back in the same area it was trapped. It showed well on top of the wall before dropping down and disappearing into the base of it.

The sky was clear and the bird had been feeding furiously right up until its capture. I felt that it would probably depart that night. Nevertheless, every effort was made to refind it from dawn the following morning, but to no avail – frustrating for all those who were waiting by their planes for news and further proof that to be guaranteed to see all the star rarities on Fair Isle, you really need to stay here for a week or two! October has replaced September as the best month to be on the isle. In five of my six seasons as warden, the rarest bird each year has arrived around the third week in October: Harlequin Duck (15th Oct 1999); Brown Shrike (21st Oct 2000); Black-faced Bunting (20th Oct 2001); Savannah Sparrow (14th Oct 2003); Siberian

Rubythroat (17th Oct 2003); Chestnut-eared Bunting (15th Oct 2004); Rufous-tailed Robin (23rd Oct 2004).

Shaw, D. 2004. The Rufous-tailed Robin on Fair Isle – a new Western Palearctic bird. *Birding World* 17, 420–423.

Rufous-tailed Robin breeds in northeast Siberia and Japan; it winters in southern China and southeast Asia.

This is the only record to date. It awaits acceptance by BOURC.

OCTOBER 2004
MASKED SHRIKE IN FIFE
Rab Shand

On the evening of Friday 29th October 2004, as Fife Bird Recorder, I received a telephone call from Willie Irvine. He told me that, during the day, Tommy Class had found a juvenile shrike at Kilrenny Common, Fife. Tommy had described it to him as a small, drab shrike with a wing pattern reminiscent of Pied Flycatcher, but unlike any shrike he had ever seen before. Kilrenny Common is one of Fife's lesser-known birding sites, but Tommy, who lives in the village, has birded this area for a long time and has found Red-backed Shrikes, Icterine Warbler and Red-breasted Flycatcher there in the past, so I took this report seriously. I telephoned Ken Shaw about it and we both thought and hoped that it might be a Woodchat Shrike – a species that most Fife birders need for their county lists.

The next morning was damp and grey, but the bird was still present, favouring the ivy along the walled garden of Innergellie House and a nearby Elder bush, and a number of Fife birders gathered. The bird was tentatively identified as a Woodchat Shrike, although a number of the observers were not convinced, as many of its characteristics – such as its general colouration, large white primary-patch, relatively long tail and slim bill – were actually wrong for that species. It was briefly considered that its strange appearance might have been accounted for by it being an eastern form Woodchat Shrike, but this possibility was soon dismissed as the same characteristics were wrong for that too.

By the time I arrived, opinion had swung towards it being a Masked Shrike – a First for Britain, although the bird appeared to show a Woodchat-like brownish cast to its wing-coverts and its important rump colouration had still not been seen clearly. The dawning realisation that we were watching a first for Britain was difficult to take in, however, and we did not want to make a mistake. To make sure that it was a Masked Shrike, a decision was made to telephone BTO Scotland to obtain permission to trap the bird. After this was agreed, Alan Lauder and Mark Oksien erected a mist-net and the bird was caught within five minutes.

They took the bird to their car to process and ring it quietly. They measured it carefully and found that all of the measurements were outside the range of Woodchat Shrike, but neatly fitted Masked Shrike. Also, the rump was dull grey as in Masked Shrike (and not whitish as in Woodchat). As they walked back to the small crowd of waiting birders, it was clear from their faces, showing a mixture of happiness and disbelief, that it was definitely a Masked Shrike!

The bird was photographed quickly in the hand and then released by its favoured Elder bush. It flew up into the trees and, after a few minutes, returned to feed by fly-catching off the ivy-covered wall. The news was quickly telephoned to Birdline Scotland and to other local birders. The bird remained in the area until dusk, by which time it had been watched by about 50 birders.

On the following morning, a Sunday, Kilrenny village awoke to the largest gathering of birders ever seen in Fife: some 450 quietly assembled for first light. Fortunately, the bird did not disappoint. It was still present and proved to be delightfully confiding; it soon performed beautifully at close range in front of the appreciative crowd. In the brighter light, it appeared greyer that it had the previous day and definitely more like the colouration of juvenile Masked Shrikes depicted in the field guides. The bird remained until 14th November and was enjoyed by a steady stream of admirers throughout.

Shand, R. 2004. The Masked Shrike in Fife – a new British bird. *Birding World* 17, 466–471.

Masked Shrike breeds from the eastern Mediterranean to Iran; it winters in southwest Arabia, Ethiopia, Sudan and west to Mali.

This is the only record to date. It awaits acceptance by BOURC.

AUGUST 1959

SYKES'S WARBLER ON FAIR ISLE

Peter Davis

A Booted Warbler (*Hippolais caligata*) was caught by R. H. Dennis and J. Bazey in the gully trap at Fair Isle in the early morning of 29th August 1959. It was released at the observatory after examination and on the 31st was seen on a cliff near-by. The only other records in western Europe are from Heligoland on 28th September 1851 and from Fair Isle on 3rd September 1936.

The following description was taken from the bird in the hand:

Upperparts, head, wing-coverts and uppertail-coverts: pale sandy grey-brown (without any olive tint), a little darker on the crown; a fairly distinct buffish-white superciliary, most obvious in front of the eye, and narrow orbital ring of the same colour.

Flight feathers: rather darker than upperparts, with buff edgings to the outer webs; outermost tail-feathers with buff-white outer webs, and penultimate pair marked buff-white at the tips of the outer webs.

Underparts and axillaries: silvery-white, with a buff tinge on the flanks and across the breast.

Soft parts: bill (slender for a *Hippolais*) with dark horn upper mandible, lower tipped same but very pale pinkish at base; inside of mouth daffodil yellow; legs pale brown with blue-grey overtone, as in the commoner *Hippolais* species; iris dark olive.

Measurements: wing 62.5 mm., bill 15.5, tarsus 21, tail 53 (outer feathers 50); bill 3.5 mm. wide at base of nostrils.

Weight: 8.4 gm. at 06.30 G.M.T. The entire plumage (including body-feathers) appeared worn and faded; the tips of the longest primaries were slightly chipped, the tail more abraded.

The specimen presented a nice problem in identification, which would have been greater had we not recently received from Kenneth Williamson his 'bird ringer's guide' to the rarer warblers (unpublished), which he had prepared after an examination of skins in the national collection at the British Museum (Natural History). One undated specimen of the closely similar eastern form of the Olivaceous Warbler (*H. pallida elaeica*) was available at Fair Isle for direct comparison; this had rather darker and greener upper-parts than our capture, no orbital ring and a broader bill. Only one person present, W. H. Tucker, had seen a live Olivaceous Warbler – the Portland bird of 1956 – and he considered that that had been a good deal darker than the bird before us.

We had to consider not only the resemblance between the Booted Warbler and the various forms of the Olivaceous, but also apparent divergences of size and colour between our bird and the available descriptions of *H. caligata*. The most detailed of these descriptions were of the typical form, to which the original western European specimens were referred. Both *The Handbook* (2: 68) and Wardlaw Ramsay (1923) state or imply that *H. c. caligata* has darker upperparts than *H. p. elaeica;* Williamson's 'guide' describes the upperparts as grey-brown in worn dress, greyish-olive (first-winter) or warm brownish-olive (adult) in new plumage. Our bird, like the Heligoland specimen described by Gätke (1895), was worn and faded, and this could account for its paleness. There is, however, a larger and paler eastern form of *H. caligata*, Sykes's Warbler (*H. c. rama*), to be taken into account; and, though it would be unwise to be dogmatic about the taxonomic position of an isolated specimen, the measurements of our bird seem more normal for a bird of the eastern form.

The typical Booted Warbler nests from the Moscow area eastward to West Siberia and south-eastward to the Caspian Sea and the southern Urals. Sykes's Warbler breeds from Transcaspia and Iran east to Sinkiang. There is a considerable area of intermediacy or hybridisation between the two forms, from the Kirghiz Steppes to western Mongolia. Both forms winter in India, mainly in the northern half of the sub-continent, but *H. c. rama* migrates to Southern Arabia also (Vaurie 1959).

On its release the Fair Isle bird flew to the cliff and settled beneath an overhanging tuft of grass. Even in the shadow it seemed a remarkably pale little warbler – the colour of weak milky tea – and when it moved into the light this was still the only feature that attracted the attention; the eye-stripe was inconspicuous and the colour seemed almost uniform from a distance of less than twenty yards. It disappeared from view, and was not rediscovered until two days later, in the cliffs of a neighbouring geo. Here it was watched for nearly an hour by R.H.D. and others. It spent the entire period restlessly hawking for flies – the prey included crane-flies (*Tipula* sp.) – or flitting about the rock-face and probing among the scattered clumps of vegetation. Though searched for later, it was not seen again.

Davis, P. 1960. Booted Warbler at Fair Isle: the problem of identification.
British Birds 53, 123–125.

Sykes's Warbler breeds in Central Asia; it winters in northern India.

There have been seven subsequent records:

Shetland Fair Isle, first-winter, 20th–27th August 1977

Shetland Seafield, Lerwick, adult, 22nd October-9th November 1993

Dorset Portland Bill, 1st July 2000

Norfolk Sheringham, 23rd August 2002

East Sussex Beachy Head, 31st August 2002

Orkney North Ronaldsay, 29th September-1st October 2003

Shetland Baltasound, Unst, 4th–8th October 2003

APPENDIX 1
Firsts for Ireland and the Isle of Man *not* recorded in Britain

IRELAND

Bald Eagle – Ballymacelligot, Co. Kerry, juvenile, 17th November 1987. Found exhausted, captured and returned to USA.

Another record, a juvenile shot near Garrison, Co. Fermanagh, 11th January 1973 and identified as a White-tailed Eagle, was belatedly re-identified in the Ulster Museum, Belfast in 1995.

Thayer's Gull – The Lough, Co. Cork, first-winter, 21st February 1990 and other locations to 5th March.

There are three other accepted records:
North Foreshore Tip, Belfast, Co. Antrim, first-winter, 1st–7th March 1997;
Killybegs, Co. Donegal, adult, 22nd February–15th March 1998;
Newport Refuse Tip, Co. Mayo, first-winter, 19th December 1998–3rd April 1999.

Elegant Tern – Greencastle Point, Carlingford Lough, Co. Down, 22nd June–3rd July 1982; same, Ballymacoda, Co. Cork, 1st August 1982.

There are two other records:
Lady's Island Lake, Co. Wexford, 8th–19th July 1999;
Mulranny, Co. Mayo, 19th October 2001.

Blue-winged Warbler – Cape Clear Island, Co. Cork, first-year male, 4th–10th October 2000.

ISLE OF MAN

Magnificent Frigatebird – Near Castletown, female, 22nd December 1998. Found exhausted and taken into care; died October 1999.

APPENDIX 2
Categories of the British List

A   Species that have been recorded in an apparently natural state at least once since 1st January 1950.

B   Species that were recorded in an apparently natural state at least once between 1st January 1800 and 31st December 1949, but have not been recorded subsequently.

C   Species that, although introduced, now derive from the resulting self-sustaining populations.

C1   Naturalised introduced species – species that have occurred only as a result of introduction, e.g. Egyptian Goose *Alopochen aegyptiaca*.

C2   Naturalised established species – species with established populations resulting from introduction by Man, but which also occur in an apparently natural state, e.g. Canada Goose *Branta canadensis*.

C3   Naturalised re-established species – species with populations successfully re-established by Man in areas of former occurrence, e.g. Red Kite *Milvus milvus*.

C4   Naturalised feral species – domesticated species with populations established in the wild, e.g. Rock Dove/Feral Pigeon *Columba livia*.

C5   Vagrant naturalised species – species from established naturalised populations abroad, e.g. possibly some Ruddy Shelducks *Tadorna ferruginea* occurring in Britain. There are currently no species in category C5.

D   Species that would otherwise appear in Category A except that there is reasonable doubt that they have ever occurred in a natural state. Species on Category D form no part of the British List.

E   Species that have been recorded as introductions, human-assisted transportees or escapees from captivity, and whose breeding populations (if any) are thought not to be self-sustaining. Category E species form no part of the British List.

(NB Ship-assisted vagrants may qualify for Category A provided that they are not fed, watered or do not receive any other direct human intervention during their journey.)

Source: BOURC.

REFERENCES

1980

Cave, B. 1982. Forster's Tern: new to Britain and Ireland. *British Birds* 75, 55–61.

Holman, D. 1990. Britain's first Yellow-browed Bunting. *British Birds* 83, 430–432.

Kitson, A. R. & Robertson, I. S. 1983. Yellow-browed Bunting: new to Britain and Ireland. *British Birds* 76, 217–225.

Rogers, M. J. & the Rarities Committee. 1981. Report on rare birds in Great Britain in 1980. *British Birds* 74, 453–495.

1981

Bradshaw, C. 2003. A 'post-Irish' review of 'firsts' for Britain. *British Birds* 96, 402–405.

Burns, D. W. 1993. Oriental Pratincole: new to the Western Palearctic. *British Birds* 86, 115–120.

Charlton, T. D. 1995. Lark Sparrow in Suffolk: new to the Western Palearctic. *British Birds* 88, 395–400.

Enright, S. D. 1995. Magnolia Warbler in Scilly: new to Britain and Ireland. *British Birds* 88, 107–108.

Gantlett, S. J. M. & Millington, R. G. 1983. Rock Sparrow: new to Britain and Ireland. *British Birds* 76, 245–247.

Grieve, A. 1987. Hudsonian Godwit: new to the Western Palearctic. *British Birds* 80, 466–473.

Gynn, G. & Gynn, E. 1983. Little Swift in Dyfed. *British Birds* 76, 578–579.

Hutchinson, C. D., Kelly, T. C. & O'Sullivan, K. 1984. American Coot: new to Britain and Ireland. *British Birds* 77, 12–16.

Nightingale, B. & Sharrock, J. T. R. 1982. Seabirds inland in Britain in late April 1981. *British Birds* 75, 558–566.

Parker, M. 1990. Pacific Swift: new to the Western Palearctic. *British Birds* 83, 43–46.

Pratley, P. 1984. River Warbler in Norfolk. *British Birds* 77, 213–214.

Riddiford, N. 1983. Sandhill Crane: new to Britain. *British Birds* 76, 105–109.

Robinson, H. P. K. 1984. Little Swift in Cornwall. *British Birds* 77, 261–262.

Rogers, M. J. & the Rarities Committee, 1982. Report on Rare Birds in 1981. *British Birds* 75, 482–533.

Thorpe, R. I. 1995. Grey-tailed Tattler in Wales: new to Britain and Ireland. *British Birds* 88, 255–262.

Wright, G. 1987. Hudsonian Godwit in Devon. *British Birds* 80, 492–494.

1982

Brown, B. J. 1986. White-crowned Black Wheatear: new to Britain and Ireland. *British Birds* 79, 221–227.

Broyd, S. J. 1985. Savannah Sparrow: new to the Western Palearctic. *British Birds* 78, 647–656.

Catley, G. P. & Hursthouse, D. 1985. Parrot Crossbills in Britain. *British Birds* 78, 482–505.

Cobb, P. R., Rawnsley, P., Grenfell, H. E., Griffiths, E. & Cox, S. 1996. Northern Mockingbirds in Britain. *British Birds* 89, 347–356.

Dunnett, J. B. 1992. Long-toed Stint: new to Britain and Ireland. *British Birds* 85, 431–436.

Howey, D. H. & Bell, M. 1985. Pallas's Warblers and other migrants in October 1982. *British Birds* 78, 381–392.

Hurford, C. 1989. Lesser Crested Tern: new to Britain and Ireland. *British Birds* 82, 396–398.

Lunn, J. 1985. Marmora's Warbler: new to Britain and Ireland. *British Birds* 78, 475–481.

Madge, S. C., Hearl, G. C., Hutchings, S. C. & Williams, L. P. 1990. Varied Thrush: new to the Western Palearctic. *British Birds* 83, 187–195.

Moon, S. J. 1983. Little Whimbrel: new to Britain and Ireland. *British Birds* 76, 438–445.

Rogers, M. J. & the Rarities Committee. 1983. Report on rare birds in Great Britain in 1982. *British Birds* 76, 476–529.

Round, P. D. 1996. Long-toed Stint in Cornwall: the first record for the Western Palearctic. *British Birds* 89, 12–24.

Tucker, L. 1982. That sheathbill. *British Birds* 75, 591.

Wallace, D. I. M. 1974. Field identification of small species in the genus *Calidris*. *British Birds* 67, 1–16.

Williams, L. P. 1986. Chimney Swift: new to the Western Palearctic. *British Birds* 79, 423–426.

1983

Carstairs, I. 1983. The Spurn Tengmalm's Owl. *British Birds* 76, 416–417.

Crosby, M. J. 1988. Cliff Swallow: new to Britain and Ireland. *British Birds* 81, 449–452.

Rogers, M. J. & the Rarities Committee. 1984. Report on rare birds in Great Britain in 1983. *British Birds* 77, 506–562.

1984

Mather, J. R. & Curtis, W. F. 1987. The Barmston Capped Petrel. *British Birds* 80, 284–286.

Rogers, M. J. & the Rarities Committee. 1985. Report on rare birds in Great Britain in 1984. *British Birds* 78, 529–589.

1985

Hume, R. A. 1993. Brown Shrike in Shetland: new to Britain and Ireland. *British Birds* 86, 600–604.

Hume, R. A. 1995. Blue Rock Thrush in Strathclyde: new to Britain and Ireland. *British Birds* 88, 130–132.

McKay, C. R. 2000. Cedar Waxwing in Shetland: new to the Western Palearctic. *British Birds* 93, 580–587.

Peacock, M. 1993. Chestnut-sided Warbler: new to the Western Palearctic. *British Birds* 86, 57–61.

Riddiford, N., Harvey, P. V. & Shepherd, K. B. 1989. Daurian Starling: new to the Western Palearctic. *British Birds* 82, 603–612.

Rogers, M. J. & the Rarities Committee. 1986. Report on rare birds in Great Britain in 1985. *British Birds* 79, 526–588.

Smaldon, R. 1990. Wilson's Warbler: new to the Western Palearctic. *Birding World* 83, 404–408.

1986

Jonsson, L. & Grant, P. J. 1984. Identification of stints and peeps. *British Birds* 77, 293–315.

Knox, A. 1987. Taxonomic status of 'Lesser Golden Plovers'. *British Birds* 80, 482–487.

Richards, B. 1989. Red-necked Stint: new to Britain and Ireland. *British Birds* 82, 391–395.

Rogers, M. J. & the Rarities Committee. 1987. Report on rare birds in Great Britain in 1986. *British Birds* 80, 516–571.

1987

Anon. 1987. 1987 – highlights of the birding year. *Twitching* 1, 381–388.

Croft, K. & Davies, A. 1987. An American flycatcher. *Twitching* 1, 93–94.

Dowdall, J. F. 1995. Philadelphia Vireo: new to the Western Palearctic. *British Birds* 88, 474–477.

Dukes, P. 1987. Wood Thrush on St Agnes – a new British bird. *Twitching* 1, 299–300.

Dukes, P. 1995. Wood Thrush in Scilly: new to Britain and Ireland. *British Birds* 88, 133–135.

Evans, G. 1987. Britain's first Lesser Scaup. *Twitching* 1, 65–66.

Filby, R. A. & Good, J. B. 1987. Philadelphia Vireo on Tresco – a new British bird. *Twitching* 1, 301–302.

Good, J. B. 1991. Philadelphia Vireo: new to Britain. *British Birds* 84, 572–574.

Grant, P. 1987. The Co. Kerry Bald Eagle. *Twitching* 1, 379–380.

Holian, J. J. & Fortey, J. E. 1992. Lesser Scaup: new to Britain and Ireland. *British Birds* 85, 370–376.

McShane, C. 1996. Eastern Phoebe in Devon: new to the Western Palearctic. *British Birds* 89, 103–107.

Rogers, M. J. & the Rarities Committee. 1988. Report on rare birds in Great Britain in 1987. *British Birds* 81, 535–596.

Wilson, T. J. & Fentiman, C. 1999. Eastern Bonelli's Warbler in Scilly: new to Britain and Ireland. *British Birds* 92, 519–523.

1988

Anon. 1989. Review of the year: 1988. *Birding World* 1, 416–420.

Barrett, M. 1992. Moussier's Redstart: new to Britain and Ireland. *British Birds* 85, 108–111.

Higson, P. & Urquhart, E. D. 1990. Crag Martins in Cornwall and East Sussex: new to Britain and Ireland. *British Birds* 83, 155–159.

Jones, M. 1988. Daurian Redstart in Fife – a new Western Palearctic bird. *Birding World* 1, 162–163.

McKay, C. R. 1994. Brown-headed Cowbird in Strathclyde: new to Britain and Ireland. *British Birds* 87, 284–288.

Rogers, M. J. & the Rarities Committee. 1989. Report on rare birds in Great Britain in 1988. *British Birds* 82, 505–563.

Saunders, D. & Saunders, S. 1992. Blackburnian Warbler: new to the Western Palearctic. *British Birds* 85, 337–343.

Willmott, J. 1988. Blackburnian Warbler on Fair Isle – a new Western Palearctic bird. *Birding World* 1, 355–356.

Woodbridge, K. 1988. Pallas's Rosefinch on Orkney – a new British bird. *Birding World* 1, 196–199.

1989

Aley, J. & Aley, R. 1995. Red-breasted Nuthatch: new to Britain and Ireland. *British Birds* 88, 150–153.

Blick, M. 1989. Double-crested Cormorant – a new Western Palearctic bird. *Birding World* 2, 53–57.

Bretagnolle, V., Carruthers, M. P., Cubitt, M. G., Bioret, F. & Cuillandre, J. P. 1991. Six captures of dark-rumped petrels in the North Eastern Atlantic. *Ibis* 133, 351–356.

Carruthers, M. P., Cubitt, M. G. & Hall, L. 1989. The dark-rumped petrels in Tyne & Wear. *Birding World* 2, 288–289.

Combridge, P. & Parr, C. 1992. Influx of Little Egrets in Britain and Ireland in 1989. *British Birds* 85, 16–21.

Cubitt, M. G. 1995. Swinhoe's Storm Petrels at Tynemouth: new to Britain and Ireland. *British Birds* 88, 342–348.

Cubitt, M., Carruthers, M. P. & Zino, F. 1992. Unravelling the mystery of the Tyne petrels. *Birding World* 5, 438–442.

Dawson, R. 1992. Blood, sweat and petrels. *Birding World* 5, 443–444.

Doherty, P. 1989. Golden-winged Warbler in Kent – a new Western Palearctic bird. *Birding World* 2, 48–52.

Doherty, P. 1992. Golden-winged Warbler: new to the Western Palearctic. *British Birds* 85, 595–600.

Ellis, P. 1989. Great Knot in Shetland – a new British bird. *Birding World* 2, 313–315.

Ellis, P. M. 1992. Great Knot: new to Britain and Ireland. *British Birds* 85, 426–428.

Hatton, D., & Varney, P. 1989. Red-breasted Nuthatch in Norfolk – a new British bird. *Birding World* 2, 354–356.

King, J. & Minguez, E. 1994. Swinhoe's Petrel: the first Mediterranean record. *Birding World* 7, 271–273.

Rogers, M. J. & the Rarities Committee. 1990. Report on rare birds in Great Britain in 1989. *British Birds* 83, 439–496.

Williams, T. J. 1996. Double-crested Cormorant in Cleveland: new to the Western Palearctic. *British Birds* 89, 162–170.

1990

Betts, M. 1990. White-throated Robin on Skokholm. *Birding World* 3, 208.

Birch, A. 1990. Yellow-throated Vireo in Cornwall – a new Western Palearctic bird. *Birding World* 3, 308–309.

Birch, A. 1994. Yellow-throated Vireo: new to Britain and Ireland. *British Birds* 87, 362–365.

Campey, R. & Mortimer, K. 1990. Ancient Murrelet on Lundy – a new Western Palearctic bird. *Birding World* 3, 211–212.

del Nevo, A. 1994. White-throated Robin in the Isle of Man: new to Britain and Ireland. *British Birds* 87, 83–86.

Heard, C. 1991. 1990: the birding highlights. *Birding World* 4, 24–28.

Hickman, D. J. D. 1995. Tree Swallow in Scilly: new to the Western Palearctic. *British Birds* 88, 381–384.

Murray, K. 1990. Naumann's Thrush in London – a British First. *Birding World* 3, 50–53.

Osborn, K. 1990. Yellow-headed Blackbird on Fair Isle. *Birding World* 3, 160.

Osborn, K. & Suddaby, D. 1990. Pallas's Sandgrouse in Shetland. *Birding World* 3, 161–163.

Rogers, M. J. & the Rarities Committee. 1991. Report on rare birds in Great Britain in 1990. *British Birds* 84, 449–505.

Wagstaff, W. 1990. Tree Swallow on Scilly – a new Western Palearctic bird. *Birding World* 3, 199–201.

Waldon, J. 1994. Ancient Murrelet in Devon: new to the Western Palearctic. *British Birds* 87, 307–310.

Wilson, J. 1990. Thayer's Gull in County Cork. *Birding World* 3, 91–93.

1991

Harrap, S. 1991. 1991: a review of the birding year. *Birding World* 4, 428–433.

Knowler, J. T. 1995. Barrow's Goldeneye in Strathclyde: new to Britain and Ireland. *British Birds* 88, 104–106.

Parrish, R. 1991. The Mugimaki Flycatcher in Humberside. *Birding World* 4, 392–395.

Rogers, M. J. & the Rarities Committee. 1992. Report on rare birds in Great Britain in 1991. *British Birds* 85, 507–554.

1992

Cudworth, J. & Spence, B. R. 1978. Spectacled Warbler: new to Britain and Ireland. *British Birds* 71, 53–58.

Dickie, I. R. & Vinicombe, K. E. 1995. Lesser Short-toed Lark in Dorset: new to Britain. *British Birds* 88, 593–599.

Harrap, S. 1992. 1992: the review of the birding year. *Birding World* 5, 461–479.

Parkin, D. T. & Shaw, K. D., on behalf of the BOURC. 1994. Asian Brown Flycatcher, Mugimaki Flycatcher and Pallas's Rosefinch – three recent decisions of the BOURC. *British Birds* 87, 247–252.

Rogers, M. J. & the Rarities Committee. 1993. Report on rare birds in Great Britain in 1992. *British Birds* 86, 447–540.

Thomas, C. C., Harbird, R. E. & Dunn, P. J. 1998. Spectacled Warbler in North Yorkshire: new to Britain and Ireland. *British Birds* 91, 225–230.

1993

Evans, L. & Millington, R. 1993. 1993: the review of the birding year. *Birding World* 6, 469–487.

Gantlett, S. 1993. The Pacific Swift in Norfolk. *Birding World* 6, 190–191.

Osborn, K. 1993. The Shetland *Hippolais* warbler. *Birding World* 6, 437–438.

Rogers, M. J. & the Rarities Committee. 1994. Report on rare birds in Great Britain in 1993. *British Birds* 87, 503–571.

1994

Alker, P. 1994. The Black-faced Bunting at Pennington Flash: a new British bird. *Birding World* 7, 94–97.

Alker, P. J. 1997. Black-faced Bunting: new to Britain and Ireland. *British Birds* 90, 549–561.

Cox, S. 1994. The Red-throated Thrush in Essex – a new British bird. *Birding World* 7, 392–395.

Golley, M. & Millington, R. 1994. 1994: the review of the birding year. *Birding World* 7, 478–495.

Hough, J. 1994. Identification and status of Black-faced Bunting. *Birding World* 7, 98–101.

Rogers, M. J. & the Rarities Committee. 1995. Report on rare birds in Great Britain in 1994. *British Birds* 88, 493–558.

1995

Evans, L. & Millington, R. 1995. 1995: the review of the birding year. *Birding World* 8, 467–476.

Ferguson, D. 1997. Bay-breasted Warbler in Cornwall: new to Britain and Ireland. *British Birds* 90, 444–449.

Rogers, M. J. & the Rarities Committee. 1996. Report on rare birds in Great Britain in 1995. *British Birds* 89, 481–531.

1996

Bullock, I. 1996. The Indigo Bunting on Ramsey. *Birding World* 9, 398.

Dennis, M. 1996. The Redhead in Nottingham – a new Western Palearctic bird. *Birding World* 9, 93–97.

Dennis, M. C. 1998. Redhead in Nottinghamshire: new to Britain and Ireland. *British Birds* 91, 149–154.

Dresser, H. E. 1895–96. *A History of the Birds of Europe*. London.

Dresser, H. E. 1902. *A Manual of Palaearctic Birds*. London.

Edberg, R. 1954. 'Steppestörnskatan *Lanius excubitor pallidirostris* Cass., och andre observationer fran Utsira 1953'. *Sterna* 13, 17.

Evans, L., Gantlett, S. & Millington, R. 1996. 1996: the review of the birding year. *Birding World* 9, 467–484.

Hartert, E. 1910. *Die Vögel der paläarktischen Fauna*. Berlin.

Hindle, C. 1996. The American Coot in Kent – a new British bird. *Birding World* 9, 137–140.

Hindle, C. 2004. American Coot in Kent: new to Britain. *British Birds* 97, 444–447.

Hutchinson, C. D., Kelly, T. C. & O'Sullivan, K. 1984. American Coot: new to Britain and Ireland. *British Birds* 77,12–16.

Larkin, P. & Mercer, D. 2004. Canvasback in Kent: new to Britain. *British Birds* 97, 139–143.

Madge, S. & Borrow, N. 1991. Separation of Canvasback and Redhead from Pochard. *Birding World* 4, 365–368.

Meinertzhagen, R. 1954. *Birds of Arabia*. Edinburgh.

Rogers, M. J. & the Rarities Committee. 1997. Report on rare birds in Great Britain in 1996. *British Birds* 90, 453–522.

Williamson, K. 1957. A desert race of the Great Grey Shrike, new to the British Isles. *British Birds* 50, 246–249.

1997

Alexander, H. G. 1955. Field-notes on some Asian leaf-warblers. *British Birds* 48, 293–299.

Clement, P. & Scott, R. E. 1999. Hume's Warbler in Sussex: new to Britain and Ireland. *British Birds* 92, 96–100.

Edwards, T. 1997. The Lesser Sand Plover in Sussex – a new British bird. *Birding World* 10, 294–297.

Hirschfeld, E., Roselaar, C. S. & Shirihai, H. 2000. Identification, taxonomy and distribution of Greater and Lesser Sand Plovers. *British Birds* 93, 162–189.

Hunt, J. 2000. Lesser Sand Plover in West Sussex: new to Britain and Ireland. *British Birds* 93, 435–441.

Madge, S. C. & Quinn, D. 1997. Identification of Hume's Warbler. *British Birds* 90, 571–575.

Millington, R. 1997. 1997: the review of the birding year. *Birding World* 10, 467–482.

Rogers, M. J. & the Rarities Committee. 1998. Report on rare birds in Great Britain in 1997. *British Birds* 91, 455–517.

1998

Bland, B. 1998. The Wilson's Snipe on the Isles of Scilly. *Birding World* 11, 382–385.

Cleeves, T. 1998. The Slender-billed Curlew in Northumberland – a new British bird. *Birding World* 11, 181–191.

Cleeves, T. 2002. Slender-billed Curlew in Northumberland: new to Britain and Ireland. *British Birds* 95, 272–278.

Crewe, M. 1998. The Scilly starling. *Birding World* 11, 113.

Millington, R. 1998. 1998: the review of the birding year. *Birding World* 11, 459–473.

Rogers, M. J. & the Rarities Committee. 1999. Report on rare birds in Great Britain in 1998. *British Birds* 92, 554–609.

Steele, J. & Vangeluwe, D. 2002. From the Rarities Committee's files: The Slender-billed Curlew at Druridge Bay, Northumberland, in 1998. *British Birds* 95, 279–299.

1999

Cleeves, T. 1999. The Short-toed Eagle on the Isles of Scilly – a new British bird. *Birding World* 12, 408–411.

Cleeves, T. R., Hepple, M. & Shaw, K. D. 2004. Short-toed Eagle: new to Britain. *British Birds* 97, 27–32.

Gantlett, S. 1999. The Magnificent Frigatebird on the Isle of Man. *Birding World* 12, 458–459.

Gantlett, S. 1999. The birding review of 1999. *Birding World* 12, 487–500.

Hume, R. A. 1995. Blue Rock Thrush in Strathclyde: new to Britain and Ireland. *British Birds* 88, 130–132.

Pullan, D. 1999. The Short-billed Dowitcher in Aberdeenshire – a new British bird. *Birding World* 12, 364–370.

Rabbitts, B. 1999. The Mourning Dove on the Outer Hebrides. *Birding World* 12, 453.

Rogers, M. J. & the Rarities Committee. 2000. Report on rare birds in Great Britain in 1999. *British Birds* 93, 512–567.

Sapsford, A. 1996. Mourning Dove in the Isle of Man: new to the Western Palearctic. *British Birds* 89, 157–161.

Willmott, J. 1999. The Booted Eagle in Cornwall – a new British bird. *Birding World* 12, 444–447.

2000

Batten, L. A. 2000. Iberian Chiffchaff in Greater London: new to Britain and Ireland. *British Birds* 93, 329–332.

Batten, L. & Wood, J. H. 1974. Iberian Chiffchaff at the Brent Reservoir. *London Bird Report* 37, 78.

Cade, M. 2000. The Sykes's Warbler in Dorset. *Birding World* 13, 274–276.

Clement, P., Helbig, A. J. & Small, B. 1998. Taxonomy and identification of chiffchaffs in the Western Palearctic. *British Birds* 91, 361–376.

Foster, K. 2000. The Siberian Blue Robin in Suffolk – a new British bird. *Birding World* 13, 412–414.

Helbig, A. J., Martens, J., Seibold, I., Henning, F., Schottler, B. & Wink, M. 1996. Phylogeny and species limits in the Palearctic Chiffchaff *Phylloscopus collybita* complex: mitochondrial genetic differentiation and bioacoustic evidence. *Ibis* 138, 650–666.

Rabbitts, B. 2000. The Hooded Merganser on the Outer Hebrides – a new British bird? *Birding World* 13, 506–507.

Richards, C. 1999. The Iberian Chiffchaff in Dorset. *Birding World* 12, 193–200.

Rogers, M. J. & the Rarities Committee. 2001. Report on rare birds in Great Britain in 2000. *British Birds* 94, 452–504.

Stevenson, A. 2000. The Long-tailed Shrike on the Outer Hebrides – a new British bird. *Birding World* 13, 454–457.

Stevenson, A. 2005. Long-tailed Shrike: new to Britain. *British Birds* 98, 26–31.

Walton, P., & Millington, R. 2000. The birding review of 2000. *Birding World* 13, 481–495.

Wing, S. 2000. The Blue-winged Warbler in County Cork – a new Western Palearctic bird. *Birding World* 13, 408–411.

2001

Blamire, S. 2004. Red-billed Tropicbird: new to Britain. *British Birds* 97, 231–237.

Croft, K. 2001. The Grey Catbird on Anglesey. *Birding World* 14, 424–425.

Croft, K. 2004. Grey Catbird on Anglesey: new to Britain. *British Birds* 97, 630–632.

Enticott, J. W. 1999. Britain and Ireland's first 'Soft-plumaged Petrel'. *British Birds* 92, 504–518.

Fisher, A. & Flood, B. 2001. The Fea's Petrel off the Isles of Scilly. *Birding World* 14, 289–292.

Fisher, D. 1989. *Pterodroma* petrels in Madeira. *Birding World* 2, 286.

Gantlett, S. 1995. Field separation of Fea's, Zino's and Soft-plumaged Petrels. *Birding World* 8, 256–260.

Jackson, B. 2001. The Snowy Egret in Argyll – a new British bird. *Birding World* 14, 460–464.

Jackson, B. 2004. Snowy Egret in Argyll and Bute: new to Britain. *British Birds* 97, 270–275.

Lees, J. 2001. The 14th annual *Scillonian* pelagic trip. *Birding World* 14, 326–328.

Madge, S. 1990. Soft-plumaged Petrels at sea. *Birding World* 3, 138–139.

Rogers, M. J. & the Rarities Committee. 2002. Report on rare birds in Great Britain in 2001. *British Birds* 95, 476–528.

Scott, M. 2002. A Brown Skua on the Isles of Scilly – the first for Europe? *Birding World* 15, 383–386.

Walton, P. & Millington, R. 2001. The birding review of 2001. *Birding World* 14, 497–511.

2002

Flood, B. 2002. Three American Herring Gulls on the Isles of Scilly. *Birding World* 15, 106–110.

Marshall, P. 2002. The Elegant Tern in Devon – a new British bird. *Birding World* 15, 209–211.

Millington, R. 2002. The orange-billed terns in summer 2002. *Birding World* 15, 287–290.

Moon, S. & Carrington, D. 2002. A Brown Skua in Glamorgan. *Birding World* 15, 387–389.

Rogers, M. J. & the Rarities Committee. 2003. Report on rare birds in Great Britain in 2002. *British Birds* 96, 542–609.

Walton, P. & Millington, R. 2002. The birding review of 2002. *Birding World* 15, 509–524.

2003

Anon. 2004. The Black Lark on Anglesey, a new bird for Britain – or not? *Yorkshire Birding* 12, 130–131.

Cederroth, C., Johansson, C. & Svensson, L. 1999. Taiga Flycatcher in Sweden: the first record in western Europe. *Birding World* 12, 460–468.

Croft, K. 2003. The Black Lark on Anglesey – a new British bird. *Birding World* 16, 238–243.

Degnan, L. & Croft, K. 2005. Black Lark: new to Britain. *British Birds* 98, 306–313.

Garner, M., Lewington, I. & Slack, R. 2003. Mongolian and Lesser Sand Plovers: an identification overview. *Birding World* 16, 377–385.

Lassey, A. 2003. The Taiga Flycatcher in East Yorkshire – a new British bird. *Birding World* 16, 153–155.

Nicholson, E. M. & Ferguson-Lees, I. J. 1962. The Hastings Rarities. *British Birds* 55, 299–384.

Parkin, D. T., Collinson, M., Helbig, A. J., Knox, A. G. & Sangster, G. 2003. The taxonomic status of Carrion and Hooded Crows. *British Birds* 96, 274–290.

Rogers, M. J. & the Rarities Committee. 2004. Report on rare birds in Great Britain in 2003. *British Birds* 97, 558–625.

Walbridge, G., Small, B. & McGowan, R. Y. 2003. From the Rarities Committee's files: Ascension Frigatebird on Tiree – new to the Western Palearctic. *British Birds* 96, 58–73.

Walker, D. 2003. The Audouin's Gull in Kent – a new British bird. *Birding World* 16, 199–202.

Walker, D. 2004. Audouin's Gull: new to Britain. *British Birds* 97, 537–541.

Walton, P. & Millington, R. 2003. The birding review of 2003. *Birding World* 16, 506–528.

2004

Coyle, S., Grant, T. & Witherall, M. 2004. The Purple Martin on the Outer Hebrides – a new Western Palearctic bird. *Birding World* 17, 381–383.

Davis, P. 1960. Booted Warbler at Fair Isle: the problem of identification. *British Birds* 53, 123–125.

Fisher, A. & Flood, B. 2004. A Scopoli's Shearwater off the Isles of Scilly. *Birding World* 17, 334–336.

Gätke, H. (1895). *Heligoland as an Ornithological Observatory*. Edinburgh.

Golley, M. 2004. The birding review of 2004. *Birding World* 17, 505–524.

Ramsay, R. G. Wardlaw (1923): *The Birds of Europe and North Africa*. London and Edinburgh.

Scott, M. 2004. The Redhead on the Outer Hebrides, the first female for the Western Palearctic. *Birding World* 17, 59.

Scott, M. 2004. The Cinnamon Teal on the Outer Hebrides – a new Western Palearctic bird? *Birding World* 17, 200–201.

Shand, R. 2004. The Masked Shrike in Fife – a new British bird. *Birding World* 17, 466–471.

Shaw, D. 2004. The Chestnut-eared Bunting on Fair Isle – a new Western Palearctic bird. *Birding World* 17, 415–419.

Shaw, D. 2004. The Rufous-tailed Robin on Fair Isle – a new Western Palearctic bird. *Birding World* 17, 420–423.

Thomson, I. 2004. The Mongolian Plover in Lothian. *Birding World* 17, 283–285.

Vaurie, C. (1959): *The Birds of the Palaearctic Fauna*. London.

Votier, S. 2001. Eastern buntings: a photo gallery. *Birding World* 14, 390–396.

Witherby, H. F. *et al.* (1941): *The Handbook of British Birds*. Vol. 2. London.

BIBLIOGRAPHY

Beaman, M. & Madge, S. 1999. *The Handbook of Bird Identification for Europe and the Western Palearctic*. Christopher Helm, London.

Byers, C., Olsson, U. & Curson, J. 1995. *Buntings and Sparrows*. Pica Press, Robertsbridge.

Chantler, P. & Driessens, G. 1995. *Swifts*. Pica Press, Robertsbridge.

Clement, P., Harris, A. & Davis, J. 1993. *Finches and Sparrows*. Christopher Helm, London.

Clement, P. & Hathway, R. 2000. *Thrushes*. Christopher Helm, London.

Cocker, M. 2001. *Birders – Tales of a Tribe*. Jonathan Cape, London.

Cramp, S. *et al.* 1977–94. *The Birds of the Western Palearctic*. Vols. 1–9. Oxford Universiy Press, Oxford.

Curson, J., Quinn, D. & Beadle, D. 1994. *New World Warblers*. Christopher Helm, London.

Dudley, S., Benton, T., Fraser, P. & Ryan, J. 1996. *Rare Birds Day by Day*. T & AD Poyser, London.

Dymond, J. N., Fraser, P. A. & Gantlett, S. J. M. 1989. *Rare Birds in Britain and Ireland*. T & AD Poyser, Calton.

Hayman, P., Marchant, J. & Prater, T. 1986. *Shorebirds*. Christopher Helm, London.

Lefranc, N. & Worfolk, T. 1997. *Shrikes*. Pica Press, Robertsbridge.

Lewington, I., Alström, P. & Colston, P. 1991. *A Field Guide to the Rare Birds of Britain and Europe*. HarperCollins, London.

Madge, S. & Burn, H. 1988. *Wildfowl*. Christopher Helm, London.

Millington, R. 1981. *A Twitcher's Diary*. Blandford Press, Poole.

Mitchell, D. & Young, S. 1999. *Photographic Handbook of the Rare Birds of Britain and Europe*. New Holland, London.

Moss, S. 2004. *A Bird in the Bush*. Aurum Press, London.

Mullarney, K., Svensson, L., Zetterström, D. & Grant, P. J. 1999. *The Collins Bird Guide*. HarperCollins, London.

National Geographic Society. 1983/1987/1999. *Field Guide to the Birds of North America*. National Geographic Society, Washington DC.

Peterson, R. T., Mountfort, G., & Hollom, P. A. D. 1983. *A Field Guide to the Birds of Britain and Europe*. Collins, London.

Robson, C. 2000. *A Field Guide to the Birds of South-East Asia*. New Holland, London.

Sharrock, J. T. R. & Grant, P. J. 1982. *Birds New to Britain and Ireland*. T & AD Poyser, Calton.

Sharrock, J. T. R. & Sharrock, E. M. 1976. *Rare Birds in Britain and Ireland*. T & AD Poyser, Calton.

Sibley, D. 2000. *The North American Bird Guide*. Pica Press, Robertsbridge.

Stattersfield, A. J. & Capper, D. 2000. *Threatened Birds of the World*. Lynx Edicions and Birdlife International, Barcelona and Cambridge.

Turner, A. & Rose, C. 1989. *Swallows and Martins*. Christopher Helm, London.

Vinicombe, K. & Cottridge, D. M. 1996. *Rare Birds in Britain and Ireland – A Photographic Record*. HarperCollins, London.

Wallace, I. 1981. *Birdwatching in the Seventies*. Macmillan, London.

WEBSITES

BirdGuides www.birdguides.com Bird News Extra rarity sightings and the invaluable Online Guide to Rarer British Birds

Birding World www.birdingworld.co.uk Magazine articles plus Books for Birders

Birds of Ireland News Service www.birdsireland.com Irish List updates

British Birds www.britishbirds.co.uk Magazine articles and an index back to 1945

British Birds Rarities Committee www.bbrc.org.uk Reports, statistics, decisions

British Ornithologists' Union Records Committee www.bou.org.uk/recreps.html

Fatbirder www.fatbirder.com Birds and birding worldwide

Irish Birding www.irishbirding.com Latest Irish bird news and Irish checklist

Irish Rare Birds Committee www.birdwatchireland.ie/bwi/irbc/irbc.html

Surfbirds www.surfbirds.com Rarity photos, life lists, trip reports, news articles

INDEX

Numbers denote the start of each First account. Numbers in *italics* denote a photograph in the plates section.